TOWN and GUN

THE 17TH-CENTURY DEFENCES OF HULL

Audrey Howes and Martin Foreman
with original artwork by Mike Frankland

Kingston
Press

in partnership with
Kingston upon Hull
Museums and Galleries

British Library Cataloguing in Publication Data.
A catalogue record for this book is available from the British Library.

First published 1999

© 1999 Audrey Howes and Martin Foreman
All maps © respective owners as indicated
original artwork © 1999 Mike Frankland as indicated

Published by Kingston Press in partnership with Kingston upon Hull Museums and Galleries

ISBN 1 902039 02 5

Kingston Press is the publishing imprint of Kingston upon Hull City Libraries,
Central Library, Albion Street, Kingston upon Hull, England HU1 3TF

Printed by Kingston upon Hull City Council Printing Services,
1-5 Witham, Kingston upon Hull, England HU9 1DA

Front cover: **The Phillips plan of Hull, probably drawn by Captain Phillips c.1716, as part of his survey of the fortifications of *North Britain*. Numerous copies were made of his plan, which was the first to approach a modern standard of accuracy; this coloured example is held at the Hull Maritime Museum.**

CONTENTS

ILLUSTRATIONS

SUMMARY

*K*ingston upon Hull was a strategic port from the outset, set on the low-lying margins of the river Humber. Edward I, who founded the town and granted it a Charter in 1299, sought to use it as a forward base for his campaigns in Scotland. It was fortified after Edward II was defeated at Bannockburn. Through the later Middle Ages, royal favour and commercial success contributed to the prosperity and independence of the town.

Domestic opposition and war abroad led Henry VIII to build one of the last great fortifications of his reign at Hull. Henry placed them under royal appointees, curtailing local autonomy. Crown insolvency forced his successor, Edward VI, to pass them back to the Mayor and Aldermen of Hull, who took only modest steps towards their maintenance and improvement.

In 1639, Charles I embarked on the disastrous Bishops War in Scotland. Hull was the principal arsenal from which his troops were armed. Charles attempted to seize arms stockpiled at Hull in April 1642, but was turned away at the gates by a Governor appointed by Parliament. Hull withstood an ineffective siege, before the formal declaration of the Civil War. In 1643, the Duke of Newcastle attempted to suborn the Governor and, when this failed, laid siege to Hull. Under Lord Ferdinando Fairfax, Hull held out against the Royalists.

Parliament maintained a Garrison at Hull through the Civil Wars and Commonwealth; their Governor at Hull presented the last opposition to the Restoration of 1660. Under Charles II, the Garrison was required both for defence against the Dutch, and for the suppression of Hull's Dissenters. In 1681, with opposition in Parliament routed, the Crown proposed the refortification of Hull. The Hull Citadel was to bridle the town as well as to guard its port, taking up a site one third the size of the town itself.

The building of the Citadel was recorded by contemporary documents, and much of its fabric has been examined by archaeological excavation. These sources combine to give a detailed picture of the progress and administration of its construction. These "stupendous works" were the most extensive and ambitious building project ever to be attempted at Hull, and were regarded as among the strongest fortifications in England.

The accession of James II, in 1685, led to rebellion in the North and West, which were suppressed by his new professional army. James' Catholicism alienated many supporters of the Crown; and fears grew that he intended to impose absolute rule over England. This led to peaceful opposition, and then to treasonable conspiracy. In 1688, William of Orange challenged James for the throne and invaded England. Hull was seized by a Williamite faction of the Garrison, on Town Taking Day, 3 December 1688.

Hull then served as a key port for the movement of troops to fight in a wide-ranging war against France. Military and civilian communities coexisted peacefully in the town. With the coming of peace, Invalid Companies provided a weak Garrison, local volunteers joining them in times of emergency. While England relied on wooden walls – the Navy – Hull's town defences were neglected; from 1774 they made way for docks.

Despite a role as a depot in the French Wars, the Citadel declined in military significance. As a fortress, it was progressively compromised by the commercial development of its surroundings. After a final tussle between town and Crown over the ownership of its site, it was razed in 1864. Its site was taken over by shipbuilding and port facilities, of commercial rather than military importance.

NOTES ON THE SOURCES

Documentary research to inform archaeological excavations of the eastern defences of Hull has been intermittently prosecuted over the period 1989-99. This research has been aptly described as partial, and has been weighted towards study of the physical fabric and setting of its subject. In this emphasis, it contrasts with previous works whose focus has been on political or constitutional matters, or on local or social historical issues.

The War Office papers in the Public Record Office, Kew (PRO), include volumes (WO46:1-2; WO55/519) dealing specifically with Hull in the period 1681-88. These have been partially transcribed, together with their PRO indices. Engineers' Papers have been selectively collected for the late 18th and early 19th centuries (WO55/714-5). Selective inspection of Treasury Bill Books (WO51/33), Returns (WO44) and Establishments (WO24) has also been carried out. Maps and plans of 18th and 19th-century date were ordered from PRO Map Room indices, or were consulted at Kew. Calendars of State Papers, and related works, were extensively consulted, but the documents they summarise have not been examined.

The Bodleian Library, Oxford, holds papers of John Duxbury (Rawlinson A475; A476 item 1); these frequently duplicate PRO material. Material from Stafford Record Office draws on Lord Dartmouth's papers (D (W) 1778), again offering coverage which overlaps with other collections. These sources inform as to later 17th-century events from an administrative perspective. Transcripts are deposited as typed copy at the National Monuments Record, Swindon; at the Brynmoor Jones Library, University of Hull; and at the Local Studies Library, Albion Street, Hull. Spelling has been modernised throughout these transcripts, and in their citation in this work.

Collections at the Kingston upon Hull Record Office (KUHRO) have been approached *via* Stanewell's Index, whose conventions are respected. KUHRO also holds the Bench Record Books (BRB) and Bench Record Letters (BRL) of Hull Corporation. Limited reference has been made to collections of the East Riding of Yorkshire Council Record Office (ERYCRO – formerly Humberside County Council), Beverley, and to published Parish Registers. Hull University holds collections of pamphlets relating to the English Civil War (Rushworth); Hull Local Studies Library also holds bound collections (Civil War Tracts).

The establishment of an Urban Database, by Humber Field Archaeology on behalf of Hull City Council, promises to provide an overview of Hull's urban development as informed by topographical research. Work on Hull's 16th-century defences continues with documentary study by Helen Good, towards a postgraduate dissertation for the University of Hull; full publication of the results of excavations on their site is still awaited.

These studies continue as redevelopment impinges upon the remaining fabric of the defences of Hull. This publication therefore illustrates the potential of diverse sources and of interdisciplinary approaches to the study of these most significant monuments, rather than offering a definitive presentation of either documentary or field evidence.

ACKNOWLEDGEMENTS

The transcription and collection of Public Record Office (PRO) material was begun by Steve Goodhand, Keeper of Streetlife Museum, Hull. Staff of the PRO (Kew); of the Record Offices at Beverley, Portsmouth and Stafford; of the Bodleian Library, Oxford and the Brynmoor Jones Library, Hull; and of the Hull Local Studies and Reference Libraries are thanked for their help. Geoff Oxley and Elspeth Rippon of Kingston upon Hull City Archives (KUHRO); and Pamela Martin and Jenny Stanley, of the Beverley Local Studies Library are warmly thanked for their help and encouragement over a decade of research. So, too, are Arthur Credland, of the Maritime Museum; and Clare Parsons and Jane Tyler, of Wilberforce House, and other staff of the Hull Museums Service. Of these, particular thanks are due to Gail Foreman and Mick Stanley, for permission to devote resources to the completion of editorial work.

The East Yorkshire Local history Society and the James Reckitt Charity, Hull, generously funded research visits, while further funding was provided by the Hull and East Riding Museum.

Private researchers and students have offered further insights from their own work, and are thanked for their generosity. They include: Judith Preston Anderson, who provided the will of Alderman Ferries; Paul Beckmann, for notes on the career of his relative Sir Martin Beckman; Norma Branton, for information on Drypool and Hull's Storekeeper James Watkinson; Martyn Clarke, for his essay on the Civil War sieges of Hull and for information as to locally-held plans; Helen Good, for her important work on the transcription of 16th-century documents; Quentin Hughes, for technical advice and comment on the design of Hull Citadel; the late Hartwig Neumann, for his advice on continental architects; Berna Moody, for assistance in the transcription of inventories of armaments; Keith Moody, for his drawn interpretation from documentary sources of the form of the Citadel barracks; Kevin Payne, for transcript material from the Hull Advertiser, and for access to his dissertation *Scarlet Fever*; and Geoff Percival, for extensive notes on the careers of the merchants and tradesmen of 17th-century Hull.

Drafts of sections of text have benefited from the informed advice of academics concerned with various topics; they include: Professors Barbara English and Donald Woodward, and Dr David Neave, of the University of Hull; and the late Professor J.P. Kenyon, formerly of the University of Hull. Andrew Saunders, Chairman of the Fortress Study Group and an authority on English fortification of the 17th century, has favoured work at Hull with his informed advice over many years, and most kindly agreed to read this text as it neared completion. Arthur Credland similarly considered drafts from a local historical perspective.

Bill Marsden photographed models and locally-held views and plans. We owe a particular debt of gratitude to Steve Howard and his collaborators at Kingston Press. Without their prompt and timely assistance, this work could not have advanced to publication.

All the above-named persons are thanked most warmly for their encouragement, help and advice. The authors regret that constraints of time and structure have prevented the more thorough exploration of many valuable points that they have raised, and take full responsibility for their very partial use of a veritable wealth of good counsel.

Audrey Howes and Martin Foreman, June 1999

CHAPTER 1

THE SETTING OF KINGSTON UPON HULL

The Humber is one of England's great waterways. Turbid and brown, it carries the waters of the rivers Trent and Ouse out to the North Sea. Before it approaches the sea, the Humber passes through a gap between low chalk Wolds to north and south. In its lower course, it traverses the low-lying rural landscapes of Holderness and North Lincolnshire. The Humber is nowhere less than 1km wide, and, after the first 3km of its course, it is between 2 and 10km wide, widening as it nears the sea.

In the last Ice Age, ice-sheets 60m thick redeposited alluvial clays across Holderness, mixing them with rock fragments from as far afield as Scandinavia. When the ice plugging the Humber Gap melted, a great prehistoric lake was to find its outlet along the course of the modern river. Subsequent alluviation masked the lowest land with further blankets of silt, and wind-blown sands accumulated in drier periods. The Humber continues to scour the claylands, as a living system of erosion and deposition both takes and makes land on either side of its course[1].

No river leads to so much of England. Prehistoric settlement spread up the great and lesser waterways of the region, occupying higher ground when climatic conditions made marsh of the lowlands. To the Romans, better known for their roads, it was rivers that permitted the transportation of bulky cargoes at a fraction of the cost incurred by wagon and mule trains. Incomers, too, travelled by water to settle as farmers, or as mercenaries and pirates to subvert and contest the rule of fertile lands. The limits of Early Anglo-Saxon settlement, or of the northern part of the Scandinavian Danelaw, were effectively defined by the access afforded to northern England by the Humber and its tributaries.

In the Anglo-Saxon period, shipments of Pennine lead and other commodities passed down the Humber to supply other regions of England, and latterly Europe. The regulation and taxation of trade in such commodities was an early development. Archaeology and history hint at contests for the control of the Humber from the 7th century AD. For the Normans, the Humber served as the boundary between their more secure southern domains, and those initially left under the control of their Anglo-Scandinavian Earls. The revolt of the Earls, in 1069, was crushed by a campaign which aimed to eradicate the peasant base on which they and their followers depended for economic support. This *Harrying of the North* left tracts of devastated land which were to retain only a particle of their former value a generation later[2].

In the course of the 12th century, the North lay open to the threat of recurrent raiding by the Scots, whose influence was strong in the upland areas to the north and west. A large-scale raid led by King David of Scotland was repelled at the Battle of the Standard, near Northallerton, in 1138. The lowlands of Holderness had become the feudal fief of the Norman Counts of Aumale by 1086. Count William of Aumale was among the leaders of the victorious English force, and was created Earl of Yorkshire for his services. William was an active supporter of King Stephen in the civil war between the King and the Empress Matilda. Perhaps because of this status, he was permitted to mint coins for Stephen from his new borough of Hedon. By the middle of the 12th century Count William had also founded the Cistercian Abbey of Meaux, providing the monks with a low-lying site about 11.5km north of the Humber.

The recovery of the region proceeded through this period, often directed by monastic houses, which colonised wasted lands. Both lay and monastic landowners were to build fortunes from the ranching of sheep for wool - sheep could be raised by relatively few hands in upland areas. The drier lowlands were repopulated, and peasants pooled their efforts in the arable farming of common fields. Their villages were often planned by feudal lords, who were anxious to harness their labour so as to draw profit from the land. Riverside and low-lying marshlands, which were too wet to be ploughed, nevertheless provided seasonal pasture for beasts. The estuarine environment was also suitable for hunting, and provided both fish and wildfowl[3].

The settlement of Wyke was founded on the west bank of the river Hull, close to its confluence with the Humber. It was probably established by the monks of Meaux, perhaps to serve as an outlet for the monastic wool crop. The river Hull was a minor tributary of the Humber, and led not only towards Meaux, but also to the long-established town of Beverley. This small but navigable river has followed the same course through the lowlands of Holderness from at least the

Roman period. As it neared the Humber, its course was less well-defined. It is likely that its waters followed a number of stream-beds, winding through marshes. Their course could be altered by human intervention, or by sudden flood. The present route of the river Hull was fixed by the later 13th century.

By 1193, wool collected at *Hulmo* was to make a significant contribution towards the ransom of Richard I. The settlement is probably to be identified with Wyke. Taxation of its trade under King John, in 1203-4, raised £35. This income ranked Wyke sixth among the ports of the south and east coasts, behind London, Boston, Southampton, Lincoln and King's Lynn. The quay along the river Hull was to be the site of the town's port or haven – the current of the Humber being too strong for the mooring of ships. Vessels tied up alongside the riverbank, at timber-framed *staithes*. These were jetties, some jutting into the river, but others incorporating wider platforms to accommodate warehouses and loading areas. The development of the staithes was to continue through the Middle Ages, intruding into the river and significantly narrowing the navigable channel[4].

The commercial potential of Wyke was recognised by Edward I, reportedly as he hunted along the marshy margin of the Humber. He ordered the area to be surveyed, and bought the site of what was to become the King's Town on the river Hull from the monks of Meaux in 1293. Edward's foundation was also informed by his intention to invade Scotland, a scheme in which Hull was to serve as a forward base for ships operating in support of his land forces. Such combined operations had served well in the subjugation of Wales, enabling the supply of garrisons or mobile forces from the sea. Edward may also have sought to establish some local balance against the power of his northern lords. These independent powers provided a buffer against Scots raids, but could equally challenge royal control from a safe distance[5].

The Kings Town upon Hull was granted a Royal Charter in 1299. This established self-government for the inhabitants, and set out their conditions of tenure, and a raft of commercial rights. These liberties were to be enjoyed without the interposition of a feudal lord, and the Borough was therefore to enjoy a direct relationship with the Crown. Streets were set out, defining rectangular plots within the town. The streets followed the north/south alignment of High Street, which ran parallel to the river Hull, and the less regular alignments of other stream-side tracks to the west. Straight east/west lanes connected these to form a loose gridiron pattern. There was a somewhat tardy take-up of the plots thus

defined. This problem was successfully addressed in the early part of the 14th century, not least by a slashing of rents. Cushioned by royal favour, the maritime trade of the town was to flourish[6].

The medieval defences

Some demarcation probably existed to define the limits of the King's Town, though its earliest form is unknown. The construction of defences, however, was recorded only after the defeat of Edward II by the Scots at Bannockburn, in 1314.

This defeat left the north of England open to raiding by the victorious troops of Robert the Bruce. Fear of the Scots impelled both Beverley and Hull to petition the King for licence to crenellate, to erect substantial defences. Only Hull was granted permission, in 1321, a clear act of discrimination in favour of the new royal foundation. This left Beverley an open town, and its Minster Chapter was reduced to composing letters in which they offered to buy off the Scots if the town were threatened. The Archbishop of York's Beverley manor was provided with a moat of defensive proportions at about this time, with an imposing drawbridge of military style; his other Yorkshire palaces may also have been strengthened[7].

The Chamberlains' Accounts for the years 1321-24 refer to the early defences of Hull as comprising a bank and great ditch, *magnum fossatum* and *le mote*; and refer to the purchase of timber boards, stakes and piles (*pro pilis*), and iron for nails. Some of these materials may have been used to construct a timber palisade on top of the bank. A sum of £40 was also spent on stone, tile - probably brick in this context, lime and sand, for use at the North Gate *and elsewhere*. This was the only gate specified at this period, and was perhaps the first to incorporate substantial elements of brick and stone. The defensive circuit encompassed three sides of the medieval town. It extended west from the mouth of the river Hull along the Humber bank; then ran along the western and northern sides of the town, returning eastwards to the Hull. The fourth side, along the river itself, was left open for the medieval port. Work on the defences had progressed sufficiently for Edward III to be highly pleased with them, when he visited Hull in 1332[8].

The defences incorporated four main gates, guarding the principal land routes into the town, some named after the older settlements to which they led. They

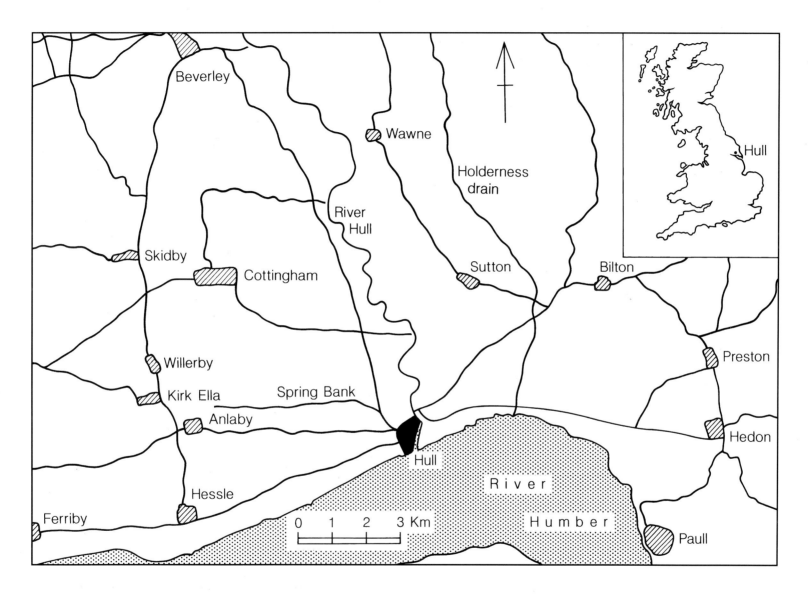

Fig 1: Location plan of Hull, showing the major routes and settlements of *Hullshire* to the west and neighbouring villages to the east.

3

were (in clockwise order) Hessle Gate, close to the Humber; Myton Gate, on the west side of the town; Beverley Gate, at its north-west corner, and North Gate, where the defences returned to the river Hull. Posterns were later added between these, giving access to the Foreland, an area of reclaimed land on the Humber shore; to Monkgate and Kirk Lane, which both ran from west to east across the town; and to Marketgate, its widest north/south street. Excavations on the site of the Beverley Gate have shown that this was a timber structure in its earliest form[9].

By 1339, work had begun on replacing the timber palisade with a brick wall. The Corporation Bench Books for that year mention *the wall of the town towards the Humber*, whilst murage grants of 1341 and 1348 specify that they were *to complete a wall, begun by them for the safety of the town and the parts adjacent, on the water of the Humber*. This might suggest either that rebuilding in brick had commenced along the southern side of the defensive circuit, or alternatively, that the stretch adjoining the Humber was required for the completion of the walls. Subsequent murage grants were made at intervals up until 1406, which suggests that the rest of the circuit was gradually replaced in brick as funds permitted[10].

The walls included 30 interval towers and posterns, and it has been estimated that it incorporated at least 4,700,000 bricks. Records for the Royal or Corporation brickyard in Hull show that its annual output during the 14th and 15th centuries averaged only about 100,000 bricks. In some years the entire output was bought by the town, in others no bricks were made. The Chamberlain's Accounts confirm that even when work on the walls was recorded, purchases of *waltighel* (brick) did not exceed the annual output of the Corporation brickyard[11].

The most energetic campaigns of construction coincided with the rise of the mercantile family of de la Pole. Richard de la Pole founded the dynasty; his son William, the first Mayor of Hull, lent large sums to the Crown; and both were knighted. As a result of royal favour, in 1337, William formed a consortium which secured a monopoly over the export of wool. The wool was funnelled through Hull, and the buying-up of bonds from lesser merchants left William richer to the tune of £2,039 when they were cashed in 1343. His son, Michael, rose as a courtier and soldier to the earldom of Suffolk, in 1385. Other merchants of Hull and Beverley shared the profits of this coup. Prosperity and civic pride found material expression in the erection of the most extensive fortifications of brick that England had seen since the Roman period[12].

Hull prospered on its overseas trade through the later medieval period. Its walls symbolised powers of self-government which were further augmented in the 15th century. Its merchants sat as its Aldermen, Mayors, and as Hull's two Members of Parliament. In 1440, Hull was granted a Charter of Incorporation, confirming its autonomy as a county. Hull had its own Sheriff, and members of the Bench of Aldermen sat as Justices of the Peace. In 1447, the jurisdiction of the County of Hull was enlarged to include outlying villages. These included Hessle, North Ferriby, Swanland, Westella, Kirkella, Tranby, Willerby, Wolfreton, Anlaby and Haltemprice; the whole area being known as *Hullshire*. This extended the town's authority westwards along the Humber shore, and up the southern foot of the Yorkshire Wolds. This status was also a rare distinction, as the Crown had been sparing in its grant of such charters; by 1603, there were only 15 Counties Corporate in England and Wales, including Hull[13].

Hull's regional influence was thus advanced under the rule of Henry VI. This was to tie the town closely to the Lancastrian interest when simmering contests for regional and national political control were to erupt as the Wars of the Roses, from 1455. This sympathy was shared by the influential Percy family of Northumberland, the predominant power in the North-East. The Percies were confirmed in their Lancastrian allegiance by a Yorkist alliance with their bitter rivals, the Nevilles of Middleham, which was agreed in 1453-54. The feud between Nevilles and Percies led to anarchy in the North through the 1450s[14].

The alarm at such events in Hull may be gauged by the deployment of guards by the town, and by a wider mobilisation of manpower for the strengthening of fortifications. In 1449, the town watch was increased from 8 to 18 men. In 1459, the night watch was raised to 24, an embargo was placed on the removal of corn from the town, and every man was to have arms appropriate to his rank. This crisis ended by November, when Yorkist power crumbled after the Battle of Blore Heath.

When war broke out again in 1460, Hull agreed to send 13 men to support Henry VI, on 5 July. The Yorkists seized the King and, with the royal person, authority, at the Battle of Northampton the same month. In September 1460, one quarter of the men of Hull was to stand watch every night. The town gates were blocked or barred through September and October, and a ditch was dug within the walls, behind North Gate. By 24 November, an archer was set to guard every public staithe. Everyone who could afford it, especially those living on the staithes, was to provide himself with a gun. A barricade of barrels filled with stones was set up in Bishop Lane, cutting off the north-eastern part of the town. Every man was to join in digging outworks before North Gate, Myton Gate and Hessle Gate. The formidable Lancastrian Queen Margaret reportedly summoned her supporters to meet with her at Hull, and, according to a foreign source, assembled a force of 15,000 men. It is held that Richard Anson, the Collector of Customs and Mayor of Hull, joined her forces and was killed in battle at either Wakefield (30 December 1460) or Towton (29 March 1461)[15].

Under the Yorkist ascendancy, Hull was intermittently called on for troops or ships to support the new regime. The ship *Mary Bedford* was fitted out for Edward IV in 1462. In 1464, Hull and its County were ordered to provide and equip a contingent of 30 men for John Neville, Lord Montague, though the pay of only five is recorded, at 1s a day. They were raised to fight against forces which included those under Lord Roos, an East Riding peer. In 1469, the rising of Robert Hildyard, or *Robin of Holderness*, was put down by Montague. In September, Hull agreed to send 20 men to aid Edward IV, with another 12 sent from the County. The true sympathies of the town were revealed on Edward's return from temporary exile, in 1471. Making a perilous landfall on the Holderness coast, Edward slipped past armed bands of Lancastrians, perhaps by reaching an accommodation with some of his opponents. He was turned away, however, from the gates of Hull[16].

In 1481, the Earl of Northumberland ordered that 13 Hull men in white jackets, and another 8 from the County of Hullshire, should be raised to fight the Scots. In June 1483, the Duke of Gloucester ordered that men arrayed for war should join him at Pontefract. By October, as King Richard III, he was to demand that as many men as possible should join him to put down Buckingham's rebellion. Hull sent 14, Hessle 4, Swanland and Ferriby 3, Kirkella and Westella and Willerby 2, and Anlaby and Wolfreton one. Both Northumberland and Gloucester had engaged in campaigns against the Scots, and, as northerners themselves, could command respect in Yorkshire. The manpower which Hull and its County could put in the field when this was required would appear to have been at a similar level to that of the town watch in especially uncertain times – as in 1459. When defence of the town was required, all could play some part according to their means, if only by digging. Heavier demands in the 1460s may have been pitched at a somewhat punitive level, but on the other hand may have met with less effective compliance[17].

The river Hull itself protected the eastern side of the town. The measures ordered on 24 November 1460 had included the mooring of Claus Orton's ship at the jetty, for the safety of the town. Local historians have speculated that this was because the vessel carried guns. On the south side of the town, at a location known as South End, a battery of four guns was later established on reclaimed ground. These primitive guns, which are illustrated by a plan of 1540 as mounted on static timber baulks rather than on wheeled carriages, were in place by that date – when they were first deployed is unknown. The battery guarded the mouth of the Haven. Its western flank was itself overlooked by a round wall tower which may have mounted guns - certainly this tower was distinct in its design from the others around the circuit of the defences. In December 1460, 100 persons subscribed for an iron chain, which was later provided with a windlass for its swift operation, to close the mouth of the river Hull. This was perhaps associated with a small round tower on the east bank; both chain and tower appear on the plan of 1540. A further £40 was spent on the walls in 1468-69, and a jetty on the eastern side of the river Hull was taken down to make an assault from that quarter less feasible[18].

In French hands, guns had contributed to a crushing defeat of English men-at-arms and archers at Castillon, in 1453. The Earl of Warwick, leader and admiral of the Calais Garrison, and mainstay of the Yorkist cause up to 1470, was a noted pioneer of their use on the battlefield. Artillery pieces and hand-guns were used in several of the battles of the Wars of the Roses. They were particularly favoured by Burgundian mercenaries, though they rarely played a decisive role. Guns available at Hull are likely to have included light pieces of a variety of calibres; many perhaps fitted to, or removed from, ships. Light swivel-mounted guns, known as *serpentines*, were mounted on the gunwhales of ships, from the later 15th century. The English warship *Sovereign*, with a displacement of no more than 1,000 tons, mounted 110 serpentines in 1495. Such guns were used, on land and sea, from the mid-15th to the mid-16th century. Later varieties would be known by a bewildering variety of names: *portingales, slings, bases, murderers, port-pieces,* and *petreiras*; most of these types came into use in the 16th century, and fell from favour in the course of the 17[th][19].

The requirements of artillery were relatively simple. A projectile required weight and hardness – early cannon shot were often made of stone, as had been the ammunition for earlier catapult weapons. Gunpowder weapons were distinguished from their predecessors, however, by the use of an explosive charge, rather than torsion, bow or counterweight, to propel the projectile. The explosion of the charge would be contained, at first in a detachable breech. The projectile would be guided on its course by a tube. Both tube and breech were fashioned of strips of wrought iron, bound by hoops, and would fit snugly together so as to limit the escape of propellant gases. They would be mounted on a stout timber bed, if stationary, or on a wheeled carriage for mobile pieces. By the later 15th century, with technological improvement in the moulding of metals, small single-piece guns were being cast of bronze. This form would be developed into the more familiar muzzle-loading guns, of bronze or iron. These would, from the 17th century, acquire the names of birds of prey: *falcons, robinets, sakers*; or of reptiles, as with *culverins, basilisks* and *dragons*[20].

The military and social implications of gunpowder weapons were to be far-reaching, however indistinctly these were glimpsed at first. Through siege warfare, they would end the ability of the powerful nobleman to defy kings or rivals who could bring guns before his castle walls. The fall of Constantinople, in 1485, saw Turkish guns breach the greatest concentric defences in Christendom. On the battlefield, an approximate parity between the fine plate-armour worn by the armoured knight and the skill of the longbowman would be disrupted. Both the knight and the longbowman were military specialists, for whom life-long physical training was the key to efficiency and survival. But, most subversive of the old order, the gun in the hands of the conscript or weakling gave him a means to penetrate the thickest armour with only a modicum of training, or to bring down the professional soldier from afar.

The fortifications of Henry VIII

The Wars of the Roses ended with the Battle of Stoke, in 1487. This final defeat of the Yorkist cause confirmed Henry Tudor's better-known victory at Bosworth, and his position as King Henry VII. Though further plots against Henry's rule were hatched, they were detected and foiled with ease. It was only under his son, Henry VIII, that the defences of Hull were to again come to the attention of the central government, having been permitted to suffer a quiet decline under the care of the Mayor and Burgesses.

It was the King's intention to divorce his wife, Catherine of Aragon, that brought Henry VIII, formerly styled *Defender of the Faith* by the Pope, to finally break with Rome. Henry's religious policies were to bring England into conflict with Charles V of Spain, the titular head of the *Holy Roman Empire*, with Francis I of France, as well as with the Papacy, which had united these earstwhile foes against Henry. These policies were also to precipitate the single most significant domestic challenge to Henry's autocratic rule. The Dissolution of the Monasteries in England provoked popular risings in Yorkshire and Lincolnshire in 1536-37, known as the *Pilgrimage of Grace*. The *pilgrims* formed a more powerful and experienced force than the royal levies raised against them. Powerful contingents from the countryside of East Yorkshire mustered in Beverley, and from there they marched on Hull[21].

Hull was besieged between 15 and 20 October 1536, by forces encamped east of the river Hull, and to the north and west of the town. When rebel reinforcements arrived from York, on 19 October, Hull capitulated, and fell into their hands. Hull therefore stood for a period in a technical state of rebellion against the Crown, though it shared a free and general pardon which Henry granted on 8 December 1536, so as to detach supporters from the revolt. The leaders of the rising were executed, after a less successful attempt to seize Hull in early 1537. By 1538, France and the Holy Roman Empire were drawing up plans for an invasion of England, to restore the Pope's authority. Any landing would become more threatening still, if it were to join with or encourage English rebels[22].

Political crises at home and abroad thus led to what has been described as the only scheme of comprehensive coastal defence to be attempted in England before modern times. Henry VIII *sent out divers of his nobles and counsellors to view and search all the ports and dangers on the coasts where any meet or convenient landing place might be supposed... And in all such doubtful places His Highness caused divers and many bulwarks and fortifications to be made.* Richard Morrison's pamphlet, *An exhortation to stir all Englishmen to the defence of their country* recommended, among other measures, *fortifying also Kingston upon Hull, Grimsby upon Humber.* Hull was one of 28 sites in England chosen by the Crown in 1539 to be fortified, after the survey ordered by the *Device by the King*[23].

Hull was, however, initially passed over in favour of the defences of the Channel coast. The intense building activity of 1539 left permanent masonry fortifications at Walmer, Portland, Camber, Sandgate, Pendennis, Hurst, Deal, St Mawes and Calshot as the first generation of Henry's *Device* forts. Elsewhere, pre-existing defences were modernised. These fortifications were intended to deny an

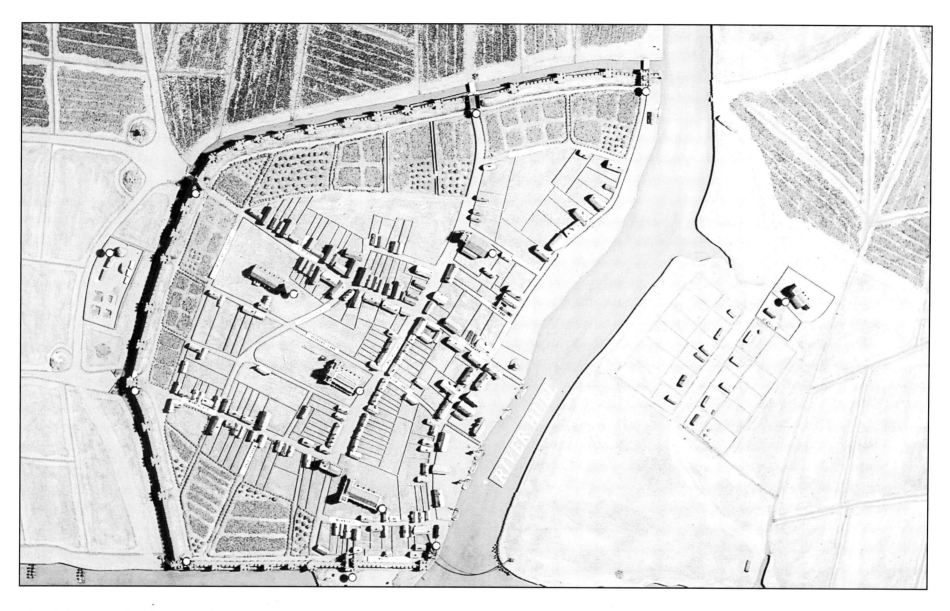

Fig 2: The town of Hull, *c*.1540, based on B.M. Cottonian Ms. Aug. 1, Supp. 4. Model by J.G. Watt, on display at the Yorkshire Water Museum, Hull.

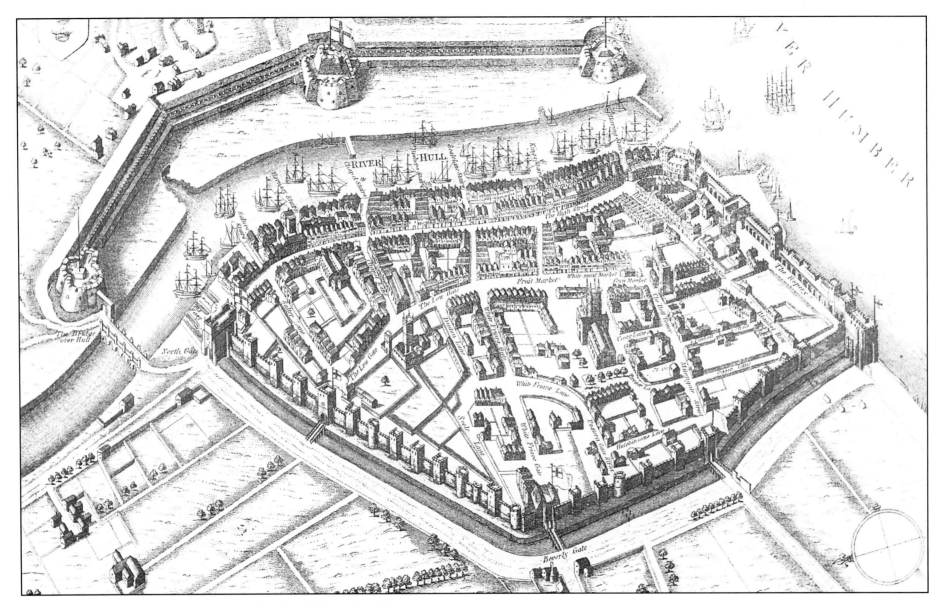

Fig 3: Hollar Plan, 1640, showing the medieval and Henrician defences.

8

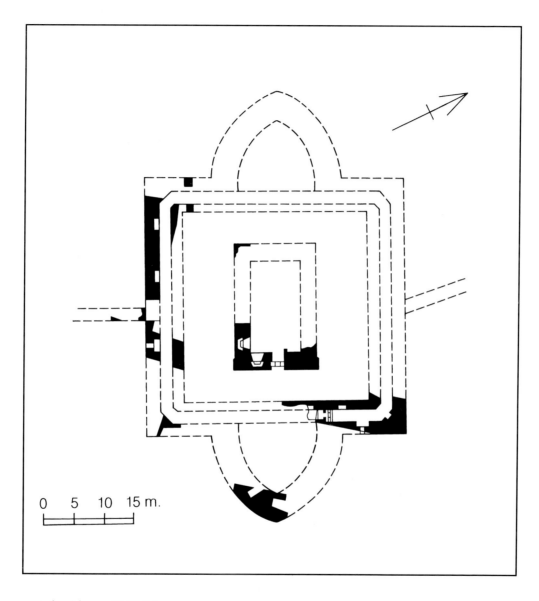

Fig 4: Plan of Hull Castle, from excavated evidence 1969-96.

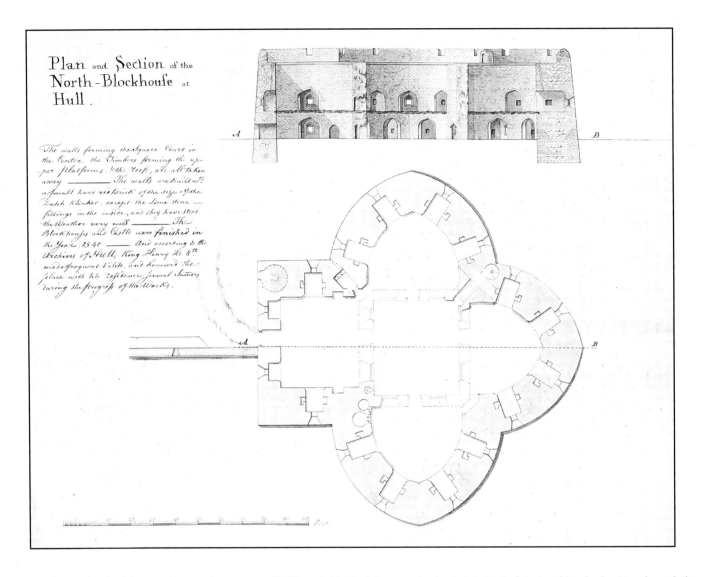

Plan and Section of the North-Blockhouse at Hull.

The walls forming the Square Court in the Centre, the Timbers forming the upper platform, & the roof, are all taken away ———— The walls are built with a small hard red brick of the size of the Dutch Klinker, except the Lime stone fillings in the inside, and they have stood the Weather very well ———— The Block houses and Castle were finished in the Year 1540 ———— And according to the Archives of Hull, King Henry the 8th made frequent Visits, and honoured the place with his residence several times during the progress of the Works.

A   B

A   B

Feet

Fig 5: Plan and elevation of North Blockhouse. Drawn between *c.*1745 and 1802, this records the brick-built fabric of both the North and the South Blockhouse, which are thought to have originally been identical in form. Gough Maps 35, fol. 24v (Plan/elevation), reproduced by permission of the Bodleian Library, University of Oxford.

invader bridgeheads for an invasion, and by the end of December 1540, 24 of the new works were already garrisoned[24].

Henry's fortifications were designed in the light of contemporary continental practice, which recognised the new ascendancy of guns in both attack and defence. To present a smaller target to the enemy, fortifications were built lower than their medieval counterparts, and with massively thick walls which could resist or deflect shot. In defence, guns would be placed on bastions forward of the main line to be defended, so as to support each other and to prevent unhindered assault on adjacent parts of the fortifications. With the spread of Renaissance ideas, these developments were rapidly adopted in northern Europe. Albrecht Durer, who advised on the fortification of Antwerp in 1520, favoured semi-circular towers with sloping parapets, and guns in defence positioned to fire into an enclosing moat, features which recur in many Henrician works. His book on fortification design, printed first in Nuremburg in 1527, was published as a Latin translation in England in 1535. Stephen von Haschenperg, a Bohemian engineer employed by Henry VIII between 1539 and 1543, may have introduced further continental features in the new fortifications built at Sandgate and Camber[25].

The Italians had been the first in Europe to develop architectural forms in response to the use of gunpowder, and Italian engineers found a place at every European court. The tradition of medieval English castle-building had developed the sophisticated use of rounded towers and concentric defences. The first generations of bastions shared the rounded form, though walls were thickened to withstand the shock of gunfire. In northern and eastern Europe, the rounded form was favoured for the strengthening of town defences in the 15th and 16th centuries. From the middle of the 16th century onwards, however, though vulnerable points might continue to be strengthened with curving elevations of masonry, an angular overall plan or *trace* was favoured. This maximised the area covered by defending guns, and could more readily assure the mutual protection of elements of an extensive fortification. Influential schemes, such as Sangallo's plans for the refortification of Rome, spread knowledge of these new techniques; while struggles between Christian and Turk for domination of the Mediterranean put them swiftly to the test. The angular bastion of the *trace Italienne* was to become the dominant form of fortification over the following two and a half centuries. In this sense, Henry's curvilinear *Device* forts represented an apogee of medieval design, rather than a method to be followed for the future[26].

Henry VIII himself visited Hull twice in 1541, to assess the importance of Hull as a fortified base in the North. His earlier, and briefer, visit was *en route* to a meeting with King James IV of Scotland, at a time of growing tension between the Scots and the English; James failed to keep his appointment with Henry. The King was lavishly entertained by the Bench during his longer stay at Hull, in October. He lodged at the King's Manor House, a central property in the town, taken over by the Crown through an exchange with its former owner, Philip Sydney. The earliest known plan of the town, dated to *c*.1540, was probably made in advance of this royal reconnaissance. Henry viewed all the defences, judged *Hull to be too weakly fortified*, and set out a scheme for their improvement[27].

The measures decided on were recorded at a meeting of the Privy Council held in Hull on 4 October. It was ordered that the town ditches should be scoured, and that some gates should be walled up. A bridge was to be built over the river Hull at the north-east corner of the town. Henry also specified *a bulwark to be made at Watergate as the King shall devise. The little round tower on Holderness side to be enlarged to bear the chain and beat the haven... The brick gate at north end to be mured up and made platform to beat the flank of the town of the one side and the flank of the haven of the other side, according to the King's device.* He also appreciated the significance of Hull's low-lying setting, ordering that the sluices controlling the drainage of the surrounding countryside should be *viewed and new made, that they may serve to drown about the town as the case shall require*[28].

Michael Stanhope, the King's *Lieutenant* - literally place-holder or personal representative - also hinted that Henry had recognised the importance of the Humber. Henry had taken a wider strategic view of its defence: *The King appointed a Master Gunner to have oversight here and at Paull - are his wages to continue... they may be no less than 12 gunners.* Paull closely overlooks the narrow navigable Humber channel, which must be followed by ships as they near Hull. It has been suggested that plans of the Humber were compiled by Italian engineers or military advisers, with the benefit of the local knowledge of Hull's Trinity House. These plans pre-date the final definition of Henry's works at Hull, *c*.1541-42[29].

The fortifications at Deal, Walmer, Sandgate, and elsewhere on the South Coast, were very similar to each other. Each had a central tower or keep, surrounded by lower rounded bastions. The bastions mounted tiers of guns. The upper guns were mounted on their roofs in the open air, to fire over their parapets, *en barbette*. The lower guns were enclosed in covered chambers, or *casemates*. Deal and

Walmer had dry moats, providing a killing-ground into which their guns could fire. The fortifications raised at Hull between 1541 and 1543 were of a different form. They comprised a *Castle* and two *Blockhouses*. The latter term was used for smaller forts; at Hull, the term was appropriate because they could close or block the river Hull to shipping by fire from their guns. The three forts were linked by a curtain wall. Together, they completed the circuit of Hull's medieval defences, by closing the eastern side of the town. They represented a considerable advance upon Henry's proposals of October 1541, and were of a form unique in England, but closely paralleled in English-held France.

The designer of the Henrician defences was an Englishman, John Rogers. Rogers had formerly been involved in non-military building projects, at Hampton Court in 1537. As Master Mason at Calais in 1541, he became involved in the fortification of Guines, on the edge of the *Pas de Calais*. The similarity of Rogers' blockhouses at Guines to those he proposed at Hull is striking. The projection of rounded towers to provide an imperfect degree of flanking fire, also a feature of Southsea Castle, may suggest that these works represent the very first moves towards the adoption of the angular bastioned system of defence. Henry probably contributed to the design work; the King emphasised that the buildings should be *mighty strong*, and ominously added, in his own hand, that Rogers should see that *those who infringe the instructions* should be not only be *corrected*, but also *punished*. As well as massive works on the eastern side of the river Hull, Rogers also planned works at the King's Manor, so that it, too, might be defended[30].

The form of Rogers' fortifications at Hull is known from a ground-plan, which survives among the Cottonian Manuscripts held in the British Museum. Versions also appear on plans dated to the later 16th century, held by Hull's Maritime Museum; and from a survey of the North Blockhouse, held by the Bodleian Library, Oxford. They appear in 17th-century plans and views of Hull, of which the Speed plan of 1610 is the earliest, and the Hollar plan of *c*.1640 one of the best known. They have also been examined by intermittent archaeological excavation, carried out between 1969 and 1997. These sources are complementary: each reveals some features upon which the others are either uninformative or misleading. Archaeological investigations on the site of the Henrician defences appear likely to continue (as of March 1999), and have not yet been comprehensively published[31].

Each fort or blockhouse mounted guns on its roof; and at first-floor and ground-floor level within. Brick and stone formed hefty foundations, which were narrowed slightly as they rose, by the use of offset or stepped construction. Above these, a massive superstructure was constructed largely of brick, with quoins and mouldings of stone. The curtain wall had a effectively vertical face, standing 13ft (3.96m) high, 14ft (4.27m) wide at base and 11ft (3.35m) thick at its top. The walls of the blockhouses were more markedly sloped or battered, so as to better deflect cannon shot, and were 15ft (4.57m) thick. The internal floors and roofs were framed in timber, and the roofs covered with lead. Moats lay to the east of the defences, and around at least the central one of the blockhouses[32].

This central, largest, fort became known as *Hull Castle*. The Castle had a rectangular keep, enclosed by a thick wall with an integral ground-floor gallery. The gallery gave access to hand-gun ports set at intervals, which would provide close-in defence, sweeping a brick-paved glacis and the surrounding moat with fire. This provision for the close-in defensive use of firepower was a feature of some of Albrecht Durer's designs, and was also employed at Deal and elsewhere. The gallery also gave access to two massive curved bastion towers, which faced east and west. These were of curved form, with their walls meeting as a beak or point. The main armament of heavy guns was mounted in, and on top of, these bastions. The keep was of three storeys, each floor being divided into two apartments. These were lighted by long narrow windows, and the upper floors were reached by two separate staircases. The only entrance to the Castle lay on its south side, and was of 5ft 6in. (1.68m) width, permitting carts and guns to be rolled into the court between the outer walls and the keep[33].

Two more blockhouses lay at the northern and southern ends of a curtain wall, which linked them to Hull Castle. These were lower than the Castle keep, being only two storeys high. They were of a trefoil shape, like clubs on modern playing cards, and were apparently identical to each other. Each lobe was a bastion, of a similar curved form to those at the Castle. The external form of the blockhouses was similar to Rogers' strong-points at Guines, though the Hull bastions were separated from each other by partitions, so as to lessen the risk of an explosion in one chamber putting others out of action. The axis of each bastion lay on the same alignment as the curtain which linked them at Hull, whereas they projected from the line of defence at Guines.

Each bastion held large guns at ground-floor, first-floor and rooftop level. At first-floor level, the bastion was divided into four chambers, comprising three gun-rooms and a lobby for access. The guns would fire through splayed embrasures or gun-ports at each level of each bastion. An entrance passage at the back of each blockhouse led to a rectangular inner court, whence spiral stairs ascended to the upper storey and the roof. The entrance passage was flanked by guard-chambers, whose walls were set with hand-gun ports[34].

Beyond the curtain wall to the east was a wet moat; though dry moats were favoured by the military theorists of the time, it would not have been feasible at low-lying Hull to keep groundwater from filling any deep trench. It is possible, though less likely, that moats may at one time have run along the western, town, side of the curtain wall. The Castle had its own moat, which did run round its western side, and which was to remain open until the later 17th century. To the west, North Bridge was constructed over the river Hull in the 1540s. The bridge was itself guarded by the guns mounted in the adjacent North Blockhouse[35].

The location of the new works on the east side of the river Hull, opposite the town, meant that ground had to be acquired for their construction. This took land from the parishes of Sutton and Drypool, and also cut off the end of the Summergangs Dike, which was provided with a new outlet into the river Hull, half a mile (c.800m) to the north. These lands had formerly belonged to Swine Priory, the Carthusian Priory or Charterhouse of Hull, and Thornton Abbey, a monastery in Lincolnshire. They had come into royal hands at the Dissolution, and had been let or leased to tenants. After the fortifications were raised, the surplus lands were granted to Sir Henry Gate[36].

The administrative and supervisory staff responsible for the project were named in a schedule signed by the King. Rogers was appointed as one of the master masons, as designer, and was also responsible for estimating the funds required, together with another master mason and the master carpenter. He was also answerable to the commander of the fortifications, because of their military significance. Rogers was to have 18d a day for himself and 6d a day for a clerk, and 4d a day extra *for every day he shall ride forth for provisions and necessaries*. Rogers' career blossomed with his work at Hull; while working there he was also sent to view fortifications at Berwick and at Wark Castle, and in 1543 was granted the sinecure of Clerk of the Ordnance, at a fee of 8d a day, and an annuity of £36 10s. The master mason and carpenter were to have 12d a day apiece. Other royal master masons were seconded to Hull from the King's works at Whitehall and Windsor in 1542[37].

Thomas Alred (or Alured) was paymaster of the works, and received 8d a day as one of the constables, and 6d a day for a clerk *to help with his book*. Rogers and the others were required to sit with the paymaster at each pay-day. At every month's end, Alred was to send up an account of the charges of the past month, which was to be signed by Rogers, the master mason and the master carpenter. £1,000 was left, *to be employed in paying out wages and provisions by those who have disbursing of it*. The Privy Council, in letters to the Mayor of Hull, ordered him to set reasonable prices on victuals, that *the King's workmen might live on their wages*[38]

The scale and character of the project is suggested by a single surviving *estimate of the wages of workmen and labourers at the King's Majesty's works at Hull 1st February 1542*. The estimate related to the cost of one month's wages. There were 20 masons employed: some taking down stones at Meaux Abbey, and others at Drypool hewing the second-hand stone. There were 20 carpenters felling and squaring timber, to make stores and work-houses. At the *bulwark next to the Humber*, which would become known as South Blockhouse, there were 60 bricklayers, working as fast as the foundations were dug. Lead from Meaux was to be taken down by 10 plumbers, who would roll it so that it could be conveyed to the works and used again. There were also 30 lime-burners, supplying material for mortar, and another 30 brick-makers. A further 60 wood-fellers were felling timber to make scaffolding; and 300 labourers were taking down stone and brick from Meaux, digging foundations, unloading ketches, keels and coal-ships, and digging chalk. The labourers received 4d a day, in line with local wages; wood-fellers 5d, and the rest 6d a day, which was a craftsman's wage. The total bill amounted to £252. Craftsmen were drawn in from outside the town, up to 200 at a time, some from York[39].

As well as Meaux Abbey, other suppressed monasteries or dilapidated churches are held to have provided materials for the Henrician works. These may have included St Mary's Church, Lowgate, and the Augustinian and Carmelite Friaries of Hull. Significant elements of these buildings, however, appear in later views and plans of Hull, so the extent of robbing must remain uncertain. Further afield, the stripping of materials from the Dominican Priory at Beverley has been illustrated by excavation, and is thought to have followed the closure of that house in 1539. The destination of timber, stone, lead, brick, tile and glass taken from there is equally unknown[40].

The formidable workforce of February 1542 may actually understate the total number of people engaged later in the year; wintry conditions would normally forbid the mortaring of brick or stone. The accounts for the construction of Sandgate Castle, for 1539, give particulars of all expenditure; there, the workforce rose to a daily average of 500. Hours of work were regulated by the 1495 Statute of Labourers, and remained virtually unchanged until the 19th century. Between 15 March and 15 September, a wage-earner had to be at work by 5 am, and was to leave between 7 and 8 pm. Out of this time, half an hour was allowed for breakfast, and an hour and a half for lunch. In Hull, however, the customary working day appears to have been between 6 am and 6 pm, with a shorter lunch-break[41].

Rogers remained based in Hull from the autumn of 1541 to the autumn of 1543. The detailed progress of the works is unknown, and they were completed for a total cost of over £23,000. From 15 February 1542 to 21 April 1543, the amount of money received and spent on the garrison and the fortifications was £14,851. The works at Hull therefore took up a significant proportion of expenditure on new fortifications in England 1539-47, which totalled £376,500[42].

The Tudor Garrison

The fortress and town of Kingston-upon-Hull was initially under the military command of its Captain, Sir Richard Long. At Deal, the upper storey of the inner keep was intended to serve as the quarters of the resident Captain. It is not known whether Long occupied the equivalent suite in Hull Castle[43].

The royal representative in the town was the King's Lieutenant, Michael Stanhope. He had charge of the money for the Garrison, *out of which he shall monthly pay the wages of himself, his lieutenant and the gunners and soldiers*. He was given a lodging at the King's Manor, having previously rented rooms at the Cloth House, in Hull's High Street, in 1543. The King's Manor had been refurbished under Rogers' direction. The addition of small bastions with hand-gun ports to its boundary walls had made it defensible, though the modest scale of these works would only have lent protection against rioters or disaffected civilians. Stanhope complained that *the chambers were too big and that all my poor implements will not furnish them. Meanwhile I have appointed the Master Gunner there. The house I have purchased at South End here is ready for me, where most of the King's Ordnance lies before the door, bent upon the Haven*. A residence at South End permitted him to keep his eye on the only large guns on the western side of the river Hull, which were positioned so as to control its mouth[44].

The composition of the Garrison under Long and Stanhope is unclear. James Utwood (or Woode) was appointed surgeon to *the retinue*, at a considerable fee of £20 a year. A number of soldiers, not named in the documents, were paid 4d a day as part of the retinue. At the royal castles of Sandown, Deal and Walmer, captains were paid 1-2s a day, porters 6-8d a day, and gunners 6d a day. The staff at Hull was probably paid at similar levels. The Master Gunner was Thomas King, who received 8d a day for himself and 4d a day for a man, or labourer, under him. As noted above, he also had oversight, of a – possibly temporary – battery at Paull, three miles to the east. The annual upkeep of Garrison, Castle and Blockhouses was claimed to have cost the Crown £900-1,000, but charges at such high levels may reflect its establishment costs in time of war. At the end of May 1542, as war with Scotland fizzled out, the Garrison was dismissed, according to royal instructions, leaving only Stanhope and his retinue[45].

The soldiers making up Stanhope's retinue were directly responsible to the King, or to Stanhope himself as King's Lieutenant. It was required *that every man shall furnish himself with harness*, or body armour. Each man had to observe a personal oath to Henry: that he would reveal to the Privy Council anything he learned that was prejudicial to the King, the realm, or the safety of the fortress. Each had to do his duty, to detect those neglecting theirs, to abstain from quarrelling, and to obey his officers. The death of any member of the Garrison was to be reported to the King[46].

Gunners were appointed by royal patent to each fort, and remained in their posts until either death or a subsequent patent removed them. They were paid directly by the Exchequer, and their appointment, training, discipline and administration was the responsibility of the Master of the Office of the Ordnance, or artillery. This central government department was responsible for fortifications, and for guns, ammunition and stores therein. From 1527, the King's Master Gunner was Sir Christopher Morris. He was to periodically *inspect the forts and their gunner detachments*[47].

Henry's Ordinance of 1542 set out the duties of gunners at the forts and castles of England. It instructed: *that the allowance of powder for exercise and the hailing of*

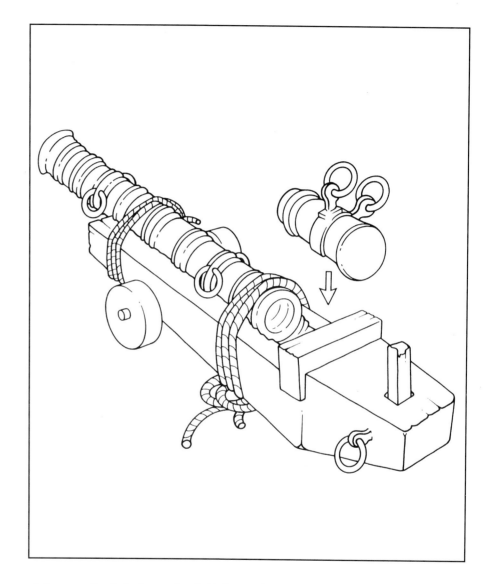

Fig 6: The Henrician port piece, the largest early breech-loading gun to be excavated from an English site on land. *Left:* As the gun and its breech were found in 1997, outside South Blockhouse. Scales 1m and 20m. *Right:* A reconstruction of the gun as it would have been mounted. The carriage is based on examples from the Mary Rose; some early guns at Hull lay on beds without wheels. Reproduced by permission of the Humber Archaeology Partnership.

ships is to be at the Governor's discretion. Nor is the captain to waste the King's powder to the danger of those that pass by. The Ordinance also stipulated *Things to be done by the inhabitants of the town: to provide iron pieces, but no brass pieces, for the defence of the town.* Munitions were to be viewed and renewed at the taking of musters, and the gunners were to keep guns maintained and ready for action. The gunners formed a tiny corps manning the castles and bulwarks of England, perhaps 200 men in all. They were, however, men of some intelligence and standing. An air of mystery and danger surrounded gunners. Their patron, shared with miners - whose occupation was similarly mysterious and hazardous - was St Barbara. A guild of St Barbara is known in Hull; it had a hall in Salthouse Lane in the 16th century, fairly close to the King's Manor[48].

One of the duties of the Garrison was the opening and shutting of the town gates at dawn and dusk. Stanhope wrote to the King's Council to ask whether this task was to be undertaken by himself or by the Mayor. Until the matter was resolved he had appointed one of his own men to this duty. The Mayor and Bench were aggrieved at this intrusion into what they regarded as their area of responsibility, as the Mayor kept the keys of the borough. Henry VIII backed Stanhope, his own appointee. He informed the Bench that he did not intend *to interfere with their liberties but that it was for their benefit, and desires them lovingly and obediently to advance the purpose.* Not only was the royal command clear, but the disloyalty of Hull at the time of the Pilgrimage of Grace may have left the Bench particularly sensitive to Henry's understated concern[49].

Stanhope and Long were also authorised, by royal commission, to levy the inhabitants for *watch and ward* on the King's behalf. *Ward* was kept by day, and *watch* by night. The town held the muster rolls for the six wards into which Hull was divided; and a night watch was first recorded in 1449. The muster rolls contained the names of able-bodied inhabitants and listed their arms, so they could be called to defend the town and the fortifications. Again, the responsibilities assumed by royal representatives overlapped with those of the town[50].

Stanhope was knighted and made *Governor* of Hull in 1547, under the new King Edward VI. The military flavour of his new title unsettled the Mayor and Bench, already offended by his exercise of what they regarded as their own functions. After the death of Henry VIII, however, Stanhope's relationship as brother-in-law to Protector Somerset placed him in a precarious position. He was accused of conspiring against the life of the Earl of Northumberland, was sent to the Tower in October 1551, and was beheaded in February 1552[51].

The execution of Stanhope permitted the Crown to mend its relations with the Bench, and simultaneously shed the financial burden of the upkeep of its fortifications. Henry VIII's wars with Scotland, in 1542, and with France, 1543-46, had proved expensive, straining the resources of the Crown. In 1553, a Royal Charter made over the care of the Castle and Blockhouses to the town: *The offices of the custody, rule, government, and charge of His Highness' Castle and two Blockhouses standing on Drypool side... That they shall safely keep and maintain all such munitions, ordnance, and implements as they shall receive of His Highness by bill... and taken part parcel and member of the said town of Kingston upon Hull and not of the said county of York*[52].

The Charter of 1553 established a highly unusual relationship between Kingston upon Hull and the Crown; comparable obligations did not fall on other fortified towns, such as Berwick, Portsmouth and Plymouth. Special financial opportunities were available: alone among the ports of England, Hull was to retain control over the collection of customs and excise duties until the later 18th century. The Corporation entered into a bond of £2,000 to keep the fortifications in repair, but only received a grant of £50 a year from the Crown, drawn from the revenues of Myton, to defray these expenses. The Garrison was now defunct. Henceforward, and until 1640, the Governor would be the Mayor of Hull. Watch and ward returned to being the responsibilities of the town. This would prove an expensive bargain; for the return of their traditional responsibilities and independence, the townsmen had undertaken to pay for the maintenance of the Henrician works on the east side of the river Hull, as well as for the upkeep of their medieval walls, towers and moats. The result, as ongoing research into 16th-century town documents has begun to reveal, was that the fortifications and their armament would tend to slip into a neglected state whenever the vigilance of central administration was relaxed[53].

The guns positioned at South Blockhouse were probably the only ones to have been in regular use since its construction, for the hailing of ships. Corporation records are silent about the payment of gunners or master gunners, though an inventory of the ordnance and stores was made at this time. Commissioners were appointed by the King to certify the list of arms and munitions made over to the Mayor. One Thomas Foxley had charge of the guns, powder and ordnance; he was permitted to graze his horses on the Garrison Ground, and so may have been a resident gunner. In 1558, guns were removed from Hull for the defence of Bridlington and Flamborough[54].

The Spanish threat

The history of the fabric of Hull's defences through the reigns of Edward VI, Queen Mary, and Queen Elizabeth I is obscure. In 1571, two Beverley bricklayers were employed on the defences. More major works are recorded in 1576, when the South Blockhouse was in need of repair, because of water getting into its foundations. The Corporation applied for some relief for the charges of the upkeep of the Castle and Blockhouses, in a series of letters to Queen Elizabeth. A survey found that, due to *the insufficiency of the timber*, at the west quarter of the Castle, *all the buildings and the lodging within the same which were framed and made of timber work are fallen down in such wise that there is nothing standing saving the outer walls*. The North Blockhouse had suffered similar problems, and collapse there had only been averted by the insertion of props. South Blockhouse was threatened by tidal erosion, against which a jetty might guard, by breaking the force of the surging waters. The Queen gave 300 trees for work on the defences, each tree providing timbers 16in. (0.41m) square and 24ft (7.32m) long. Ropes also had to be provided, to lash the logs together. The Hull Bench purchased 120 spades, 120 shovels and 60 pickaxes, items which suggest that extensive excavations formed part of the works. A new jetty, called South Jetty, was built to protect the Blockhouse, and much of the timber may have been used in this structure[55].

By 1583, Hull had spent a total of £624 6s 10d on the repair of the Castle and Blockhouses over the previous seven years. The revenue to offset these charges, from the rents of the manor of Myton, amounted to only £350. Hull claimed to have paid out £440 6s 10d, including £170 more on gunpowder than was allowed for. Lord Burghley summoned representatives of the Corporation to London, to account for their neglect of Hull's fortifications. The hauling of *great trees* to the top of the defences was recorded in 1584. Plans of the Castle and Blockhouses, which have been loosely dated to *c*.1600, refer to new timber roof-framing, and might relate to work at this time[56].

The renewed interest of central government in the condition of defences was impelled by tension with the Catholic powers of Europe. In 1559 there had been fears of a French invasion. These prompted the Spanish Minister to ask: *what treasure what other furniture for defence? Is there one fortress or hold in all England that is able one day to endure the breath of cannon?* Lord Burghley had a map of the East Riding produced in 1560, which was annotated with information about potential landing places. Under Elizabeth, the government had continued the construc-

tion of the massive Italianate bastioned defences of Berwick on Tweed, 1558-70, at a cost of £130,000. These guarded the frontier with the Scots, who were traditionally allied to France. Contemporaries criticised the works at Berwick as being poorly constructed and militarily ineffective, though such judgements were offered in the ideal light of modern military theory, rather than that of borderland necessities. In the 1580s and 1590s, Portsmouth and the Isle of Wight, and defences at Plymouth, Pendennis and the Isles of Scilly, would be refortified against the threat of Spanish invasion[57].

The threat of invasion by Phillip II of Spain was sharpened by the presence of a Spanish field army in the Netherlands. Armadas, or armed fleets, were assembled in 1585, 1588 - that known as the Great Armada - and in 1596. In most cases, severe weather was to prove more effective than naval force in their dispersal. The Tudor state had no standing army to repel invasion or suppress revolt. In dire need, the sovereign could summon the county militia. Only the better sort would serve, to keep arms from the hands of the lower classes. In 1558, a man qualified by a considerable income of £10 *per annum* was required to provide one *alim*, one bow, one bill and one *hackbut*, or hand-gun - and, presumably, retainers to wield these weapons. If he was worth £40 he was to provide two *Almain rivet*, which were flexible suits of light body armour as made particularly in Germany, one bow and one bill; or two armoured horsemen and two foot-soldiers. From 1573, the system for home defence was reviewed, and *trained bands* began to be selected and armed to provide a more reliable militia[58].

The reforms of 1573 led to the compilation of muster rolls. Each county borough entered in its muster roll a record of the men and equipment available, and the state of their training. The central government periodically collected and tabulated the rolls to show the reported strength of the militia in each county. The six wards of Hull were used as administrative divisions for this purpose, and had 714 men aged between 16 and 60 eligible for service in 1584. They were under the tuition of James Nettleton, the Muster Master. *Training of the shot is the first most requisite part of the muster master*, but he was also assigned a variety of other functions. The Muster Master was a paid officer appointed by the Lord Lieutenant or the Mayor, whose wages were charged to the town. Only a certain number of those listed in the muster rolls were selected for training. In 1577 Hull chose 10 men for training with the *arquebus*, or hand-gun. This was not a welcome duty: Robert Armyn, a freeman, alleged that his son had been chosen out of ill-will towards himself. The Mayor imprisoned Armyn for these malicious words, and Armyn's appeal to the Earl of Huntingdon, President of the Council of the North, led to the confirmation of his sentence - until such time as he apologised to the Mayor[59].

Reports of the assembly of a Spanish fleet in early 1585 prompted rapid and unseasonable activity on the defences at Hull. Over five weeks in February and March, new ditches were dug on the site of the Henrician defences. Thirty men were employed for the first week, rising to 98 and 92 for the last two weeks; in all 330 labourers were at work. All were paid 6d a day; this was a craftsman's rate, and was perhaps intended to ensure that an adequate labour force could be rapidly assembled. The work here may have concentrated on the scouring of the Henrician moat. As rumour of the departure of the Spanish fleet from Lisbon, on 30 May 1585, filtered through England, preparations against invasion intensified in Hull and the East Riding. What form these took is uncertain, though the town militia was called out and mustered, and did *watch and ward* duty. Hull did not maintain a garrison in its fortifications, though Keepers served as caretakers on behalf of the town. In 1585, John Bysbye was Keeper of the Castle; one Alcock or Ancoke was Keeper of South Blockhouse; and Henry Hubert was Keeper of North Blockhouse[60].

In February 1588, the fear of invasion by the Great Armada prompted the Bench to order a range of precautions. They closed all the town gates except Beverley Gate and North Gate, which were to be guarded by two warders at either end of the gate passages. *The planks of the posterns* were to be taken up. The watches were organised with particular attention to their supervision, and an active regime of hourly guard-changes was to be imposed. Four men, with *calivers* (hand-guns), powder and shot, were to remain at the guard-house at South End. Aldermen, serving a weekly rota, were to *lie one at the South House and another at the Water House or a sufficient man for him and with either of them 6 men every night*. The staithes were to be mended, and fitted with good gates with iron locks. The Constables of the County, the local hinterland of Hull, were to warn *every man charged with any furniture* (military equipment) *to be in readiness with his furniture*. Each night the chain was to be drawn across the mouth of the haven. A Night Watch of 18 men, comprising two men and a constable from each of the six wards, was sworn in. They remained on duty from the closing of the gates at 9 pm in summer, to 4 am the next morning[61].

The town employed Edmund Gorrel to repair the corslets, armour and calivers with which its militia was to be equipped. The East Riding was also to provide 21 light horsemen and 1,600 foot to resist a Spanish landing. This inexperienced force would probably have stood little chance in battle against the veterans of the Duke of Alva's Spanish army. A plan by W. Browne, dated *c*.1588, illustrated irregular star-shaped earthworks proposed around the North and South Blockhouses, and a pair of eared bastions, to lie at and to the north of the Castle. The plan also indicated point-blank cannon ranges, projected from batteries which were to lie in the well-sheltered bastion flanks. The plan also highlights projecting masonry structures at the town gates. The rebuilding of the Beverley Gate and the addition to it of guard-chambers, recorded by excavation, may date to this period; and other town gates may also have been modified. Later plans, however, show no trace of new earthworks about the eastern defences; this extensive scheme was probably not implemented[62].

Early warning against invasion was to be provided by a chain of beacons across the East Riding. The manning of the beacons was one of the most important duties performed by local people. The peak of activity in building and maintaining beacons in the North corresponded to the international crises of 1585-92, and of 1595-9. Duty on watch at the beacons pressed heavily on the local villages. Two watchmen were required at each through every day, and three at night. Only honest householders of over 30 years of age - steady men of property with a stake in the country - qualified for this task. They were instructed that *If the said watchman on the sea coast or Humber do see any great number of ships which to them be apparent to be enemies, and that they offer to land to invade, then the said watchman shall set where there be beacons on fire*. Detailed instructions as to how the beacons were to take light, one from another, were also provided. The nearest beacon to Hull was at Marfleet. Many other sites may still be identified, as at the Beacon Hills at Kilnsea and Patrington; Beacon Field, Boreas Hill, near Paull; Beaconsfield, Bridlington; and Beacon Farm, Bainton. People living on the coast were also ordered *to drive away all stock from the land where the enemy shall be or may land*, to deprive them of supplies[63].

In 1597 came further rumours of the Armada's return. When it appeared, it took the country by surprise, as the government had expected it to sail the following spring. By 30 October, the formidable nature of the threat was realised, and garrisons were strengthened. All people were put on the alert against those who spread *false rumour and mutinous reports*. The Privy Council ordered that Catholic prisoners should be removed from the Blockhouses, presumably as a security measure should they come under attack. The Castle and Blockhouses were reported to be in good repair; watch and ward was kept when deemed necessary; every householder stood ready with his weapons, and forty or fifty men were on watch every night[64]

The threat of invasion by Catholic Spain had heightened fears that English Catholics would act as a fifth column on behalf of the invaders. Penal Statutes, passed from 1558 onwards, laid down penalties for failure to conform to or attend the Church of England, and these legal instruments were enforced with intermittent vigour. After an abortive northern rising in 1569, central government was represented by the Council of the North, based at York. Archbishop Whitgift, successor to the Earl of Huntingdon as President of the Council, was responsible for rounding up *recusants* - those admitting to Catholic loyalties. These were detected by *searchers*, who made an unsavoury living by tracking and informing against offenders, and spies who infiltrated communities of secretly practising Catholics[65].

The Castle and Blockhouses served as prisons for those arrested, as prisoners of conscience, from about 1577. They were again used for this purpose from about 1580; and in 1586 the release of Thomas Leeds, a *recusant and prisoner in the Castle and South Blockhouse* is recorded. Twelve recusants were held there in 1581 and in 1585, and in 1597 sixteen. The ground-floor chambers, in particular, proved grim quarters: *some have been kept three or four years in low houses without fire, where the houses have been overflowed with water at high tide, so that as they walked, the earth was so raw and moist that their shoes would cleave to the ground. Neither had any place of ease* (toilets) *but by their bedsides, and when the keeper came, morn and even, to carry it in their hands and throw it into the haven.* Accounts of those who suffered for their faith at Hull, from the later 16th century and through the 17th century, are presented by Hirst in his account of *The Blockhouses of Hull and who went there*[66].

Footnotes

1: Ellis and Crowther 1990.
2: Raistrick and Jennings 1965; Myres 1935, 250-62; Farley 1783.
3: English 1979.
4: Ayers 1979, 3-9.
5: Frost 1827.

6: Ayers 1979; Allison 1969.
7: Allison 1989, 178; Foreman in prep.
8: Evans 1995; Evans 1999; Horrox 1983, 58-9.
9: Evans 1999.
10: Evans 1995; Allison 1969.
11: Bartlett 1971; Brooks 1939; Evans 1995; Evans 1999; Allison 1969.
12: Gillett and MacMahon 1989, 17.
13: Boyle 1905; Allison 1969, 29.
14: Dockray 1992.
15: Gillett and MacMahon 1989, 66-67; Dockray 1992.
16: Gillett and MacMahon 1989, 68-9; Haigh 1997, 189-93; Bruce 1839, 1-30.
17: Gillett and MacMahon 1989, 69.
18: Gillett and MacMahon 1989, 66-7; KUHRO BRB 1, 75, 1449-1552; de Boer 1973, pl. 10; Gillett and MacMahon 1989, 69.
19: Smith 1988; Smith 1993; Smith 1995.
20: Hogg 1963, 5.
21: Dickens 1964, 178, 298.
22: Neave 1996a, 120; KUHRO D564; Saunders 1976, 9.
23: Colvin 1982, 369; LPFD Henry VIII xiv (1), 655.
24: Saunders 1989, 37-52.
25: Hughes 1974; Hale 1965, 466-74; Saunders 1976, 12-13; Saunders 1989, 45; O'Neil 1945, 155.
26: Hughes 1974; Spiteri 1993, 106; Malachowicz 1977; Pepper 1976; Spiteri 1994.
27: Allison 1969, 93; de Boer 1973, 84-5.
28: LPFD Henry VIII xvi, 579; PRO SP 1/167, fos 83-4, cited in de Boer 1973, 82; LPFD Henry VIII xvii, 1541, 62-5.
29: LPFD Henry VIII xvi, 1541, 4 October 1541; de Boer 1973, 85-7, pls 11-12.
30: Shelby 1967, 46; pls 2, 5 and 8; 34-46, pls 10-13.
31: B.M. Cott. MSS. Aug. 1, Supp. 4; Hull Maritime Museum, unaccessioned later 16th-century plans, perhaps collected for lawsuit claiming title to Citadel, *c.*1858; Bod. Lib. Gough Plans, 35f: 25; Bartlett 1971; Eddy 1976; Foreman 1989; Foreman 1994; Foreman 1995; Foreman 1996; Foreman 1997.
32: PRO WO46:1, Estimate, 18 July 1682; Foreman 1996.
33: Saunders 1976, 12-13; Saunders 1989, 37-47; Hirst 1913, 4-7.
34: Shelby 1967, pls 2-5.
35: Foreman 1995, 26; Foreman 1996, 26.
36: Blashill 1903, 12, 68.
37: LPFD Henry VIII 1542, no. 140; Colvin 1982, 379.

38: LPFD Henry VIII 1542, no. 155.

39: LPFD Henry VIII 1542, 34; Woodward 1995, 172; Colvin 1982, 474-5.

40: Hirst 1913, 2-3; Foreman 1996, 258-60.

41: Morley 1963, 11-12; Hoskins 1976, 108; Woodward 1995.

42: LPFD Henry VIII xviii (1), 438; Colvin 1982, 374.

43: LPFD Henry VIII 1542, no. 161; Saunders 1976, 26.

44: LPFD Henry VIII 1542, no. 140; Shelby 1967, pl. 13; Horrox 1978, 20; LPFD Henry VIII 34, no. 358; Horrox 1978, 92.

45: LPFD Henry VIII 1542, no. 140; Saunders 1976, 15; Hadley 1788, 105; LPFD Henry VIII 1542, 30 May, no. 358.

46: LPFD Henry VIII 1542, 64-5.

47: Hogg 1963, 160.

48: LPFD Henry VIII 1542, no. 154; Hogg 1963, 155; Lambert 1891, 111.

49: LPFD Henry VIII 1542, no. 358; LPFD Henry VIII 1542, no. 130.

50: KUHRO L15, 1541; Gillett and MacMahon 1980, 64.

51: KUHRO L16, 1550; Stephens and Lee vol. 18, 908-9.

52: KUHRO: Charter of Edward VI, 1552-53, D597.

53: KUHRO BRB 4, 88; Brooks 1951; pers. comm. Helen Good.

54: KUHRO M46,1552; Gillett and MacMahon 1980, 147.

55: Woodward 1995, 165; KUHRO BRB 4, 147, L17-21, M56, L17-21, M78; Woodward 1995, 46, 93.

56: CSPD Add. 1580-1625, 97; Eddy 1976.

57: Rodriguez-Salgado 1988, 68-9; English 1990, 136; Saunders 1989.

58: Boynton 1967.

59: Allison 1969, 4; KUHRO M137A; Boynton 1967, 106; Brooks 1951, 101-3; Boynton 1967, 116.

60: Woodward 1995, 99; Gillett and MacMahon 1980, 149; Hirst 1913, 80, 107, 113.

61: KUHRO BRB 3, 245v; Gillett and MacMahon 1980, 149, 64.

62: Gillett and MacMahon 1980, 149; BM Cott. MSS Aug. Vol. 1, No. 83; Evans and Sitch 1990; Evans 1999.

63: Poulson 1841, 85-8; Nicholson 1887, 42, 46, 32, 33, 31.

64: Palliser 1983, 28; Boynton 1967, 149; CSPD Add. 1566-99, 179; Gillett and MacMahon 1980, 128.

65: Hirst 1913, 16-48.

66: de la Pryme [1986], 49; KUHRO L56; Hirst 1913, 69-129.

CHAPTER 2

HULL BESIEGED

By the end of the 16th century, Hull's administrative independence seemed assured. Hull was ruled by a *Bench* of 13 Aldermen, drawn from among the most prominent and wealthy merchants of the town. New Aldermen joined them only on the nomination of sitting members, confirmed by elections held among themselves. Those elected held office for life. The Mayor was elected annually from among the Aldermen. As a closed corporation, the Bench ruled the town, made its regulations, and sat as magistrates to enforce them. Like all town corporations, the Mayor and Bench were proud and jealous of their liberties, which had culminated in a political drive towards independence.

From 1440, the Royal Charter had settled the form of local administration. The Bench exercised both executive and judicial functions in the Town and County of Hull. Their hereditary grip on political and economic power was buttressed by royal support. During the personal rule of Charles I, the King was to favour the rich merchant oligarchies of the corporate towns by protecting their position with restrictive trading practices. At Hull, they ruled over a population living mainly within the medieval circuit of walls; by the end of the 17th century, the population of Hull still numbered no more than about 7,000[1].

The defences under James I

Royal favour carried a price: the upkeep of Hull's fortifications had cost the town £3,522 between 1552 and 1599. The Bench was aggrieved at the unwillingness of the Crown to help defray the costs of the maintenance of the Henrician Castle and Blockhouses. These had far exceeded the revenues of £50 *per annum* which the Crown had allocated as the contribution of the government to their upkeep. The Bench claimed that customs duties, such as taxes levied on the trade in foreign grain in the town, should go towards their expenditure on the upkeep of their piers and fortifications. Attempts to attach the costs of maintaining the eastern bank of the river Hull to those of the eastern defences would be intermittently revived until the mid-19th century[2].

The costs incurred by the Bench included the staffing of the fortifications as well as the maintenance of their fabric. On the death of the Keeper of South Blockhouse in 1598, the Corporation employed Edward Brown, a mariner, in his place, at a cost of £13 6s 8d a year. In 1625, William Biggins was hired to serve as a full-time gunner. In the 1630s, Edward Haslam and Robert Coulinge were Keepers, at the North and South Blockhouses respectively. Though charged with the maintenance and delivery of arms and ordnance, both were also referred to as gunners from time to time. Retired seamen would often have been acquainted with gunnery through naval service, and would thus be suited to such positions[3].

Hull was almost entirely Puritan in both sentiment and religion. The enforcement of religious conformity devolved, like all else, on the Bench and its appointed officers. This point was most painfully obvious to the Catholic recusants who continued to be detained in Hull, where they were victimised or exploited by the Keepers of the Castle and Blockhouses. In 1613, four Catholics imprisoned for refusing to swear the oath of allegiance to James I were removed to the South Blockhouse *for their better ease and conveniency* - as South Blockhouse was more prone to flooding at high tides than the others, this may have been a grimly ironic comment. Northern Europe was in the throes of the Thirty Years War, a conflict embittered by religious division, and England declared war on Catholic Spain in 1626. Hull contributed to this struggle with the payment and billeting of 1,300 foot soldiers *en route* for the German town of Stoad, to fight for the Protestant cause[4].

In 1626, the Privy Council ordered that Hull should be fortified against the possibility of a Spanish raid, which might be launched from the Netherlands, and that the trained bands should be armed and exercised. The Mayor petitioned the government for a supply of ordnance for the defence of the town. In about February 1627, the President of the Council of the North asked that the Master of Ordnance supply £300 worth of gunpowder, 300 muskets and as many corslets, or suits of body armour, from the Tower Armoury in London to Hull, to refurnish the king's storehouse. In 1628, the Bench asked the King for 20 guns, gun carriages, powder and shot, to *fortify and make stronger the town*[5].

Some of these guns were to arm a *curtain sconce near the South Blockhouse built by the Mayor and Burgesses* in 1627 (it is possible that *curtain* is a misreading of *certain*; however, the new fort surrounded the South Blockhouse, making the former reading apt). This is first mentioned in a detailed survey of the defences in

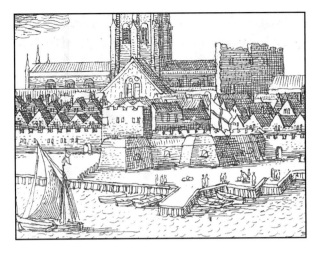

Fig 7: South End Fort, as seen from the Humber. Views by Hollar (1640), Hibbert (1737) and Buck (1745). From the collections of Wilberforce House Museum, Hull.

22

1634, and comprised a rectangular fortification immediately to the east of South Blockhouse. At this time the sconce mounted four guns. It is illustrated as an earthwork on a plan by Joseph Osbourne, datable to either 1660 or 1680, and appears ruinous in a sketch by Francis Place, dated to 1680. The same survey detailed the armament of the Henrician defences, and the other military stores held there. At South Blockhouse, 15 guns were on the roof and 9 below; at the Castle there were 9 guns above and 20 below, some in store; and at North Blockhouse 10 on the roof and 14 below[6].

A fort at South End, on the other side of the river Hull, was also built in 1627. It was later described as *a great rampart or open fort at South End which had cost them (the town) above £1,000.* It is illustrated by the Osbourne plan as a D-shaped structure of brick. It was substantially built, with foundations descending to a considerable depth. The South End Fort replaced earthworks first recorded *c.*1540. In 1716, these survived as hummocks immediately west of the new work. In 1634, South End mounted 11 guns of varied calibre, together with shot and all other essentials housed in a storeroom. As guns here could provide a valuable crossfire with those at South Blockhouse, enhancing control over the mouth of the Hull, this battery would later be renovated, *c.*1686, and would continue in use until the mid-19th century. Twelve iron *sakers* were lent by the King, and shipped from London to Hull in May 1630. About 1630, the Crown ordered the Mayor, in his capacity as Governor of Hull, to have the town ditch scoured, the walls repaired and the Blockhouses mended[7].

Corporation expenditure on the fortifications up to 1635 totalled £11,367. If the 16th-century payments of £3,522, and the wages paid to gunners and Keepers, are deducted from this total, it appears that much of the remaining £7,845 laid out must have related to measures taken to secure the mouth of the river Hull. The will of Alderman Thomas Ferries, of 1630, left the town the considerable sum of £250: *so soon as conveniently may be in good oaken timber and planks for repairing of the North Bridge of this town and platforms in the Castle and Blockhouses here and other needful places.* This is the first such bequest to be identified, but other worthies may similarly have contributed private resources to the defences of the town[8].

The report of Commissioners appointed to view the defences in March 1634 led the Mayor to issue further orders for repairs in June. *The celebrating on November 5th by firing of guns to commemorate God's great deliverance from gunpowder treason* was an opportunity to demonstrate both Hull's Protestant loyalty to the Crown, and the readiness of its refurbished defences. Work was continuing the next year, when overtime was paid to labourers working on earthwork defences[9].

Despite this municipal investment and effort, the artificial defences of Hull would still have to be regarded as weak and outmoded when compared to contemporary works on the continent, or at other places in England. The low-lying setting of the town, on the other hand, offered the prospect of defence through the flooding of the surrounding countryside. Such an operation had been carried out at Antwerp in 1584, to the discomfiture of its Spanish besiegers. The Dutch engineer Simon Stevin had advocated this method of defence most particularly for those towns which stood either by the sea or by a river with a large tidal variation - locations where tides were high and strong. The Humber tides are among the highest in England, and no English town was better placed than Hull to exploit them in time of need[10].

The Bishops Wars

Under Elizabeth I, national unity had been cemented by the prospect of foreign invasion. The equation of Catholicism with treason was underlined by the Gunpowder Plot of 1605, against James I. In the later years of James' reign, and under his son Charles I, external factors began to lose their power to distract critical attention from the shortcomings of an impecunious and incompetent central government. From 1629 until 1640, Charles I was to rule without calling a Parliament. The expedients to which he resorted in order to fund government alienated one powerful interest group after another. With the growth of Puritanism, conflict between *Court* and *Country* was increasingly articulated in moral and religious terms[11].

In 1638, matters came to a head when Charles tried to impose the authority of Bishops over the traditionally independent and strongly Protestant clergy of Scotland. This policy led to open revolt in Scotland, where an army sworn to defend their religious independence assembled in 1639. Hull, because of its strategic position, was central to Charles' plans to bring the Scots to heel. Its magazine was to be stocked with munitions brought in by sea from London and abroad. These were to be issued to the militia, who would then march on to assemble at York, the main base for the campaign. Berwick and Newcastle were advanced collecting points for the troops[12].

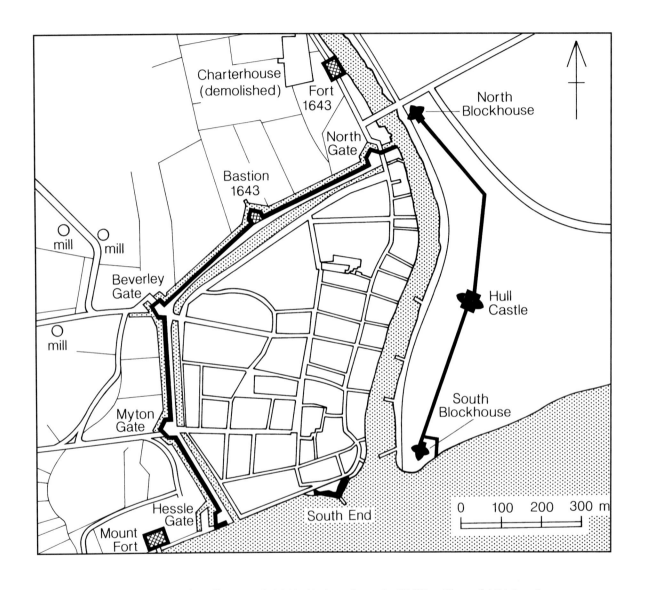

Fig 8: The Civil War defences: the earthwork defences of Hull, erected 1640-43, based on the Phillips Plan of 1716 and contemporary accounts. Cross-hatch indicates works erected or renewed about the time of the siege of 1643

24

In January 1638, Captain William Legge, Master of the King's Armouries, conveyed royal instructions to the Mayor. The moats of Hull were to be cleaned, new drawbridges were to be added to three of the town's gates, and the others were not to be used. These instructions were implemented under threat of a lawsuit against the Bench, which was alleged to have neglected the care of Hull's defences. Once the King was satisfied by Legge's report on progress, the lawsuit was dropped, in 1639. The Crown also offered more positive assistance. *His Majesty is pleased, for the better encouragement of the inhabitants, to fortify the town, to lend them six demi-culverin of iron, with their field carriages, mounted on unshod wheels, with ladles and sponges belonging to them.* The guns were delivered to John Spencer, one of His Majesty's gunners[13].

The King's Manor, now property of Henry Hilyard, was once more to be taken over *for the King's service and the safety of the town,* so as to serve as a magazine for stores of war. Hilyard consented to this in August 1638. The magazine was in the charge of Alderman James Watkinson, a wealthy merchant. Legge, with the nominal assistance of the Mayor, was to take receipt of arms arriving at Hull. These included a consignment *of 800 muskets complete, and 2,000 pikes, and all other provisions which are to be brought out of the Low Countries by Sir Jacob Astley;* and other stores shipped up from the Tower of London. Legge was to issue powder, match and musket-shot to the commanders of the militia that would form Charles' expeditionary force to Scotland. These commanders were to include the Lords Lieutenant of Nottingham, Derby, York, Lancaster, Chester, Stafford, Northumberland, Cumberland, Westmoreland and Durham. The Keepers of the North and South Blockhouses were similarly authorised to keep and issue arms and munitions. With practical and administrative measures for the assembly of an arsenal at Hull in place, the royal Mandate to *close and fortify the town* was issued on 1 February 1639[14].

Charles himself came to Hull from York in April 1639, to view progress in his martial preparations. The trained bands lined the streets where the King was to pass. A force of 100 musketeers were dressed in coats provided at the town's expense, and armed out of the stores at the Castle and Blockhouses. They paraded under the captaincy of the Mayor, William Popple, and his officers. A later comment hints that the trained bands of Hull wore grey coats - the use of undyed cloth was common in the equipment of soldiers raised in the North, while the trained bands of Beverley were provided with grey coats. All this made a brave show, and the king was pleased. He then examined the magazine and the arms and ammunition stored there, and the guns were fired, apparently to his satisfaction. He stayed that night in the house of Sir John Lister, in High Street. Having assured himself that his Mandate had been fulfilled, the King left for York the next day with a ribbon - the *Hull Favour* - in his hat[15].

Sir Jacob Astley had already informed the King that 1,000 men could hold Hull in a siege. As well as the gunners and the uniformed company provided by the town, Hull could draw on the Holderness trained bands and Sir John Hotham's regiment at Beverley. In 1639, it was proposed that outer defences should be constructed for (in clockwise order) Hessle Gate, Myton Gate, Beverley Gate and North Gate, though these works were apparently only begun the next year[16].

The militia of the northern counties who gathered to collect arms from Hull, and who were billeted on the surrounding countryside, were a sorry sight. Sir Edmund Verney reported in May 1639: *Our men are very raw, I daresay that there never was so raw, so unskilful, and so unwilling an army brought to fight.* The First Bishops' War ended in June 1639, when an English force bolted in the face of a Scots detachment under Leslie, resulting in the *Pacification of Berwick.* Arms were returned to stores at Berwick, Carlisle and Hull in November. At Hull, Legge was initially to be provided with £500 out of *imprest* - locally collected customs revenue - to refurbish weapons. He estimated the total cost of repairs required to be £1,561 4s 6d[17].

In 1640, the King again raised troops for war against the Scots. In March, 2,000 horse were to be raised, to receive their arms at Hull, and to be quartered in the neighbourhood. The Earl of Northumberland asked that all assistance should be given to the quartermaster in accommodating this force. In June, 1,650 soldiers under Colonel Edward Fielding were to be sent to be *ready to assist the works of fortification if there should be cause,* and their lodging was under discussion. In July, the Mayor and Sir Jacob Astley were seeking to reduce the numbers of troops billeted in the town, by various means. It was determined that the soldiers should be billeted in the surrounding villages, and the King decided that troops should not be billeted in Hull. News of plague in London sharpened anxieties lest Hull should be packed with strangers. Two more companies arrived, and thanks to the Bench were recorded in August 1640 for credit, *for some few days pay,* afforded the soldiers[18].

The trained bands were to be kept in readiness against a Scots invasion, and the Mayor was asked to carefully perform instructions to this end. In August 1640, a ramshackle force marched north. Later the same month they were routed at Newburn, outside Newcastle, being scared from the field by the Scots' artillery. The King sent Sir Thomas Glemham to be Governor of Hull, for the safety of the town and the magazine there, in September 1640. His regiment of foot was to serve as a garrison. The Mayor and Aldermen resented this appointment most strongly, as an infringement of the Charter of 1553. They complained to the Earl of Strafford, President of the Council of the North, who urged their submission. The Mayor was eventually persuaded when the King himself threatened to come to Hull, and delivered the keys of the town, Castle and Blockhouses up to Glemham[19].

Glemham, with 1,000 men - a full-strength regiment of foot - duly took possession of the town. The arrival of Glemham's regiment was followed by the first recorded work on defences outside the medieval walls of Hull, as had been proposed in 1639. On 10 September 1640, Captain Thomas Dymoke reported that *our regiment was sent to fortify Hull, the place now aimed at by the enemy, and the town is strengthened daily by the soldiers, who are continually busy in framing an outward defence.* The works begun in 1640 encircled the medieval defences of the town[20].

The extent of these earthworks is most fully illustrated by plans dated to 1660 and c.1716, and their profile by a section view of 1742. The larger part of the outer defences would appear to have been as envisaged in 1639. Projecting defences or *half moons* were thrown up before Hessle Gate, in a rectangular form. Myton Gate, Beverley Gate and North Gate were strengthened by angled bastions. Breastworks linked these four bastions, forming a continuous perimeter. The outer ditch before these defences was often referred to as the *Bush Dyke*, and was fed by the Spring or Julian Dyke which carried water to Hull from springs in Anlaby, close to the modern Waterworks Street. Near the Humber, it was referred to as a common sewer[21].

Later descriptions give an impression of the character of these defences. Thomas Baskerville visited in 1677; probably entering at Beverley Gate. He described his approach to Hull as follows: *Being now got near it, ready to enter, we saw a drawbridge and a deep and broad moat full of water surrounding this part of the town. Leaving this behind us we came to another deep moat with a drawbridge over it where there is a strong gatehouse, and portcullis, and a strong wall on the inner bank surrounding this moat. Then, allowing room for defence where men may stand and use their arms, we came at length to another strong gate which led us into the town, with a wall*

surrounding their houses. This account records a drawbridge over the outer moat of 1640; another spanning the medieval moat; and a berm, or level space, between this moat and the medieval town walls. Of the two inner gates, either the first was in a barbican forward of the walls, and the second in the gatehouse itself; or both were at the gatehouse[22].

The garrison remained at Hull for 10 months. Towards the end of this period, a group of soldiers murdered a Captain Withers, on 7 June 1641, and then defied their officers, demanding pardon for their actions, from the security of the Blockhouses. The same month, the keys of Hull were returned to the Mayor; the soldiers' accounts for lodging and stabling settled; and Glemham's regiment marched to York, where it disbanded. A further five regiments gathered at Hull were paid off and sent home, in mid-July 1641[23].

In September 1641, soldiers were loading ammunition at Hull to be transported back to London. The Scots War was ended by the Treaty of Ripon, on 26 October 1641. The expense of the war, however, had broken Charles' ability to rule without a Parliament to raise taxes. In April 1640, Charles had summoned the *Short Parliament*, which was called on the advice of the Earl of Strafford. This Parliament would not grant money unless the accumulated grievances of Charles' personal rule were addressed. They were not, and Parliament was dissolved in May. Charles then summoned a Great Council of Peers in York in October 1641, but they were fearful of independent action, and could only advise that a full Parliament should be called. The Treaty of Ripon dictated that Charles should pay £850 a day to maintain the Scots army ensconced in Newcastle. The royal coffers were empty. These demands made the summoning of a Parliament imperative, and the *Long Parliament* was summoned on 3rd November 1641. Parliament took this opportunity to curb royal power; impeach Strafford and Archbishop Laud, who were executed; and to use its tax-gathering powers to enforce its primacy. It was Charles' break with the Long Parliament that led to civil war[24].

The first siege of the Civil War

On 15 January 1642, Charles ordered the Earl of Newcastle and Captain Legge to secure Hull on his behalf; the Earl of Newcastle being appointed as Governor. He came with Legge, armed with the King's Commission. Legge wrote: *the best means I had was to prevail with the burgesses of this town by themselves to secure the place for his Majesty's service and that work is very well brought to pass, for last night arrived an express from Sir John Hotham with an order from Parliament for him to be Governor and a power to draw in such forces as he thought fit; likewise a letter from him to the magistrates for preparing and lodging and billet for his regiment, his admission was quite denied and a letter to the Parliament dispatched under the chief hand of the Burgess' to excuse themselves from receiving any garrison, they of the town being able to secure the place for his Majesty's service. The Earl of Newcastle is Governor of Kingston-upon-Hull whereof the townsmen have manifested great affection to the King and excused their not receiving of Sir John Hotham, but they were overruled by Parliament.* The town was thrown into a dilemma, first refusing, then accepting Newcastle, and finally admitting Sir John Hotham with an order from Parliament appointing him as Governor. All this transpired on the same day, 21 January 1642[25].

Sir John Hotham was Colonel of the trained bands of the East Riding of Yorkshire, and Member of Parliament for Beverley. He was installed as Governor, with 1,000 troops. His son, Captain John Hotham, Member for Scarborough, came into the town with five companies of the East Yorkshire trained bands. Parliament had authorised him to raise these troops for the security of Hull; they were to be billeted on the town. Sir John Hotham was to be the Governor of the town and fortress of Hull, by Parliamentary sanction. Henry Barnard, the Royalist Mayor, relinquished the keys of the town to Hotham, protesting that as Mayor he should be Governor as of right. For this, and for his opposition to the quartering of troops on the town, he was called to the Bar of the House of Commons, and was admonished by the Speaker[26].

With their nominee established as Governor in Hull, Parliament petitioned on 20 April for the magazine to be removed from Hull to London by sea. The magazine at Hull was, because of the recent war against the Scots, one of the two principal stores of arms in the Kingdom, the other being the Tower of London. The Hull magazine had contained 120 field pieces, 20,000 arms, and 7,000 barrels of gunpowder after the Scots Wars in 1641, though some ammunition had been sent back to London, in September 1641[27].

Charles moved from York to Hull, and on 23 April 1642, Governor Hotham denied him entry to Hull. Hotham lined the walls of Hull with the men of his trained bands, who stood guard with loaded muskets. Other soldiers kept the citizens confined to their houses until sunset, while the Mayor was also put under

guard. Soldiers guarded the gates, with drawn swords in hand, under orders to kill anyone that came near them. Having declared Hotham a traitor, the King, humiliated, retired to Beverley. With Hull occupied by Parliamentarian troops, the ordnance in store was removed by sea to the Tower of London in May. It took four ships to carry away military stores which now included 49 brass cannon with their carriages, 906 barrels of gunpowder, enough shot to blow away an army, and other arms and stores. At the same time, Charles' plans to seize an arsenal at Portsmouth were also frustrated[28].

There followed three badly organised undercover operations by the Royalists against Hull; all failed. In June, a spy reported on the tight security imposed at Hull: *This night I was at Hull, and there they fortify daily. At the North Gate, next the river an earth wall is built for two rows of musketeers, the gate blocked up with earth. So is Myton Gate. At Hessle Gate they have planted a piece (gun) in either side, one in top of the gate. Within every gate two (sentries) look us in the face as we go in. And in every gate, three pieces, one in either side and one aloft*[29].

In July 1642, the King marched from York to Beverley to make a further attempt against Hull. According to a Parliamentarian source, he was accompanied by an army numbering 3,000 foot and 1,000 horse. A Royalist source described a force of 700 foot and 400 horse, and the enrolment of other supporters. The King proclaimed that none should provision Hull. Sir John Pennington was to enforce this order by naval blockade, while 200 horse were sent into Lincolnshire, to secure Barton-on-Humber and prevent reinforcements reaching Hull from that direction. Hull was besieged between 8 and 27 July[30].

On the evening of 4 July, Governor Hotham, taking advantage of a high spring tide, had ordered the sluices raised and the Humber banks cut. He blew up the Charterhouse, to the north of the town, and cleared all the remnants of Myton town, to the west. This was *for fear the Royalists should get possession of them and make lodgements against the town.* Local accounts disagree as to whether clearance to the west of the town preceded or followed the siege of 1642, though they agree that this was Hotham's work. The opening of the sluices led to an anguished petition of complaint from the leading gentry of Holderness, and some 300 others, to the King at Beverley. A counter-declaration from Parliament, offering compensation for flood-damage, was issued on 12 July. The same day, Charles offered pardon to all in Hull, if only they would lay down their arms. [31].

Royalist land forces burnt three mills belonging to the town, and cut the fresh-water dyke supplying the town. Charles had consulted earlier that year with Sir Thomas Glemham about a strategy to beseige Hull, his earstwhile command. *Cannot I starve Hull by cutting off the fresh water supply?*, asked the King. Glemham replied that the King had been misinformed, *for though you may cut off from them the fresh spring that runs to Hull, yet the haven is fresh at low water and every man can dig at his door. They cannot bury a corpse there, but the grave first drowns him ere it buries him.* The effectiveness of this measure was questionable, but, like flooding and burning, it was perhaps intended as a demonstration to those whose loyalties were still wavering[32].

The inhabitants of Hull had raised a well-armed force of 1,000 townsmen, *who generally entered into pay and duty.* For their part, Parliament ordered that captains and lieutenants for these 10 companies, and money to pay arrears owed to some of the garrison, should be sent to Hull. They also raised 2,000 men in London *by beat of drum* to reinforce them, under the command of Frances Fairfax. Sir John Meldrum, a Scottish captain who had seen service in Germany and elsewhere on the continent, was sent to assist Hotham[33]

The Navy and seamen went over to the Earl of Warwick *en masse*, on his appointment as Admiral by Parliament in July 1642. Crucially, he sent two ships to help Hull. In mid-July, Warwick wrote to Parliament informing them that a royal messenger had commanded that he should send the 40-gun ship *Lion* to his Majesty before Hull, and deliver up the Captain of that ship. Warwick refused the King's order, on the instructions of both houses of Parliament. Parliamentarian superiority at sea was to permit both supplies and reinforcements to enter the town, running an ineffectual Royalist blockade. It was reported that *Sir John Hotham has taken in two vessels laden one with corn, the other with wine whereby he succours himself and prevents his opposers.* The Parliamentarian ships protecting Hull and the Humber were the *Raine-Bow* (or *Rainbow*), of 790 tons with 40 guns and a crew of 260; the *Unicorn*, of 767 tons with 46 guns and 250 crew; and the merchant ships *Mary-Flower* (or *Mayflower*), of 450 tons with a crew of 121 and *Hercules*, of 350 tons with 150 crew. The merchantmen were, in size at least, broadly equivalent to third or fourth rate *men-o-war*[34].

Two Royalist ships arrived from Holland between 8 and 12 July, but were separated from each other by a storm at the mouth of the Humber. The *Providence*, under Captain John Strachan, ran aground at Keyingham, east of Hull. This 304 ton vessel had been built in 1637, and was armed with either 14 or 30 guns. It landed no more than eight guns, which together with warlike stores were carried off in ten carts to serve the King against Hull. A battery was established outside the walls, and sailors from the ship manned the guns. There can have been few professional gunners with the King at this stage. A Cornish engineer named John Lanayon was employed as engineer in charge of the siege. Another Royalist ship, *coming up very boldly towards Hull*, came under fire from the town - presumably from guns mounted either at South Blockhouse or South End - and was driven off, landing guns on the south bank of the Humber[35].

Royalist forts were raised at Paull and Hessle, and on the south bank of the Humber in Lincolnshire. *These fired on ships sailing to and fro on the Humber; but there* (at Paull) *they broke one of their guns, and another at Hessle.* It is unclear whether these losses were caused by Parliamentarian ships, or were the result of accidents – the overcharging of small guns in a desperate attempt to damage passing ships would have been especially likely to burst their barrels. Three guns being taken to the south bank of the Humber by a yacht, however, were intercepted by the Parliamentarian frigate *Mayflower*, and were taken back to Hull. It was reported from Hull, on 15 July, that *Captain Paget that let the Providence loose for want of care, has now played his part and redeemed his credit, in taking a Hoy and three great guns that was going to be planted on (?)Cuntolpher side for stopping passage by water to us, and did beat all the musketeers, and made them run ashore by the west, to fly his ordnance.* On 19 July, *We sent out a small pinnace towards Becton* (Barton), *where espying some of the Cavaliers that would starve us we shot two or three guns amongst them; and now resolved to kill them if we can, that would starve us if they can*[36].

On land, Meldrum launched aggressive sallies from Hull. At the end of July, he led a party of 500 who routed the Royalist trained band foot regiment of Robert Strickland, which failed to stand against them. Meldrum's men chased the Royalist horse, thus left unsupported, northwards towards Beverley, killing two of them - *the first blood, as they say, that was shed in these unnatural wars* - and capturing 30. Soon after, another sally killed more, took another 15 prisoners, and destroyed the Royalist magazine at Anlaby, routing its guards and removing some arms[37].

Harassment on land, the loss of guns from the forts, and the failure to impose a naval blockade, persuaded Charles to hold a Council of War. Here, because precious time was being wasted, he resolved to cut his losses, abandon the siege, and withdraw his forces. He was to raise the Royal Standard as a formal declaration of war on 22 August, at Nottingham. The focus of hostilities then moved south, the forces of King and Parliament contesting the approach to London at the indecisive Battle of Edgehill, on 23 October 1642.

The Hotham Conspiracy

On 22 February 1643, the Queen landed at Bridlington Quay with three ships carrying a massive store of armaments purchased in the Netherlands. A safe passage having been cleared, a convoy of 500 wagons transported this arsenal over the Yorkshire Wolds to York. The convoy reached Burton Fleming on 5 March; Malton on 7 March, and York on 8 March. During the summer of 1643, the royalists, operating from bases at York and Scarborough, extended their control over the whole of the East Riding, with the exception of Hull and Wressle Castle[38].

The next Royalist attempt on Hull came in June 1643, and depended on the weakening enthusiasm of the Governor for the Parliamentarian cause. Sir John Hotham had worked in vain to reconcile King and Parliament in the weeks before the Battle of Edgehill. Copies of his correspondence fell into the hands of *those that bore him ill will in the House of Commons; upon which jealousies were much increased against him.* Sir Thomas Fairfax, who had been involved in fighting at Leeds in January 1643 together with Hotham's son, already half-suspected him of treason against Parliament. Sir John Hotham was again in communication with the Royalist Earl of Newcastle, from April 1643. On Parliament's order, he was placed under the covert surveillance of Sir Matthew Boynton, in June 1643. On 24 June, his son escaped from captivity at Nottingham, where he had been detained by Oliver Cromwell for misconduct and desertion; an episode which further embittered Hotham against Parliament[39].

On 28 June 1643, Sir John Hotham was reported to be plotting the betrayal of Hull. His betrayer is held to have been a minister, and relative, sent to discover his real intentions toward the King. The events that followed, by night, were reported as follows. The Mayor, having learnt of the plot, informed some Aldermen, Boynton and others. They *would not be seen to act* - presumably as it was uncertain who among Hotham's force might be involved in conspiracy. They secretly informed *such as were most zealous for Parliament* among the townsmen. By 4 am, about 1,500 men were in readiness, waiting on the Mayor's command.

The townsmen, *every man armed, with his musket charged and match lighted came forth and drew up in several bodies; seized first upon the commanders and the main guard, next upon all that had any relation to the Governor, and particularly on Captain Hotham (his son); then on the Magazine, and all the ordnance on the walls, and the Guards at the Gates, and the three Blockhouses, and the Castle; so that the whole town, and all that belonged to it, was in less than about an hours time secured, without one drop of blood, or so much as a musket discharged*[40].

Sir John Hotham fled. Having then notice of what was done, got out of his house, and meeting a man riding into the town made him alight, and mounted his horse, and so passed through Beverley Gate, the guard having yet no order to stop him. But the pursuers immediately coming thither, and seeing him gone, one from the walls shot a musket, and a gunner discharged a piece of ordnance at him. Fearing a pursuit, he quitted Beverley Road, and turned down to a ferry, intending to have got over into Holderness; but then missing of a boat, was forced to ride on to Beverley. He was apprehended there by Sir Matthew Boynton's son, Colonel Boynton, who had by now been warned of Hotham's flight. A royalist force came to Beverley the next day, perhaps expecting a friendly reception from their partisans, but, *finding a stout resistance, they retired.*

The counter-coup staged by the townsmen of Hull had forestalled a covert attempt by the Royalists to seize Hull. The Hothams, father and son, were taken to London, tried, and eventually executed in January 1645. On 1 July 1643, the Parliamentarian general Lord Ferdinando Fairfax learned of events at Hull. Fairfax was at Leeds, in headlong retreat from the Royalist army of the Earl of Newcastle, having been defeated at Adwalton Moor. He decided to make for Hull, and, breaking through enemy lines at Selby, arrived in Hull in the early hours of 3 July. His son, Sir Thomas Fairfax, after an adventurous and circuitous journey pursued by the Royalists, at last came under the supporting guns of a Parliamentarian ketch at Barton-on-Humber, and so joined his father at Hull[41].

The townsmen at Hull had appointed the Mayor, Thomas Raikes, as an interim Governor, at the head of a committee. This committee took over the payment of the Garrison, at a weekly cost of £700, *having no other means to keep the soldiers from disbanding.* They appealed to Parliament for arms to stock the Magazine anew; money to raise troops; and permission to pass money seized at Hotham's house to Fairfax for his soldiers. They opposed the rumoured appointment, by Parliament, of Sir Matthew Boynton as their new Governor. In his stead, they petitioned that Lord Fairfax should hold the post. Lord Fairfax was duly installed as Governor on 22 July, taking the residence of James Watkinson for his son, Sir Thomas. Watkinson, the former Storekeeper of the Hull Magazine, had joined the King at York. On 3 August, the town was asserting its traditional complaint that the appointment of Lord Fairfax as Governor was against their liberties; this concern was to pale into insignificance with the descent of the victorious northern Royalist army of the Earl of Newcastle[42].

The great siege of 1643

Lord Fairfax had called for recruits to gather at Beverley on 7 July. Sir Thomas Fairfax assembled an army of 25 troops of horse, a force variously stated to comprise 1,600, 1,800 or 2,000 foot, horse and dragoons, and five or six guns, which he quartered in and around the town. Fairfax's memoirs state that: *Our first business was to raise new forces and in a short time we had about 1,500 foot and 700 horse.* Fairfax's command - also specified as of horse and 600 foot - were stationed in Beverley to avoid overcrowding within the walls of Hull. By late July, there was *a general averseness in the common people, who (following the stronger party) come in very slackly to our assistance.* Hull faced a range of difficulties: *the potency of the enemy; the weakness of our forces; the danger of being restrained within these walls (whereby we are likely to be debarred of all contribution from the Country, levies of men, and other assistance); and the unwillingness of the Lord General's forces to recruit; which (as we conceive) is for lack of assurance of pay*[43].

The Earl of Newcastle, newly titled Marquess by the King, advanced on Beverley with an army of 16,000. From lists of officers compiled after the Restoration, his army would appear to have comprised something less than 20 regiments of foot; about 25 cavalry units; and three or four regiments of dragoons. Both horse and foot units were of widely variable strengths. Sir Francis Wortley's "troop" of Horse, for example, comprised 600 men, a respectable regimental strength; while the Foot "regiments" of Colonel Henry Clayton and Sir Francis Cobbe were both small units from East Yorkshire, perhaps of company size. Newcastle's strength in artillery is not known, though this would be essential for his conduct of a siege. Later events show it included two larger guns, four smaller pieces, and a mortar or mortars. Sixteen guns had been planted against Gainsborough, Lincolnshire, in June and July 1643, and *several pieces of ordnance* had been taken at Adwalton Moor in June. As Newcastle's forces were split between Yorkshire and Lincolnshire, guns may have been deployed from Gainsborough. Used as battering guns, 18 guns of demi-cannon and culverin class firing at close (c.400m) range could breach fortified defences in ten hours. It is unlikely that such a powerful battery could have been assembled before Hull[44].

Though Sir Thomas Fairfax had been ordered to hold his ground against the Royalist army, this was clearly impossible for his outnumbered force in Beverley, a town without significant defences. Sir Thomas Fairfax abandoned Beverley, which was sacked by the Royalists, and fell back on Hull on 28 August. A body of musketeers checked the royalists near Newland, killing one horse and man, and the Royalists fell back on Beverley. On 29 August they took Cottingham, whence Parliamentarian sympathisers fled to Hull, while their forces drove what stock they could into the town. On the 30 August, Parliamentarian horse and foot drove the Royalists through Cottingham, killing some and capturing others. On the 31 August, however, the Parliamentarian foot were drawn out as far as the west end of Cottingham Ings, whereupon a large Royalist force sallied out from Cottingham and drove them back in disorder[45].

From 2 September, the Royalists began the erection of field fortifications. The first was at Newland, *about the way from Beverley.* The site of one of the first forts to be raised may have been close to that of the 19th-century Newland House. Guns were *placed upon a bank which was the highway,* the *causey* or raised embankment of the Beverley Road, permitting the besiegers to bring guns within range of Hull[46].

The Royalists then came to Stoneferry Clow - the sluice on the bank of the river Hull, *and there made works and brought guns thither.* As was appropriate to the progressive construction of siegeworks, *they every day wrought nearer and nearer Hull and made several forts both betwixt Newland and Hull, and also betwixt Sculcoates and Hull.* The work at Sculcoates was referred to as a *battery royal,* a term distinguishing an imposing fieldwork armed with guns. It lay *a half mile from the walls where afterwards besides other ordnance two brass demi-cannon... shot bullets 36lbs into the town.* On 5 September, the Royalists raised *another work upon the banks of the river Hull, east from the former* (battery royal), *over which they laid a bridge of boats that they might assure passage and re-passage into Holderness, where they had two more pieces of cannon.* The position of one of these forts was later to be indicated by the discovery of four cannon balls at Wilmington, during the construction of the railway swing-bridge which remains today[47].

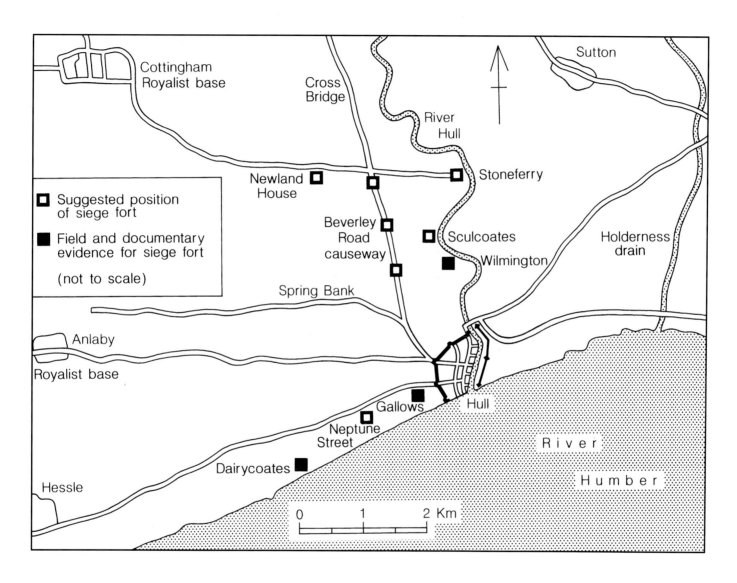

Fig 9: The siege of 1643, showing the direction of the Royalist siege-lines, and the position of major incidents in the fighting at Hull, based on the Phillips Plan of 1716 and contemporary accounts.

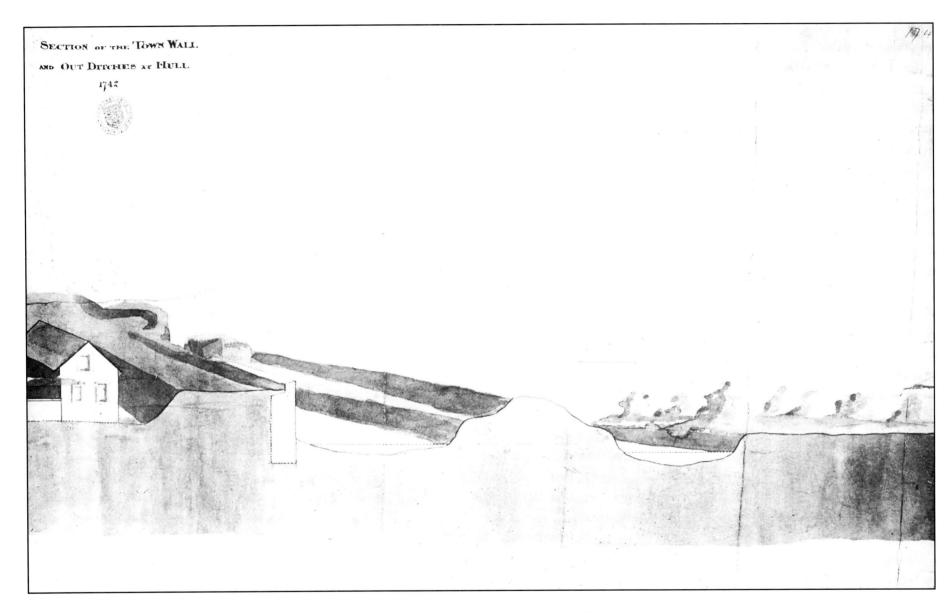

SECTION OF THE TOWN WALL.
AND OUT DITCHES AT HULL.
1742

Fig 10: Profile of the town defences, 1742. From the collections of Wilberforce House Museum, Hull.

These accounts describe the progressive advance of two lines of siege-works. One advanced southwards from Newland, on the raised line of the Beverley Road, and comprised at least three forts. These were perhaps within musket shot (c.200m) of each other, so that troops in the first to be built could cover the raising of the next, and so on. The other line of attack ran to the west of the river Hull, perhaps starting from the battery at Stoneferry sluice. A fort at an improvised bridge of boats may have formed part of this line. The river Hull itself provided a natural obstacle to secure the Royalist left flank.

A third line of siege-works advanced on Hull from the west, as a continuous entrenchment. *They had made great and large works likewise between Hessle and Hull. They began to work at a place on Humber side, called Gallow Shore, and so came slanting along with earthworks at least the half a mile in length, with strong forts, half moons and breastworks, slanting nearer and nearer towards the town, till they had gotten a strong fort made, hard by the gallows which was very near the west side of the town.* There were *high works on the bank of the Humber*, which may have been built up with *gabions*, earth-filled baskets. Other forts were possibly built up on the side facing the town, but left open behind[48].

The position of the gallows is identified by Aitken's *map of Kingston upon Hull as it appeared in AD 1800*. The fort here, threatening the west side of the town, was armed with six guns. These comprised a large demi-cannon, a demi-culverin, four small drakes in one carriage, a saker-cut and two large brass drakes, along with three and a half barrels of powder and many shot. This represents a range of guns: from larger pieces for bombardment, to smaller ones most useful for use against troops at close range. The quadruple drake had barrels which lay like *organ pipes upon a broad carriage*, and were fired by a train arranged so as to ensure a simultaneous discharge; the shot weighed one pound. According to Meldrum, the largest guns were positioned further back along the line of siege-works, perhaps in the third or fourth fort in the line. In this case, those guns first advanced close to the defences would have been lighter pieces[49].

The position of forts or other features relating to the western siege-works may be surmised from further discoveries made in the 19th and early 20th centuries. Two iron cannon-balls, of 5in. (127mm) and 3½in. (89mm) diameter, and numerous lead musket balls, some unused, were found *in a low rectangular mound*. The east end of the mound was cut by rails serving sheds of the North Eastern Railway in 1902. A cannon ball found in Neptune Street, about 300yds (274m)

from the Humber, may mark the position of another element of the siege lines[50]. The distance of these fortifications from the northern lines might at first appear to represent a deficiency in Newcastle's plan of attack. However, the numerical superiority of the Royalist force would have made any attempt to engage them in the field dangerous for the shaken defenders of Hull. With grazing available for their mounts, the Royalist cavalry were able to maintain themselves as a mobile and dangerous force. The gap in the siege lines may therefore have been more apparent than real, and may even have been intended to tempt Fairfax to venture out.

The Parliamentarians sought to impede these advances with works set forward of the main defensive line around the town. One was built on the site of the recently-built house of Thomas Swan in the *Grainswicke*. Swan's new house had been demolished on Hotham's order, in 1642 or early 1643. *The close wherein the house stood was by the said Sir John Hotham's command cut up and a great mound or sconce raised and made therein for better defence of the said town.* This fort was called *the Mount*. The Mount was described as *lately raised in the Grainswicke*, and was subsequently ordered to be *thrown down and levelled*. It is likely that this should be identified with a fort guarding the West or Ragged Jetty, on the Humber shore. This was built – or perhaps, given the likelihood of earlier activity there, rebuilt - on 16 September. It mounted three guns, and was itself supported by other works, probably including the *half moon* before Hessle Gate. The West Jetty is illustrated by the Phillips plan of c.1716; at that later date, a rectangular ditched enclosure lay nearby, perhaps marking the position of the close occupied by the Mount[51].

The advance of Royalist siege-works from the north and west progressively limited the options open to the Parliamentarians. A raid on the Royalist headquarters at Anlaby on 9 September, which thrust between the besiegers' lines, was repulsed with loss to both sides. On 13 September, the Royalists cut the dyke supplying fresh water to Hull. Neither the outlying forts, nor guns in the half moons or on the walls, secured enough ground to graze cattle or cavalry mounts: *they could no sooner straggle twice twelve score* (480 yards – c.440m) *from the town but they were snatched from us*. The cattle were accordingly slaughtered to provision the garrison. The cavalry mounts *were now useless and many died every day having nothing but salt water about the town.* Between 16 and 20 troops of cavalry under Sir Thomas Fairfax were shipped south across the Humber to Lincolnshire on 26 September, joining Cromwell's forces there[52].

On 14 September, Lord Fairfax ordered the Humber banks to be cut, *whereby the waters much annoyed the besiegers in their works.* The flooding *drowned the land for two miles about the town.* This may, in particular, have prevented assault against the eastern defences - at any rate, no action here is recorded. This ground was intersected by numerous east/west ditches, which would have impeded an orderly advance even before the sluices were opened. Later claims seeking compensation for flood damage stressed *that Drypool's meadows and grounds were quite spoiled* (in 1642). Following Fairfax's action in 1643, *they have laboured still* (in 1647) *to keep out the waters from breaking in upon the country.* In 1643, John Burnsell of Preston, about four miles from Hull, had *buried writings and other things of value and worth* to save them from the *insolence and rage of the soldiers, but by reason of water and the moisture of the ground they utterly perished*[53].

The siting of guns on raised causeways and earthworks permitted them to continue in use, though work in the Royalist entrenchments became increasingly miserable as autumn wore on. There was heavy rain in September, and in October the high tides swelled the floodwaters. *The Spring tides did overflow all their works and made them wet lodgings there.* Sir Phillip Warwick visited the royal army, and commented *that those without the town seemed likelier to rot than those within to starve*[54].

The defenders suffered their own misfortune on 16 September. *A great part of the North Blockhouse was blown up by the carelessness of a cannonier; who, with his light-match, went to fetch cartridges, where were nine or ten hand grenadoes that took fire, rent the floor, slew him and four more; but ten barrels of powder, that were in the next room, were not touched.* Later estimates for repairs suggest that this had occurred in the south bastion of the North Blockhouse. The circumstances of the accident suggest that guns here were already in action; presumably against Royalist works in the Sculcoates area. On 28 September, a Royalist magazine at Cottingham was fired; as Parliamentarian accounts claimed no credit, this, too, was perhaps an accidental detonation[55].

The advancing siege-works permitted the emplacement of guns to fire on Hull's defences. These *included two very great guns which were called the Queen's pocket pistols, one of which lay betwixt Sculcoates and Hull* (the northern lines), *and the other towards Hessle* (the western lines - this gun was possibly moved closer to the town). These large guns fired over 80 heated shot, each weighing 35lbs (15.8kg), into the town. Newcastle's farrier, Francis Moore, had been employed *making instruments to charge the ordnance with red hot bullets, to be used at the siege of Hull.* Heated shot was an incendiary weapon, and Lord Fairfax ordered that tubs of water should be set at every door, and that hemp, flax, tar and pitch should be kept in cellars to lessen the chance of a major conflagration. One cannonade was aimed at the tower of Holy Trinity on Sunday morning, 1 October, while the garrison was at prayer. Two balls went wide, and one skated over the leads. One man, a woman and a child were killed, but many others *were miraculously delivered through God's mercy*; suggesting that the bombardment had been a notable ordeal for the townsfolk. The Royalists also employed a mortar or mortars, which *sent their granadoes towards us which came short or wide of the town and did no harm*[56].

This barrage nettled the defenders into mounting a sally, on 4 October. A force of 500 townsmen and soldiers attacked the northern siege-works towards Newland: *we made them run like cowardly hares and took three of their works, demolished them, took six or eight prisoners, but cannot tell how many we killed, only we heard one Colonel Vavasor was slain and buried at Cottingham* - though his burial does not figure in the parish register. Two of the forts overrun were afterwards repaired, though the nearest to the town was not[57].

The next day, 5 October, a force of 500 men under Sir John Meldrum disembarked from Parliamentarian ships to join the garrison of Hull. On the same day, to the north of the town, Fairfax had an earthen rampart raised on the site of the Charterhouse. This was intended to counter royalist guns at Sculcoates. The work was carried out under enemy fire. The women of the town were prominent in its construction, assisted by others, perhaps camp-followers accompanying Meldrum's troops. *They killed a woman servant as she was carrying earth for the raising of the earth an hundred more of her sex were disheartened and deserted the work, but afterwards all the women even those of the best rank stranger and others willingly helped forward the works.* This was later described as *a fort hard by the ruins of the Charterhouse, upon which they planted a great brass gun.* The discovery of five large cannon balls at Wincolmlee suggests that this fort was positioned immediately upon the west bank of the river Hull[58].

It is possible that a further bastion was constructed at this time; at the mid-point of the earthworks protecting the north walls of Hull. De la Pryme, writing in about 1700, described *a new fort flanking the Fort Royal, 12 score yards* (240yds – c.220m) *west of the Charterhouse battery.* The only feature matching this location is that bastion on the north side of Hull, opposite Lowgate. This was not enumerated among the works erected against the Scots three years before, and was of different form, and may therefore represent a further counter against the Royalist siege works[59].

Heartened by the arrival of Meldrum's men, the defenders planned a sally for Monday 9 October. In the event, the Parliamentarians were themselves surprised. *In the morning, before the break of day, a chosen company of the enemy came privily and secretly from their own works and got betwixt the town and our works, our men supposing them to be their friends suffered them to come to our works which they took.* The combined accounts of this action suggest that the attack was against the bastion projecting before Hessle Gate. It was commanded by *Denton Strickland, and one Little a countryman of mine* (a Scot: this is Meldrum's report), *who commanded in chief.* The Parliamentarians were chased to *our other fort* or *half moon* with the Royalists in pursuit[60].

This emergency was countered by Meldrum, who led 100 musketeers from *the Mount* to reinforce the defenders: *gunners and soldiers* under two English commanders and a Scot. The Royalists were then repelled with the loss of 14 or 15 men *knocked down*, including their commanders, who were killed, and other fatalities. The rest of the Royalist storming party retired 240yds (220m) to the nearest part of their own lines. Another account describes this engagement as follows: *Their first attempt on the half moon which they scaled and entered, but were beaten out again - within pistol shot of the West Jetty galled their rear - but failing in their purpose they advanced to the battery which they attempted to scale - not a shot fired but club law. Their commander was Captain Strickland who with many more men demanded a surrender - beaten down and ran.* This had been a most dangerous threat; the Royalist party had apparently taken the bastion before Hessle Gate. With a little more time, they might either have entered there, or have driven their way north towards the Myton and Beverley Gates[61].

This nasty shock encouraged the more thorough planning of the next sally by the Parliamentarians. A Council of War was convened by Fairfax the same day, and arranged a coordinated attack for the morning of 11 October. Two parties, of 500 musketeers apiece, under *Colonels* Lambert and Rainsborow, were to *issue forth, and to beat them forth of their next works approaching to ours.* Rainsborow is elsewhere described as a captain in command of a party of 100 sailors from the ship *Lion*, and townsmen were also numbered among the force. The troops were marshalled at 5 am, *without beat of drum; and order was given to the guards on the north*

side of the town, to flash powder as if they were lighting many hundred of matches, that so the besiegers might expect the attack on that side. Guns were also fired from the northern defences, to reinforce the impression that an attack was to be launched from that quarter[62].

At 9 am, *townsmen, soldiers, and seamen from on board the Parliament ships in the road, and four troops of horse, sallied out towards the west.* One party made a frontal assault on the Royalist gun position by the gallows. Meldrum led another against *their left flank,* and a third force advanced from the West Jetty fort to charge *their high works on the bank of Humber.* The four troops of horse supported the latter party. Meldrum described the attackers as *marching along the enemy's line of approach, on every side*[63].

The Royalists fought bravely, but after a quarter-hour were driven from one entrenchment and, *after a sharp dispute,* from another. The assault, however, lost cohesion, and Newcastle's men were reinforced by fresh troops from their Leaguer, or camp, a quarter of a mile away. This must have been a mustering-point in their line of entrenchments, as the Royalist quarters were centred at Anlaby, three miles to the west. The fresh force comprised only 100 pikemen, but advancing as a formed unit, *charging the van of our foot, scattered and in disorder did drive us backward again, regained their ordnance* (in the forts formerly overrun), *and enforced us all to a shameful retreat.* Guns mounted on the town walls, however, dissuaded *a great body of the Marquess's horse, who stood a mile off* from intervening to ride down the retiring Parliamentarians. They fell back in two parties: one group *into Myton Carr Lane* and the other *towards the Mount*[64].

Fairfax and Meldrum, appalled at the collapse of their attack, *used all endeavours to rally their men, and forgot no arguments, to encourage them; so that they quickly got them into order.* The horse may have played a part here: *the troopers riding among those who pursued them* (the retiring foot), *the enemies fled.* Meldrum noted that the rout was halted on Fairfax's order to close the gates. With their retreat thus barred, the men *recovered the sense of their own carriage*[65].

The Parliamentarians attacked again. One party of foot seems to have broken into the rear of the contested gun positions, the other again making a frontal attack: *then our foot men flanked up the backside of their works one other part forced over the works and drove them away.* The foot *once more made themselves masters of the several forts, and turning the besiegers own guns upon them, gave them five shots in the rear.* The renewed assault pressed further than before, and the Parliamentarians *recovered all the ordnance lost and gained a half-cannon and a demi-culverin of brass, which we had not possessed in the first charge*[66].

The captured positions were occupied until the guns - including one of the *Queen's pocket pistols* - had been dragged back to the town, and then were evacuated under intense Royalist pressure. Fighting lasted for three hours, in the course of which *above an hundred pieces of cannon were shot from the walls and the fort-royal* - the latter possibly the fort at Charterhouse. Meldrum commented: *our ordnance hath done them a great deal of mischief; and if we had had a fresh body of foot, they had been put to a great straight.* He also came very near to death himself: *I had a blow on the side by a slug of cutted iron shot from the great piece but thanks be to God, am not the worse, I believe her sacred Majesty if she had known where the shot would have lighted, would have checked the gunner for not charging full home*[67].

The Royalists at last recovered from their surprise, and *their whole body of foot with forty colours* (implying forty companies, a paper strength of over 4,000) *draws themselves within pistol shot to the Ragged Jetty.* The Royalist counter-attack pressed hardest here: musketeers fired from *the jetty, the half-moon, and the banks... yet the besiegers came up within pistol-shot of the jetty, and lined a bank with their musketeers, against whom a party sallying-out, forced them to run in such disorder, that they left most of their muskets behind them; upon which loss, the besiegers betook themselves to their works, and the fight ceased*[68].

The defenders of Hull had captured 60 prisoners and six guns, and had killed a number of the enemy. Of their force, no *men of note* were lost except Captain Rainsborrow, who was captured. He became a prisoner of Captain Bushell, and was later ransomed for £500[69].

The reverse broke the royalist will to continue with the siege, and they drew away their remaining guns overnight. The Parliamentarian account stated: *they marched away with half their number, notwithstanding the many troops they took up by commission of array throughout all parts of the country, so many were killed, and took their opportunity to run away.* Newcastle's withdrawal to York, and the complete wrecking of the sluice at Stoneferry and of bridges over Setting Dyke and Newland Haven, was covered by guards at Newland and Stoneferry. Their entrenchments closer to Hull, however, stood empty the next morning and were immediately demolished by the townsmen. On Lord Fairfax's orders, the 12 October was observed as a public thanksgiving by the town[70].

The reasons for Newcastle's withdrawal from Hull are unclear. Clarendon's *History of the Rebellion* maintained that orders to mask Hull, and to march south through East Anglia should the siege prove difficult, were initially unacceptable to Newcastle's officers. Their men, raised in Yorkshire, refused to leave Hull untaken. Their own homes and families were threatened by raids mounted from the town. It has also been suggested that jealousy between Prince Rupert and Newcastle made Newcastle reluctant to participate in a wide-ranging strategy. The Parliamentarian victory at Winceby, also on 11 October, left no effective Royalist forces in Lincolnshire. Newcastle's wife ascribed his withdrawal to reverses in Lincolnshire[71].

The extent of casualties on both sides in 1643 cannot be firmly established. The reports cited above indicate *a number* of Royalists killed - only three are named. Another 14 or 15 were *knocked down*, and over 90 captured. The Royalist descent on Beverley of 29 June, which was repulsed, had left 13 men *of the King's party* to be buried next day, as recorded in the parish Register of St Mary's, Beverley. Disease and desertion must surely have cost Newcastle's force of 15,000 a greater number than are known to have fallen in battle. The fight of 11 October must have largely been a clash of pikes and clubbed muskets until its closing stages, a point on which the low losses of the defenders of Hull are revealing[72].

The registers of Holy Trinity, Hull, record 32 burials in August 1643, 44 in September, 46 in October and 59 in November. One of these was a Lieutenant Appleyard, and another a Captain Waters. A Captain Waters was a member of the Earl of Newcastle's First Regiment in 1642, but it is not known if this was the same man, and indeed if any of these burials might relate to the siege. At St Mary's, Lowgate, Hull, there were three burials in August, and seven in both September and October; a Captain Collings was one of the latter. The Register of St Mary's, Cottingham, records four deaths in September and six in October. Holy Trinity churchyard was held by de la Pryme to be full, and he records that a garden in Trinity House Lane might be used for extra burials. His implication that there had been great loss of life is, however, unsupported by other evidence[73].

The failure of the Earl of Newcastle to take Hull did not result in major defections from the predominantly Royalist gentry of the surrounding countryside. The *Queen's pocket pistol*, renamed *Sweet Lips* after a well-known Hull whore, would go on in Parliament's service to batter Royalist strongholds at Newark and Scarborough for its new masters. The garrison at Hull continued to mount small-scale raids across the East Riding, as at Kilham, Bridlington, Driffield and Whitby in 1644. Newcastle's army would only be broken at Marston Moor, on 2 July 1644. The importance of Hull in 1643 was ultimately that, like Plymouth and Gloucester, it held one of three Royalist armies at bay, at a time when a concentration of forces on London could have won the war for the King[74].

Footnotes

1:      Gillett and MacMahon 1989, 85-94; Hill 1980, 94.

2:      Allison 1969, 415; CSPD 1619-23, 574; Chancery Judgement 1860.

3:      KUHRO BRB 4, 311, 318; BRB 5, 72; KUHRO D842, D842a.

4:      Gillett and MacMahon 1989, 119-31; Hirst 1913; KUHRO D797; Rushworth Coll. vol. 1, 425; KUHRO M145; CSPD 1627-8, 111, 146, 233, 244, 272.

5:      KUHRO M146, L216-7; CSPD 1625-49, 199.

6:      KUHRO M154, appendix 1; Evans and Sitch 1990, 21; Foreman 1988, 5-6.

7:      KUHRO L488; Sheahan 1864, 346-7, 352; KUHRO M154; de Boer 1973, pl.10; Phillips plan, 1716; BL Add. 16370, fo.107; PRO WO44/195, report on the armament of the Citadel, December 1846; KUHRO BRB 5, 222; de la Pryme [1986] pt.1, 62.

8:      Allison 1969, 415; Borthwick Institute, vol. 41, fos 353-4.

9:      KUHRO M153; BRB 5, 176; Woodward 1995, 126.

10:     Hughes 1974; Duffy 1979, 61; Sheppard 1958, 1-7.

11:     Stone 1972.

12:     CSPD 1640, 171; CSPD 1639-40, 513; Tindall Wildridge 1886, 21-2; Rushworth Coll. vol. 4, 722.

13:     KUHRO L274, M153, M155, M151; Rushworth Coll. vol. 4, 721-4.

14:     KUHRO L273; CSPD 1640, 71; Rushworth Coll. vol. 4, 721-4; KUHRO D842a.

15:     KUHRO BRB 5, 250; Bell 1849, vol. 1, 414-15; Norfolk 1965, 4; KUHRO M167.

16:     CSPD 1638-9, 310; KUHRO L260; CSPD 1638-9, 411.

17:     Firth 1902, 13; CSPD 1639-40, 109, 157, 168.

18:     KUHRO L292, L294, L295-6, L298-9, L300, L301, 303; Tindall Wildridge 1886, 27.

19:     KUHRO L303-4; Corelli Barnet 1970, 76; KUHRO L305, L304a.

20:     de la Pryme [1986], vol. 2, 71; KUHRO L305, 305a; CSPD 1640, 39.

21:     Evans and Sitch 1990, 21; KUHRO Woolner and Phillips plans; Wilberforce House plan F.1/9; KUHRO D796a, D797a.

22:     Woodward 1985, 37-8; Evans 1999.

23:     Fletcher 1981, 32; KUHRO DMT5; CSPD 1641-3, vol. 465, 14.

24:     CSPD 1641, 122.

25:     CSPD 1641-2, 253-4; KUHRO M173.

26:     KUHRO M173; Gillett and MacMahon 1980, 168.

27:     CSPD 1641-3, 253; Fletcher 1981, 185; CSPD 1641, 122.

28:     de la Pryme [1986] vol. 2, 74; CSPD 1642, 307, 333; Ryder 1989, 139-48; Kenyon 1978, 140-4.

29:     Barclay 1992; Gillett and MacMahon 1980, 169-70; Kings Pamphlets vol. 58, art. 17, from York, June 17th 1642, in *Civil War Proceedings in Yorkshire*, YAS 1882, vol. 7, 76.

30:     Rushworth Coll. vol. 5, 610-12; YAS 1882, vol. 7, 385, citing *Kings Pamphlets* vol. 61, art. 37; Neave 1996b, 123.

31:     KUHRO BRB 5, 597; de la Pryme [1986] part 2, 80; Rushworth Coll. vol. 5, 610; YAS 1882, vol. 61, art. 44, 240, *The Humble Petition of the Gentry and Inhabitants of Holderness with His Majesty's answer 6th July 1642*; Rushworth Coll. vol. 5, 611; YAS 1882, vol. 7, 383, citing *Kings Pamphlets* vol. 62, art. 4, *His Majesty's proceedings at Hull. From the 8 of July to the 12* 1642.

32:     Boyle 1882, 27-8.

33:     YAS 1882, vol. 7, 383 *loc. cit.* in note 31; Rushworth Coll. *loc. cit.* in note 31; YAS 1882, vol. 7, 383-5; CSPD 1625-49, 641, *Order in Parliament*; Gillett and MacMahon 1980, 170-1, 174; Firth 1902, 29n.

34:     Oppenheim 1896, 240, 255; CSPD 1642, 360; Rushworth Coll. vol. 5, 610; YAS 1882, vol. 7, 390, citing *His Majesties Command to the Earl of Warwick*, in *Kings Pamphlets* vol. 63, art. 31; YAS 1882, vol. 7, citing *Kings Pamphlets* vol. 61, art. 37; Tucker 1972, 76-7.

35:     YAS 1882, vol. 7, 383-5, *Order in Parliament, Kings Pamphlets* vol. 62, art. 4; Neave 1996b, 123; Roy 1964, 15; Ross 1984, 28, citing *Civil War Tracts* E108, 40. YAS 1882, vol. 7, 385, citing *Kings Pamphlets* vol. 61, art. 37, *Exceeding True News from Hull*.

36:     YAS 1882, vol. 7, 398, *Kings Pamphlets* vol. 63, art. 12, *Extract of all passages from Hull, York and Lincolnshire*.

37:     Newman 1985, 19; Rushworth Coll. vol. 5, 610-12.

38:     Neave 1996b, 122-3.

39:     Markham 1870, 9; Barclay 1992.

40:     Rushworth Coll. vol. 3, 274-81.

41:     Fairfax [1910], 89-90.

42:     Clay 1893, 112; KUHRO M175; Tindall Wildridge 1886, 36, 41-3, 46.

43:     KUHRO M180a; Stamp 1991, 30; YAS 1882, vol. 7, 383-5; Fairfax [1910], 95; Markham 1870, 114; Tindall Wildridge 1886, 43.

44: Reid vol. 1, 14, 33, 39; vol.2, 67, 80, 83, 101; vol. 3, 104, 108, 109, 111, 121. 124, 134; vol. 4, 158-9, 161-2, 168, 170, 186, 199; Rushworth Coll. vol. 3, 279-80; Ross 1984, 52-7.

45: Fairfax [1910], 89-90; Miller *et al.* 1982; Neave 1996, 122; Stamp 1991, 30.

46: Rushworth Coll. vol. 3, 280; *Civil War Tracts* no. 46, 14; Hadley 1788, 623; Stamp 1991, 30; Fairfax [1884], 218.

47: Stamp 1991, 30; *Civil War Tracts* no. 46, 15; de la Pryme [1986] pt. 2, 89; *Civil War Tracts* no. 46, 15; Rushworth Coll. vol. 3, 280; Sheppard 1904, 38.

48: Stamp 1991, 31; Rushworth Coll. vol. 3, 280-1; Stamp 1991, 32.

49: Stamp 1991, 31-3; Rushworth Coll. vol. 3, 280-1; *Civil War Tracts* no. 46, 21; Ross 1984, 38-9; McNicol 1987, 33.

50: Sheppard 1902, 11; Ordnance Survey 25in. plan, 1910; Sheahan 1866, 168.

51: McNicol 1987, 32; Reckitt 1952, 131-2; Tindall Wildridge 1886, 159; Travis-Cook 1905, 44; Rushworth Coll. vol. 3, 280-1; *Civil War Tracts* no. 46, 16; McNicol 1987, appendix 3.

52: Neave 1996, 122; Fairfax [1910], 103; Stamp 1991, 31; Rushworth Coll. vol. 3, 280.

53: Rushworth Coll. vol. 3, 280; YAJ 1884, vol. 8, *Civil War Tracts* no. 46, 218; Phillips plan 1716; ERYCRO CSR 12/1; 16/1.

54: *Civil War Tracts* no. 46, 17; Reckitt 1952, 95.

55: Rushworth Coll. vol. 3, 280.

56: Stamp 1991, 31; CCAM 1642-56, pt. 2, 1430; de la Pryme [1986], pt. 2, 90; *Civil War Tracts* no. 46, 14-5.

57: Stamp 1991, 31.

58: Rushworth Coll. vol. 3, 280; *Civil War Tracts* no. 46, 18; *ibid.*, 14-15; de la Pryme [1986], vol. 2, 89; Sheahan 1866, 168; Bellamy 1965, vol. 2, appendix 6, 16-17; *Hull Advertiser* 27 August 1847; *Goad Insurance Plan* no. 21, April 1893.

59: Phillips plan, 1716.

60: Stamp 1991, 32; McNicol 1987, 32; Stamp 1991, 32.

61: McNicol 1987, 32; Stamp 1991, 32; *Civil War Tracts* no. 46, 18.

62: McNicol 1987, 32; Stamp 1991, 33; Rushworth Coll. vol. 3, 280.

63: McNicol 1987, 32-3; Rushworth Coll. vol. 3, 280.

64: *Civil War Tracts* no. 46, 16; McNicol 1987, 33; Stamp 1991, 32.

65: Rushworth Coll. vol. 3, 280; Stamp 1991, 32; McNicol 1987, 33.

66: Stamp 1991, 32; Rushworth Coll. vol. 3, 280; McNicol 1987, 33.

67: McNicol 1987, 34.

68: McNicol 1987, 33; Rushworth Coll. vol. 3, 280.

69: Stamp 1991, 33; *Civil War Tracts* no. 46, 21; Binns 1991.

70: *Civil War Tracts* no. 47, 5, 23; Stamp 1991, 33; Rushworth Coll. vol. 3, 281.

71: Clarendon vol. 3, 150; Gardiner 1904, vol. 1, 194; Stephens and Lee vol. 3, 1275; Firth 1906, 50.

72: ERYCRO St Mary's Cottingham, Parish Register.

73: Holy Trinity Hull, Parish Register, vol. 2, 1552-1653; Peacock 1874, 10; St Mary's Lowgate, Hull, Parish Register, 1564-1657; de la Pryme [1986] vol. 2, 92.

74: Neave 1996b, 123; Kenyon 1988, 84; Newman 1985, 45; Reckitt 1952, 100.

CHAPTER 3

HULL AND THE COMMONWEALTH

After the siege of 1643, Hull was to see no more serious fighting. It was, however, to continue to serve the Parliamentarian cause as a port and arsenal. Hull also continued to be held by a garrison. The fears expressed by the Bench, of a loss of autonomy and historic liberties, proved to have been justified. The Second Civil War, of 1648-51, saw a Scottish army invade England, in support of Charles I. After the execution of Charles I, in January 1649, and the defeat of the Scots and the young Charles II, Oliver Cromwell became *Lord Protector* of a Commonwealth. All England lay under military rule until after his death[1].

A perpetual Garrison

From 1643, the Governor of Hull was a military officer appointed to his post by the government. He enjoyed full power to correct offenders for, according to the Articles of War, *no magistrate of town or country shall without licence imprison any soldier unless for capital offences.* In 1646, *for further safety of the Town,* Colonel Muleverer (or Mauleverer) took charge of the keys to the fort at South End. From November of the same year, the guards stationed there were to be *assisted by soldiers*[2].

The Royalist siege of 1643 had been broken by a mixed force. This had comprised elements of Fairfax's army; townsmen in arms; the East Yorkshire trained bands; and soldiers and sailors sent from London. The *New Model Army,* raised by Parliament in 1644-45, was of a very different complexion. The New Model was a regular red-coated force, whose members were imbued with fiercely Independent or Puritan beliefs. In 1645, Parliamentarian soldiers quartered in Hull entered the churches and burnt the Book of Common Prayer in the Market Place, to the sound of trumpet and drum. By 1648, Colonel Robert Overton was Governor of Hull. Overton was suspected to favour the *Fifth Monarchists,* an extreme sect whose members awaited the imminent earthly kingship of Christ.

He led a regiment of similarly fundamentalist persuasion. The soldiers of the Garrison took over the chancel of Hull's Holy Trinity with their own Independent minister in 1650, erecting a wall between nave and chancel. They were still holding separate services there in 1659. John Canne, a radical minister nominated by Overton, preached to them there[3].

In 1645, Sir Thomas Fairfax succeeded his father, Lord Fairfax, as Governor. The Bench refused to provide his soldiers with lodgings, and, in the face of this defiance, troops were forcibly billeted on the people of the town. In 1647, Parliament established a Garrison for Hull, of 1,000 men. This was to be a perpetual standing garrison, to be kept at the public charge of the nation. The composition of the Hull Garrison is difficult to establish. Troops would be allocated from one regiment to another, and their officers might be called on for service elsewhere. From 1647 onwards, the strength of the Garrison is never stated. Its composition may only be inferred from references to the officers commanding various companies, and to its overall cost[4].

In 1649, Cromwell set off to subjugate Ireland. Hull was one of only four English towns he left to be invested with a garrison regiment, the others being Carlisle, Lynne and Weymouth. Pamphlets later claimed all garrisons and forts to be useless, hurtful and unnecessary. In 1657, William Prynne described the behavior of troops in garrison: *soldiers spend their days eating, drinking, whoring, sleeping and standing watch at night, but only to gaze about and call to one another "who goes there".* They *also made off with wives and daughters and leave not a few great bellies and bastards on the inhabitants' and the country's charge*[5].

The Bench was required to house and feed the soldiers, and regarded this, added to the cost of its fortifications, as insupportable. The town pleaded against it, *but for all these complaints and threatenings the Parliament settled it, in spite of their teeth and they must not lift up a finger against it or say a word against their arbitrary master.* A list, of 27 April 1657, details the accommodation of over 130 soldiers. Of these, all appear – by this date - to have been married, and 90% had children, with up to five children in each family. The list relates to four of the six wards into which the town was divided. In Humber Ward there were 23 soldiers named, 16 in Trinity Ward, 17 in Austin Ward, and 65 in Whitefriargate. Another five names were added to the bottom of the list. Other, undated, lists include 20 names for Trinity Ward; 42 names in North Ward, among whom appeared one George Overton and his child; and 38 soldiers in Austin Ward, some of whom were single men. Though incomplete, these lists give some indication of the impact of a military presence on the daily life of the ordinary citizens of Hull. In peacetime, or when, as in 1645, this arrangement was forced upon them, it was especially resented[6].

These irritations were compounded by the taxation levied to keep up a standing army 40,000 strong, of which the Hull Garrison was part. The main part of government revenue came from customs and excise and a land tax, which were levied with a ruthless efficiency which royal administrations had never managed. A monthly assessment was extended over the whole country; Hull's portion was £40 a month. The town claimed this to be excessive, in view of the commercial loss it had suffered: both from a diminished foreign trade, and from supplying ships for Parliament. Hull goldsmiths had a particular complaint, in that their trade had fallen off because citizens had been forced to donate money and plate towards the cost of the garrison. William Sykes, a prominent supporter of Parliament, was imprisoned for debt in Hull in 1648. His impoverishment had arisen from his loyalty: to fund Lord Fairfax's garrison he had lent money, £8,000 more than his estate, in cash, arms and plate. An additional charge, for the support of maimed veterans, was levied on parishes across England in 1647[7].

Some of the wealthiest merchants in Hull had been Royalist sympathisers in the Civil War. These suffered the punitive sequestration of property, being forced to *compound* by paying swingeing fines to Parliament in reparation for the costs of the war and the army. Among them were Alderman James Watkinson, who had left Hull to join Charles I in 1642; Matthew Topham, a merchant who had similarly fled to York; and Thomas Swan, whose new house had been demolished to counter Royalist siege-works in 1643. Robert Cartwright, a draper, had served under the Earl of Newcastle; Edward Dodson was also a draper. The Royalist gentry of East Yorkshire were similarly penalised. They included Christopher and Robert Hilyard; Sir Michael Warton, of Beverley, and his son; and Sir Henry Griffith of Burton Agnes, who had surrendered after Marston Moor. The latter was at first fined £7,547, though this was reduced to £5,122. Sir Francis Cobb, an esquire of the King's bodyguard, was also fined and his goods sequestrated[8].

Soldiers were recruited by impressment in time of war up to 1651, but as volunteers recruited *by beat of drum* thereafter. The Garrison comprised a variable number of companies, whose strength usually stood at 70 men. Emergencies would be met by raising the number of men in particular companies to 100, while econo-

my would be achieved by reductions later - the paper-strength of companies in the New Model Army had originally been set at 120 men. In 1651, the level of garrison troops was reduced from eight to four companies. By September 1651, as well as garrison companies, the field regiments of Colonel Ingoldsby and Colonel Goffes were also at Hull. In 1652, the four companies were further reduced to three companies, of 120 men apiece[9].

In 1651, Parliament voted that a regiment of 10 companies under Colonel Overton should form part of a standing army in Scotland. Five companies went to Scotland, leaving three at Hull and one at Scarborough - one company is unaccounted for, though it may also have remained at Hull. The regimental musters of the army in Scotland in January 1651 show that Overton's men were drawn from Hull, Scarborough and other Yorkshire garrisons. Overton himself had first marched into Hull with Hotham's trained bands, and had served under Fairfax during the sieges of Hull. In 1649, Timothy Scaife was a major in this regiment, perhaps the same man who had marched from Scarborough to Hull in July 1643. Captain John Overton, Colonel Overton's son, commanded a company at Hull in the 1650s. In 1660, William Daniel was to be made Colonel of Overton's regiment. The Daniel family came from Beswick, near Driffield, East Yorkshire; a John Daniel was subsequently to serve the restored monarchy as an ensign in Lord Belasyse's Garrison Company in 1661, becoming a lieutenant in 1663[10].

Parliament fell behind with the payment of garrisons from 1644, and increasing sums were owed in arrears of soldiers' pay. In October 1649, £129 12s 4d had to be borrowed to pay the Hull Garrison, but this still left them owed further arrears of £229 13s 4d, despite the importance of this post. The Governor of Hull had been paid £5 a day in 1645-6. The surgeon of the Garrison, appointed in 1656, was paid 2s 6d a day, rising to 3s in 1657. The total cost of the Hull Garrison in 1655 was £486 a month, which covered its wages and allowances for heating and lighting, known as *fire and candle*. Hull was by then the largest garrison in the country after Berwick upon Tweed[11].

The rates of pay for soldiers fluctuated over the period of the Commonwealth. Between 1642 and 1645, a foot-soldier was paid 8d a day. Cheese, and bread or biscuit, were provided as staple rations. These could be supplemented with meat bought out of the soldier's pay - the weekly cost of a beef diet for a single man 1650-59 has been calculated as 2s 8d. A weekly deduction of 9d covered the cost of clothing. A soldier's pay fell to 6d a day in 1646, but rose again to 9d for those in garrison, in 1649. The provision of *Free Quarter* had been abolished at the foundation of the New Model Army; its soldiers were supposed to enjoy regular pay, though as this was already in arrears by 1647, the cost of lodgings still fell first upon householders who rented rooms to soldiers. Pay fell back again to 8d in 1655, with the cost of living, and remained fixed at this level until 1660. The fire and candle allowance was always tied to the number of soldiers present in Garrison; in December 1657, this rose from 2s 6d to 4s a day at Hull[12].

In 1652, each of four companies at Hull were reduced in strength by two men, saving 6s 8d a day overall, and a chaplain was added to the establishment. In August of that year, *Captain Gregson is willing to take two wounded Dutch seamen into pay in his company.* The lot of a soldier may have been preferable to that of a prisoner, though this was a remarkable appointment as it was hostilities with Holland which had prompted reinforcement of the Garrison! In June 1654, the Storekeeper of the Magazine was to *deliver 140 muskets, 100 pikes and 400 bandoliers for the use of six companies of a regiment quartered at Hull.* This level of provision might suggest a force divided into pikemen and musketeers at a ratio of 1:4, with 83 men in each company. In 1655, a foot company of 68 men, under Captain George Westoby, was added to the Hull Garrison. In 1658, with his appointment as Governor of Hull, Colonel Henry Smith's foot company was to join the Garrison establishment, while Westoby's was placed as a company of Colonel Salmon's regiment[13].

As an army officer, the Governor was frequently called away on active service. In such circumstances, his command devolved upon the Deputy or Lieutenant-Governor. Lieutenant-Colonel Edward Salmon, second-in-command of Colonel Overton's regiment, also served as his Deputy-Governor at Hull, from 1650 to 1653. Overton returned to Hull in 1653, going back to Scotland in September 1654. In December 1654, he was imprisoned in the Tower of London, on suspicion of treason. He was replaced as Governor, in 1655, by Colonel John Bright. Bright did not live in the town, and was removed in 1658. From 1654, Major or Lieutenant-Colonel Richard Elton was Bright's Deputy-Governor. Elton was more intimately engaged with Hull, and married Mrs Elizabeth Hollis, a widow of the town, in April 1657. In 1657, Major John Waterhouse was serving as Deputy-Governor, and in 1658 Colonel Henry Smith was made Governor. At his appointment, it was required that he should live in the town. Smith was given the Governorship of Inverness in 1659, though it seems he did not take up this post. In July 1659, Overton, now 50 years old, was released from prison, and was reinstated as Governor of Hull. He remained in his post until March 1660[14].

In 1659, as moves to restore the monarchy gathered pace, troops of horse were brought into the town. On 20 September 1659, three companies of the Hull Garrison were ordered for service in Cheshire; a further two were to join the army marching from Scotland to London under General Monck. The three companies leaving Hull were each to recruit four men to make up their numbers to 75 apiece, but the five remaining in Garrison were left at a lower strength[15].

Battered bastions

The maintenance of the fortifications was now the responsibility of the Governor. He was responsible for paying for repairs, and submitting a detailed account of payments and all works performed to the Council of State. The work was checked by a number of persons, including the Mayor and the Storekeeper of the Garrison. On 3 June 1645, Peregrine Pelham, Member of Parliament for Hull, wrote to the Mayor about the upkeep of the fortifications. In September, trees were to be provided for repairing a Blockhouse. Trees for the repair of the Blockhouses, and other places not specified, were supplied in April 1646[16].

The defences of Hull had taken a battering in 1643: from enemy action; from the accidental explosion in North Blockhouse; and, not least, from the damage which had arisen from their occupation by the soldiers of the Garrison. In 1646, the cost of repairs was estimated to total £6,605[17].

Necessary repairs to the Henrician fortifications, on the east side of the river Hull, were enumerated in detail. Two platforms at the North Blockhouse, probably roof-level gun positions, required repairs to the value of £200. The *South Quarter* of North Blockhouse, however, needed £1000 for its repair, and £300 for brickwork: the scale of these works may suggest that this had been the site of the accidental explosion in 1643. The Castle required repairs valued at £300, *after damage done by fire* while it had been under the command of Sir John Hotham. The South Blockhouse had been *much damaged and burned by the soldiers,* and would cost £120. The *platform and walls of South Blockhouse decayed by the late service* needed another £100. Bridge repairs were to cost £300. *The Jetty on the Garrison Side over against the Castle,* and the *Jetty on the Garrison Side betwixt the Castle and South Blockhouse spoiled by the soldiers* required £120 and £40 respectively[18].

The western walls and defences had also suffered; many of these damages again arising from their military occupation. *Thirty score yards (600yds – 548m) of woodwork betwixt the jetty and the lime kilns have been stubbed and carried away by the soldiers for firing*, at a cost of £600. *The jetty works... nigh into the hornwork at Hessle Gate* needed £50 of repairs. The *stonework at Hessle Gate* itself, damaged *by the hornwork lately raised upon it for fortifying the town* needed £200. Other timber-work related to the defences raised in 1640-43 needed £75 worth of repairs. The provision of *40 platforms... against the town walls for the ordnance*, at a cost of £300, suggests the level of armament deemed appropriate to their defence - a gun would occupy each platform. The addition of earthworks to the medieval wall also dictated that *52 buttresses must be made of brick stone timber for... behind the North Gate*. This was the single most expensive item required, being estimated at £2,600[19].

The outward collapse of 50yds (*c.*46m) of the town wall between Myton Gate and the postern to the north, *into the ground to the very foundations*, was reported on 12 November 1646. This was thought to have occurred because of the artillery positioned here; the weight of soil piled behind it, and heavy rain, were considered as contributing to the collapse. On 8 June 1647, it was ordered: *That the Town Walls* (be) *lined with earth from Myton Gate to Hessle Gate and that a* (?subscription) *shall be made through the town for paying of the soldiers that shall be employed in the said works*[20].

Between January and May 1648, in a petition against having to pay for the upkeep of the defences, the Bench claimed that the town had paid £10,000 to repair the fortifications of the town and Castle and Blockhouses. This claim was in part retrospective, as it included costs incurred in 1627. In 1648, Francis Thorpe, Hull's other Member of Parliament, informed the Mayor that a grant had been made for the fortifications. Of this, the first £100 was raised as a loan from Thomas Munnor of London. By June 1649, an order directed £2,000 for the fortifications of Hull to the Governor, Overton, and his deputy, Lieutenant-Colonel Salmon. In 1650 or 1651, an engineer named Captain Oakeshott used wood to repair South Blockhouse, but was called away to London before he could deal with North Blockhouse[21].

In 1652, £600 was paid for materials and works at Hull. The works included repairing one of the Blockhouses, and, in 1653, the *making up the boom* to close the mouth of the river Hull. In June 1655, a bill for repairing the *Ropery, Blockhouses and breaches of the line* was ordered by Deputy-Governor Elton. The Council of State requested that Colonel Hugh Bethel, Matthew Locke, Thomas Somerscales - perhaps a burgess of Hull, Joseph Drake the Storekeeper and Major Robert Ripley survey the repairs and estimate their cost. This was met from the Army Contingency Fund, at a cost of £87 8s 11d. These repairs were required because of war with the Dutch, and were accompanied by measures to defend shipping. Seamen were impressed for naval service, and a ship of 20 guns was set to patrol the mouth of the Humber, to deter the privateer raiders known as *Dunkerkers*[22].

These levels of expenditure failed to keep the fortifications in good order. Repairs at the garrison were still estimated to require £5,051 10s in August 1657, of which only £1,000 was forthcoming from the Army Contingency Fund. The money for the fortifications was placed in the charge of Alderman John Rogers. This allocation became a convenient source to pay for repairs to weapons, rather than permitting more major works. In December 1657, redundant *sling pieces*, light breech-loading guns held in the Hull Magazine, were to be sold to finance repairs. In May 1658, £500 was allocated to repair of the Garrison. Between April and July 1658, soldiers were working in gangs of between three and twelve on the river bank, pointing and driving piles, while others helped land timber and assisted with the piling. This was to consolidate banks close to the fortifications, though exactly where is unknown. In April 1659, Thomas Parry presented bills for £100 for *expenses and pains about the garrison* to Governor Smith; and £400 *for repairing forts, blockhouses at Hull* to Colonel Charles Fairfax[23].

Work was also intermittently in progress on the landward defences of the town, in which the town had a longer-established interest. In 1653, 1s 6d was *given by the Mayor's order to the labourers to drink when he and some of the aldermen went to view the work and gave order for making the cross bank at Hessle Gate*. In 1656, Stephen Walker spent two-and-a-half days *making a frame for turning the arch* of a new bridge over the moat[24].

In summer 1656, a major project was undertaken to replace the *dolphin*. This was a structure of timber posts in the mouth of the river Hull, used to warp vessels in and out of the haven, and hence was of both commercial and military significance. The work cost £152 12s 10d, and involved making *the new dolphin and taking up the old one* under the supervision of Matthew Rowton, *our chief workman* at Trinity House. The emplacement of a stanchion, robust enough to swing ships round, required the use of *the gin to drive piles*. The dolphin first appears on a plan of *c.*1716[25].

The Magazine

The Magazine at Hull remained an important facility under the Commonwealth, providing both ships and soldiers with powder, shot and other supplies. Hull was also well-placed for the storage of the largest siege-guns. Hauling such guns along the roads of the day involved teams of 16 horses or oxen under optimum conditions, and became difficult or impossible in wet weather. Heavy guns could be most speedily and conveniently transported by water[26].

The Magazine remained in the former King's Manor until 1660. The Bench requested rent for it, which the Army failed to pay, a situation only resolved in June 1659. The Magazine was in the care of the Garrison Storekeeper. In 1652, Joseph Drake occupied this post. The Storekeeper was under the command of the Governor, and was required to maintain an updated inventory of all guns, powder and shot held in the magazine, together with other arms and supplies, and to arrange for their repair[27].

After the defeat of the Royalist army at Marston Moor, in 1644, northern garrisons holding out for the King were to be reduced with the aid of guns supplied from Hull. Guns were dispatched to York, Scarborough and Wressle Castle in 1644, by order of the Parliamentarian army. In 1645, Sandal Castle was bombarded with four *cannon royal* brought from Hull; 60lb (27kg) shot fired by these guns were discovered during excavations of Civil War deposits at that site. Scarborough Castle was besieged by Sir John Meldrum in 1645; the gun *Sweet Lips*, captured by his men before Hull in 1643, served there. The reduction of Royalist strongholds in the Second Civil War again saw siege guns sent from Hull. Pontefract castle was *bombarded with six good battering guns none less than demi-cannon*, along with two or three of the biggest mortars firing shells. These were shipped *via* Hull in 1648, along with shot and gunpowder; Pontefract surrendered in March 1649, after a five-month siege[28].

When the Royalist strongholds had been battered into submission, their stores were removed to Hull, and were thence shipped on to London. Redundant garrisons were similarly disarmed. In November 1651, *guns and their equippage with round shot, bullet and other necessaries* were to be sent from Nottingham Castle to Hull. On 10 March 1652, the Council of State ordered the movement of guns from Hull: *there are several brass ordnance in your garrison which may be spared except one cannon of eight and a brass basilisk. Send them up to the Tower whether serviceable*

or not. We have sent orders to other places for sending their brass guns to Hull to be forwarded to London and desire you to send them as they arrive. Two days later, they were ordering payment for *the messenger that is to go to York and Hull to see the ordnance sent from Cliffords Tower to Hull and thence shipped away*. The guns were to go to the Tower of London, in a convoy comprising the *Godspeed* and five other ships of Hull[29].

The issue and receipt of other military stores was similarly the responsibility of the Storekeeper. In June 1651, Nehemiah Bourne was to ship ammunition to Leith, in Scotland, for the use of the Army. In March 1653, 150 barrels of gunpowder were sent from Hull to Portsmouth. In September, the Governor was required *to deliver on order 500 shot to the Admiralty Committee for the Navy*, to arm ships[30].

The armament of the Garrison itself, however, fell into disrepair. In December 1657, 150 firearms and 100 pikes were to be sent from the Tower of London to Hull, and broken weapons already at Hull were to be mended out of money allocated for the fortifications. The repair of *decayed carriages* for guns was also ordered at this time. On February 9 1658, Colonel Henry Smith, the Governor, was ordered to deliver 40 of the largest types of iron gun: cannon, demi-cannon and culverins for the Garrison. On 25 March, the Admiralty Commission were to consider what was necessary for the Garrison, *as carriages are wanted for the guns at Hull not having been supplied for long*, and four days later were asked to supply carriages[31].

Plots and prisoners

The order for repair of fortifications at Hull issued in June 1649 was accompanied by a reminder to the Governor to take special care for the safety of Hull. Scarborough had declared for the King in 1648, and other towns were expected to be invited to join the Royalist cause; Great Yarmouth had already rejected such a summons. The Prince of Wales, the future Charles II, was expected to sail north in search of support against Parliament. Hull was to be guarded well, most particularly against attempts to suborn its Garrison. Here, the town could play its part, watching its military masters just as they were to watch the town[32].

Parliament wrote to Hull's Bench in July 1649: *the more the enemy increase in the north the greater are our apprehensions for the safety of Kingston upon Hull*. They wrote again in August: *The town of Hull is of consequence to the Commonwealth and we would admit nothing that condones to its safety. The enemy have their eyes much upon it, and will use all means to get it into their power, by corrupting any that may contribute thereto. We doubt not that the Governor and the officers of that Garrison will do their best and we recommend all things there to your care*. Francis Thorpe, one of Hull's Members of Parliament, writing to the Mayor in August, stated *his confidence in the Town's steadfastness*. This was thought to arise from the influence of its maritime community in particular; Sir Hugh Cholmley, former Governor of Scarborough, wrote of Hull that: *the seamen who had great influence on this and other maritime towns, found it stood with their interests and stick to Parliament*[33].

Prisoners-of-war, and other enemies of the Commonwealth, were detained at Hull. A Captain Cotterill was held at Hull in 1651, together with a number of Scottish prisoners, for whose keep £34 9s 6d was sent to the Deputy-Governor. In 1656, Sutton Oglethorpe was brought from York to Hull Castle, whence he petitioned for release. He had been arrested two years before, at the age of 16. A plot in Yorkshire, in 1654, had led to the trial and conviction of eight *men of quality*, who were sentenced to confinement at Hull. Robert Brandling, a prisoner at Hull Castle, appealed to Oliver Cromwell in 1657, imploring *his liberty after three years of captivity... imprisoned on false suspicion that I was privy to the late insurrection in Yorkshire*[34].

The most prominent political prisoner held at Hull was Sir Henry Slingsby. Slingsby had been arrested for his supposed involvement in the planning of the Yorkshire plot, and was detained without charge at Hull Castle from March 1655. The Commonwealth, nettled by the continuous plotting of Royalist exiles and their sympathisers, resolved to make an example of him. He was brought to trial on 25 May 1658 at Westminster Hall, London. He faced a charge of high treason: *That he did traitorously advisedly and maliciously combine together and plot to betray and yield up the said Garrison of Hull unto Charles Stuart... from 30 April last (1657) and divers times since 10 October 1656... to withdraw Ralph Waterhouse, John Overton (the Governor's son), George Thompson etc., officers of the same from their obedience to His Highness Oliver Lord Protector*[35].

This was a show trial, before a High Court of a Judge sitting without jury. Slingsby was not permitted Counsel. The case against him rested on a commission by which, it was alleged, he had sought to enrol officers of the Hull Garrison into the service of the exiled King. Slingsby claimed that: *The commission was procured by no intercourse with any person beyond the seas, but a blank one I have had four years together*. It seems that Lieutenant George Thompson had been sent to Hull by Cromwell as a double-agent to entrap Slingsby. Royalists in exile recognised, too late, that *Sir Henry Slingsby is in great danger, being discovered by Waterhouse the Deputy-Governor of Hull, who held him a long time in treaty*. Slingsby had clearly spoken unwisely before his custodians. His sole defence, that his remarks had been made in jest, was unavailing. Despite the widespread opinion that *he had very hard measure*, he was found guilty, and was beheaded at Tower Hill on 30 June 1658[36].

In 1659, prisoners at Hull were still considered dangerous enough to be kept under restraint; two, named Stamford and Townsend, were permitted to leave so as to appear before the Council of State, on presentation of massive sureties of £3,000 apiece. Others held there at this time were Robert Waters, Colonel John Lord Belasyse (or Bellasis), and Lord Willoughby. Lord Belasyse was removed from Hull Castle after a month there, to the Tower of London. Belasyse had been Slingsby's brother-in-law, and it may have been deemed inappropriate for him to remain where his relative had attempted the subversion of the Garrison. He passed his time at the Tower writing his memoirs, and was released on 2 November 1659[37].

In 1658 Oliver Cromwell died. With its charismatic leader gone, the arrears of pay owed to the Army now strained its loyalty to the Commonwealth. By 1659, the arrears owed to the Hull Garrison alone stood at £6,222; £658 towards this was paid out of the excise in July. The army grew restive as its total arrears mounted to £890,000; disaffection was reported in the Garrisons of Hull and York[38].

On June 20 1659, Colonel Overton was released from the Tower and reinstated as Governor of Hull. Colonel Smith, the former Governor, was given *ten loose companies* to be formed into a new regiment which he was to command. In July, Smith was appointed Governor of Inverness. It is believed that he never went to Scotland; he was still in Hull as late as September 1659, though his soldiers may have marched north. In July 1659, the government's Committee of Safety ordered the Hull regiment to be *filled up*, with Colonel Rogers as its Lieutenant-Colonel[39].

There is some uncertainty about troop movements at this time – and of the number of regiments at Hull - a John Wigan is also listed as Lieutenant-Colonel of Colonel Overton's regiment in July 1659. By 8 August, the Hull Foot had been paid some of its arrears, and had set off for Scotland. Overton was to command only a foot company at Hull. *He was not so wedded to his regiment as not to accept the Committee's pleasure but would rather nominate some officers for the Committee's good liking, than have a new regiment.* There were four companies at Hull, *but none of the companies have orders to recruit*[40].

Overton had owed his imprisonment to Cromwell's suspicion of his radical anti-Monarchist opinions. While Overton ensured that his troops at Hull would be led by officers who shared his own views, General Monck had set in motion events which would end with the Restoration of the Monarchy. The court-in-exile speculated as to whether Monck and Overton could be drawn to serve Charles. Monck was tractable. Overton was not. He ordered the Yorkshire Militia Horse into the town; a troop of cavalry were quartered there by 8 August. In November 1659, Overton, Lord Fairfax and Skippon, who had all fought for Parliament in the Civil War, were circulating papers opposing the restoration of monarchy. By early 1660, Overton's officers had all signed declarations in which they opposed the return of *Monarchical bondage*. Overton forced out from the Garrison two companies which had agreed with Monck's proposition for a free Parliament[41].

General Monck sent Major Smith and Colonel Aldred to talk Overton out of his opposition to the Restoration. Monck considered it possible that Overton was intending to prepare Hull for a siege, and so left a regiment at York to guard against the forces which remained under Overton's command. This regiment was led by Colonel Charles Fairfax, uncle of the Parliamentarian General Lord Thomas Fairfax. Overton remained vague about his allegiance, and on 10 March 1660, the Council of State ordered him to attend on them forthwith. He was also ordered to accept into the Hull Blockhouses two companies of Colonel Fairfax's regiment, and to dismiss *that part of the Militia Horse of Yorkshire lately admitted into the Garrison; after their dismissal you are to cause them to be disbanded and their arms secured in York Castle*[42].

The discontent of unpaid soldiers afforded leverage to those working for the Restoration: General Monck wrote to all the provincial garrisons in 1660, pointing out that only a properly constituted Parliament could raise the taxation needed to satisfy their demands for the payment of arrears. £1,000, *on account of pay of the forces belonging Hull Garrison*, was paid to Major Nancy, of Overton's regiment, to be drawn from receipts of customs and excise. By 16 March, Overton submitted, surrendering Hull to Colonel Charles Fairfax. On reporting to London, Overton was arrested, and once more found himself imprisoned in the Tower. Monck ordered the remaining soldiers of his regiment to Scotland on 17 March[43].

Having offered the first defiance of King Charles I in 1642, Hull had also presented the last obstacle to the Restoration of his son in 1660. Colonel Charles Fairfax served as Governor in Overton's place, but after ten days his companies were withdrawn, and a regiment commanded by John Streeter was recommissioned on March 26 as the Garrison regiment of Hull. This served until its disbandment on 5 October 1660, when four companies were retained. Charles II came to the throne in May 1660, amid popular rejoicing. Colonel Fairfax was later pensioned off with £100 a year, drawn from the customs collected at Hull, in recognition of his service. He was replaced as Governor, on 31 December 1660, by the veteran Royalist Lord John Belasyse, former prisoner at Hull, *who by his wounds and imprisonment hath sufficiently testified his honour and loyalty to his majesty*[44].

Footnotes

1:     Singleton and Rawnsley 1986, 66.

2:     KUHRO L486; Firth 1902, 312; KUHRO BRB 5, 743; *ibid.*, 741.

3:     Firth 1902, 147; Tickell 1798, 491; CSPD&C 1659, 45-6; CSPD 1659-60, 86; KUHRO L414-5.

4:     CSPD 1645, 237; CSPD 1647, 563; KUHRO L352, L486-7, M237.

5:     Firth and Davies 1940, xxiv; Schoerer 1974, 62.

6:     KUHRO L489; de la Pryme [1986], 95; KUHRO DMT 5/8/3/4; *ibid.*, 5/8/3/2; *ibid.*, 5/8/3/1.

7:     Correlli Barnett 1963, 115; Firth 1902, 131; Bennett 1988, 117; CCAM 1642-1656, pt. 2, 1648, 942; Hutton 1985, 129.

8:     Clay 1915, 350; Reckitt 1952, 129-31.

9:     Firth 1902, vol. 2, xxvii; CSPD&C 1652, 251, 424.

10:    Firth and Davies 1940 vol.2, 549; Stephens and Lee vol. 14, 1281; Rushworth Coll. vol. 3, 277; Firth and Davies 1940 vol. 2, 555, 559.

11:    CSPD 1649, 371; CSPD 1645-6, 237; CSPD&C 1656-7, 239; CSPD&C 1655, 238.

12: Correlli Barnett 1970, 96-7; Woodward 1995, 282; Firth 1902 vol. 1, 186-9, 234; CSPD&C 1656-7, 239.

13: CSPD 1651-2, 221; KUHRO BRB 5, 61; CSPD&C 1653-4, 219; *ibid.* 1655, 357; *ibid.*, 1658, 34.

14: Firth and Davies 1940 vol. 2, 515; 555-9; Sykes 1893, 470.

15: CSPD, Council of State, Ray's Proceedings, 216.

16: KUHRO L369, L397, L446.

17: KUHRO BRB 5, 744-6.

18: KUHRO BRB 5, 745.

19: KUHRO BRB 5, 745-6.

20: KUHRO BRB 5, 744-5, 761.

21: KUHRO L490, M237, M239; CSPD 1649-50, vol. 2, 574; KUHRO M363.

22: CSPD 1651, 619; CSPD&C 1653-4, 485; CSPD&C 1655, 182, 199, 309; CSPD&C 1655-6, 206.

23: CSPD&C 1657, 52, 217; 240, 239; CSPD&C 1658, 33; Woodward 1995, 99; CSPD&C 1659, 597.

24: Woodward 1995, 151, 18.

25: Woodward 1995, 7; 77; KUHRO Phillips plan.

26: Ross 1984, 42.

27: KUHRO M281, M283, D867; CSPD&C 1652, 524.

28: KUHRO L405; KUHRO M191, M218; Butler 1991, 94; Kenyon 1988, 194.

29: CSPD 1651, 481; CSPD&C 1651-2, 173; *ibid.*, 177; CSPD&C 1652, 554.

30: CSPD&C 1651, 268; CSPD&C 1653-4, 232, 431.

31: CSPD&C 1657, 217, 240; CSPD&C 1657-8, 280, 345, 348.

32: CSPD 1649-50, vol. 2, 574; KUHRO L506, L508.

32: CSPD 1649, 312; KUHRO L508; Binns 1986, 106.

34: CSPD&C 1652, 609; CSPD&C 1657-8, 49; Firth 1902, 271; CSPD&C 1657, 80.

35: Parsons 1836; Stephens and Lee vol. 17, 376-7; CSPD&C 1659, 372, 172.

36: CSPD&C 1659, 372; Routledge 1970 vol. 4, 46.

37: CSPD&C 1659, 172, 181; Routledge 1970, vol. 4, 330; Peacock 1874, 15.

38: CSPD&C 1658-59, 577; Hutton 1985, 115.

39: CSPD&C 1659, 31; Firth and Davies 1940 vol. 2, 515; CSPD&C 1659-60, 155; 172; CSPD&C 1659, 375; 382-3; CSPD&C 1659-60, 17.

40: CSPD&C 1659-60, 56, 86; CSPD&C 1659, 383, 216.

41: CSPD&C 1659-60, 265, 261, 86.

42: Firth and Davies 1940, vol. 2, 559; Firth 1902 vol. 2, 505-6; CSPD&C 1659-60, 43; Kenyon 1988, 299; CSPD 1659-60, 381-88; 393; Firth and Davies 1940, vol. 2, 417; CSPD 1659-60, 338, 389.

44: Firth and Davies 1940, vol. 2, 435, 559; CSPD Charles II 1660-61, 429.

CHAPTER 4

THE RETURN OF THE KING

The Restoration expressed a popular revulsion against all the trappings of military rule. The administration of Charles II, however, was forced to behave with moderation towards those who had served the Commonwealth. Charles sought to avoid the excesses of arbitrary rule which had led his father to the scaffold. Puritans and Independents, known as Dissenters because of their disagreement with Anglican practice, were perceived as offering an ever-present threat to the restored monarchy. For the first years of Charles' rule, the Crown trod a fine line between conciliation on the one hand, and the repression of dissent on the other.

Restoration rule

By the time Charles II was crowned, in May 1660, all but one of the 20 permanent garrisons of the kingdom were under the command of men who had fought for his father in the Civil War. As in the case of John Lord Belasyse at Hull, these posts were granted to reward the loyal, and in compensation for their suffering under the Commonwealth. Such officers could be relied upon to harry the Dissenters. The King also sought the election of Royalists to the Bench of Hull, and to Parliament. The advancement of royal power over the Bench was not to be easily achieved. Thus, Governor Belasyse supported the election of his Deputy-Governor, Anthony Gilby, as one of Hull's Members of Parliament in 1661. He could not, however, prevent the election of Andrew Marvell, a professed republican, to Hull's other parliamentary seat. The Governor or Deputy-Governor promoted royal policies in Hull, but often against the wishes of the Bench. He could exert direct control only over the Garrison[1].

In January 1661, the Fifth Monarchists attempted a rising in the City of London, under the leadership of Captain Venner. Overton, the former Governor of Hull, had been suspected of sympathy with their aims. After a brief period of liberty, he was arrested again in December 1660, and, save for a brief period in 1663, remained in close custody until his death in 1668. In 1660, Richard Goodgroom, John Rye and John Portman were imprisoned at Hull, by Special Warrant of the King; in 1667 they were still to be kept as close prisoners, as they were regarded as factious and seditious persons. The same year, Robert Duckenfield was released on bail from Hull Castle, *where he had long been a prisoner*[2].

After Venner's rising, the government was on its guard against subversion. In November 1662, an *information* was given against Francis Creame, a collector's clerk at Hull. It was alleged *that he had formerly served Oliver and the Rump* (Parliament under the Commonwealth), *and for trying to keep up the old interests, and employing four dangerous officers in the late army*. In 1663, the Deputy-Governor of Newcastle was embroiled in the *Yorkshire Plot*; he was arrested in London, and in 1664, 20 men were hanged in Yorkshire for their part in the conspiracy. In Hull, however, it was reported *that no considerable persons were engaged in it. People in the town hope there will be no rising in the north, as it would prejudice their party and advantage the King's*. Though there was opposition to the government in the town, it did not extend to treasonable activity. The Governor reported that *the province and Garrison being in so good position none dare attempt them*[3].

James, Duke of York, visited Hull in August 1665. James was to view the fortifications, as England was again at war with the Dutch (the Second Dutch War, of 1665-67). He was met in the East Riding by two troops of well-armed train bands horse, and many local gentry. James stayed two days as the guest of Deputy-Governor Gilby, in his house on High Street. This visit occasioned protestations of loyalty by the Bench: the Mayor presented the Duke with a purse of £50 in gold, and dined him in town, along with the aldermen dressed in their scarlet gowns. The Duke reported pleasure with the reception he received in the North, and *left great marks of his vigilance and industry at Hull and in other parts of the provinces*. His armed escort was, however, retained, as *there is some apprehension of the fanatics*. In December 1665, another plot in Yorkshire was reported. Four conspirators were *acquainted with the master of the Magazine at Hull and hope to get two or three horse-loads of arms and guns from the Magazine*[4].

In July 1666, the town again played host to courtiers when the Duke and Duchess of Buckingham, the Earls of Shrewsbury and Cardigan, *their ladies and other persons of quality* visited. They dined with the Governor, and banquetted with the Mayor and Aldermen; the Buckinghams then stayed on with the Deputy-Governor. Lord Fauconberg inspected the fortifications at Hull in July 1667. The Peace of Breda ended the war with the Dutch in 1667, though the settlement attracted criticism in Hull, duly reported by Gilby: *the peace is generally acceptable, yet some begin already to declare their suspicion that it is not an honourable one. It is impossible to satisfy disaffected people of whom there are too many*[5].

A year later, in 1668: *A multitude of disaffected persons speaks much against the government, and I believe that never were more private meetings than present.* Lord Arlington instructed the Governors of Carlisle, Berwick, Hull, Plymouth and Portsmouth that: *The King has heard of an increase of unlawful meetings on pretence of religion. You are to prevent or disperse them; proceed against them, the teacher, master of the house where the meeting is held and other ring-leaders according to the law, and to seek needful assistance from the town's magistrates.* The Governor and Deputy-Governor, however, were engaged in dispute with the very Bench of Magistrates whose help they were referred to. In May 1670, Gilby reported, *there have been great disturbances in the Garrison by the seditious meetings in conventicles during my 10 days absence and though Captain Bennet endeavoured to prevent them he was unable to do so for want of help from the Civil Power.* The disturbances included the preaching of a non-conformist sermon from the pulpit of Holy Trinity, with the connivance of the Mayor, Alderman Acklam. As Mayor, Acklam was also head of the Bench of Magistrates; Gilby was uncertain how to proceed against him[6].

In June, faced with an uncooperative Bench, Gilby was forced to take his own measures against the Dissenters. He *prevented the meeting of sectaries by placing spies on every street.* In July, government opinion was that: *The Presbyterians are so high at Hull - openly speak against the government - that they generally think that the King cannot reign long - two-thirds of the people here are Presbyterians.* By August, however, *the meetings at Hull are not so frequent as formerly, but there are still a few who are now and then prosecuted as directed by the Act.* A year later, Gilby found *the fanatics here pretty quiet*[7].

Reports of plots were received in the 1670s with increasing scepticism. A spy reported a conversation heard in a tavern, about a plot to capture Hull, to Sir Robert Hilyard. No further action is known to have followed; the suspects were presumably merely grumbling in their cups. There were further garbled reports of French spies and arsonists abroad in 1676; Gilby dismissed these tales as *rumours, groundless reports when looked into*[8].

Dissenters were debarred from public office by laws requiring public conformity with the Church of England on the part of all office-holders. Conformity carried with it the recognition of the King as Head of the Church of England, and an implicit assent to the unity of Established Church and State. Legislation enforced this policy: the Act of 1661, required those employed by Corporations to take the Anglican Communion. In 1666, the Act of Conformity specifically required those taking up government posts to swear an Oath of Allegiance and Supremacy, recognising the King as the legitimate head of the Church of England. The Oath operated to disqualify both Dissenters and Catholics from office. As well as running counter to extreme sectarian opinion, it also denied Catholic doctrine, according to which the Pope was the sole head of the Church. Lord Belasyse was sent overseas, to serve as Governor of Tangiers. He was forced to resign this post too, by the Act of 1666, as he was a Catholic. Ten soldiers in the garrison at Hull also refused the oath at this time, these were Irishmen, probably also Catholics[9].

In 1673, the Test Acts required government employees to take the Anglican Communion, and to make a written denial of Catholic doctrine. Governor Belasyse was again forced to resign office. He was replaced by the Duke of Monmouth. Monmouth was an illegitimate son of the King with a reputation for irreproachable Protestantism. The enforcement of legislation against Catholics was politically contentious because James, Duke of York, the King's brother and heir-apparent, was himself a Catholic[10].

The *Popish Plot*, of 1678, saw an anti-Catholic scare whipped up by the Whig opponents of the government. The *Exclusion Crisis*, in 1679-81, saw them raise the political stakes with an attempt to exclude James from the Succession, on the grounds of his Catholicism. The Duke of Monmouth, an Exclusionist, was replaced as Governor of Hull by the Earl of Mulgrove, on 1 December 1679. Through his friendship with James, Mulgrove gained several preferments at Monmouth's expense. In 1681, the Hull Bench voted by four to three, with six abstentions, to declare their loyal opposition to the Exclusion Bill then being promoted by the Whigs. This position of only nominal support – in reality tacit opposition - was again underlined in 1682. The Bench then decided by a majority of seven to four against sending an address to the Crown expressing abhorrence at attempts to debar James[11].

Hull returned Members of Parliament who favoured Exclusion, despite the efforts of successive Governors to secure the election of candidates who would support James' right to succeed to the throne. On the death of Andrew Marvell, Monmouth had recommended Captain John Shales, a protege of James', as Member of Parliament in his place. Shales was forced to withdraw for lack of support. A merchant of Hull, William Ramsden, was elected instead. The General Election of 1679 saw Monmouth put forward Lemuel Kingdom,

Paymaster to the Army. Kingdom was elected along with Ramsden; however, Alderman William Gee, an unsuccessful candidate, petitioned against his return on the grounds of menaces and compulsion. In a second election Gee was returned, along with Sir Michael Warton of Beverley[12].

The King's soldiers

The power of the Governor to influence events in Hull rested on his command of the Garrison. The Commonwealth, however, had so embittered opinion against military rule that an obtrusive military presence only went unchallenged in time of emergency. The Army was paid off and discharged as soon as money could be raised, in the autumn of 1660. The remaining forces were *Guards and Garrisons*, as at Hull. These, through the Governor, were under the command of the Crown. In view of the town's record in the Civil War, Charles II forbade Hull to raise its own militia. The Lord Lieutenancy of the East Riding, which controlled the militia, was placed in the hands of the Governor of Hull. When militia had to be raised, they were to be drawn from East Yorkshire, which had been generally Royalist in the Civil War, and they would be deployed under the Governor's control[13].

In March 1660, there were three companies of soldiers in Hull: the remnants of Overton's Garrison. On May 10, they numbered 250 men, kept in Hull at a cost of 7 ¾d each per day. The Disbanding Act of 1660, which received the Royal Assent on 13 September, specifically excepted *companies guarding the arsenals at Hull and the Scottish border at Carlisle and Berwick* (which were to be) *retained in pay until the completion of the disbandment*. In October, a commission was granted to William Broxholme to raise a company of 100 men at Hull, of which he was to be Captain, *for the safe guard of the place*. Some disbanded men may have re-mustered with Broxholme. Six companies were to be raised under Lord Belasyse. The Letters Patent of 5 December 1660, which appointed Belasyse as Governor of Hull, fixed his fee to include the cost of a body of 20 men. This probably represented a personal guard, as an institutional legacy of the retinue employed by the Governor of Hull up to 1552. In the 1680s, they were to form part of the first, Governor's, Garrison Company of 100 men[14].

In January 1661, at Belasyse's request, two companies of foot were to be raised within the town. A. Dorman and Alderman William Dobson were to serve as captains of one company, with George Osbourne, the Master Gunner at Hull, as lieutenant. Hugh Lister, a member of a prominent family of Hull Royalists, and Mr William Thompson, a seaman, were respectively captain and lieutenant of the second company. Mr Arthur Saltrain and John Horner were to serve as ensigns. Lord Belasyse made this request in his capacity as Lord Lieutenant of the Town's County, suggesting that these forces were initially to be classed as elements of the militia, rather than with the *Guards and Garrisons*[15].

On 12 March 1661, pay for a garrison of six companies was ordered for Lord Belasyse's command, at a total charge of £767 18s a month, with £825 arrears. The payment was back-dated to 1 December 1660 for three companies, and to 26 January 1661 for the other three. Payments at this rate were recorded from November 1661 to July 1662. They represented wages for 600 men. In 1662, Captains Robert Hilyard, Francis Cobb, Michael Warton, William Broxholme and Belasyse – the latter either the Governor or his son – were mentioned[16].

In September 1663, the Royal Regiment of Guards, commanded by Lord Thomas Wentworth with a strength of 24 companies, were ordered to garrison Hull, Berwick, and other towns in the north of England. The Hull Garrison was halved, to make room for three companies of the Guards, in the autumn of 1663. In 1662, the company of Sir Henry Belasyse, son of the Governor, had been disbanded. The Yorkshire Plot of 1663, however, encouraged the postponement of the disbanding of Sir Robert Hilyard's company. Further appointments to three companies, in January 1665, show them to have been commanded by a father and son, both named Robert Hilyard, and by Richard Hilyard. The Hilyard family, from Winestead in the East Riding, had been prominent supporters of Charles I in the Civil War. Commissions were awarded to loyal local Royalists, and it was these reliable captains who were retained at a time when the government was alert to conspiracy in the North[17].

Provision was also made, though haltingly, for other impoverished veterans. In 1664, Abraham Warton, *one of the late disbanded officers who faithfully served the King*, was commissioned as ensign in Sir Francis Cobb's company of foot at Hull. Cobb himself had been among the East Riding Royalists fined under the old regime. A *reformando*, or former Commonwealth officer, was commended by General Monck - now Duke of Albemarle - for service at Hull, in September 1664. This was Lieutenant-Colonel Thomas Duncan, who requested *that he may be mustered in his* (Belasyse's) *company as a reformando free of duty as commanded by* the Duke of Albemarle. *Also for some office of relief of his wife and children who he has not seen for five years.* Duncan was still attempting to take up his place in May 1665. In 1666, Colonel Stephen White sought a pensioner place at Hull, which was *void by the preferment of Captain Morrough Flaherty to service in Tangiers.* The posting of an Irishman to Tangiers is a reminder of the fate of many Catholic or Dissenter soldiers, who were tidied away to die in this colonial campaign. Military posts also provided pensions for other deserving cases. Again on Albemarle's request, a *dead pay* - the wage of an unfilled post - was granted to 74-year-old John Rudston, who had been *miraculously preserved when the London frigate was blown up*[18].

The Dutch Wars

Commercial rivalry with the Dutch flared into war again in 1665. As a principal East Coast port, Hull was again recognised as being at risk. In June 1667, national provision was made for the establishment of 12 new regiments of foot to fight the Dutch, each of ten companies with 50 men apiece. At Hull, the Garrison now comprised the Governor's company, and three others. Twelve men were to be added to the Governor's company, and 20 men to each of the others, bringing them to 100 men apiece. A further two new companies were to be raised, each of 100 men, taking the strength of the Garrison to 500 men - a figure which excluded the Governor's company - and its annual cost to £4,076 16s[19].

On 16 June 1667, three companies of *Hull Guards* - as noted above, a detachment of the Royal Regiment of Guards - were prepared to march from Hull to London. Meanwhile, Belasyse called the trained bands of the East Riding to muster at Beverley. Sir Francis Cobb, apparently as acting-commander in Belasyse's absence, requested two companies of foot of 100 men apiece for Hull garrison, to be added to *the four who were there before the arrival of the guards now commanded away* - to keep up a garrison strength of six companies. By 21 June, the militia had arrived to fill up the Garrison: *Three companies of train bands have come from Beverley under Colonel Warton and Captains Bethell and Vavasour. Captain Moontan's company all lusty able men have come in and expressed readiness to serve King and country*[20].

Reviewing the mobilisation of 1667, in August, Lord Belasyse considered that the reduction of the Garrison had over-stretched local defences. The Garrison should in future be maintained at a minimum level of six companies: *600 men being scarce sufficient to perform the duty of the Garrison and the train bands of the East Riding not sufficient to guard the coast in case of danger.* The train bands could not patrol the countryside and watch the coasts if they were simultaneously tied to duty in Hull. The pay of all garrisons was at least four months in arrears by December 1667. Payments by the Treasury from excise, between May 1668 and June 1669, reflected an establishment of six companies, or at least its arrears of pay for 1668[21].

Independent Companies raised for garrisons in 1667 were largely drawn from pensioned or superannuated soldiers, who were thus rewarded for past service. They wore a red coat for full dress, as did other foot. Their day-to-day clothing consisted of a grey cloth coat lined with *bayes* (beige); a pair of lined *kersey* breeches; a hat edged with lace and a hat-band; a sash, and a sword-belt. Non-commissioned officers wore similar dress. The coat cost £2 13s, the cost of which was divided equally between the soldier, out of his *off-reckonings* or deductions, and his commander[22].

The Governor and Deputy-Governor continued to arrange for the defence of shipping in time of war, as they had under the Commonwealth. This was a welcome service to a maritime community. In February 1665, *40 Holland and Zealand men-o-war are on the coast and coals have risen very high, no ships venturing to Newcastle.* The coal shortage was resolved in July, by sending Deputy-Governor Gilby with a prize ship, which as a captured vessel might be mistaken by the enemy for one of their own, to fetch coal from Newcastle for the Garrison. Gilby was sailing his *privateer* from Hull in November 1666. In view of the Dutch threat, the convoy system was revived; in March 1667, *five or six vessels have come from London, one with ammunition for the garrison*[23].

Ships of the Royal Navy off-loaded prisoners captured at sea; in August 1667, 180 prisoners arrived at Hull in three ships. The confinement of so many could be troublesome, and whenever possible they would be paroled to be of good behaviour. In 1666, as a special security measure, Dutch prisoners on bail were committed to close custody by the Governor. Numbers of prisoners died while held at Hull, and were buried in the graveyard of Holy Trinity[24].

The refusal of Parliament to fund the upkeep of a standing army, once the forces raised for the Dutch war were disbanded, left funds for the Hull Garrison at a level appropriate only to a caretaker establishment. The King was forced to pay for his troops out of his hereditary revenues, rather than from taxation. Allocations in January 1670 were for *John Lord Belasyse Governor and Captain of 20 soldiers 10s a day, 8d a day to 20 soldiers from time to time to be placed there, for one year to Xmas last*, or a year in arrears. The orders for payment from the excise for 1670, in January, were at a rate of £81 14s 8d *for Hull and Blockhouses*. Meanwhile, Deputy-Governor Gilby protested that the suppression of Dissenters in the town could not be continued without recruitment of the companies. In January 1671, the total charge of Hull Garrison - for the previous year as payment was in arrears - was £425 16s 8d[25].

In May 1671, the King ordered 540 recruits to be *distributed among the garrisons of Berwick, Plymouth, Hull, Portsmouth, York and Windsor... to supply the places of nine companies sent to Rochester* - implying that these were 80-man companies. The Garrison was settled, in May 1671, at a level of *three garrison companies and the two companies of the Admiralty Regiment at Hull. Twelve recruits to each company being 60 men making in all 560 soldiers at 8d a day; all which we have settled by an establishment under our hand to commence the 6th day of May 1671.* The Storekeeper was supplying *six* companies with arms between March and June 1672. This may suggest that the Governor's Company remained a separate force at this time[26].

The Garrison was strengthened in 1671 in preparation for the renewal of hostilities with the Dutch. In the Third Anglo-Dutch War (of 1672-73), Hull became a transit point as the Crown shuffled its small forces about the kingdom. Most standing regiments were stationed near the East Coast and the Channel ports. Companies briefly swelled the Hull garrison, only to be redeployed after a few days or weeks. Overall, priority was afforded to the defence of southern ports, which had experienced alarming raids in the war of 1665-67. In April 1672: *Last Friday being our Market Day the proclamation of War was published at the Market Cross where all the soldiers were drawn up and was generally owned by beat of drum.* In March, a detachment of 28 soldiers, and others, joined the frigate *Richmond*; Captain Bennet's company from Hull arrived at Sheerness later the same month. In May, the new raised companies of Captain Radcliffe (or Ratcliffe) and Captain Talbot, part of Colonel Fitzgerald's regiment, reinforced the Garrison[27].

Troop movements continued late into the year. In December, *Captain Sidney's company came here from Berwick to reinforce this garrison, in the room of Sir Robert Hilyard's which marched on 6 November for Plymouth.* On 4 December, the depar-

ture of a foot company for Colchester, under Lieutenant Griffith and Ensign Yarborough, was reported. On 8 December, *Sir Walter Vane's and Sir Thomas Woodcock's foot companies* (were) *all now settled in their quarters, and tomorrow we suppose will march here Major Ratcliffe's and Captain Talbot's foot companies, they having already secured their quarters.* The latter two companies had perhaps arranged accommodation when they had arrived as newly levied forces in May. On 28 January 1673, Captain Talbot's company was reported as having arrived at Walton-on-Naze, near Landguard Fort, Essex. In March, a company drawn from Hull under the command of Ensign Elvidge was at Lincoln, awaiting arms and further orders. In June 1673, Captain Walter's company of dragoons arrived; in August, five companies of 100 men marched from Hull for Yarmouth[28].

Hull shippers could profit from these hectic days, whether carrying munitions or soldiers. In 1672, the Storekeeper paid £2 14s for carriage of goods in George Huntingdon's ship from Hull to the Ordnance wharf at the Tower of London. Towards the close of 1673, troops went from Hull to Holland; 60 men under Captain Green of Carlisle sailed in the *Charity* of Hull in early December. The sounds of naval gunfire, which carried from the indecisive running battle of Southwold Bay in May 1672, were reportedly audible in Hull, and served as a reminder of the value of the Garrison to the town[29].

The settled Garrison was listed under the heading of *Hull Blockhouse*, on the appointment of the Duke of Monmouth as Governor, in April 1673. It amounted to two 60-man companies, each with a captain, lieutenant, ensign, two sergeants, three corporals and a drummer. The Governor was Captain of one of the companies, the Deputy-Governor drew Captain's pay for the other. In addition, there was a Master Gunner, paid 2s a day, and seven other gunners receiving 1s 6d a day - over twice the pay allowed for a private soldier. The Storekeeper received 8d a day, a soldier's wage, and an additional 4d. The gunners and Storekeeper were later listed along with 10 soldiers as elements of a 20-man command under the Governor. The fire and candle allowance for heating and lighting was set at 4s a day. The total annual cost of the Garrison amounted to £2,745 5s 4d. It was still maintained at this level in 1679[30].

The passage of troops through Hull had made it difficult to enforce an *Ancient order in the Garrison of Hull* against the recruitment of married men. As the companies of the Governor and Deputy-Governor were now fixed forces, *constantly residing in the garrison which are not subject to be removed as the others are*, this regulation was re-stated by Monmouth in June 1675. A dispensation was granted for those already married, allowing them to retain their posts. This suggests that a degree of integration was possible between a fixed garrison and its host community, and that this had indeed occurred at Hull. Overton's regiment had included local men from the outset, and by 1657 the majority of soldiers known to have been living in Hull shared lodgings with their wives and children. The re-mustering of most of these men, who had no trade to follow and yet had families to support, would have been necessary where it was intended to keep a garrison in being[31].

There is little evidence for the disorder traditionally associated with a military presence. Only the most serious cases would come before the Bench, and such cases were infrequently reported. In 1664, a town jury gave a *post-mortem* verdict on the body of Gervase Dighton, a corporal in Gilby's company, killed by Theophilus Garlike, a sergeant in the same company, in a duel. Petty crime, as with a soldier accused of stealing clothes - probably from his lodgings - figured in correspondance between Gilby and the Mayor, in 1675. A case which had arisen in November 1674, when a Lieutenant Morgan of the Garrison struck a corporal who later died of his injuries, was referred to the civil authorities for trial in 1676. In April 1678, Monmouth wrote to Sir Robert Hilyard about deserters who *are run from their colours and now shelter themselves in Hull. I order you to make search for them... the captain tells me they are well known to the Town Major therefore it will befit to use his assistance*[32].

The Town Major was a most important figure in maintaining cordial relations between the military and the town. This officer was responsible for finding lodgings for soldiers in the houses of the inhabitants, in a time before it was accepted that barracks should be provided. In July 1666, Colonel Walter Whitford, *disabled from field service by 18 wounds received in the late king's* (Charles I) *war*, had petitioned for the post of Town Major of Hull. It is uncertain whether his application was successful. John Johnson, *once Town Major*, was buried in St Mary's Lowgate, Hull, in January 1685. Edward Carew was appointed to the post in 1685, followed by George Barrett in 1687[33].

The tensions arising from the quartering of soldiers seem to have become especially acute at the mobilisation of 1667, perhaps because the post of Town Major was unfilled at that time. In November 1667, the Bench wrote *concerning the removal of the wives and children of soldiers removed or disbanded*, money owed for quartering the troops, and debts left unpaid when the Hull Guards had marched up to London. Correspondence about these claims continued through December, between the Bench on one hand for the town; and William Lister, Deputy-Governor Gilby, and Governor Belasyse for the Crown on the other. In 1669, further correspondence *concerned the removal of Lieutenant Wise and his company from Hull*. More extensive troop movements in 1673 were managed smoothly, perhaps because an officer responsible for liaison between the civil and military communities had been appointed[34].

The *Popish Plot* of 1678 generated particular concern in Hull, when the Garrison was reinforced, as sectarian fears exacerbated the financial and practical difficulties to be expected. Gilby denied reports that *most of the four companies of Monmouth's regiment coming to Hull were papist*. These regular soldiers were to be placed under the officer in command at Hull, to raise its establishment to six companies. In 1679, Gilby received orders for the admission of four companies: Sir Baurchier Wray's, Captain Bagot's and Captain Lyttleton's from the Duke of Monmouth's regiment, and Captain Richardson's of the Holland regiment. Other troops collected arms at Hull, *en route* for other postings. Money was unavailable to pay for subsistence for the Duke of Monmouth's regiment: payments of £10 were made in June 1679 to William Barnes, John Cawley and Ambrose Butler, in respect of what they were owed by *several of Captain Gilby's soldiers in the Duke of Monmouth's regiment*. Such problems recurred whenever the Garrison was reinforced with outsiders: *William Abernathy late quarter-master to the Earl of Roscommon's troop of horse regiment is indebted to several inhabitants of Hull for his own and some soldiers quarters of the said troop and he denies he owes any such quarter*[35].

The Garrison offered useful services to compensate for such inconveniences. In 1666, after the Plague of the previous year, Gilby was issuing passes to officers, *Hull being free from the plague and all other infectious diseases*. In 1676, a file of musketeers escorted merchants' wagons from Gainsborough, Lincolnshire, to London. The sergeant in charge of the party was *to take special care that the soldiers all along the march behave civilly and duly pay for whatsoever they may have occasion for*. His responsibility for defences on both banks of the river Hull encouraged Monmouth, in 1678, to order Gilby to assign two soldiers to row ferry boats used to cross the river. Soldiers would take turns, each pair spending a week on this duty. Boatmen had formerly been hired, using *dead pays* to finance their charges[36].

The defences neglected

The armament of Hull's defences was listed on 15 June 1660, one month after the Coronation of Charles II. This survey dealt with the type and quantity of guns, rather than their quality or state of readiness. It indicates that, under the Commonwealth, the majority of pieces remaining in Hull had been under the control of the Garrison, and that the defence of Hull against naval attack had been the priority governing their deployment.

South End Fort, guarding the mouth of the river Hull, held 19 guns, including a large *basilisk*, a *cannon of eight*, three *culverins* and nine *demi-culverins*. South Blockhouse, and *the forts* below it, were also strongly armed, with 21 guns. North Blockhouse, commanding North Bridge, held 10 guns. The Castle, however, held only eight *sakers*, the lightest class of guns. The Hessle Gate Fort, perhaps the earthwork defences advanced before the gate itself, had three *sakers*. Beverley Gate Fort had three *sakers* and a *demi-culverin*, a slightly stronger armament for the main landward entrance to the town. Myton Gate Fort and the Main Guard or guardhouse had two *sakers* apiece, and two *demi-culverins* were at the Magazine. The total of 71 guns was distributed so as to afford significant protection to the mouth of the river Hull, and nominal defence of the landward approaches to the town. Though armed in the Civil War, the ramparts raised behind the medieval walls now mounted no guns[37].

The stores of the Garrison included 9,696 round-shot for guns, 264 stone cannon-balls, 343 rounds of case-shot, and 103 other specialised projectiles such as *sangar* shot, *cross-barrel* shot, *burr* shot and *chain* shot. These were mainly for use against shipping. For infantry use, there were 1,126 hand grenades, for use in sieges; match and shot for muskets; between 600 and 700 *backs and breasts* of body armour for pikemen, and 766 pots or metal helmets; along with other broken, antique or unsorted pieces and ammunition. A store of 793 barrels of *acorn powder* was also held[38].

The condition of the eastern defences was briefly reviewed in 1660, when it was found that *the South Blockhouse which commands the Humber* (is) *in good repair, the other two somewhat decayed*. A Royal Warrant, of 18 February 1661, directed that timber *seized or embezzled in Sherwood Forest* was to supply the Governor, Lord Belasyse, *with timber felled in the forest for the repairs of the fortifications* of Hull. A Warrant paying him £500 *towards the repair of the fortification at Hull* was dated 11

August 1662, and £300 of the money was transferred in June 1663. A further Warrant, of 27 July 1663, authorised him *to use materials, by sale or otherwise, of the North Blockhouse at Hull which is very ruinous, to put the necessary part of the Blockhouse into serviceable condition*[39].

The interpretation of instructions *vis a vis* the North Blockhouse was later shown to have been eccentric, even by the standards of the day. The works of 1663 were investigated long after Lord Belasyse had left office, in 1680. The timber and lead from North Blockhouse had been *used for other purposes*. The bricks had been taken away by Deputy-Governor Gilby, who had used them to build himself a new house at Sunk Island, to the east of Hull[40].

The mobilisation of 1667 saw 60 loads of timber brought to Hull, which Belasyse used to make carriages for the guns - these had been recognised as decayed nine years before, and were *almost past using*. The work, using 205ft (*c*.76m) of timber, was undertaken by Alderman Robinson. These repairs were deemed to have brought the Garrison to a state of *very good equippage* by 26 June 1667, though ten days before there had scarcely been 10 guns mounted on working carriages. The gunner's stores from the *Little Victory* were also added to the Garrison, in July 1667. The defences were inspected in 1665 and 1667, by the Duke of York and Lord Fauconberg respectively. Estimates for repairs at the Castle, Storerooms and South Blockhouse were prepared by August 1674, though it is uncertain if they led to action[41].

The town defences were similarly neglected in the 1660s. In May 1669, the Bench employed a man at 8d a day, for spending five days *laying in wait to prevent soil throwing down at Beverley Gates and the manor side*. In March 1670, Thomas Bennett and 15 other Commissioners at Hull *by desire of Lord Belasyse the Governor... viewed the drawbridge and gates which are much in decay and estimate that the repairs will cost £85*. Belasyse undertook to repay the cost of the drawbridge repairs at Beverley Gate; the Bench claimed the charge for the work fell to the Crown. They similarly disclaimed responsibility for repairs to a jetty, and breaches in the Humber banks *on Holderness side* - to the east of Hull - *if it is not repaired the South* (Block) *House will be an island*. The Crown found the town liable for repairs to the jetty, and ordered their speedy execution. It is uncertain when these works were carried out, if at all[42].

In 1673, Richard Blorne visited Hull, and emphasised its strong defences. *It is seated on the mouth of the river Hull where it falleth into the Humber, and is a place of exceeding great strength, being able to bid defiance both to a navy, and a land-army, and that by reason of its strong block-houses, castles, walls, forts, trenches, and the inhabitants and soldiers within it being at present a considerable Garrison of His Majesty's, under the command of the Right Honourable John Lord Belasyse, Lord Lieutenant of this Riding.* The Garrison was indeed the enlarged war-time establishment for Hull, but the fortifications had seen only the most urgent repairs carried out since 1640[43].

The most significant building undertaken by the Governors of Hull up to 1680 was actually within the town. In March 1679, the Duke of Monmouth asked Aldermen Skinner, Lambert and Maister to direct and inspect work on a new Guardhouse, *to be built at the upper* (south) *end of the Market Place near the Prison.* The guardhouse it replaced was also nearby, but had proved *inconvenient to the inhabitants and the frequenters of the Market.* A 2ft (0.6m) wide part *of a chamber built adjoining the pinfold and taken lately into the Guardhouse, lately built for the soldiers of the Garrison,* was recorded on 8 December 1679[44].

The money supplied to Charles II by Parliament had provided ships and men in time of war, but could not cover the costs of extensive building as well. In April 1681, the Board of Ordnance began to consider where money might be found for work on the fortifications at Tilbury, Sheerness, Portsmouth and Hull. The southern forts, begun earlier in the reign, already required extensive repairs, while Hull had seen no major works since 1640. The renovation of defences was justified not merely for local defence, but in the interests of internal stability: *at this time, when the misguided multitude are so much disposed to mischief and the malice of disloyal and ambitious persons, so mysteriously contriving the disturbance of his Majesty's government.* The works which were thus set in train would express, through their massive form, a new turn in the relationship between town and Crown, and town and gun[45].

Footnotes

1: Hutton 1985, 139; Gillett and MacMahon 1980, 182.
2: Rogers 1966, 112-21; Stephens and Lee vol. 14, 1281-3; CSPD 1666-67, 498, 161.
3: CSPD 1661-62, 457; Walker 1934, 349-59; CSPD 1663-64, 291, 223.
4: CSPD 1664-65, 520, 523; de la Pryme [1986] vol. 2, 99; CSPD 1665-66, 115.
5: CSPD 1665-66, 534; CSPD 1667, 291, 344.

6: CSPD 1667-68, 481; CSPD 1668-69, 655; CSPD 1670, 240; KUHRO L807; CSPD 1670, 289.
7: CSPD 1670, 270, 309, 389; CSPD 1671, 206.
8: KUHRO L869; CSPD 1676-77, 101.
9: Hirst 1913, 22-3; Stephens and Lee vol. 2, 142-3; CSPD 1666-67, 292.
10: CSPD 1673, 194.
11: KUHRO BRB 7, 633-707; CSPD 1679-80, 293; Stephens and Lee vol. 18, 13-15.
12: Gillett and MacMahon 1980, 183-4.
13: Hutton 1985, 138; CSPD February-December 1685, 300.
14: CSPD 1660, 436; CSPD 1660-61, 314; CTB 1669-72, 777.
15: KUHRO BRB 2, 343.
16: CTB 1660-67, 233, from November 1661 for four months pay drawn on receipts of customs at Hull - £3,071 12s; *ibid.*, 307, in February 1662 - £1,535; *ibid.*, 358, in May 1662, covering a period up to the preceding March - £3,839 10s; *ibid.*, 393, and in July 1662, for two months pay between March and May - £1,535 16s - *ibid.*, 404; KUHRO BRB 5, 472.
17: Walton 1894, 5; Routledge 1970 vol. 5, 333; CSPD 1667, 382; Dalton 1960, vol. 1, 13-14; CSPD 1663-64, 282; CSPD 1664-65, 186, 193.
18: CSPD 1663-64, 234; CSPD 1664-65, 612, 2, 225, 371; CSPD 1665-66, 320; CSPD 1664-65, 161, 431.
19: CSPD 1667, 178.
20: CSPD 1667, 382, 198; CSPD 1666-67, 216; CSPD 1667, 198; 219.
21: CSPD 1667, 219; 382; Childs 1976, 57; CTB 1667-68, 572, 588, 640; CTB 1669-72, 185, 234. Payments were as follows: in May - £2,169 9s 4d; July - £1,200 9s; and September 1668 - £1,081 14s 8d; and in February - £2,163 9s 4d; and June 1669 - £1,622 12s.
22: Childs 1976, 217, 57.
23: CSPD 1664-65, 225, 493; CSPD 1666-67, 221, 587.
24: CSPD 1667, 390; CSPD 1666-67, 108; ERYCRO PE158/3.6.
25: Wilson 1965, 211-15; CTB 1669-72, 777, 515, 252-3; CSPD 1670, 270.
26: CSPD 1671, 220; CTB 1669-72, 919, 921; PRO WO51/20, TBB Ser. 2; CTB 1669-72, 1345.
27: Childs 1976, 98; CSPD 1672, 358, 189, 241, 473.
28: CSPD 1672-73, 203-4, 243, 255, 488; CSPD 1673, 194, 335, 488.
29: PRO WO51/20, TBB 1677, 34, Ser. 2; CSPD 1673, 442-3; CSPD 1672, 102.
30: Bod. Lib. Rawl. A475, nd, probably January 1686, Duxbury to Board; PRO WO24/3, Establishments Returns 1673; CTB 1679-80 extra; CTB 1672-75, 107.
31: CSPD 1675-76, 164.

32:     KUHRO M312, L855-6; CSPD 1676-77, 297, 311; CSPD 1677-78, 123.

33:     Sykes 1893, 12, 474; Dalton 1960, vol. 2, 40, 47.

34:     KUHRO L761-2, L768, L770-2, L791a, L784.

35:     KUHRO L902; CSPD 1678, 519-20; CSPD 1679-80, 165; CSPD 1677-78, 85;
        CSPD 1679-80, 15; KUHRO L907, L918; CTB 1679-80, 366.

36:     CSPD 1665-66, 286; CSPD 1676-77, 346; CSPD 1677-78, 172.

37:     PRO WO46:1, 2, Account of Ordnance.

38:     Stafford Record Office D (W) 1778/C/55(1), Abstract of Ordnance belonging to
        the Garrison.

39:     Lankester 1846, 162; CTB vol. 6, pt. 3, appendix 1, 1530; CSPD 1661-62, 448;
        CTB 1660-67, 351; CSPD 1662-63, 184.

40:     See below, Chapter 5; KUHRO M362.

41:     CSPD 1667-68, 162; CSPD 1666-67, 198; CSPD 1667-68, 193; CSPD 1666-67,
        233; CSPD 1667, 293, 291; PRO WO46:1 (index), 216, Estimates, 15 August
        1674.

42:     Woodward 1995, 108; CSPD 1670, 131; KUHRO M324; CSPD 1670, 189, 587.

43:     Woodward 1985, 28-9.

44:     CSPD 1679-80, 104, 105; KUHRO D904.

45:     Stafford Record Office D (W) 1778/I/639, Board of Ordnance, 22 April 1681.

CHAPTER 5

BUILDERS AND BUREAUCRATS

The decision to refortify Hull set in motion the last great military project of the reign of Charles II: the construction of the Hull Citadel. This would continue under his successor, James II, and was to be completed for William III in 1690, after the Glorious Revolution of 1688 had placed him on the throne as the first constitutional monarch of England.

The enterprise was directed and funded from the seat of royal government in London. Having established the character of the works to be undertaken, the Crown appointed Commissioners at Hull to oversee the implementation of its designs. The administrative relationship between the central government and its Commissioners produced a voluminous documentary archive. This detailed the nature, cost and chequered progress of the works, and illuminated the varied concerns of those involved in them at every level. It also provided a striking illustration of the day-to-day mechanisms by which government under the later Stuarts was capable of getting things done.

The Board of Ordnance

The planning of the new works at Hull was directed from the Office of the Board of Ordnance, a department of state based in London, at the Tower. The Board was responsible for the building and maintenance of garrisons; the erection of new defences throughout England, and their supply with all manner of stores and armaments, as well as the supply of guns to the Navy. These were, for the 17th century, the logistical responsibilities of the modern Ministry of Defence. In 1667, wide-ranging reforms had seen the Board take over responsibility for construction or repairs from the individual Governors of forts and garrisons who had formerly exercised, and abused, these powers[1].

The nominal head of the Board was the Master-General of the Ordnance. He reported to the King and the Privy Council. In his military capacity the Master-General served as Commander-in-Chief of artillery and engineers, and in a civil capacity as the head of the Board. This post was filled by Sir Christopher Musgrave up to 1681, and by George Legge, Lord Dartmouth, from 1682 to 1689. Dartmouth was a particularly capable administrator, and the procedures which he set out were to be followed, with only minor alteration, until the abolition of the Board in 1855. These rules detailed the duties of every employee, and gained their legal force through Royal Warrant. Further Warrants legalised the extension of the activity of the Board when, as at Hull, new projects were to be undertaken[2].

The day-to-day work of the Board of Ordnance devolved upon five Principal Officers, who met twice weekly at the Tower to transact their business. The Ordnance Treasurer, Charles Bertie, solicited funds from the Treasury, and received and paid out monies. The Board's finance was governed by an annual allocation from the Treasury. In the 1660s and 1670s, estimates for all Ordnance services calculated an overall charge of £30,000, rising to £60,000, *per annum*. Of the other members of the Board, the Lieutenant-General, Sir Christopher Musgrave, held a general brief as a day-to-day manager, supervising the tabling of estimates and contracts. The Surveyor-General, Sir Jonas Moore, saw to the estimating and measuring of works, and the passage of bills. This was a technical position; Moore was a noted mathemetician, a writer on military architecture, and had produced a practical handbook entitled *Modern Fortification* in 1669. The Principal Storekeeper, Mr Edward Conyers, was responsible for stores held at forts and garrisons, and at the Tower. The Clerk of the Ordnance, Sir Edward Sherbourn, was not only a general scribe serving the others, but also the hub of accounting under whose hand passed debentures, bills of imprest, issues and returns of money, and who also monitored the state of the Ordnance debt[3].

A sixth individual, the Chief Engineer, though serving under the Board, also had direct access to the King and Privy Council. Sir Bernard de Gomme had filled this post and, for nearly 20 years, had been responsible for fortification design and construction in England. From 1682, de Gomme combined this post with that of Surveyor General, bringing him formally onto the Board as one of its Principal Officers. He had designed and built major works such as Plymouth Citadel, the town defences of Portsmouth and Gosport, and the riverside forts at Tilbury and Sheerness. His former employment under Charles I had seen him erect more temporary, if extensive, defences, as at Oxford and Liverpool, during the Civil War. He brought a distinctively Dutch flavour to the design of English fortifications in the later 17th century, which was most appropriate to Hull.

In the 1680s, largely without recourse to Parliament, the Board tapped diverse resources to pay for works at Hull. In 1681, it was proposed that £30,000 should be raised, to cover repairs at Tilbury, Sheerness, Portsmouth and Hull. A Royal Warrant permitted the sale of 2,000 barrels of surplus gunpowder, to employ the proceeds on these projects. Major contractors who engaged directly with the Board would also be paid by them. Funds for the first works at Hull were scraped together. Part was paid in kind: 299 barrels of surplus gunpowder, at the rate of 50s per barrel, worth £725. A further £250 came from the sale of the Artillery Ground in London. Finally, the largest sum, £2,485 16s 10d came *out of the first payment of money into this office out of His Majesty's said Kingdom of England* (i.e. from the Treasury allocation)[4].

Ordnance estimates for works in 1682 identified costs of £14,759 3s 6d. These were partly met by a loan of £3,000 from Henry Genew of London to the Exchequer, at 6% interest and 2% *reward*, secured by £4,000 worth of timber to be felled in Sherwood Forest. The repayment for money borrowed for work at Hull was ordered by the Board in February 1683. Another £2,000 was raised in the same way in 1683. Funds were paid from Customs duties collected in Hull, in 1684, 1687 and 1689. In 1686, £2,000 from a fine paid by a Mr Williams was paid *via* the Exchequer to the Board for Hull[5].

In 1688, the first year for which an overall figure was stated to have been allocated for Hull, £12,000 was assigned to the year's work. Money from the Excise duty on wine and vinegar was allocated in three tranches, of £1,000, £1,500 and £4,000. The recovery of a wreck off Hispaniola (Haiti) provided a further £4,000[6].

In 1689, £2,000 was ordered to be paid speedily, and the Treasury consulted John Fitch *upon his proposal for £6,372 10s for the works at Hull* for the following year, which was to be raised by wood sales in the New Forest. A loan also provided £1,302 *for the sluices of Hull*, paid on the order of the Prince of Orange. The last large outlay was recorded in the year 1691-92: £7,823 12s 2 ¼d for the *Reparations at Hull*, probably a retrospective payment. The total expenditure on the Hull Citadel was to amount to £100,000. In 1699 it was opined that a further £75,000 would be required to finish the works to the original plan[7].

The Board sent out officers in the early stages of planning a project; either military or civilian staff. Once approval had been gained for work to begin, a Royal Warrant conferred powers upon locally-based Commissioners. This procedure had precedents at Plymouth, Portsmouth and Sheerness, where similarly extensive works had been undertaken. Orders agreed by the Board would be conveyed to Commissioners by letters written the same day. The Commissioners held their own meetings, provided progress reports for the Board, and in turn issued orders. In case of disagreement, the Board was empowered to overrule their local delegates, though a contentious case might be argued back and forth for weeks.

Breaking ground

From January 1680, the Board launched extensive enquiries as to the whereabouts of building materials set aside for the defences of Hull in 1663. Their enquiries were initially directed to the former Governor, Lord Belasyse, as the officer responsible for the fortifications at that time. The scope of enquiries widened to embrace Aldermen and tradesmen of Hull: these included Mr John Baker, Alderman Lambert, Alderman Maisters, Mr Abraham Warton, and the merchants Mr Skinner and Mr Brown. Of these, Aldermen Lambert and Maisters in turn examined Mr Osbourne, the Master Gunner[8].

Osbourne's statement alleged that Deputy-Governor Gilby had used the bricks to build himself a house at Sunk Island, east of Hull. Some in Hull, notably John Baker, were keen to discredit officials like Gilby, who had been responsible for efforts to suppress Dissent among the townsfolk. An Order in Council required that the Mayor should prosecute Baker as an *author and publisher of false news to be bound to be of good behaviour.* In May, he was *discharged with a severe reproof from the recorder and the whole court* of the Bench, for publishing *false news relating to Captain Bagot then Deputy-Governor of Hull.* There were countervailing efforts to deflect the course of enquiries. Gilby *misdirected* a Mr Woodstock, who had been sent *to view the defects of the two Blockhouses.* A Major Ogleby - perhaps one of Gilby's officers - denied that Woodstock had even carried out his inspection. The investigation ground on. By September, it was established that 70 pieces of timber and 30,000 bricks had disappeared. Gilby would eventually be presented with a certificate of debt *under account of embezzlements of lead, stores etc.,* in November 1681. Former Governor Belasyse had to pay £129 to the Treasurer of the Ordnance, in respect of his own responsibility for misappropriated stores[9].

On 18 April 1681, a King's Warrant was issued *for causing the works and repairs at Hull to be undertaken.* In May 1681, the Board ordered Major Martin Beckman to

Hull – in place of de Gomme, who was ill with gout. Beckman was an accomplished mercenary soldier, intermittently employed by the Crown since 1661, as Second Engineer under de Gomme from 1675. His particular *forte* was the deployment of artillery. An early employment as a *fireworker* had involved him with experimental munitions, as well as with formal displays. He invented naval and incendiary weapons, and is thought to have been a developer of the howitzer, a field gun firing shells on a parabolic arc like a mortar. He had fought in the early 1660s at Tangiers, where he designed defensive works, and would return there to supervise demolition works, in 1683. Subsequently, he would fight on land in the bitter Irish War of 1689-91, commanding batteries in both siege-works and on the battlefield. At sea, he would later lead a strikingly successful naval bombardment of the French Atlantic coast[10].

Beckman's first task was to provide a reliable plan of the existing defences. He drew up his survey in early June, including large-scale plans of South Blockhouse. By the middle of June he had presented a damning report: *The fortification in this place is come most to a total ruin, the moats about the town most grown up; the ramparts without parapets like a dyke on a sea side, the stone wall about the town, all decayed, cracked, and ready to fall down, which it has in one part, but repaired by the town. It has not one inch of parapet nor a gun about the walls that can do service. The Blockhouses are very much out of repair; the North Blockhouse is altogether dismantled, all the lead and wood converted to private uses. The moats about the Blockhouses is altogether grown up even with the ground about it, and not a drop of water in it. The King has not one foot of ground beyond this old moat and as it is altogether necessary that the Blockhouses be repaired I will say nothing of any new works.* Beckman also noted the political lie of the land. He commented that: *There is a great difference between the Deputy-Governor of this place, and Mr Baker, and indeed all the loyal party of this place do avoid this Baker's company: I am in opinion therefore, that either the Deputy-Governor or Mr Baker ought to be excluded from having conference in this work, lest the King's service should by their quarrel be interrupted*[11].

A new waterside gun platform was appended to Beckman's estimate of the repairs required at South Blockhouse. This schedule specified the reroofing of the Blockhouse, repairs to its walls and parapets, the construction of a new drawbridge and gate, and internal fixtures such as a staircase. The curtain fort around South Blockhouse was to be rebuilt, and the moat scoured. The overall cost was estimated at £2,772 3s 2d[12].

Beckman sought to involve himself in the search for suitable contractors. Mr Catlyn, a Hull builder, had been asked in December 1680 to send the Board *draughts and estimates* for works at South Blockhouse. In June 1681, however, he repeatedly declined to undertake the repairs. Beckman ascribed this reluctance to the rates offered by the Board: *there is none here that does adventure upon it without being assured of £6 15s per square (10ft square, and 1ft thick – 3.05m square by 0.31m) of timber, and £6 10s per rod (9ft, being a half-perch – 2.74m; a rod could also be a measure of 16½ft square and, usually, 1ft deep – 5.03m by 0.31m) of brick-work; the first because the girders will be so long and troublesome to get, and the second because you will have a rod wall of 1½ brick to be 14in thick.* John Baker had been asked by the Board to inform Beckman of the prices of materials in the town, along with Mr Watkinson, the Ordnance Storekeeper at Hull, and a Mr Fareside. Baker agreed to assist Beckman, and two days later had supplied the information required. Though perhaps tempted to tender for the work on Catlyn's refusal, Baker, also, was to decline further involvement[13].

Beckman then made a strong case in favour of a Mr Trollop, with whom he had worked before. *I know he can do it cheaper than any you can get. Since he has his own quarry of stone, burns his own brick and lime and always keeps a good stock by him of timbers and planks. This is he that built Clifford's Fort near Tynemouth and that at Holy Island and designed and built the 'Change (a stately piece) at Newcastle. Trollop has your Commission as Master Workman in these northern parts, who is as able a workman and as reasonable in his rates and just in his undertakings as I know.* Beckman was aware that Mr John Fitch, a substantial London builder, was also in the running to receive the first contract. Fitch had worked at Portsmouth for Sir Bernard de Gomme, Principal Engineer of England, and Beckman's immediate superior. Beckman conceded that *I suppose you will accept of him* (Trollop) *or Mr Fitch who you know better than myself, but if he would do so well here as at Guernsey, he would be worthy of the choice.* The grudging acknowledgement of Fitch's ability, set against the fulsome tributes paid to Trollop, has the ring of faint praise[14].

Mr Woodstock was ordered by the Board to draw up estimates to compare with Fitch's rates. He returned to Hull, a journey for which he received £20 expenses. Beckman was *ordered to give him the particulars of the said works and all encouragement.* The same instructions, pointedly ordering *his utmost assistance in viewing and estimating the repairs*, were sent to Gilby. The Board received Mr Woodstock's report, and sent it on to Beckman a month later. Sir Bernard de Gomme, as Chief Engineer, was required to comment on the two estimates. The King's Warrant,

For strengthening Hull with a new fortification and for contracting for which ground shall be found necessary to be taken in for the same and to appoint Commissioners, was issued on 24 June 1681. The new Warrant extended the scope of that issued two months before, with its references to the acquisition of land and a new fortification[15].

Beckman was ordered *to return to London and to bring his designs and draughts of the fortifications.* On 23 July, de Gomme and Beckman were ordered *to attend His Majesty with the design of the works to be done.* The plans were approved: on 10 August 1681, a Warrant was issued to Commissioners appointed to oversee repairs and a new fortification at Hull, *according to the design of Major Martin Beckman*[16].

On the same day, a contract was signed between the Board and *Sir Thomas Fitch Knight and John Fitch Esquire* for the opening works at Hull. The contract listed the works which would open a nine-year campaign of construction: the renovation of South Blockhouse and the repair of drawbridges leading to North Gate, Myton Gate and Beverley Gate, all parts of the old defences; and new earthwork bastions and moats around South Blockhouse and Hull Castle. Sir Thomas and Mr John Fitch were brothers, substantial London builders, and associates of Sir Christopher Wren. In the 1660s and 1670s they had been engaged for the construction of Sir Bernard de Gomme's works at Portsmouth and Gosport. Their metropolitan connections with the Board of Ordnance placed them in a strong position when competition for lucrative contracts on the works at Hull arose. They also enjoyed royal favour; in 1682, John Fitch succeeded Philip Lanyon as Workmaster to the Ordnance. This appointment was later recognised as having set an undesirable precedent, and a later administration would refuse to renew it[17].

The form of works at Hull was closely defined by these very detailed contracts, which reiterated the terms of estimates which they were intended to implement. Where the documentary evidence may be compared with surviving structures, these confirm their reliability as a guide to what was actually built. The Fitches' contracts for Hull outline the construction of major masonry elements of the Citadel. The contracts name both brothers. It was John Fitch who was most closely engaged with the Hull Citadel, and who drew upon himself and his proceedings a wealth of critical attention. Complaints of particular gravity were addressed to both Thomas and John, having been filtered by the Board from the letters of the Commissioners and their other officers[18].

The first contract, of 10 August 1681, set out repairs at South Blockhouse and the associated earthworks. That of May 1683 arranged for the construction of the East Point of the Citadel's southern side, and the Main Gate and sally ports in the east curtain, and was implemented the following year. A smaller contract, for the construction of a new drain at South Blockhouse, was agreed in April 1684. The major contract for the first *water bastion* – as commonly cited, though the term properly refers to a bastion advanced beyond low water-mark, which this was not - was agreed with the Board on 31 March 1686, and an ancillary contract for a breakwater was signed on 22 June. A contract of April 1687 was for the curtain scarp or sea wall built that year. The second water bastion was contracted for on 29 March 1688, along with barrack buildings for 200 men. A supplementary contract was awarded to the Fitches for earthworks in May of that year, with an upper limit of £1,000 set on their cost. Under William III, in March 1690, John Fitch signed the final large contract for the effective completion of the Citadel, both brick and earthwork together[19].

Payment for major contracts was delivered in stages, permitting materials and workmen to be provided and hired, while retaining control over the execution of work through the threat of withholding further installments. The contract of May 1683 was typical. An estimated cost of £4,119 19s 1d was to be divided into four quarters. The first was paid at the signing of the contract. The second would be paid when one quarter of the work was done, and another when three quarters were finished. The final payment depended on the certification of the work as complete, by His Majesty's Engineer - Beckman. This could include *overwork*: tasks omitted from the contract but carried out by the contractors and agreed as necessary to its fulfilment[20].

The most costly contracts were for the waterside bastions and the curtain between them, built along the south side of the Citadel between 1686 and 1690. These embraced piling and timber foundations, brick and masonry walls, and the earthworks behind them, and cost over £8,000 apiece. In all, over £40,000 was paid to the Fitches, of £100,000 spent on the Citadel[21].

The Warrant to the Ordnance Commissioners at Hull was *for causing the said fortification to be built according to the said design, and for buying up the ground.* Land purchase was the necessary precursor to the extension of royal works beyond the Henrician fortifications. By 1 September 1681, Beckman had reported on the prospects for this. His report was presented to the Council of State; de Gomme was to be consulted as to the procedures invoked to buy land for his works at Plymouth; and the Board itself was to refresh its knowledge of the legalities of compulsory purchase. Beckman feared that *the agreement and buying of the ground on the other side of the Blockhouse will prove a tedious business.* He reckoned that the works on land already owned by the Crown would be finished before this issue was resolved[22].

His pessimism was unjustified, for agreements were set in train only two days later. They were between Commissioners appointed by the Board, and landowners in the parish of Drypool. The major proprietors were Hugh Blaydes, George Bronflott or Broomfleet, and John Dalton; draft conveyances were also gathered from Christopher Gurnby and others. Legal opinion was sought by the Board on these transfers, and conveyances were ordered to be drawn up on 15 September[23].

Some landowners drove harder bargains than others, and one who broke ranks in negotiating a price with the Commissioners made himself deeply unpopular, as Beckman reported. *We are already sufficiently cursed by the people for not allowing the owners of the ground 20 years purchase* (*i.e.* a price equivalent to the value of 20 years rental), *and Mr Dalton is in danger if ever the rabble of this town gets him, for being willing to sell to His Majesty his ground for 16 years purchase, for the other two owners could not pretend more than he did. But Hugh Blaides stood hard for 20 years purchase at 25 shillings per acre for good and bad, 'tis therefore a folly to offer less than what is agreed upon, unless you be willing to break the bargain and not buy it at all.* Dalton at least received the satisfaction of being paid before the other landowners[24].

The Bench at Hull now belatedly revived their claim to the land occupied by the Henrician defences, basing it on their Royal Charter of 1553. This may have been an attempt to tap the flow of funds which the new project now seemed likely to release. *The claim of the Mayor and Aldermen to the Blockhouse* was brought to the attention of the Board in October. They referred this and the other conveyances to their legal advisors, to the Governor of Hull, Lord Mulgrove, and to Sir Christopher Musgrave of the Board. These were asked to *examine the pretensions of the Mayor and Aldermen.* By late October, the conveyance of the privately owned land was in hand, and on the last day of the month Beckman was intending *this morning to break ground on the other side of the Blockhouse* - on the newly acquired land to the east. The Commissioners were ordered to get the paperwork sealed, and to draw bills for the money, in February 1682[25].

Beckman had gained permission to break ground on the land disputed with the town, to the west, in advance of their protests and the completion of negotiations relating to the rest of the site. With the purchase of the eastern land in hand, the way was clear for him to open works there as well. By nimbly working between private and municipal interests he thus embarked on the construction of a modern fortress which was intended to occupy an area of 30 acres (12.1ha); one third the size of Hull itself[26].

The design of the Citadel

On Beckman's return to Hull in August 1681, he had consulted the Board about showing his plans to the Mayor and Aldermen. In doing this, he *made them believe that the whole town will be fortified, they are here very well satisfied... the four carpenters that came on Sunday last I have employed to repair the drawbridges about the town, to the great satisfaction of the townspeople.* Beckman's intention was to update the royal fortifications on the east bank of the river Hull. To begin with, however, he let the town believe that their own defences to the west were also to be refurbished. The construction of earthwork defences around the Henrician fortifications was not a new idea. Armada-period proposals had figured bastioned forts armed with guns around each of the three Blockhouses. These earthworks had not got off the drawing board. Beckman may have intended to give the impression that these long-deferred plans were at last to be put into effect; he commented that *the whole town is sensible of the design*[27].

The art of fortification had developed rapidly in the later 16th and 17th centuries. These developments were particularly striking in the Low Countries, where the Dutch had waged a protracted struggle against Spanish rule. Here, earthwork construction was substituted for masonry fortifications. Earthworks were lower, could be thrown up rapidly, and presented a smaller target for the guns of attackers. Earth was also more resistant to gunfire, absorbing the shock of impact which could smash brick and stone into lethal splinters. The raw material for earthworks was also to hand in such locations which, like Hull, were devoid of readily available stone and timber. The Old Dutch School of fortification was developed in a flat, low-lying landscape, and employed wide water-filled moats as obstacles to assault[28].

The English Civil War had seen the erection of extensive fortifications around towns like London, Oxford, York, Liverpool and Hull, and many more tempo-

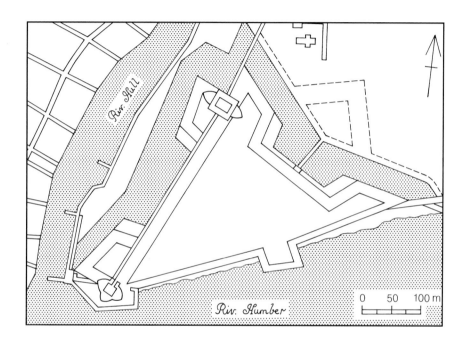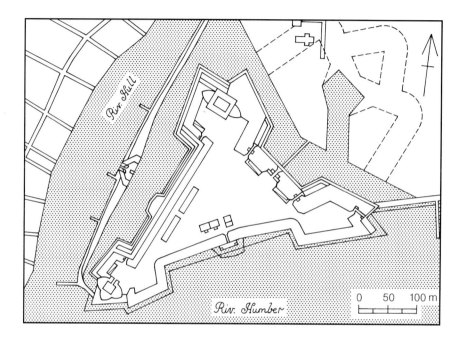

Fig 11: The design of the Citadel, *c*.1681-85. Left: de Gomme's initial proposals, dating to the summer of 1681; redrawn from Dartmouth Papers (no. 32) held at the Yale Center for British Art, New Haven, Connecticut. Right: Beckman's revised plan, of *c*.1685-88; redrawn from B.L. Egerton Ms. 16370, fo.1, Leeds Papers, Citadel of Hull.

61

rary forts, batteries and entrenchments set up as siege-works or improvised defences. The direction of engineering works had been the effective preserve of continental engineers employed by the warring parties; Sir Bernard de Gomme, a Dutchman, had served first as Prince Rupert's engineer, and then as Principal Engineer for Charles I. Martin Beckman's younger brother, Diderich, had worked with de Gomme on the fortification of Oxford. Both de Gomme and Martin Beckman owed positions under Charles II to their previous personal or family connections with his father's cause[29].

The sophistication of earthworks increased through the 17th century. A variety of methods of attacking and defending fortified places were developed over this period. Improvements in defence included the arrangement of angular bastions to afford more effective mutual support. In this respect, the spacing of bastions took into account the limited range of infantry arms as well as that of larger guns: smooth-bore muskets had an effective range of no more than 200m. The various methods by which fortifications were raised were also to be codified in the course of the 17th century, as the challenges offered by different sites were met, and technical solutions were absorbed into the engineers' repertoire. The permanent English fortifications of the later 17th century were erected in coastal settings. The problems of waterside construction added a new dimension to these massive projects. Major English works in the 1660s and 1670s, at Tilbury, Sheerness, and Portsmouth in the south; and at Tynemouth, and elsewhere, in the north, contributed a body of recent experience - and mishaps - to inform subsequent works. Technical innovation was to continue at Hull in the 1680s, as the intractable nature of the site became clear.

The earliest draft plan of the Citadel has recently been encountered in the collections of Yale University, where it appears to have arrived following the dispersal of the papers of Lord Dartmouth. It is drawn in the hand of Sir Bernard de Gomme, and sets out the Citadel proposed for Hull. It presents a triangular plan, more regular in form than that which was actually to be followed. Its context is uncertain; it may have been prepared for the meeting with the King on 23 July 1681. The plan also envisages the repair of North Blockhouse, which was never attempted; this could conceivably suggest a slightly earlier date, preceding Beckman's survey in May. The use of indented salients is typical of de Gomme's designs, permitting the two short faces to flank each other, and preventing a narrow point being knocked off by bombardment. This convention was to be observed as the works progressed, being formed between what were described as

pairs of *half-bastions*. Along the south, or Humber, front, however, de Gomme's plan shows that his initial intention was for fortifications to follow the existing shoreline of the Humber, as an elongated curtain. This would have significantly weakened the seaward defences of the Citadel. The use of both bastions and a *tenaille* or scissor-shaped front shows that Beckman was more venturesome than his superior, projecting his building works out into the river, so as to present more guns, and a smaller target, to an attacker[30].

By June 1681, after Beckman's survey, a *new fortification* was integral to the works proposed at Hull. Its triangular form was apparently decided by the middle part of 1681, estimated for in 1682, and confirmed by the contract of May 1683. This form was economical in so far as the extent of the perimeter to be defended was concerned. It also lent itself to a position at the confluence of rivers: here, the Humber to the south, and the Hull to the west. The new fortification was to take in parts of the Henrician defences, and much of the curtain wall between them: the Castle and South Blockhouse would form strongpoints within the two western bastions. Here, earthworks would strengthen the earlier defences. To the east they would be set out from scratch, while to the south they would be faced with a stone-faced scarp or *sea wall*, to protect them from the Humber tides. This was designed as a *tenaille* front. The *tenaille* form had been followed by Ferabosco at Comorra, on the Danube; by Paul Ive at Castel Cornet, Guernsey, in 1593; and in 1660 at Gdansk Glowa, Poland[31].

The triangular form proposed for the new work was appropriate to its position between two rivers. It also resembles that recommended by Sir Jonas Moore, in 1669, for *Citadels, castles or forts of the least sort, which are built to bridle the town or place, lest the burghers should be rebellious... They are commonly of 4 or 5 bastions, and no more, and are set so there may be two faces and a curtain towards the town.* As Surveyor-General, Moore was one of the signatories of the contract which set works at Hull in motion. Beckman's design was to meet Moore's specification precisely. The title of Citadel, used to describe the new work at Hull, in the 17th century carried with it a connotation of domination, rather than simply describing a strongpoint. In England, Citadels were built only at Hull and at Plymouth – both were seaports which had held out against Charles I throughout the Civil War[32].

Given his expertise as an artilleryman, Beckman's design for the positioning of guns at Hull Citadel is revealing. The curtain facing the town formed a long continuous battery with provision for the mounting of 27 guns. These would face the quays along the river Hull. Similar batteries, designed to control river traffic, had been constructed by de Gomme at Tilbury Fort on the Thames, and at Beckman's Clifford's Fort, at Tynemouth. The threat which these guns posed to the town of Hull was implicit, but clear. This battery was fronted by a foot-bank, so musketeers could assist guns in close defence. Guns were mounted *upon the curtains and flanks of the stone wall next to Humber*, in August and September 1688. Guns in the flanks could sweep the shoreline with fire, while the channel approaching the mouth of the Hull was under the curtain battery. Later commentators perceived the south front as weak. However, the strong Humber tides made it impossible for a sailing ship to moor offshore of the Citadel to engage it, while the entry of a vessel into the river Hull could only be carried out under its guns[33].

The guns in the bastion flanks of the Citadel were conventionally positioned so as to sweep the faces of adjacent bastions and the curtain, fulfilling a role in close-in defence. Their firepower was doubled by the use of *base flanks*: these were low-level gun positions set in front of the main ramparts. These were derived from the *fausse braye*, and were features of the Dutch System of fortification much-favoured by de Gomme. Engaging ships, they would also offer gunners an opportunity to skip shot into the waterline of an attacking vessel. Beckman was to introduce a slight asymmetry into the triangular design of the Citadel. This brought the eastern approaches to the town, North Bridge, and the mouth of the river Hull, into their line of fire. Though shorter on every side than the line of the Henrician fortifications, the Citadel was just as capable of controlling access to the town. Like these earlier royal defences, it could theoretically be held without regard to the sympathies of the town.

The governing concept of this plan was control - the physical welfare of the town was incidental to such a scheme. In this crucial aspect, the Citadel presented a marked contrast with the earlier town defences, whether the medieval walls or the earthworks of 1640 are considered. These had been erected and maintained by the town, or at least with the interested cooperation of its citizens. They had defended the town by surrounding it, and by sheltering its people and property from external threat. The Citadel was a gun platform. If it were conceived as defending Hull - and the town was never to come under attack while it stood - this was to be accomplished by deterrence.

The Citadel was not to be completed to Beckman's original design. Outworks planned to defend its eastern side were begun, but never finished. Financial constraints were to be influential on this abbreviation of his original scheme, as were the political developments of 1688. So too, however, was the proven ability of flooding to hamper an attacking force, as had happened in 1642 and 1643. Outworks were intended to prevent an enemy from establishing his guns in positions where they could threaten the main body of a fortification. The opening of sluices to flood the countryside around Hull could accomplish this in time of need, and was to remain integral to defensive plans until the 19th century[34].

The King's Commissioners

The Board of Ordnance was represented by Commissioners for the purposes of its works at Hull. The Board turned to formal consideration of the composition of their Commission three days after the issue of the Warrant empowering it to act on their behalf. Lord Montague wrote, *touching fit officers or persons to be commissioned to oversee the works*, on 13 August 1681. The Governor, Lord Mulgrove, nominated several persons a week later, and issued their instructions the week after that. In February 1683, Lord Dartmouth signed a further warrant nominating and appointing two further Commissioners, and ordered Captain Lloyd to join them; and the Board to consider *of works most necessary to be done*. The Governor informed existing Commissioners of the new appointments, in April 1683. The post of Commissioner was an unpaid one, and so would only be exercised by persons of ample means, and those with a stake - professional or financial - in the progress of the works[35].

The Commissioners included the Governor of Hull, on the rare occasions when he was present in the town, and, more frequently, the Deputy-Governor. From 1682, this was Lionel Copley. Other officers, of the regiment in Garrison at Hull and of the Garrison Independent Companies - Lieutenant-Colonel Purcell, Captains Stirling, Collingwood, Hildyard and Middleton, and Lieutenants Williams, Wheeler and Gower - served as Commissioners at various times. The Ordnance Storekeeper at Hull, John Watkinson, also attended. Beckman supplied technical expertise as the Engineer, and junior engineers sent by the Board would also join the Commissioners: Captain Charles Lloyd in 1683, Talbot Edwards in 1684, Richard Wharton in 1687, and Jacob Richards in 1688. The Corporation of Hull was represented by a selection of wealthy and politically reliable Aldermen. These included Anthony Lambert; Robert Mason, the Collector of Customs at Hull; Henry Maisters, a member of a prominent local merchant family; and the apothecary Alderman Matthew Hardy, who served as surgeon to the Garrison from 1685. Edward Carew, the Town Major, was included in 1683 and 1686. The number of Commissioners present varied from one meeting to the next. A maximum number of 13 are recorded at any one time; the quorum was apparently four, and letters would usually be signed by at least three members. Beckman noted it as unusual, in November 1682, that there was *not one Commissioner on the place or in the town but me*[36].

The Commissioners supervised the implementation of the Crown's plans for the refortification of Hull. This entailed oversight of the Fitches' works, to ensure that they fulfilled the contracts agreed with the Board. The Commissioners' control over the Fitches was indirect, as they had to refer their opinions back to the Board. The Commissioners contracted directly on the Board's behalf with lesser contractors, or with local suppliers of materials. They enjoyed a degree of initiative in the assignment of these smaller contracts and, as the works progressed, they increasingly set piece-work rates, or payment *by the measure*. This was an alternative to the payment of craftsmen or labourers *by the day*, the method favoured by the labourers themselves, or an all-in price for a contract, known as payment *by the great*. Beckman was particularly insistent on this point. By 1688, the Commissioners had been brought round to share this view: *That Sir Martin Beckman Knt. having reported to us the inconvenience of working by the day, it is ordered that a letter be writ to the Office of the Ordnance that our opinion is, it would be better for His Majesty's service to let it by the floor, giving them our reason for the same*[37].

The Commissioners were to meet from 1681 until 1688. The frequency and attendance of their meetings is inferred from the papers they generated; this must provide somewhat uneven coverage of their activity. In general, they seem to have convened as circumstances demanded, rather than according to a pre-arranged schedule. In 1682, there were apparently about 10 meetings, the last in July. In May 1683, Lloyd, the engineer, *received your lordship's letter and accordingly summoned the Commissioners to meet but amongst all the number none agreed except myself and Mr Hardy*. In November 1684, *Major Beckman was pleased to call a meeting of the Commissioners communicating unto them the unseasonableness of working any further with brick and stonework this winter which caused them to give a stop to all such works at present*. Another meeting saw competing contractors brought together to hammer out a compromise solution to a bitter dispute, and was described as *a convocation of the Commissioners, Mr Fitch and Mr Blaides*[38].

About 18 meetings were held in 1683, which was a short but troublesome year on the site. The number of meetings in 1684, on the other hand, is uncertain. In 1685, there were three meetings in June, one a month in July and August, and two more towards the end of October and November. In 1686, there were 15 meetings, though again more than half were convened at a time when the allocation of a large contract became a bone of contention between the Commissioners and the Board, in May and June. There were two meetings recorded in July, and none after that till October, when the Commissioners assembled at the beginning, middle and end of the month. In 1687, meetings in April and June sufficed until mid-August. Thereafter, there were 11 meetings held at irregular intervals, most frequently in October when the Commissioners met almost weekly. In 1688, the Commissioners met two or three times monthly between March and May. In June there were two meetings, but letters to the Board were signed only by Lord Langdale, James II's Governor of Hull. The pace of works accelerated as the crisis of 1688 developed. Exceptionally, the Commissioners were empowered to draw up a major contract with John Fitch in November for *new works to be raised at Hull for the better security of that place amounting in the whole to the sum of £5,000*[39].

Beckman wryly noted his own inclusion, in an aside from a request for money owed him, *now you have made me a small Lord Commissioner*. Two nominees, Sir Ralph Warton and Mr Fairside, were out of town, and copies of the Board's instructions were sent to them. The others *were here on the place*. At this time, they included Captain James Stirling, Commander-in-Chief (of the Holland Regiment companies); and Captain Francis Collingwood and Lieutenant Francis Williams, his officers. Along with Warton, their first official function was to sign agreements to buy land for the works[40].

For the first four years of the works, Beckman spent as much time as was possible in personal supervision of their progress. He was in Hull from August to late November 1681, to oversee their opening. He was staying outside the town - probably to the north. This may be deduced from his claim for travelling expenses of 12d a day, for boat-hire: *I am not able to go every four miles (c.6.5km) off and on, to the works in the clay up to the ankles and stand all the day in wet and walk in the clay; Sir Christopher can satisfy you which way I have to march every day, I made bold to guide him all that way, because he might pity my case but he took no notice of it here, and made nothing of it himself; I could have wished he had not been so good a walker for that time*[41].

In 1682, Beckman was in Hull from June; was ordered from there to Berwick in mid-August and briefly to York in mid-October; and returned to London in late November or December when the money for the year's works was spent. In 1683, he visited to certify the works of the previous two years in January, returning to London in March. He left his detailed instructions for his deputy, Captain Lloyd, in April, before going overseas to supervise demolition works at Tangiers. He returned to Hull, for how long is uncertain, in September[42].

In 1684, Beckman and John Fitch were ordered to Hull at the end of April. They were late in coming, and Beckman eventually arrived in mid-June. He was to play an active part in the works that year, harrying John Fitch mercilessly when he eventually arrived, and returned to London just before Christmas. He was back, measuring on the site and drawing up certificates for work achieved over the last year, in January 1685. He then returned to the Board of Ordnance in London, where he was in early April[43].

From 1685, and the accession of James II, Beckman's personal involvement at Hull became more intermittent. In May he was in Hull, but drafted instructions for his junior engineer, Wharton, and the Commissioners, in early June, and left a few days later. He returned in mid-September. He was intending to return to London on 7 October, but was back in Hull later in the month, to ensure that the works were placed *in the best posture of defence*. He also took up the cudgels with the Bench over the damage which their neglect of the riverbank threatened to the adjoining Citadel sluice. Beckman is last known to have been in Hull in late November, when he signed an order of the Commissioners intended to place the works in care over winter[44].

Beckman and Wharton returned to Hull the next year, arriving at the end of April 1686. Beckman spent May instructing his subordinates at Hull, and making arrangements for the year's works, which were the most difficult yet embarked upon, as they involved building out into the Humber. Beckman was not in Hull as disputes flowed from the allocation of contracts related to this project over the summer, but was back from September. His bill for travelling expenses also mention visits to Hull, arriving on 1 July after a six-day journey, and from Hull to Tynemouth in October, which entailed six-day journeys there and back. In early December he was preparing for a visit to survey and design a fort at Bristol. In 1687, he was ordered to Hull with Wharton at the end of April, and issued detailed instructions to Wharton and other overseers in early June,

leaving for Berwick a week later. He was involved in the planning of improvised if substantial additional works at Hull in August, and remained an active Commissioner in a season which saw heavy involvement of soldiers on the works. He wrote to announce his intention of closing the works for winter in early December[45].

In 1688, Beckman presented the Commissioners with his plans for the year in April. Though present in early May, when he was involved in allocating contracts, he apparently left town in June, *having made much greater progress than he had expected* with the year's works. On 22 June, the Governor commented that *there is a great want of Sir Martin Beckman, whom I hope the King will send*. On 1 November, Beckman's proposals, for an extra £5,000 to be spent *for new works to be raised at Hull for the better security of that place*, were approved by the Lords of the Treasury. Beckman may have been in Hull when William of Orange landed in the West Country on 5 November; his instructions for the Clerk of Works to complete the new works are dated 11 November. He was next in Hull about 18 months later, when viewing riverbank works with the Mayor and Bench of Hull. By this time, his Citadel was as complete as it ever would be, and the Commissioners charged with its erection had apparently disbanded[46].

As Engineer, Beckman led the Commissioners, leaving detailed written instructions when called away on other duties. He also communicated on their behalf with the Board until the arrival of John Duxbury, who was to serve as their Clerk of Works, and who in later years was occasionally to be referred to as *Clerk of the Cheque*. Duxbury's first report from Hull was dated 25 September 1681. His subsequent letters cast an invaluable light on both his own career, and the progress of the project as a whole. Duxbury had served as second clerk to the Surveyor-General in the 1670s. He was born in Guisbourne (now Gisburn), North Yorkshire, and had served the Board since 1667. He was married, with ten children. Up to 1685, he left his family in rented rooms in London, travelling to Hull in spring, and returning home over winter. His family was later able to join him where he lived, in St Mary's Ward, in the north-eastern part of Hull[47].

Duxbury's primary function was record-keeping, and keeping track of a range of duplicate copies, including his own personal filing system. He kept a Journal in which he entered letters to, and orders from, the Board. Copies of all contracts, great and small, signed by the Board, were entered in the Contracts Book. Duxbury asked the Board about *the payment of the monies for the lands, for instruc-*

tion *how to enter such concerns in his books*, in March 1682, perhaps because he was uncertain as to which ledger should be used. Another Journal served for orders issued by the Commissioners, and any subsequent alterations. He also kept an Account Book of monies paid weekly to the workforce, in which any monies returned were also included. His bill of 7s 6d for quills and ink, between 1683 and 1685, was surprisingly modest. Finally, Duxbury was responsible for a voluminous correspondence from Hull, which detailed weekly, and sometimes daily, progress there[48].

Correspondence between Board and Commissioners was by letter. Government mail services were centred on London, at the Post Office, the headquarters of the service known as the Grand Letter Office. Inland letters were dispatched from London in the early hours of Tuesday, Thursday and Saturday mornings. They were carried by mounted messengers, equipped with post-bag and horn, who could change horses at post-houses situated at 15 mile intervals along the major routes. Letters arrived in London on Monday, Wednesday and Friday nights. The Hull Post Office received mail in the early hours of every morning except Tuesday, and sent out letters at 3 pm every day except Sunday. An urgent enquiry could actually expect a reply within a day or two, though there was more normally an interval of about five days between a letter being sent and dealt with. In particularly grave circumstances, as on the death of Charles II, an *express* messenger might be sent[49].

A dispute over wage-rates, in 1683, serves to illustrate the possible pace of dialogue between the Board and the Commissioners. On 27 June, the Commissioners raised the daily wage for labourers at Hull, informing the Board of their action. On 14 July, the Board quashed the decision, and the Commissioners responded on 17 July. The Board replied to this letter on 20 July, having shown it to Lord Dartmouth, and sent a formal confirmation the next day[50].

In his capacity as Clerk of Works, Duxbury received and checked all materials supplied by local merchants and craftsmen. In November 1684, he noted that *I am now in arrears of salary since Christmas last*, and could not afford the journey to London at the end of the working year. He requested *the Master Gunner's place at Hull, which is now vacant, if your Lordship would be pleased to bestow it on me, it might be something towards a certainty for my continuance here in the winter which would be convenient to look after the works, being quite weary of waiting at London from October*

last (1683) till March, except when the office sent me a-travelling which proved severe this harsh winter... which pay would be some satisfaction for the extra charges I have been at this sharp winter, in being parted from my family, which is now large... I have disbursed a great deal of moneys out of my pocket in travelling charges. In 1685, he applied for the post of Storekeeper at Hull, as the health of the previous incumbent was failing. The nature of the work was similar to what he was already doing. He hoped, moreover, that this might provide him with more security; having been *20 years in an unfettered state, weary of many removals and going to London each winter, my family being here* (London); *I have a great ambition to be a small fixed star in this terrestial orb*[51].

His application was successful, and as Storekeeper, Duxbury would be responsible for compiling regular *returns*, and the issuing and receipt of stores. These were varied: *there is a great quantity of old unserviceable stuff, which is neither worth sending up to the Tower, nor the keeping here, but does encumber the storehouse, which might serve for much better uses.* As well as military *materiel*, this included mouldering tons of tobacco stalks - presumably confiscated contraband - which *have lain in this store house above this 20 years.* Their disposal, which was to be accomplished by touting samples round the tobacco merchants of the town, distracted Duxbury between September and December 1685. The gunpowder in the stores required re-packing, *for when the barrels came to be moved the hoops were so rotten that they all flew in pieces and the powder was much damnified for want of being turned*[52].

With Monmouth's rebellion in 1685, the attendant business of arming newly-raised troops, and an active role on the works, Duxbury began to feel the strain. He asked the Board for an assistant: *The necessity of my being constantly upon the works and for want of a labourer that I can trust with the stores, open the doors and receive in and deliver out upon ordinary occasions - please allow me a labourer that I may not be necessitated to go with the keys upon all trivial occasions.* Another letter detailed his duties, and concluded: *I have only the nights to make up those accounts for all the day I cannot be off the works*[53].

The Storekeeper's post was worth £40 a year, with a £10 annual bonus, though security was required of the post-holder - Duxbury's was provided by his brother James, a London silversmith, and Sir John Slater, a Southwark plumber. Duxbury collected a further 8d a day as a soldier mustered into the Governor's Garrison Company. He also attempted to contract for minor elements of the works on the Citadel. By this combination of means he prospered. This brought with it the need to cultivate *friends* in London, to dress as a gentleman, and to juggle debts and bonds with bankers. His brother Andrew, a lawyer at Stadies Inn in Holborn, helped to deal with the transfer of credit notes on his behalf, together with his attorney, Mr Hubbald. These necessary relationships were lubricated by casks of Hull ale, sent up to London on ships transporting stores between Hull and the Tower. There was a hint of *parvenu* snobbishness in his letters at this time; he excused the importunities of his brother James to one of his bankers: *I fear my brother has been too troublesome to you, and more urgent than he need to have been, for tradesmen are very greedy*[54].

One of his less agreeable duties was to act as scapegoat for his superiors. When Captain Lloyd botched earthworks in 1683, Duxbury was censured for having failed to enter his instructions into his book.. He had been *in a great fright whether to disoblige him, or them* (the Commissioners)... *I thought it was better to rely upon him who was the sole instrument or agent from our office, than upon those who till now did take no notice of it.* He wrote to Lloyd, *that the Commissioners had written to the Office concerning your error... but they are so against me for not putting it in the Journal I am liable to be ruined thereby... therefore I hope I cannot be blamed for anything except obeying your commands, which fault I hope you will be so just as to quit me of.* The Commission acknowledged that Duxbury was *commanded to the contrary by Capt. Lloyd whom (whether out of fear of displeasing or to prevent discord and contentions among us) he has rather obeyed than performed his duty to us.* Lloyd was duly carpeted before the Board in 1684. In a dispute over materials provided in 1686, Duxbury was libelled by the contractor John Fitch - he provided an easier target than Beckman and the Commissioners. On this occasion he defended himself with vigour, and Fitch conceded the point[55].

Duxbury's letters show that a somewhat unlikely friendship developed between the Engineer, Beckman, and his Clerk of Works. Beckman grew to rely on Duxbury, not least for his perceptive advice on the administration of the project to which both men were committed. They collaborated on the measuring and certification of the works. Over the winters of 1683-84 and 1687-88, Duxbury was one of a pair of officers entrusted with the daily checking of the stability of the earthworks. Beckman also valued his supervisory ability, considering him capable of covering the posts of any two overseers: *Duxbury... understands both direction, and the workmen's most audacious intrigues as well as any five that can be sent.* He was appointed as one of four overseers in 1687 and 1688, with a particular brief to monitor undertakers' adherence to their contracts. In November 1688, in the hectic weeks before the Glorious Revolution, it was Duxbury who Beckman left in charge of the completion of the works, with specific orders to prevent Fitch becoming involved with wider works for the defence of Hull[56].

The two men were united in their loathing of Beckman's immediate superior, Sir Bernard de Gomme. After de Gomme's death, in November 1685, Duxbury commented: *I wonder how I came to be cut off £10 6s for my bill of salary... I suppose it was one of the last just and charitable acts done by the Great Knight before he died, prognosticating that it would not be in his power to wrong me as he used to do.* Duxbury would sometimes supplement his official reports with less formal accounts for Beckman. On the subject of repairs required at South Blockhouse, he digressed as follows: *Our officers intend to make great revelling on top of the South Blockhouse on the Coronation day* (James II), *having invited several females, intending to fire a great many guns; if the house should fall with such a heavy weight, the women would be in a sad pickle.* Another letter concluded: *I shall ever own and acknowledge* (you) *for my best friend and greatest benefactor.* On receiving news of Beckman's knighthood, Duxbury enthused: *After my hearty congratulations of the meritorious honour which His Majesty has at last been graciously pleased to confer upon you, wishing that you may enjoy it with much peace and happiness, and to get better cheer than bread and cheese. At first coming of the news hither, your good health was drunk here with much joy by several.* Duxbury was to die in Hull, and was buried in St Mary's Church, on January 7 1689[57].

After the Engineer and his Clerk of Works, the most important individual member of the Commission was the Treasurer. The Treasurer kept his own Journal of Accounts, which his colleagues would sign, and which would be submitted at intervals to the Board. This would then be compared with Duxbury's accounts. The Treasurer's post required sufficient private means to bridge shortfalls in cash when the Board was late in providing for the works. Money was sent to Hull as imprest, or bills, which would be changed in Hull for cash to pay small local contractors and the mass of unskilled labourers employed on the site. In November 1681, Alderman Lambert was to be paid for lead supplied to plumbers working on South Blockhouse. He was expected to collect his payment from the Board in person, as he was one of a deputation from the Bench delivering a formal Address to the King. Alderman Maisters, another Commissioner, had also supplied lead for the works. It was Lambert, however, who was to be appointed as Treasurer, in June 1682. Lambert was a wealthy Hull merchant, and would become Mayor in 1683[58].

From June to December 1682, monthly imprests of £100 to Lambert covered the wages of labourers and the supply of ancillary goods and services. The payments were not always timely. In July, the Commissioners appealed to the Board for money, *showing the ill consequence that will attend the works without it.* In August, Lambert wrote about the lack of money, and about the meaning of the word *imprest.* Both Duxbury and Lambert wrote in similar vein in October. Duxbury encouraged Lambert to delay sending his accounts up to London until the last £100 of a total of £600 was spent. The final accounting for the works of 1682, an abstract signed by Captain Collingwood, Beckman and Storekeeper Watkinson, showed that £500 13s 8d had been paid out by the Commissioners for earthworks, and just under £110 for other works and minor contracts. Lambert was ordered *an allowance for his care and pains as Treasurer* by the Board, in January 1683[59].

In March 1683, the Board ordered Lambert to continue as paymaster, notifying him that Alderman Mason was to pay him an imprest of £500, in his capacity as Collector of Customs. By mid-April the Commissioners detailed their expenditures to date, and their concern that no more money was ordered. They ordered: *That a letter be written to the Office of the Ordnance to acquaint them how that Alderman Lambert so positively refuses to pay any money till he receives the bill or order from the Office for the said £500 imprested to him.* Two days later, they stressed that *the men do daily increase and if they should but once miss of their weekly payment they would be so much discouraged that they will quite forsake us.* The Board made arrangements for a further payment to be drawn from Alderman Mason[60].

In June, Lambert was still pressing for payment of money owed to him, as Mason held £1,200. Duxbury reported: *we have but £430 15s 3 ½d remaining in cash of the £1,605 14s 5 ½d you imprested to Alderman Lambert, which sum (if the weather be good and men continue) will be quickly exhausted, therefore we desire that you will be pleased to be mindful of ordering down another bill of imprest to our said Treasurer, that we may not be at a stand for want thereof.* The Board secured £1,500 from the Treasury, and ordered Mason to pass £1,254 10s 5 ½d as imprest to Lambert. The failure of the Board to find further funds forced a premature halt to the works in July[61].

In August, the Board ordered that Lambert receive a £15 gratuity, along with a bill and debentures for £1,579 19s 5d; his accounts were to go to the Ordnance Treasurer. In September, he wrote to the Board to tell them that he expected an allowance for receiving and paying funds on their behalf. From this time, the Commissioners ordered Lambert to pay the funds he received to Mason, who thereafter became their *de facto* Treasurer. A final allowance for Lambert, at the rate of 10s for every £50 which he had handled, was agreed in November 1684[62].

As Collector of Customs at Hull, Mason was well-placed to implement orders for locally gathered revenue to be directed to the works. This appointment was at Duxbury's suggestion: *Concerning the payment of the monies, which the office need not pay for returning of it from London, and from Alderman Lambert (who has positively refused to be any further concerned), for they may have an order from the Customs House at London to pay you here as we have occasion for it, and then you may order who you please to pay it to the labourers without any great charge, and the Custom House pay here is very good and punctual without any scruples. I hope you will be pleased to pardon me for presuming either to advise or direct you herein, but I have seen such differences and scruples since you was here, that I have been put to a great deal of trouble, and the labourers have been unpaid for three weeks together.* Lambert officially relinquished the Treasurer's post in June 1684, though he continued to serve as a Commissioner. He was replaced as Treasurer by Mason[63].

Although local transfers of cash were henceforward less complicated, the difficulties with central funding persisted. The release of fixed sums by the Board had always impeded the ability of the Commissioners to react to changing local circumstances. In July 1685, Mason advanced several weeks wages, but refused to continue to do so until the Board supplied more money. In August, *having received £1,000, when the bills last ordered are all paid there will remain but £5 1s 9d* being now at a much greater charge weekly, because of the unexpectedly high cost of turfs. In September, an imprest of £1,300 was set against payments of labourers' wages totalling £1,455 8s 4d, leaving Mason in debt to the tune of over £155; Mason expected *a better consideration than he had last*[64].

Mason continued, however, to serve as Treasurer. In 1687, Mason was dealing with a fellow banker: the Commissioners ordered him to *pay unto Mr John Saunders for the use of John Fitch Esq. the sum of £96 13s 4d by way of imprest in part for erecting a wall to support South Blockhouse from settling any more.* Towards the end of 1687, Mason promised that earthworks would not be delayed for a matter of £100 or £200 coming late as bills of imprest. Smaller tradesmen engaged on the works suffered longer delays in the payment of their bills: the carpenters Robinson and Shields executed repairs in the spring of 1685, but were only to report the listing of debentures which would enable payment in February or March of the following year[65].

Meeting temporary shortfalls of cash devolved *in extremis* upon other members of the Commission. Chronic financial problems became acute in 1684; Beckman and the Commissioners were forced to pay labourers' wages from their own pockets to get the works under way. Beckman raised £100 credit with his sister to ensure the works would be kept up. To pay for emergency repairs, Captain Collingwood, Deputy-Governor Copley and Duxbury all had to lend money at one time or another. A wage bill incurred by the Master Gunner in November 1688, for labourers shifting guns about the defences, was only settled in June 1689. Duxbury's payments to labourers employed to sift powder, provide locks, or clean arms in store were similarly settled retrospectively[66].

Footnotes

1: Tomlinson 1973, 5-25.

2: Tomlinson 1979.

3: Tomlinson 1979, 34, 168; pers. comm. Andrew Saunders.

4: Stafford Record Office D (W) 1778/1:/639, Office (of Ordnance), 22 April 1681; CSPD 1680-81, 297; PRO WO55/1785, Contract of 10 August 1681.

5: CTB 7, part i, 1681-85, 578; PRO WO46:1 (index), 262, Orders of Board, 22 February 1683; CTB 7, part ii, 1681-85, 743, 27 March 1683; CTB 7, part i, 1681-85, 1215, 9 July 1684; CTB 8, part iii, 1685-89, 1561, 25 October 1687; *ibid.*, 2134, 23 November 1688.

6: PRO WO55/519, Board to Commissioners, 8 May 1688; CTB 8, part iii, 1685-88, May, October, November 1688; CTB 8, part iv, 1685-88, vol. 3, 2039, August 1688.

7: CTB 9, part i, 37, June 1689; CTB 8, part ii, 397, 4 June 1689; CTB 3, part vi, 2158, 1 January 1689; CTB Declared Accounts Ordnance 1689-90, part i, vol. 9; Allison 1969, 416, citing Luttrell State Papers iv, 487.

8: PRO WO46:1 (index), 250, Orders of Board, 18 January 1680; *ibid.*, 27 January 1680; PRO WO46:1 (index), 266, Letters from Office, January 27 1680; *ibid.*, 267, 29 January 1680; *ibid.*, 268, 8 February 1680.

9: KUHRO M362; CSPD 1679-80, 252; PRO WO46:1 (index), 269-70, Letters from Office , 12 April 1681; *ibid.*, 300, 19 April 1681; *ibid.*, 270, 23 April 1681; PRO WO46:1 (index), 253, Orders of Board, 30 August 1681; *ibid.*, 6 September 1681; CTB 7, part i, 1679-80, 306, 17 November 1681; *ibid.*, 333, 10 December 1681.

10: PRO WO46:1 (index), 212, King's Warrants, Signification from the Master and Commissioners, 18 March 1681; PRO WO46:1 (index), 250, Orders of Board, 14 May 1681; information E.P. Beckman..

11: PRO WO46:1, 301, Beckman to Board, 1 June 1681; *ibid.*, 302, 13 June 1681.

12: PRO WO46:1, 217, Estimate, 15 June 1681.

13: Neave 1983, 8-10; PRO WO46:1 (index), 266, Letters from Office, 22 December 1680; *ibid.* (index), 301, Beckman to Office and Baker to Office, 11-13 June 1681; *ibid.*, 302-3, Beckman to Office, 15 June 1681; *ibid.* (index), 271, Letters from Office, 17 May 1681; *ibid.*, 300, Letters to Office, 4 June 1681; *ibid.*, 301-2, 8 June 1681, 13-14 June 1681.

14: PRO WO46:1, 302, Beckman to Office, 15 June 1681; *ibid.*, 303, 15 June 1681.

15: PRO WO46:1 (index), 252, Orders of Board, 6 June 1681; *ibid.*, 252, 9 August 1681; *ibid.*., 251, 23 June 1681; *ibid.*, 271, Letters from Office, 25 June 1681; *ibid.*, 251, Orders of Board, 23 July 1681; *ibid.*, 251, 21 June 1681; PRO WO46:1, 214, Kings Warrants, Signification from the Master and Commissioners, 24 June 1681.

16: PRO WO46:1 (index), 251, Orders of Board, 272, Letters from Office, 12 July 1681; *ibid.*, 252, Orders of Board, 23 July 1681; CSPD 1680-81, 396.

17: PRO WO55/1785, Contract, 10 August 1681; Woodward 1987, 130; pers. comm. Andrew Saunders; PRO WO46/6 29065, 22 May 1705.

18: Foreman and Goodhand 1997.

19: PRO WO55/1785, Contract, 10 August 1681; *ibid.* 24 May 1683; PRO WO46:2, 315, Estimates and Contracts, 22 April 1684; PRO WO51/33, TBB series 2, 91; PRO WO55/519, Orders of Commissioners, 10 July 1686; *ibid.*, Board to Plymouth, 30 April 1687; PRO WO55/1785, Contract, 29 March 1688; *ibid.*, 19 May 1688; *ibid.*, 13 March 1690.

20: Stafford Record Office D (W) 1778/V/68; PRO WO55/1785, Contract, 24 May 1683; e.g. PRO WO46:2, 327, Measurement of Works and Overwork, 29 January 1685.

21: PRO WO51/33, TBB series 2, 91; *ibid.*, 191.

22: CSPD 1680-81, 396; PRO WO46:1 (index), 253, Orders of Board, 1 September 1681; *ibid.*, 307, Beckman to Board, 7 September 1681.

23: PRO WO46:1 (index), 234-5, Several Things Touching Lands Taken in for Fortifications, 9 September 1681; KUHRO M363, M365; PRO WO46:1 (index), 236-7, 240, Several Things Touching Lands Taken in for Fortifications, 9 September 1681; *ibid.*, 276, Letters from Office, 15 September 1681.

24: PRO WO46:1, 308, Beckman to Board, 21 September 1681; *ibid.* (index), 317, Letters to Office, 20 November 1681.

25: PRO WO46:1 (index), 310, Letters to Office, 8 October 1681; *ibid.*, 279, Letters from Office, 11 October 1681; *ibid.*, 254, Orders of Board, 14 October 1681; *ibid.*,

279, Letters from Office, 15 October 1681; *ibid.*, 314, Beckman to Board, 22 October 1681; *ibid.*, 314, 31 October 1681; *ibid.*, 284, Letters from Office, 10 February 1682.

26: PRO WO46:1, 307, Beckman to Board, 14 September 1681.

27: PRO WO46:1 (index), 305, Letters to Office, 22 August 1681; *ibid.*, 306, 27 August 1681; PRO WO46:1, 307, Beckman to Board, 7 September 1681.

28: Duffy 1975; Duffy 1979; pers. comm. Andrew Saunders.

29: Smith 1997; Saunders 1989.

30: Foreman 1989, 40; Hughes 1989, 10-11; Yale Center for British Art, New Haven, Connecticut, bearing printed no. 37 [annotation ?from Dartmouth Collection] - pers. comm. Andrew Saunders

31: PRO WO46:1, 220, Estimate, 18 July 1682; Foreman and Goodhand 1997; PRO WO55/1785, Contract, 22 May 1683; pers. comm. Quentin Hughes.

32: Moore 1673, 86; pers. comm. Paul Beckmann; PRO WO55/1785, Contract, 10 August 1681.

33: British Library, Egerton Ms. 3359, f.1, Leeds Papers, Citadel of Hull, County of York; Saunders 1989; Kear 1986; e.g. PRO WO434/195, Report on Armament of the Citadel, December 1846.

34: PRO WO30/59, 57-72, Proposals for the Defence of the Humber, *c*.1803.

35: PRO WO46:1 (index), 273, Letters from Office, 13 August 1681; *ibid.*, 305, Letters to Office 22 August 1681; *ibid.*, 275, Letters from Office, 30 August 1681; *ibid.*, 215, 295, 233, King's Warrants, Signification from Master and Commissioners, 13 March 1683; *ibid.*, 296, Letters from Office, 7 April 1683.

36: CSPD Feb-Dec. 1685, 61; PRO WO46:1, 340, Beckman to Board, 20 November 1682.

37: PRO WO55/519, Commissioners to Board, 2 May 1688; *ibid.*, Orders of Commissioners, 1 May 1688.

38: Bod. Lib. Rawl. A475, Lloyd to Board, 2 May 1683; Bod. Lib. Rawl. A476, item 1, Duxbury to Board, 19 November 1684; *ibid.*, undated 1686 .

39: PRO WO55/519, Board to Langdale, 1 November 1688.

40: PRO WO46:1, 307, Beckman to Board, 7 September 1681; KUHRO M363.

41: PRO WO46:1 (index), 306, Letters to Office, 27 August 1681; *ibid.*, 282, Letters from Office, 29 November 1681; *ibid.*, 315, Beckman to Board, 9 November 1681.

42: PRO WO46:1 (index), 330, Letters to Office, 26 June 1682; *ibid.*, 287, Letters from Office, 16 August 1682; *ibid.*, 336, Letters to Office, 14 October 1682; *ibid.*, 340, Beckman to Board, 20 November 1682; *ibid.*, 292, Beckman's Certificate, 27 January 1683; *ibid.*, 344, Letters to Office, 24 March 1683; *ibid.*, 347, Beckman's Instructions to Lloyd, 17 April 1683; PRO WO46:2, 94, Board to Hull, 20 September 1683.

43: PRO WO46:2 (index), 22, Orders of Board, 29 April 1684; Bod. Lib. Rawl. A476, item 1, Duxbury to Board, 30 May 1684; PRO WO46:2 (index), 224, Letters from Hull, 14 June 1684; *ibid.*, 301, Beckman to Board, 12 December 1684; *ibid.*, 327, Bill of Work 19 January 1685; *ibid.*, 301 *et seq.*, Measurement of Works and Overworks, 29 January 1685; Bod. Lib. Rawl. A476, item 1, Duxbury to Board, 5 April 1685.

44: PRO WO55/519, Beckman's Instructions for Wharton, 2 June 1685; Bod. Lib. Rawl. A475, Duxbury to Board, 16 September 1685; PRO WO55/519, Bill of Works, 7 October 1685; *ibid.*, Report of Commissioners, 26 October 1685; KUHRO BRB 6, 147; PRO WO55/519, Order of Commissioners, 29 November 1685.

45: Bod. Lib. Rawl. A475, Duxbury to Board, 30 April 1686; PRO WO55/519, Estimate, Order of Commissioners, Commissioners to Board, and Beckman's Instructions, 14 May 1686 to 22 May 1686; *ibid.*, Order of Commissioners, 11 September 1686; PRO WO51/33, TBB series 2, 82, 132; PRO WO55/519, Beckman's Instructions, 3 June 1687; *ibid.*, Commissioners to Board, 11 June 1687; *ibid.*, Order of Commissioners, 12 August 1687; *ibid.*, Order of Commissioners, 7 December 1687.

46: PRO WO55/519, Order of Commissioners, 19 April 1688; *ibid.*, Commissioners to Board, 11 May 1688; HMC Dartmouth Mss, 136, Langdale to Dartmouth, 6 June 1688; CSPD 1688, 450a; PRO WO55/519, Board to Langdale, 1 November 1688; *ibid.*, Instructions to Duxbury, 10 November 1688; KUHRO BRB 10, 9 July 1690.

47: PRO WO46:1 (index), 308, Letters to Office, 25 September 1681; Tomlinson 1979, 227; Bod. Lib. Rawl. A475, Letter from Duxbury, 24 March 1686; *ibid.*, Duxbury to Hubbald, 30 March 1686; Bod. Lib. Rawl. A476 item 1, fo. 20, Duxbury to ?Dartmouth, 11 April 1685.

48: Bod. Lib. Rawl. A475; A476 item 1, Duxbury's Papers and Transcripts; Bod. Lib. Rawl. `A475, Order of Commissioners, 26 May 1683; PRO WO46:2 (index), 323, Letters to Office, 1 March 1682; PRO WO46:1 and 2, Ordnance Papers relating to Hull Citadel; PRO WO55/519, Papers of the Commissioners at Hull; PRO WO51/32, TBB series 3, fo. 1.

49: Latham 1983, vol. 10, 333-4; Hull Directory 1791, 45; CSPD 1684-85, 278.

50: PRO WO46:2 (index), 44, Orders of Commissioners, 27 June 1683; *ibid.*, 4, Orders of Board, 14 July 1683; *ibid.* (index), 45, Orders of Commissioners, 17 July 1683; Bod. Lib. Rawl. A475, Board to Commissioners, 20 July 1683.

51: Bod. Lib. Rawl. A475, Orders of Commissioners, 7 May 1683; Bod. Lib. Rawl. A476, item 1, Duxbury to Board, 19 November 1684; *ibid.*, undated; *ibid.*, Duxbury to Board, 13-14 April 1685.

52:   Bod. Lib. Rawl. A475, Duxbury to Board, 16 August 1685; *ibid*., Duxbury to Board, 7, 14 and 20 October, and 1 December 1685.

53:   Bod. Lib. Rawl. A475, Duxbury to Board, 26 August 1685; *ibid*. 20 October1685.

54:   Bod. Lib. Rawl. A475, Duxbury to Board, 22 March 1686; *ibid*., Duxbury to ?Beckman, 16 June 1686; e.g. *ibid*., John Duxbury to Andrew Duxbury, March 1686; *ibid*., Duxbury to Hubbald, 12 June 1686; e.g. *ibid*., Duxbury to Winteringham, 13 January 1686; Duxbury to ?, 24 March 1686; *ibid*., 16 June 1686.

55:   Bod. Lib. Rawl. A476, item 1, Duxbury to Board, 25 June 1684; *ibid*., Duxbury to Lloyd, 25 June 1684; PRO WO46:2, 227, Commissioners to Board, 25 June 1684; *ibid*. (index), 29, Orders of Board, 31 July 1684; PRO WO55/519, Duxbury to Board, 21 July 1686; *ibid*., John Fitch to Board, 21 July 1686.

56:   e.g. PRO WO46:2, Measurement of Works and Overworks, 29 January 1685; *ibid*. (index), 48, Orders of Commissioners, 16 October 1683; PRO WO55/519, Instructions for Duxbury, 20 March 1688; *ibid*., Beckman to Board, 12 May 1686; *ibid*., Instructions for Duxbury, ?5 April 1688; *ibid*., Instructions for Duxbury, 10 November 1688.

57:   Bod. Lib. Rawl. A475, Duxbury to ?, 8 February 1686; Bod. Lib. Rawl. A476, item 1, Duxbury to Beckman, 15 April 1685; Bod. Lib Rawl. A475, Duxbury to Beckman, 16 January 1686; *ibid*., Duxbury to Beckman, ?8 April 1686; Sykes 1893.

58:   PRO WO46:2 (index), 165, Letters from Hull, 29 August 1683; PRO WO46:1 (index), 255, Orders of Board, 5 November 1681; *ibid*., 316, Duxbury to Board, 16 November 1681; *ibid*. (index), 256, Orders of Board, 21 December 1681; *ibid*., 258, Orders of Board, 27 June 1682; KUHRO BRB 8, 66.

59:   Stafford Record Office D (W) 1778/V/64 (52), Lambert's Accounts, 15 July 1682, 22 July 1682, 29 July 1682, 5 August 1682, 12 August 1682; PRO WO46:1 (index), 258, Orders of Board, 16 August 1682; Stafford Record Office *loc. cit.* 19 August 1682, 2 September 1682, 9 September 1682; PRO WO46:1 (index), 259, Orders of Board, 23 September 1682; *ibid*., 334, Letters to Office, 29 September 1682; Stafford Record Office *loc. cit.* 7 October 1682, 14 October 1682; PRO WO46:1 (index), 259, Orders of Board, 21 October 1682; Stafford Record Office *loc. cit.* 21 October 1682, 28 October 1682; 4 November 1682; PRO WO46:1 (index), 260, Orders of Board, and 290, Letters from Office, 7 November 1682; *ibid*. 260, orders of Board, 16 November 1682; *ibid*., 331, Letters to Office, 31 July 1682; *ibid*., 333, 22 August 1682; *ibid*., 336-7, 15-16 October 1682; *ibid*., 340, Duxbury to Board, 20 November 1682; Stafford Record Office D (W) 1778/V/64 (51), Abstract of Payments for 1682, 9 December 1682; PRO WO46:1 (index), 261, Orders of Board, 27 January 1683.

60:   PRO WO46:1 (index), 262, Orders of Board, 27 March 1683; *ibid*., 346, Letters to Office, 14 April 1683; Bod. Lib. Rawl. A475, Orders of Commissioners, 14 April 1683; *ibid*., Commissioners to Board, 16 April 1683; *ibid*., Board to Commissioners, 24 April 1683.

61:   PRO WO46:2 (index), 153-4, Letters from Hull, 25 June 1683; Bod. Lib. Rawl. A475, v15, Commissioners to Board, 25 June 1683; CTB 7, pt ix, 1681-85, 1215, 10 July 1683; PRO WO46:2 (index), 3, Orders of Board, 10 July 1683; *ibid*., 5, Order of Board, 21 July 1683.

62:   PRO WO46:2 (index), 10, Orders of Board, 30 August 1683; *ibid*., 172, Letters from Hull, 21 September 1683; *ibid*., 46-47, Orders of Commissioners, 22 September 1683; *ibid*., 48, 16 October 1683; *ibid*., 36, Orders of Board, 22 November 1684.

63:   Bod. Lib. A476, item 1, 2-3, Duxbury to Beckman, 12 April 1684; PRO WO46:2 (index), 226, Letters from Hull, 23 June 1684; *ibid*., 120, Letters of Board to Hull, 20 June 1684; *ibid*., 122, 28 June 1684.

64:   HMC Dartmouth MSS, 128; Bod. Lib. Rawl. A475, Duxbury to Board, 5 August 1685; *ibid*., August-September 1685; *ibid*., 7 September 1685.

65:   e.g. PRO WO55/519, Order of Commissioners, 29 October 1687; *ibid*., 24 August 1687; *ibid*., 26 October 1687; Bod. Lib. Rawl. A475, John Duxbury to Andrew Duxbury, undated, but between 18 February and 3 March 1686.

66:   PRO WO46:2, 49, Orders of Commissioners, 13 June 1684; *ibid*. (index), 233, Letters from Hull; Bod. Lib. Rawl. A476 item 1, Commissioners to Board, 25 June 1684; Bod. Lib. Rawl. A475, Osbourne's Account, 6 May 1683; *ibid*., Commissioners to Board, 16 April 1683; *ibid*., Duxbury to Beckman, 20 February 1686; *ibid*., Duxbury to Hubbald, 30 March 1686; PRO WO51/37, TBB 8 series iii, 1688, 123-4, 17 June 1689, 127, November 1688 ; TBB 8, series ii, 1688, 44a, September 1688.

CHAPTER 6

THE PROGRESS OF THE WORKS, 1681-90

The later defences of Hull have been the subject of recent archaeological study. Documentary research has been set alongside the extensive surviving structural evidence, providing a detailed picture of the construction of the Citadel between 1681 and 1690. The sequence of the works has been established in detail for 1681-85, and in more summary fashion for the later stages of the works, 1686-90[1].

The execution of the work may be followed along two strands of documented activity. The first comprised the formal steps of estimation, contracting, and certification. The subordination of Beckman, as Second Engineer, to Sir Bernard de Gomme, the Chief Engineer, and, from 1682, Surveyor-General, left every stage of the process open to criticism or interference. A strained relationship between the two men was lent additional piquancy by the grant of the post of Chief Engineer to Beckman *in reversion*. This meant that Beckman could look forward to becoming Chief Engineer on de Gomme's death. The fact that he did not also succeed to the Surveyor-General's post may hint that this conflict was also one between Beckman, as professional engineer, and de Gomme, serving more as an administrator in his later years. The second strand of documentary evidence was provided by responses to the problems presented by an intractable site, by weather, tide, and other circumstances. From 1686, when Beckman inherited the post of Chief Engineer, there were fewer procedural difficulties. The distractions of office, however, forced Beckman to increasing reliance on capable subordinates.

1681

Sir Thomas and John Fitch had secured the all-important first contract of August 1681. The Board ordered Storekeeper Watkinson to supply wheelbarrows to Mr Felton, for use by their men. A month later, however, presaging further difficulties, *Here is not materials, undertakers, or master workmen yet arrived*. The repair of South Blockhouse began with the mending of its great parapet by two bricklayers[2].

At the end of September, John Fitch was complaining about the weather and the workforce. By November 1681, Beckman was also developing his low opinion of Fitch; generally with regard to his claiming completion, and particularly of his techniques for earthworks. John Fitch expected completion of brickwork by early October, but, in late November, Beckman reported: *I have till your further order made a stop to the brick and major works yet remaining to be done, till March next upon the South Blockhouse, for I have no reason to hazard His Majesty's money, being no cause or necessity for it, for if it should now be longer continued the winter or frosty weather would spall it, and so consequently be spoiled.* The next March, bricklayers and masons were finishing the parapet. It was coped with stone set in waterproof *terras* mortar, cramped with iron set in lead[3].

The Henrician curtain wall was cut to the north and south of the Castle, and to the north of South Blockhouse. This was initially to permit access for workmen, and was subsequently to render the western bastions of the Citadel accessible from within the new fortifications. Demolition between the Blockhouse and Castle was undertaken by a gang of 51 day-labourers under Beckman's supervision, in 1681. The fabric to be removed included *60 rodds (c.165m) of wall, which is hard as flint*. Other clearance operations entailed the dismantling of a summer house which had been built close to the Castle by John Russel, a Gunner at Hull; and the demolition of *the garden wall near the South Blockhouse* (and) *the Traverse Wall at the same house and the demolishing of two small spurs that laid before the gates of the South Blockhouse and the Castle.* The garden wall perhaps ran up to the north side of South Blockhouse, while the traverse wall may have been a relict of the Corporation's curtain fort of *c.*1627. It was described as *the long wall which reaches from South Blockhouse to the pierhead, jetting out towards the South End of the town through which the graft will go*[4].

The roof of South Blockhouse was taken off and replaced with a structure of oak beams up to 30ft (9.1m) long and joists 15in. (*c.*380mm) apart, to be covered with deal boards. The lead sheeting over it was to be replaced. Above this, new platforms to support the weight of guns were to be framed with slightly larger girders and joists, and planked with 2in. (51mm) oak. Oak beams and joists, covered with deal, would form a new floor for the first floor within the Blockhouse. The lobes, or *quarters*, of the Blockhouse were dealt with in turn: first the west quarter, then the north, finally the south. New lead was mixed with the old, to make it run better when recast. The south quarter was being covered, and new drainpipes being cast, on 28 November 1681. Carpenters were framing the timber for the first of the gun platforms, *but all the timber for the platforms is not yet come, though one the carpenters is gone to Gainsborough (Lincolnshire) to hasten it away*[5].

The late start to the works meant that 1681 was an exceptionally short working year; they closed in December. The most progress was achieved in the refurbishment of South Blockhouse. This year also saw a substantial start made on earthwork bastions to strengthen the South Blockhouse and Castle. The construction of ramparts in 1681 entailed the piling of earth against the north side of the Blockhouse, masking at least one of its original gun-ports. The moat was 8-12ft (*c*.2.45-3.66m) deep; the bastion at South Blockhouse was for the time being considered as complete except for its parapet; and the bastion at the Castle was under way. These works were to be carried on the next year[6].

1682

John Duxbury was in Hull in January 1682, noting that the trenches on the site were filled with water, and that the sluice to drain them required attention. Mr Felton was engaged on these repairs in February. Wintry conditions did not obstruct indoor repairs at South Blockhouse. The building was weatherproofed by the repair of eight stone windows, the repair of 200 square foot (*c*.18.6m^2) of old glass, and the provision of 300ft (*c*.28m^2) of new quarry glass. On 13 March 1682, *yesterday it proved wet weather and now does snow which will hinder our proceedings*. Indoor work could be carried forward regardless of the weather: Fitch's craftsmen were *fitting up the rooms within, lathing, plastering and flooring*. Contracted internal repairs included the building of a newel stair of oak, the rebuilding of two sentry houses with passages leading to them, and four new doors, of a double thickness of oak plank with hinges, locks and bolts[7].

Attempts to start earthworks before Beckman's order were blocked by the Commissioners. They were begun early in March. Substantial building was under way by April; complaints against the Fitches again arose; they centred on the quality and supply of materials: planks which failed to arrive, or which were of poor quality when they did; and the use of salt water when mixing mortar[8].

In June, two persons were to undertake earthworks. Beckman's Certificate, of January 1683, drew attention to the failure of the Fitches to ram earthworks in 1681, and to their lower cost in 1682: *This is to be observed: that the earthwork in the*

year following did not cost His Majesty more than 6s 11d per floor (a measure of volume 18ft square and 1ft deep – *c*.9.2m^3), *although the bastions were brought higher and larger, and the moat larger or broader. The digging, wheeling, levelling, ramming, scaffolding and all other materials therein included. Nor do I conceive but that the said Sir Thomas and his brother were obliged (by contract to be at the charge of digging and wheeling it) for 7s per floor*. Significant progress was nevertheless achieved. Building works included the effective completion of the Saluting Platform, adjacent to South Blockhouse, and a new drain, which was under construction in November. The earthworks of the previous year were continued. The bastion at the Castle was being clad with turf in September: *we have laid four courses round the half bastion at the Castle which being very large, takes a great deal of work to go through with it*[9].

1683

In 1683, the Board contracted for further new building works at the Citadel with the Fitches. It is perhaps significant that Sir Bernard de Gomme was to calculate the first instalment of their payment; that Beckman's authority regarding earthworks was restated; and that *the Commissioners at Hull* (were) *to take notice if the works contracted for are cheaper than promised*. Mr Catlyn of Hull, who had declined a part in the works in 1681, submitted an estimate of the costs required to implement those planned for 1683; his costing is possibly that for £4,119 19s 1d lodged with Lord Dartmouth's papers. Bernard de Gomme commented on these proposals, and Beckman's estimate which they were to implement. Beckman fielded his criticism, with some irritation, and with passing reference to de Gomme's own works at Portsmouth, in April. In May, the Commissioners enquired if the Board could *let us know whether you have concluded anything concerning Mr Catlyn's contract for the stone wall and sallyports which we expected to have received an account of from Major Beckman*. The Board were considering these proposals. On 24 May, however, they signed a contract of 66 articles with the Fitches. This was to be implemented the following year[10].

The works of 1683 began in March, but were brought to a premature close in July, following a strike by the labourers. From April, the works were left under the supervision of Captain Charles Lloyd. Beckman provided Lloyd with instructions and explained them to him in detail. This proved, however, an unfortunate appointment: Lloyd antagonised his colleagues on the Commission, and appears to have bullied Duxbury into withholding his instructions from the Journal in which they should have been entered. Lloyd's manner was matched by his incompetence, and his direction of earthworks was gravely bungled.

Relicts of the *old moat by the long curtain wall* were filled. Stretches of the old curtain were to be removed north of the Castle, to make way for the Citadel moat. For this, Beckman initially ordered iron drills to be made by a Mr Silver. Later payments indicate that gunpowder had to be used to demolish the wall here by blasting, so the drills may have been used to make holes for the insertion of charges. The remaining extent of the Henrician curtain between the Castle and South Blockhouse served as an outer revetment for the earth ramparts forming the west curtain of the Citadel. The instructions of April 1683 stipulated that Mr Conden (or Condon), a gunner at Hull who served as a *sodlayer*, was to set men to *fill up the vacancies of the stone curtain*. By 18 June, the rampart was 45ft (13.7m) thick, excluding the wall itself; and by late August was held to be complete. In early 1684, the rampart was *52ft (c.15.9m) broad and 14ft (c.4.3m) in height from the water in the old moat*. Further earthworks were set out in front of this main rampart, to be manned by infantry[11].

Beckman specified that Mr Conden should carry out the earthworks. From references to him in the instructions for Lloyd, he appears to have enjoyed Beckman's trust. However, Conden was taken ill in May. A Mr Newton was also contracted by the Commissioners, *for digging and wheeling away the earth*, and they contracted with Mr Felton, who was to carry out earthworks on the Fitches' behalf. A contract with John Harkon, for *taking up the old foundation wall against the Castle bastion* set out a rate of 18d for every *floor* carried away, *to be measured by the Clerk of Works and paid for as the work is finished*. Mr Felton was *very hardly used by the Fitches, for though he got them clear by his pains and care £700 clear, yet they owe him £400, and will not pay him what he contracted for, nor for any extraordinary works, which has almost broke his heart*. In reviewing the works of 1683, Duxbury suggested assigning earthworks as a single fixed-price contract: *I think if it was all let by the Great (except the ramming work) it would be the cheaper way, for we cannot possibly make the labourers work for the King, as they will for the undertakers*[12].

In May 1683, Joseph Blaides (or Blaydes), a prominent shipwright and carpenter of Hull, was contracted by the Commissioners to build a new sluice controlling water flow between the river Hull and the Citadel moat, with the approval of the Board. This project entailed the supply of *so much good blue clay to be brought from*

Blacktoft as shall be required for making a firm foundation for laying the new trunk (sluice) upon, for which he is to be allowed the sum of 25s for each keel containing 20 ton, and 18s a keel to the owner of the ground where this clay is got[13].

In August 1683, the new sluice threatened to collapse. With the early closure of the works, there was no-one on the site to take immediate action. Duxbury reported to the Board, who in turn informed the Commissioners: *that the last high tides came to the top of the dam and soaked through the loose earth on both sides of it, which together with the rains has caused a great quantity of earth to flounder down to the trunk's mouth and more will follow except some day-labourers be appointed to cut away the earth to lay the wing towards the Haven. That they would please to order the preventing any further damage by directing such day-labourers to be put upon the same as shall be needful, and for raising the bank 6ft higher to its full height*. As the sluice was Blaides' work, he was ordered to mend it, and to submit his bill for overworks to the Board[14].

Duxbury returned in September, to take charge of the mending of the dam in front of the sluice. He had an open brief *to employ so many hands as was requisite for the finishing the great dam to prevent the Haven breaking in upon the trunk*. A further two breaches in the Humber bank to the east of the Citadel were also to be mended in October, and again he had leave from the Commissioners, *to employ so many carpenters and labourers as shall be necessary to repair the two great breaches beyond the east bastion next to Humber to prevent the next high tides from further damnifying the bank to the furthest extent of His Majesty's ground*. The sluice was eventually to be finished by Blaides in September 1684, and was attached to the riverbank revetments the following year. Duxbury spent the winter in London, though he was able to report on the good condition of the works on his return to Hull the next April[15].

1684

An inspection in March 1684 found *the mortar is shaken off round the parapet of South Blockhouse, and some of the brick shattered to pieces which Mr Fitch must repair*. Repointing with decorative scoring along the mortar between bricks may be ascribed to these repairs. Fitch was ordered to replace underfired *salmon bricks*. In February 1684, South Blockhouse was broken open by thieves. A new doorway was required, not only for its security, but also because of flooding within and around the Blockhouse: *That whereas the water stands within the half-bastion at South Blockhouse it is thought convenient to pave the same with cobbles and to make a gutter to carry the water hence through the gate into the new drain made by Mr Fitch within South Blockhouse. That the old great door or gate going into South Blockhouse being too low for making the said gutter through to carry the water into the new drain; it is ordered that a new door be made for the same.* An estimate of July 1684 included an item *for raising the floor in South Blockhouse and paving.* Beckman complained: *We cannot go in our formalities into the South Blockhouse but knee deep in clay, and water having no passage I intend.... to have a current to the last drain that was made in the middle of the court in the South House*[16].

The new works of 1684 began in June with the re-forming of Lloyd's earthworks, and continued with the building of a casemated entrance at the Main Gate of the Citadel, and sally ports to run through the east curtain. These all formed vaulted tunnels, flanked by antechambers, magazines and guardrooms, and were masked by the rampart except for their entrances, which were framed in neoclassical style. Beckman proposed additions to the agreed building works. These changes, which aimed to achieve a more balanced layout flanking the Main Gate, were accepted once de Gomme had been convinced that they would indeed *prove very serviceable as well as ornamental.* This year also saw the start, at its eastern end, of the south side of the Citadel. This was to comprise a brick sea-wall faced with limestone ashlar for its lower extent, resting on a piled and planked foundation. Building close to the shoreline was difficult and dangerous; the specifications for every aspect of the construction were revised as the problems presented by unstable soils and percolating water became clear[17]

These works comprised a substantial programme of building, and there ensued a stream of complaints against John Fitch. He sent inferior local lime rather than the Knottingley lime specified in the contract for a drain. Low river levels impeded the delivery of stone, which he was to provide. Sir Thomas and John were taxed with their *omissions,* which included a failure to send adequate numbers of masons and bricklayers: *if they do not immediately dispatch and lead them away the work will be but half done for this year, that they are come no further than even with the surface of the ground which is an insufferable thing.* In October, still, *the masons work here has been a great hindrance to others and I fear will yet retard our works*[18].

Beckman could find *nobody that cares for the undertaking of the earthwork but are all for day work.* Talbot Edwards, an employee of the Board - and related to Beckman by marriage - was contracted by the Commissioners for the digging of foundation trenches and the construction of foundations and dams, and for the covering of casemated structures with earth, at a rate of 8s 6d per floor of material moved, and at an estimated cost of £293 11s 8d. Beckman took on similar tasks and earthworks as a contractor the same year, at an estimated cost of £247 19s. He undertook the work at the Board's order, *for method's sake*[19].

When it became clear that stone could not be brought from quarries at Roche (or Roach) Abbey, near Leeds, Beckman made alternative arrangements. *I have taken a bond of £500 from the Mason of this town, one Mr Roebuck, to provide as durable and serviceable stone for this work as that of Roach Abbey is, from Tadd and Don(caster), and he is obliged upon his own charge to make good any particular stone that shall fleave or moulder away at any time hereafter.* As Fitch had placed Beckman in this position through the failure of his own materials to arrive, and Beckman was not certain of Roebuck, he was also charged an equivalent bond[20].

Faced with such delays in the supply of materials and craftsmen, Beckman's patience wore thin: *Esquire Fitch's Parliament have adjourned themselves till the arrival of stones and plank, in the meanwhile these rabble members live merrily and lug and tug one anothers ears; but I hear the fat vizier Mr Fitch is approaching this way, there being some of his jannisaries gone to meet him in order to carry the horse tail before him, a signal of war, but against whom is not yet known except it be against himself who does indeed deserve a little strangling for remembrance sake.* Beckman vented his spleen with these unflattering comparisons of his contractors to the officials of the Turkish Empire. Matters were not improved by the collapse of Fitch's old sluice, which had been built as a temporary fixture in 1682. In October, Sir Thomas and John Fitch were formally warned by the Board, *touching their neglect in carrying on the works and that they must expect to answer all damages through their default.* The autumn weather closed in, and, in early November, *we have paid nothing the last week the weather being so various and wet we could not work two whole days*[21].

John Fitch was ordered to Hull in November, to ensure the completion of his works for the year. This was unfortunate timing; the next day Beckman was reporting an accident on part of Fitch's work. He opposed a hurried completion: *If Mr Fitch doth finish this years work in ten days time after his arrival as he has promised... then will I finish the whole Citadel in five days. One as possible as the other... I am well assured that it will not be for His Majesty's service, nor anybody's credit to meddle and hazard with any mortarworks in this season.* Having carried this point, a week later Beckman noted that *here is not yet one stone upon the place (for an unfinished cornice) ... he says it will be here the next tide, and so it was to be here 8 days before I went to Scotland, but it seems Mr Fitch's tides and times have no influence by the moon.* This was an unhappy time for John Fitch and his masons: *He says he was not right understood in the office; for he meant the 10th day the day of his finishing, and the first day must not have a beginning before some time the next week and so to continue in progression. Always with the provision that all such days Mr Fitch keeps his chamber or gives audience to his apothecary and a cylinder of leeches must not be one of the ten days; but when all is done his expedition is remarkable for he makes the stone-cutters hew the stones in the vaults till 10 o'clock at night at candlelight*[22].

1685

Beckman certified the Fitches' works and overworks in January 1685, though he could not resist inserting a note that they largely fulfilled the Contract *which was to have been finished in the year 1683*. These did not survive the winter unscathed. By April, the new drain had been *blown up* by water and Fitch's Agent was awaiting permission to repair it; repointing of brickwork and other minor tasks were again required[23].

The drain was repaired, and orders issued in June 1685: *That the rubbish be taken out of the lower rooms of South Blockhouse, and paved with pebble stones... And that all the moist and watery places in the lower rooms be digged out and well filled up with good strong clay, but not to dig lower down than the foundation.* A month later these works were complete: *paving the Sourth Blockhouse, and the Castle, being in all 1,604 yards which for sand, cobble, gravel and workmanship has cost us above £120.* Fitch sent William Heath, bricklayer, to effect repairs to an arch, probably that covering the drain, *which he has done in good and workmanlike manner and in our opinion very firmly and substantially*[24].

The documents reviewed to date are virtually silent in so far as the Castle is concerned, though the raising of the north bastion around it is amply described. It was probably in better condition than South Blockhouse, being further from the Humber, and may therefore have required less attention. Archaeological excavations have shown some features likely to date to the construction of the Citadel,

which are best attributed to the period 1685-87. The original ground-floor hand-gun ports were blocked with brick. This was perhaps associated with proposals drafted by Beckman, late in 1686, for the support of the west quarter of the Castle with four pillar buttresses along with other brickwork, at an estimated cost of £30 14s[25].

The plugging of the Castle moat with clay was glimpsed by excavation. Edward Raven was paid in 1686 for *digging and wheeling 44 floors and 244ft of earth out of the new graft to fill up the old moat at the Castle.* The main gate of the Castle was rebuilt, being widened by *c.*1m. An *open gutter to be made in the Castle yard... to convey the water through that side where the low flanker is to be facing the North Blockhouse (i.e.* northwards) figured in instructions of June 1685; and the Castle had been paved with cobble bedded in gravel by early August. These works appear to have been similar in character to those documented at South Blockhouse, and, like them, improved access to elements of the Henrician defences[26].

The main works of 1685 completed the eastern bastions and curtain, the most substantial unsupported earthworks to be raised at the Citadel. In early 1685, tools were repaired, at a cost of £14 2s. By mid-July, there were 400 labourers at work, moving from the bastions to the curtain, then to the berm before the curtain. A parapet *quite around Drypoolside* was ordered to be built on 26 October, to cap these extensive works. To turf the earthworks, the Commissioners contracted with *the proprietors of the Summergangs common for £20 an acre* (0.41ha), *so far as we shall cut the sod, and £20 for leading through their grounds*, combining purchase and transportation as separate items within a single contract. The year also saw the clearing of further relics of the Henrician curtain to the north of the Citadel[27].

Joseph Blaides was contracted to fence the eastern side of the site; *to make a house of office at the Saluting Platform* (a toilet projecting from the point) *according to Major Beckman's instructions*; to *repair and make good the* (artillery) *train carriages*; and to complete the fixing of his sluice to the riverside revetments. This could not prevent other damage over winter. *We have had such an abundance of rain that it has filled the Citadel almost full of water, and yet the ground is not high enough to carry it into the drains, which has caused it to press so much upon the new curtain, especially between the further drain to the angle of the curtain, where it always had a vent or (?)quirksan that it has caused the lower berm or foreland to fall in the belly for about 18ft (c.5.5m) from the drain to the angle of the curtain.* Duxbury spent in the region of

£40 at his own initiative on piled and planked repairs and clay packing, in January 1686. He inserted *spouts* to draw off springing water the following month[28].

1686

Sir Bernard de Gomme died in November 1685, to the satisfaction of Beckman, to whom the office of Principal Engineer now passed in reversion, and who was knighted. The Commissioners ordered: *That a contract be made with Edward Raven for levelling the earth within the Citadel to 50ft (c.15.25m) in breadth from the bottom of the curtain.* This was required to prevent further damage by standing water. It involved widespread raising of the ground-level, by about 2ft (c.0.6m), at an overall cost of £61 7d[29].

The water bastion of 1686 was the first of three major elements which were to form a sea wall along the south side of the Citadel. The Fitches' men landed materials for its construction below the tideline on the Humber shore, and complaints about salty sand and cheap lime again surfaced. Terras (waterproof) mortar was only to be mixed under close supervision[30].

The vigour of these contentions was magnified when the Commission contracted for a breakwater jetty to protect the proposed water bastion. This was required to prevent the Humber tides from washing away the bastions to be built out into the river. Beckman identified the requirement for the jetty in May 1686, estimated for this work, and calculated its cost at £901 14s. The Commissioners sought the approval of the Board; this was granted, and an imprest of £200 was sent to begin the work. The Commissioners contracted with Joseph Blaides on the recommendation of Beckman, on 14 June, advancing him £100 for materials. Three days later, however, John Fitch outflanked the local interest by contracting directly with the Board in London[31].

The Commissioners defended their decision: *we hope you will not suffer us the penalty of the law by the contracting with Mr Fitch, who is so incapable of performing this work that he cannot, nor could possibly proceed with, his contract for the water bastion, if he be not furnished with plank and timber from this Mr Blaides.* Fitch directed his counterattack at Duxbury, who was stung into a detailed rebuttal: *Yours of the 15th instant I received with the enclosed copy of Mr Fitch's letter, wherein he endeav-*

oured to make me a notorious liar, which (if proved) might have utterly destroyed my credit and reputation with your honour and all the north and consequently have ruined my fortunes... And notwithstanding his common discourse has made him incredulous to all that know him, yet I shall endeavour to prove him so in several particulars - which he did. Fitch, having secured his contract, retracted his attack on Duxbury. This episode *so incensed the Commissioners here that they are almost resolved never to act more in these affairs*[32].

Duxbury was a partisan of Beckman's; neither, however, was now in a position for a contest with the Fitches. Duxbury had sought the Storekeeper's post at Hull in 1685, for which security had to be provided. He had also entrusted to John Fitch a letter in which he requested the stipend of Master Gunner, pleading his indebtedness as a reason. He had been granted the Storekeeper's post, but from December 1685 had fielded enquiries which seemed to cast doubt on this appointment. His financial affairs in London remained troublesome, and he had himself tendered unsuccessfully for a small part of the works of 1686. Beckman's hand was weakened by his new responsibilities as Principal Engineer, by his direct subordination to Lord Dartmouth, and by the need to avoid obvious entanglement with local vested interests on the Bench at Hull - he was to submit his estimates for the repair of their own defences in October[33].

John Fitch appears to have exploited these circumstances with considerable skill. The Board upheld the contract with Fitch - and its own authority - and cancelled that reached with Blaides, though it provided that Fitch should *take off the timber and materials provided by the said Joseph Blaides towards the work.* Duxbury rehearsed the logistics involved: Blaides had *above 40 ton of timber for the use of the jetty in vessels, which lay above a week on board, because he has not room on the Garrison side to land it, for Mr Fitch's materials took up all the ground at the landing place, so that Mr Blaides was forced to put the piles into Mr Harlow's dock and the rest at his own sawpits, which is now sawn into planks for Mr Fitch's use at the new wall, all which came out of my Lord Castleton's parks from Bawne, Whitby etc*[34].

1687

From 1686 to 1688 the lower part of the south scarp or sea wall was completed in three annual stages: in 1686, the east water bastion, which projected into the Humber; in 1687, the south curtain, and probably also a wharf at its centre; and the west water bastion, which met the Platform before South Blockhouse, in 1688. These works saw the further development of technical solutions to varied problems. These included the construction of dams to permit trenching at the water's edge; the modification of piling, permitting localised subsidence to strengthen the union of the masonry scarp and the earthworks piled behind it; and the sloping or canting of massive walls to achieve the same effect. These major undertakings, including some of their earthwork components, were to remain the preserve of the Fitches until 1690. The documentary record of their actual execution is sparse, though the archaeological record amply compensates for this[35].

The supply of turf for finishing earthworks had proved unexpectedly expensive in 1685. For 1687, though Summergangs Common was still to provide the turf, its cost was to be calculated *after the rate of 30s per square* (100ft square – *c*.9.3m^2) *for cutting, leading and parching*, with £10 impressed for the proprietors, via a Mr Buly. This cost included every stage of sodwork, as later specified by Beckman: *for cutting, leading with carts, laying, trimming, wheeling the sods upon the rampart and pins* (for fastening the turfs in place) *included*. The extent of earthworks in this season may be gauged by the number of labourers employed, which rose above 1,000 at one point[36].

The provision of tools and scaffolding by the Commissioners helped them to secure lower rates for labour. In 1687, Alderman Trippitt was paid *for deals, baulks, spars and other materials for erecting of stages* (scaffolding), *bridges etc.*; Laurence Evans, carpenter, *for making of wheelbarrows and setting up stages and bridges*; and John Shields for 150 new wheelbarrows. Further payments were made in the course of the year: to Thomas Carter, blacksmith, *for nails, spades spurs etc.*; and to Shields, Evans, Trippitt and Carter[37].

The erection and dismantling of scaffolding, and the repair of tools, was to be by piece-work, at Beckman's insistence: *That the carpenters be allowed for first setting up the stage (the King finding all materials) after the rate of 6d per foot (0.31m) running measure, and 4d per foot for removing the same, and to be 4d for mending each barrow (when broke). And 6d apiece for new hafting the rammers, and 4d apiece for shafting the pickaxes with good ash. For removing of stages I have agreed for 4d per foot running measure they finding their own, which has cost before twice as much when they did by days work, and the King found nails. The repairing of wheelbarrows I have agreed for 4d per piece one with another, where a wheel or whole frame were in pieces*[38].

Beckman's detailed analysis of the works of 1687 showed that the employment of soldiers and labourers on piece-work for earthworks had been far too expensive. Tasks such as digging, wheeling, spreading and ramming, reckoned as separate tasks, had cost 20s a floor (*c*.9.2m^3) in his absence; *when he has had it done in his presence for 8s or 9s per floor. And being that he cannot expect always to be upon the place, nor to stand always over them...* he recommended the Commissioners to include earthworks for 1688 in a contract with *a substantial undertaker*. The earthworks fell to the Fitches, though the Crown would supply wheelbarrows, tools and scaffolding, which the Fitches were to maintain[39].

The structural problems at South Blockhouse had still not yet been finally resolved. In August 1687, a contract was agreed with John Fitch, for *erecting a new wall to support South Blockhouse from settling any further*. On 26 September, Beckman reported *that I have had a troublesome business with the pinning up of South Blockhouse*; which was certified as complete in November. The wall was revealed by excavation, in 1997 and 1998, as a substantial brick structure resting on planked foundations, and shared various characteristics with other works of 1687[40].

The intersection of the old moat around South Blockhouse with the new Citadel moat demanded particular attention. A substantial brick wall formed a lining for the inner side of the new moat. This would appear to have been intended to revet the softer soils of the old moat around the Blockhouse where the line of the new one for the Citadel cut through them. The construction of the wall may have been associated with the operations to pin up South Blockhouse. These entailed an estimated cost of £290 1s 4d, substantial overworks of £329 11s, and *works not mentioned in contract allowed by the Board*, of £101 9s[41].

In 1687, Beckman also reached an agreement with Mr William Robinson: *for making of 2 million bricks on His Majesty's ground on the Garrison side at Hull*, for the next year's works. This direct negotiation would deny Fitch the opportunity of buying cheap and selling dear to the Board. Robinson had contracted to sell his bricks to Fitch at 9s per thousand, with Fitch fetching them from the clamps, which would raise their price to 11s per thousand, his normal rate for sale in the town. The best bricks, for facing walls, were more expensive, at 20s per thousand. The Commission concurred with Beckman's initiative; *all the advantage accruing to His Majesty hereby is the taking away of so much earth*. The digging of clay, for bricks to complete the sea wall, was probably intended to help complete wide ditches intended as outworks to the east[42].

Beckman designed a spade suitable for digging the stiff Hull clay, with a narrow blade, a thicker iron, and a shaft let deeper into the socket than was usual. He sought and gained the Board's approval for a contract with the blacksmith, Thomas Carter, for making the spades at 2s apiece. The Board approved the contracts with Robinson and Carter together. The circumstances of these negotiations hint that Robinson's brick pits were to lie on the eastern edge of the Citadel. They perhaps achieved the partial definition of the triangular ravelin before it. Beckman contracted for 500 of the new spades; a number appropriate to a major campaign of construction, rather than to brick-making alone[43].

1688

In 1688, the lower part of the southern side of the Citadel was completed. Barracks for 200 men were also contracted for. These were to be built within the Citadel, along with a slightly smaller lodging for officers. The two barrack blocks were to be 156½ft (47.7m) long and 37½ft (11.43m) wide. They were to be brick-walled and roofed with pantiles, rising 11ft (3.35m) to the wall plates, with gables at either end above. They were divided at ground floor level by a partition supporting a staircase, which led to an upper gallery. The rooms were to have wooden floors, a generously proportioned window and a fireplace, lath and plaster ceilings and plastered walls, and were lit by garret casement windows. The officers lodgings were to include panelled chambers downstairs, and more spacious rooms, which were to measure 9ft (2.75m) from floor to ceiling. The certificate recording the completion of these works mentions two officers' houses. The Officers Barracks illustrated by the earliest plans of the Citadel formed a single range. Immediately to the east lay the Governor's house; when this was constructed is less certain, though it figures in a plan of the Citadel dated to 1685-88[44].

As events moved towards the Glorious Revolution, the western defences - facing Hull - were upgraded. Many of these measures had been envisaged by the contract which set out the works planned for the year. They included *passages to the lower vaults through the Castle wall*, which were sallyports which gave access to *base flank* batteries; and a *cut through the Castle wall for the passage and drain and* (demolition of) *a piece of wall at the steps to the wall*, which may have conveniently coincided with this. Sally ports leading to the *base flanks* here, however, were revealed by excavation to have been less robust in their construction than similar features raised under Beckman's oversight in 1684, perhaps as a result of their hurried completion[45].

On 10 November, Beckman left his *instructions for Mr John Duxbury to see such works finished as is contracted for with Mr Fitch for the present defence of His Majesty's town and Citadel of Hull*. This was a package of measures, hurriedly agreed at an estimated cost of £5,000, against the possibility of a seabourne assault on Hull and its unfinished fortification. For the Citadel, these entailed palisades, some already in place, probably along the south front, where only the lower part of the scarp had been completed. The further manufacture of iron-tipped *stockadoes* was to halt when 2,000 had been made. Earthworks at the western *base flanks* served by the new sallyports, and the clearing of moats there, were to be completed by labourers under the Governor's control. A parapet was to *be cut out of the great banks* at East Point, rendering it defensible. The *Small Hornwork* was mentioned for the first time; the most likely position for this is on the Humber bank to the east of the Citadel. An outlying redoubt here guarded a sluice in the banks, and was itself covered by guns at East Point. The sluices were to be secured and locked, and the keys lodged with the Governor. Other works were to be completed before the North Gate of Hull and the North Bridge, and apparently comprised extensive earthworks and a water-filled moat. These were again to be completed by labourers; Duxbury was ordered: *That Mr Fitch have no hand in the half bastion before the North Gate and Town Bridge but that the said works be continued by the town and country people as long as my lord the Governor shall think fit to employ them*[46].

Payments to John Fitch continued to be made, in instalments of £250 or £500. The emergency of 1688 had overstretched the finances of the Board of Ordnance: *A great charge has also been cast upon the office by the necessary defence of Hull Garrison, proposed by Sir Martin Beckman, for which the contract amounted to upwards of £5,000, and of which only £2,150 has been paid; so that Mr Fitch, who has finished the most part of his work, is likely to fall under an inevitable ruin unless his Lordship interceded with the Treasury*. Transactions continued in 1689, under William and Mary[47].

1689-90

In 1689, as government was purged of the adherents of James II, little activity is recorded at Hull. The Fitches retained responsibility for maintenance tasks.

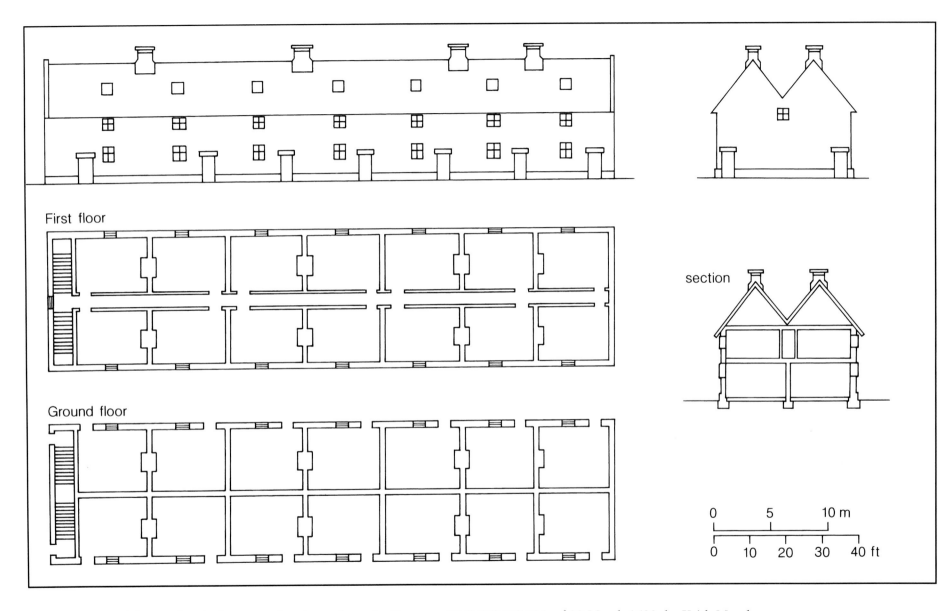

First floor

Ground floor

section

0   5   10 m

0   10   20   30   40 ft

Fig 12: The Citadel Barracks. An interpretation drawn from the Contract, PRO WO55/1785, of 29 March 1688, by Keith Moody.

Their *maintaining and upholding the work and fortifications at Hull was suspected to be ill done*. In 1690, however, under the new Williamite regime, they raised a brick wall to complete the upper part of the south side of the Citadel along its whole length. The final form of the ramparts here was demi-revetted, with earthworks forming the top of an otherwise brick and stone-faced elevation. Though further work was intended, it was never done[48].

The unfinished elements included a triangular ravelin guarding the bridge across the moat to the Main Gate, and a further suite of wide earthworks and ditches beyond it. The earthworks required to back the wall of 1690 were *to be made with earth fetched from without the Citadel in carts from such places as the Engineer on the place shall order which will contain 1,970 floors (c.18,000m³)*. The excavation of this large volume of clay may have formed what were to be recorded as irregular ponds by the Phillips plan of 1716, lying to the east of the finished works. They were never, however, to be formed into any coherent defensive pattern[49].

As a beneficiary of the redistribution of offices and appointments after the Glorious Revolution of 1688, John Fitch was to die a wealthy man, in 1705. In 1694, he had received a payment as *Workmaster of the Ordnance*, being paid £240 *on his fee* for two years between 1692 and 1694. In an extraordinary comment on this succesful career, the Duke of Marlborough wrote: *Mr John Fitch (who by the favour of my Lord Treasurer Danby) had a patent constituting him Major Workman of all her Majesty's Forts and Fortifications, by virtue of which patent it is true Mr Fitch always made his pretensions to such works. But we are very well assured he never was employed pursuant to that patent, this Office taking patents of that nature to be of very dangerous consequence and even contrary to law, because such patentees then might have a right to demand extravagant prices for what works they should undertake*[50].

Footnotes

1:      Foreman and Goodhand 1997; *ibid.*, fig. 4.
2:      PRO WO46:1 (index), 252, Orders of Board, 16 August 1681; *ibid.*, 307, Beckman to Board, 7 September 1681.
3:      PRO WO46:1, 308, Fitch to Board, 25 September 1681; *ibid.*, 318, Beckman to Board, 26 November 1681, 23 November 1681; *ibid.*, 324, Duxbury to Board, 13 March 1682.
4:      PRO WO46:1, 312, Account of Day Labourers, 13 October 1681; *ibid.*, 308, Beckman to Board, 24 September 1681; Borthwick Inst., Wills vol. 59, fo. 454; PRO WO46:1, 311, Beckman to Board, 15 October 1681; Foreman 1997, 58; PRO WO46:1, 308, Duxbury to Board, 25 September 1681.
5:      PRO WO46:1, 217, Estimate, 15 June 1681; *ibid.*, 316, Duxbury to Board, 16 November 1681; *ibid.*, 319, 28 November 1681.
6:      Foreman 1997, 11, 58; PRO WO46:1, 318, Beckman to Board, 26 November 1681; *ibid.*, 316, Duxbury to Board, 16 November 1681.
7:      PRO WO46:1, 322, Duxbury to Board, 28 January 1682; *ibid.*, 7 February 1682; PRO WO55/1785, Contract, 10 August 1681; PRO WO46:1, 324, Duxbury to Board, 13 March 1682.
8:      PRO WO46:1, 322, Duxbury to Board, 7 February 1682; *ibid.*, 13 March 1682; *ibid.*, 285, Board to Watkinson, 11 April 1682; *ibid.* (index), 326, Letters to Office, 22 March 1681; *ibid.*, 285, Letters from Office, 27 May 1682.
9:      PRO WO46:1 (index), 328, Letters to Office, 26 June 1682; *ibid.*, 292, Letters from Office, 27 January 1683; Foreman and Goodhand 1997, 149; PRO WO46:1, 334, Duxbury to Board, 25 September 1682.
10:     PRO WO46:2 (index), 1, Orders of Board, 2 June 1683; *ibid.*, 2, 9 June 1683; Stafford Record Office D (W) 1778/V/68, Estimate, 1683; PRO WO46:1 (index), 230-1, Estimates, 1683; *ibid.*, Beckman to de Gomme, 26 April 1683; Bod. Lib. Rawl. A475, Commissioners to Board, 9 May 1683; *ibid.*, Board to Commissioners, 12 May 1683; PRO WO55/1785, Contract, 24 May 1683.
11:     PRO WO46:1, 345, Duxbury to Board, 9 April 1683; *ibid.* (index), 263, Orders of Board, 8 May 1683; PRO WO55/519, Commissioners Certificate, 12 May 1685; PRO WO46:1, 347, Instructions to Lloyd, 17 April 1683; PRO WO46:2, 151, Duxbury to Board, 18 June 1683; *ibid.*, 89, Lloyd's Particular of works done, 30 August 1683; Bod. Lib. Rawl. A476, item 1, 2-3, Duxbury to Beckman, 12 April 1684.
12:     PRO WO46:1, 347, Instruction to Lloyd, 17 April 1683; Bod. Lib. Rawl. A476, item 1, 2-3, Duxbury to Beckman, 12 April 1684; PRO WO46:1, 351, Duxbury to Board, 21 May 1683; PRO WO46:2 (index), 42, Orders of Commissioners, 9 June 1683; Bod. Lib. Rawl. A476, item 1, 4, Duxbury to Beckman, 12 April 1684; Bod. Lib. Rawl. A475, Orders of Commissioners, 27 April 1683.
13:     PRO WO46:1 (index), 263, Orders of Board, 3 May 1683; Bod. Lib. Rawl. A475, Orders of Commissioners, 4 May 1683.
14:     PRO WO46:2, 9, Order of Board, 23 August 1683; *ibid.*, (index), 87, 28 August 1683.
15:     PRO WO46:2, 91, Board to Commissioners, 13 September 1683; *ibid.*, 48, Orders

of Commissioners, 5 October 1683; *ibid*., 256, Beckman to Board, 13 September 1684; PRO WO55/519, Commissioners' Estimate, 4 July 1685; Bod. Lib. Rawl. A476, item 1, 4, Duxbury to Beckman, 12 April 1684.

16: Bod. Lib. Rawl. A476, item 1, Duxbury to Plymouth, 29 March 1684; Foreman 1997, 11, 59; PRO WO46:2, 19, Order of Board, 8 April 1684; *ibid*. (index), 194, Letters from Hull, 16 February 1684; *ibid*., 52, Order of Commissioners, 17 September 1684; *ibid*., 309, Estimates, 17 July 1684; *ibid*., 259, Beckman to Board, 17 September 1684.

17: PRO WO46:2, 126, Board to Commissioners, 3 July 1684.

18: PRO WO46:2, 315, Contracts 22 April 1684; Bod. Lib. Rawl. A476, item 1, Duxbury to Board, 30 May 1684; PRO WO46:2 (index), 39, Orders of Commissioners, 16 July 1684; *ibid*., 26, Order of Board, 3 July 1684; *ibid*., 287, Wharton to Board, 25 October 1684.

19: PRO WO46:2, 225, Beckman to Board, 16 June 1684; *ibid*., 317, Contract, 7 July 1684; *ibid*., 309, Estimates, 17 July 1684.

20: PRO WO46:2, 244, Beckman to Board, 30 July 1684; *ibid*., 247, 9 August 1684.

21: PRO WO46:2, 242, Beckman to Board, 23 July 1684; *ibid*., 256, 13 September 1684; *ibid*. (index), 145, Board to Hull, 28 October 1684; *ibid*., 291, Duxbury to Board, 12 November 1684.

22: PRO WO46:2 (index), 149, Letters of Board, 18 November 1684; *ibid*., 295, Letters from Hull, 19 November 1684; *ibid*., 295, Beckman to Board, 19 November 1684; Bod. Lib. Rawl. A476, item 1, Duxbury to Board, 19 November 1684; PRO WO46:2, 299, Beckman to Board, 26 November 1684; *ibid*., 300, 6 December 1684.

23: PRO WO46:2, 327, Certificate, 29 January 1685; Bod. Lib. Rawl. A476, item 1, Duxbury to Board, 5 April 1685.

24: PRO WO55/519, Commissioners' Certificate, 2 June 1685; Bod. Lib. Rawl. A475, Duxbury to Board, 6 July 1685, Board to Beckman 5 August 1685; PRO WO55/519, Commissioners' Certificate, 28 August 1685.

25: Foreman 1996; Cook 1971, 5; Eddy 1976, 3; Foreman 1996, 28; Brit. Lib. Add. 16370, fo. 107, Estimate, 14 October 1686.

26: Cook 1971, 5; PRO WO55/519, Order of Commissioners, 11 September 1686; Foreman 1996, 10-11; PRO WO55/519, Instructions to Wharton, 2 June 1685; Bod. Lib. Rawl. A475, Duxbury to Board, 5 August 1685.

27: Bod. Lib. Rawl. A476, item 1, Duxbury's Certificate, 9 April 1685; Foreman and Goodhand 1997, 151; PRO WO55/519, Commissioners to Board, 13 June 1685.

28: PRO WO55/519, Postscript to Certificate, 2 June 1685; Bod. Lib. Rawl. A475, Duxbury to Board, 16 January 1686; *ibid*., Duxbury to Beckman, 20 February 1686.

29: Bod. Lib. Rawl. A475, Duxbury to ?, 8 February 1686; PRO WO55/519, Orders of Commissioners, 1 May 1686; *ibid*., Beckman to Board, 25 March 1686; Foreman 1998a; PRO WO55/519, Order of Commissioners, 6 October 1686.

30: PRO WO55/519, Order of Commissioners, 1 May 1686; Stafford Record Office D (W) 1778/I/i/1173, Commissioners to Board, 21 June 1686; PRO WO55/519, Instruction to Duxbury, 21 May 1686.

31: Stafford Record Office D (W)1778/I/i/1171, Contract (with Blaides), 14 June 1686; PRO WO55/519, Estimate, 14 May 1686; *ibid*., Commissioners to Board, 17 May 1686; Stafford Record Office D (W) 1778/I/i/1166, Board to Commissioners, 25 May 1686; PRO WO55/519, Order of Commissioners, 14 June 1686; Stafford Record Office D (W) 1778/I/i:/1172, Board to Commissioners, 17 June 1686.

32: PRO WO55/519, Commissioners to Board, 21 June 1686; *ibid*., Duxbury to Board, 21 July 1686; Bod. Lib. A475, Duxbury to ?Beckman, 30 June 1686; PRO WO55/519, Fitch to Board, 21 July 1686; *ibid*., Order of Commissioners, 10 July 1686.

33: Bod. Lib. Rawl. A476, item 1, Duxbury to Dartmouth, 13 April 1685; *ibid*., Duxbury to Musgrave, to Dartmouth, 19 -27 April 1685; Bod. Lib. Rawl. A475, Duxbury to Plymouth, 29 June 1685; *ibid*., Duxbury to Board, 23 December 1685; *ibid*., Duxbury to Winteringham, 13 January 1686; *ibid*., Duxbury to ?Board, 8 February 1686; *ibid*., Duxbury to ?Beckman, 30 June 1686; Brit. Lib. Add Ms 16370, fos 102 and 107, Estimate.

34: PRO WO55/519, Order of Commissioners, 10 July 1686; *ibid*., Duxbury to Board, 21 July 1686.

35: PRO WO55/519, Beckman's Instructions, 3 June 1687; e.g. PRO WO55/1785, Contract, 19 May 1688; Foreman and Goodhand 1997.

36: Bod. Lib. Rawl. A475, 5 August 1685; PRO WO55/519, 20 September 1687, 24 September 1687; Stafford Record Office D (W) 1778/I:/1233, Beckman to Board, 24 September 1687.

37: PRO WO55/519, Orders of Commissioners, 24 September 1687; *ibid*., 8 October 1687; *ibid*., 15 October 1687; *ibid*., 29 October 1687.

38: PRO WO55/519, Orders of Commissioners, 20 September 1687; Stafford Office D (W) 1778/I:/ 1233, Beckman to Board, 24 September 1687.

39: PRO WO55/519, Commissioners to Board, 2 May 1688; *ibid*., Board to Commissioners, 8 May 1688; PRO WO55/1785, Contract, 19 May 1688.

40: PRO WO55/519, Order of Commissioners, 12 August 1687; Stafford Record Office D(W) 1778/I:/1233, Beckman to Board, 26 September 1687; PRO WO55/519, Commissioners to Board, 21 November 1687; Foreman 1997; 1998.

41:     Foreman 1998, 13-4, 67-8; PRO WO51/35, TBB series 2, 191b, 10 January 1688.

42:     PRO WO55/519, Board to Beckman, 24 August 1687; *ibid.*, Board to Commissioners, November 1687; *ibid.*, Orders of Commissioners, 26 October 1687; *ibid.*, Commissioners to Board, 31 October 1687.

43:     PRO WO55/519, Commissioners to Board, 5 November 1687; *ibid.*, Orders of Commissioners, 21 November 1687.

44:     Foreman and Goodhand 1997, 179-80; Foreman 1989, 41; PRO WO55/1785, Contract, 27 March 1688; PRO WO51/38, TBB series 2, 52; Brit. Lib. Egerton Ms 3359, fo. 1.

45:     PRO WO55/1785, Contract 29 March 1688; Phillips plan *c.*1716; Foreman and Goodhand 1997, 179-80.

46:     PRO WO55/519, Instructions to Duxbury, 10 November 1688.

47:     CTB vol. 8, part 3, 1685-89, November 1688, 2136; HMC Dartmouth Mss, 222, 1 December 1688; CTB vol. 8, part 3, 1685-89, December 1688, 2142; CTB vol. 3, part 5, January 1689, 2158; CTB vol. 9, part 1, February 1688-89, 3; *ibid.*, June 1689, 37; *ibid.*, July 1689, 193; *ibid.*, July 1689, 26; *ibid.*, September 1689, 57.

48:     PRO WO51/40, TBB, series 2, 43, 17 February 1690; PRO WO55/1785, Contract, 13 March 1690; PRO WO44/100/HK5970 X19, Beckman, 10 December 1690.

49:     Brit. Lib. Egerton Mss, fo. 1; PRO WO55/1785, Contract, 13 March 1690.

50:     CTB vol. 10, part 1, 734; CTB vol. 10, part 1, 479; PRO WO46/6 29065, 22 May 1705.

CHAPTER 7
TO BUILD A FORTRESS

The works at Hull included a range of distinct elements. Along the western side of the Citadel, the Henrician defences were repaired and modernised, being converted to serve new purposes within the new fortification. The South Blockhouse and the Castle provided strong-points and storerooms within the north and west bastions of the Citadel, and the curtain wall between them supported earthworks. To the east, where no earlier defences existed, ramparts were set out on the Dutch model, with passages and chambers beneath them. To the south, along the Humber shore, a great masonry scarp formed a sea wall to protect earthworks behind it. The moats surrounding the Citadel were to be filled with water, whose control presented further challenges in this low-lying location.

These varied works demanded a wide range of techniques. Documents and archaeological records illustrate every stage of these complex works: from the initial setting out of features on the site, right through the execution of complex structural projects. The methods employed were to be refined in the course of the intense activity on this intractable site.

Plans on the ground

Martin Beckman had drawn up detailed plans of the Henrician defences. The proposals for their improvement, in which both Sir Bernard de Gomme and Beckman had a hand, passed before the King. The use, understanding and explanation of plan, profile and elevation drawings was expected of an engineer, together with the mathematical calculation of stresses and loads necessary for the economical design of structures. The designs also had to pass from paper drafts - and sometimes models, as were occasionally recorded at the Tower of London - and contracts to the ground, where the fortifications were to stand. At Hull, some of the most informative episodes about this process are recorded from those occasions when it went awry.

When handing command of the works at Hull over to Captain Charles Lloyd, in 1683, *Major Beckman has promised to draw a draft of those works with Captain Lloyd and full instructions how to progress the same.* Lloyd was referred to the *Ground Plot, Profiles, the Uprights of the frontispiece and the Contract, wherein you will find all proportions to an inch,* and to *the Draught of the Citadel.* Beckman's instructions for Wharton, in October 1684, referred him to the *Profiles, Ground Plot and Upright,* and his *Draught for His Majesty's Arms.* The latter had been fashioned incorrectly; having spelled out the detail of their proper form in minute detail, Beckman urged that *it is therefore requisite that you show this paragraph to the masons that they may not run into further errors.* The craftsmen were expected to be literate and, moreover, capable of implementing complex amendments to their work according to written instructions[1].

Beckman took a personal hand in the setting out of the works. Some details of earthworks in 1681 were to be proportioned *as the Engineer upon the place shall order and appoint;* though obviously sensible, among the documents viewed for Hull this latitude appears to have been uncommon, and was to become rarer still later. Beckman himself set out the embrasures for gun-ports at the Saluting Platform and the eastern *base flanks.* His instructions to Lloyd referred to parapets and embrasures, which *I have staked and marked out,* and to other completed illustrating the forms to be achieved. The exact form of embrasures changed according to their position in the defences - as an artilleryman, Beckman took a particular interest in their placement. Thus, embrasures for guns placed in the flanks of bastions were to be slightly lower than about their faces, permitting guns there to be depressed to fire on attackers at close range. Foot-banks or fire-steps had to be raised high enough to allow infantry to fire over parapets, or through small embrasures for muskets. Beckman also *set out the ground where the new jetty is to be built into Humber.* Again, this was because the exact placement of the jetty was vital if it was to serve its intended purpose: the protection of the adjacent bastion from tidal erosion[2].

A lockspit, or trench, defined the limit of works. This could carry groundwater off from the immediate vicinity, to enable work to proceed in relatively dry conditions. More extensive earthworks could also be part-formed in places, so as to indicate how the remainder should be finished. In 1683, Lloyd misunderstood his instructions, *though the Major (Beckman) had left a sufficient pattern in his works by taking it down in steps leaving room for a sufficient slope. Lloyd ordered the carpenter to make the bevel according to his directions.* The wooden template was to be used to show what Lloyd erroneously believed to be the correct sloping of the earth. He had given *particular orders... to Raven and Birt and Shields to make the bevels, and.... constantly attended that work*[3].

Work at the Main Gate in 1684 was contracted to follow the *Ground Platt*, and *the Draught signed by Major Beckman... in the place he has staked it out and is to be seen in the Ground Platt*. Contracts were formally read before being entered in the Journal, so their provisions would be known to all the Commissioners. A well-attended meeting of the Commissioners, in 1683, ordered *That Sir Thomas and Mr John Fitch's Contract being this day read at board, it is ordered that it be entered in the Book of Contracts and punctually observed by the Commissioners*. Lloyd had refused to do this with his instructions, or to enter them in the Journal, claiming that *he was wholly entrusted in giving directions about the works, which he would communicate to none, but those who were personally employed*. In 1688, the Governor was instructed: *desiring your Lordship will please with the rest of the Commissioners and the said Chief Engineer at his arrival to order a meeting, and cause the whole contract to be directly read*[4].

Raising the ramparts

Earthworks formed the principal part of the new works of 1681-83 and 1685. They also formed an important subsidiary element of other works, as in 1686 and 1688. The earthworks were constructed according to prevailing conventions of military engineering, and constituted the primary defensive capacity of the Citadel. The raw material, a stiff, plastic alluvial clay, was immediately available as the predominant subsoil on the site. On the east side of the Citadel, its ramparts were to be 120ft (36.5m) thick. Where faced with brickwork, to the south and west, they were to be 60ft (*c*.18.3m) thick. All round, they were to rise to a height of between 10 and 15ft (*c*.3-4.5m). The ramparts were crowned by a parapet, which was intermittently interrupted by embrasures or gun-ports. The upper surface of the ramparts was gently sloped, with a fall towards its outer side. In the long term, this helped preserve them, by preventing rainwater from standing on top. In case of an attack by cannon fire, the slope would serve to deflect shot, which would hopefully bounce over the heads of troops sheltering behind the ramparts[5].

The bastions at the three corners of the Citadel, and its east curtain, were to stand largely unsupported. The design of earthworks was itself a specialised task, and their construction required informed supervision of an unskilled workforce. This was most dramatically illustrated when Lloyd took charge of the works, and failed to understand his instructions. As a result, he piled perpendicular mounds of earth, without allowing any angle of repose for the soil. The earth subsequently fell away all around the works[6].

At Hull, the ramparts were raised to about half their planned thickness one year, and completed as a separate operation the next year, or later. The full width of the moats, whence the clay for ramparts was initially dug, was also achieved in stages. Thus, though the digging of moats was under way from 1681, they were enlarged to their minimum width of 50ft (15.25m) only in 1686. The clay for earthworks was quantified in floors, a measure equivalent to one cubic yard of soil. It was dug from the line of moats in the early stages, and later from their outer edge or beyond the works as they approached their full extent. Special strengthened spades were designed in 1687, in preparation for the digging of the most extensive outworks[7].

Once dug out, the earth would be wheeled in barrows to be spread where it was required. The wheeling of earth from a distance entailed the clearance of obstructions, as in 1681, when the Henrician curtain wall was partly demolished. Later, as new works stood with moats before them, temporary bridges were required. In 1685, Duxbury was to negotiate cheap prices for deals, spars and stays for bridges. These temporary fixtures could be of an imposing size. In 1690, *a new bridge at the East Point for the conveniency of carts*, crossing the moat, was to be 307ft (*c*.93.6m) long and 12ft (3.7m) wide, with rails on either side. It was to be built at a cost of 15s per foot. Bricklayers and masons used wooden scaffolding, which formed raised working platforms or *stages*. The diversion of labourers from earthworks to wheeling duties, in *wet weather that the men cannot go up the stages*, suggests that it also formed barrow-runs up slopes. Earth piled up during foul-weather working *must not be rammed but levelled and deal boards laid in several places for the wheelbarrows*. The scaffolding was apparently fixed into the ramparts as they rose, and would be removed when work was complete. In October 1682, men were employed *making up the gaps where the stages came up to the parapet of the south bastion*[8].

The clay brought to form a rampart would not merely be piled, but would also be compacted by hand. This process was termed ramming, and labourers

Fig 13: Profiles of the Citadel ramparts; from top to bottom showing the form of the west, east and south ramparts; PRO MPHH 97 [1], reproduced by permission of the Public Record Office, Kew.

engaged in this arduous work were paid 2d more a day than those who dug or wheeled the earth. The heavy two-handed tools employed were familiar to those engaged in agriculture or building work. For farming, rammers were made from *old everings* (wagon axles) *harrow balls or such things as have holes: they put into the holes two rungs to hold by, the lowest for the right hand more than three-quarters of a yard from the foot of the rammer, the uppermost about a quarter of a yard higher than it.* At the Citadel, ramming entailed the deposit of thin layers of minced clay, and their compaction to half the original thickness. Adjacent surfaces were alternately raised and rammed until the desired configuration was reached. A typical requirement was for 6in. (150mm) of clay to be rammed to 3in. thickness, though this specification would vary with the location and purpose of earthworks; 4in. (100mm) reduced to 2in, or 8in. (200mm) to 4in. are also recorded. The rammer used for work on fortifications was usually a *double rammer*, weighing 70lbs (31.8kg), and would be lifted above the knees[9].

The earthworks raised under the supervision of John Fitch were criticised by Beckman because they had not been properly rammed. *For I ought not (he will say) ram but the sods and not the earth behind, according to contract - the truth on it is I expect nothing but a battle with him, and I am ready to give the first blow.* Fitch followed de Gomme's method, as practised at Portsmouth, compacting only the turf cladding of ramparts. Beckman did not consider this appropriate: *I have told him I am not obliged for His Majesty's services and any credit to follow the rule of Portsmouth and that Engineer (de Gomme) that have given such direction ought to have his ears cut off, to be nailed to his great toes to cure him of the gout, for I will prove to any of sense that he deserves it.* The excavation of elements of the earthworks of 1681, which had generated this trenchant criticism, showed them to comprise banded layers of soft clay, with spreads of softer soil and rubbish between them. More correct treatment of other ramparts, dated to 1681-2, produced a notably resistant outer surface of clay[10].

The extent of ramming was varied according to its position and purpose. Along the scarp of the eastern defences, if the ground was bad, *best clay* was to be rammed between a trench and the scarp of the rampart, 7ft (2.1m) wide at base and 4ft (1.23m) wide at the top. This formed a thick skin for the inner face of the clay-dug moat. Ramming could also consolidate rubble if this were used to back-fill foundation trenches, or to prepare particularly poor ground on which earthworks were to be raised. Wharton was instructed, in 1685, *if the foundation proves muddy, then take off the old rubbish that lay behind the great brick wall, and ram that 6*

or 12in. (c.150-300mm) more or less in the mud or sand, and 5 or 6ft (1.5-1.8m) wide. At the end of the month, he reported: *We have made a firm foundation (though the ground proved very bad) with stones and chalk rubbish well rammed for the scarp of the berm at the east bastion near the Humber, and have brought up the said scarp with sods about 5ft high*[11].

Ramming also followed the laying of sods of turf to protect the earthworks from erosion, though as noted above, this was no substitute for the proper treatment of the ramparts themselves. The sod-layers were valued specialists in their own right. The Commissioners maintained that there was *not one in a thousand that can understand or undertake this business which is not only labourers work of raising up turf but it is the cutting and paring and trimming of it in conclusion.* Two steel spades were supplied for cutting turf. Extensive sod-laying took place in at the western bastions in 1683, and in 1685 along the eastern scarp. Turf was initially cut close at hand, by the river. From 1685, it was brought in from Summergangs, an area of common land north-east of the Citadel. Turf would be trimmed, laid and pounded in place. The laying of turf on the eastern bastions in 1685 was to be preceded by the cutting of a trench *of 7ft (2.1m) wide and 18in. (460mm) deep, lower than where the moat is deepest, and then lay your first course of sods... of 9in. (228mm) long and half inch (c.13mm) thick at the upper end,* with clay rammed behind them. In especially wet locations, turf was less suitable, and other surfacing would be used. In 1686, the berm between the moat and the rampart of the Citadel was to be paved, as water overflowing from the moat might wash away turf laid here[12].

The grey turf-lines marking the position of this grassy cladding were noted during the archaeological excavation of trenches across the ramparts. At the west bastion, they rose at a 45° angle, appropriate to the stable ascent of an earthen bank. The splayed embrasures in earthwork defences, which were vertical faces, were framed with 3in. (76mm) oaken plank. The planked revetments provided support for the earth rising on either side of the embrasure. This was recorded for *the ports of the south bastion,* in 1682. Subsequent views and plans of the Citadel showed the low earthen hummocks left behind after the removal or decay of wooden frames[13].

The list of tools remaining at the end of organised works in 1683 illustrates some of the requirements of a busy season of earthworks. The gear belonging to the Crown included 44 spades; 9 shovels; 317 wheelbarrows; 32 double rams and four single rams; 17 *paring and turning spades* for sod-work; 4 iron crowbars; 12

pickaxes without shafts; 8 bevels; 5 levels; 3 sledges; and 6 wedges. There were also 23 stages of scaffolding, containing 1,380 boards. Tools belonging to the contractors Fitch and Felton were repaired in preparation for the working season of 1685, in which earthworks were similarly important. They included 256 wheelbarrows, 34 pickaxes hafted with ash, six double and two single rammers. Preparing for the works of 1688, Beckman had 500 of his own design of clay-digging spade made. These would improve upon the hand-tools provided by the labourers themselves[14].

Casemates and chambers

Where access was required through the ramparts, this was provided by vaulted passages. These were effectively tunnels, built from the level of the original land surface, with the soils of the rampart packed round and above them. As well as leading through the ramparts, the passages also gave access to *casemated* chambers and magazines. These were protected by vaulted roofs, and by the earth tamped carefully over these. This covering was intended to render them *bombproof*, so they could resist the plunging fire of mortars.

The largest passage was the Main Gate of the Citadel, at the mid-point of the east curtain. This was a barrel-vaulted passage wide enough for the passage of carts and gun carriages. A Soldiers' Guardhouse and a smaller Gunner's Vault lay on one side of the passage, and an Officers' Guardhouse and a Prison Vault on the other. The Guardhouses were lit by pairs of arched windows in their western walls, which looked out over the interior of the Citadel.

These features were required to withstand the lateral pressure exerted by the ramparts as well as the lesser weight of earth above. The Main Gate passage was to be supported by the walls of the chambers on either side. Beckman detailed this aspect of his design: *Which guardhouses and the prison vaults being the chief supporters of the whole arch or passage under the said rampart, the bottom of which I have made is to be supported by the guardhouses for otherwise, if standing alone, the wall for the support of the arch must have been reinforced in thickness, and to raise the arch and gates without any support and without earth or the guardhouses joined to it will look most odiously and with certainty come down again.* They were also to be secured against damp, to provide accommodation for men or powder[15].

The same configuration, though on a smaller scale, was used for sally ports. These passages provided access to the *base flank* gun batteries, which lay outside the main rampart. Four sally ports lay in the angles where bastions met adjacent curtains. These had small chambers on one or both sides to serve as expense magazines, so that powder required by the gunners could be stored under cover. Double-leaved doors were set at either end and at the mid-point of the passages. A fifth sally port lay at the East Point, with larger magazine chambers on either side. The ends of passages were flanked by brick-built *wings*, which retained the ramparts on either side[16].

The Main Gate and the eastern *base flank* sallyports were built in 1684, being inserted into part-formed ramparts which were to be completed the following year. The larger chambers and passage at East Point are thought to have been work of 1686. The base flank sally ports to the west were built in 1688, being hurriedly inserted into the re-entrant angles of ramparts which had been effectively completed six years before[17].

The digging of foundations was omitted from the contracts for 1684, and was undertaken by Beckman for £50. The trenches contained *planked foundations*, comprising *sleepers and cross-planks* at the Main Gate. The excavation of a sally port built in 1688, on the west of the Citadel, revealed no such provision, perhaps the result of skimped and hurried construction. Planks of 3in. (76mm) pine have been recorded below a wall near South Blockhouse in 1687, and the form of foundation adopted for the casemated features may have been comparable to this[18].

Above the foundations, brick walls were raised. In keeping with their role as supporting elements for the vaults above, the walls of the Guardhouses were contracted to be of battered construction, narrowing by 1ft (c.0.3m) as they rose, *3ft (c.0.9m) in and 6ft (c.1.8m) above the ground*. The support of the arches required *buttments and spandrels* in addition, which were to be brought into the Bill of Overworks. Passage walls elsewhere were of an even thickness. Walls were of coursed brick skins, with mortared rubble cores. Solidly coursed brickwork was used for narrower parts, and at doorways; this may have been the result of breaking into the fabric for the insertion of door cases. At the Main Gate, the walls rose 12ft (c.3.7m) from the foundation to the springing of the arch, and another 3ft (c.0.9m) to the crown of the arch[19].

The facade of the chambers at the Main Gate had a *water table* or damp-course of limestone ashlar at a low level, and internal water tables for the chambers with-

Fig 14: The South or Soldiers' Guardhouse at the Main Gate, looking south-east. The entrance passage is in the foreground; a fireplace is at the mid-point of the wall on the right, and a wing and a small cistern lie at its right-hand corner. From 1988 excavations by the Humberside Archaeology Unit.

Fig 15: An excavated sally port, on the east side of the Citadel, looking from the outer gun positions (flooded) westwards, down the passage. At its midpoint lie twin expense magazines. Scale is 2m long. Photo by D.H. Evans, from 1988 excavations by the Humberside Archaeology Unit.

in. The wings, which were slightly angled, and which rose to meet a stone cornice, were also clad in stone at this level. Stone was used for the decorative framing of the Main Gate with pilasters, and for a curved pediment at both ends of the passage. Similar conventions were followed for the more modest adornment of the sally port doorways. Stone was also used for internal door cases; for chimneys rising from the Guardhouse fireplaces, and for the coping of the wings. The use of *terras* mortar was specified for the pilasters of the Main Gate and for the coping stones, to prevent the infiltration of moisture[20].

Wooden *centering* was required to lay the bricks forming vaults over the passages and chambers, and was also used to form window arches for the Guardhouses. The barrel vaults were intended to be two and a half bricks thick. They were covered externally with bricks set on edge in terras mortar 6in thick. Interior surfaces of arches and chambers were plastered with terras, again to waterproof them; the use of this appropriate material was an afterthought brought into the Bill of Overworks. The chambers were then panelled *with good sound dry deal boards pitched on the backside and fastened with oaken pins to good sound oaken rails of 2 and 3in. (51-76mm) scantling placed 15in.(380mm) distance.* Floors were of large cobbles for the Main Gate passage, 3in. paving slabs for the Guardhouses, and brick-on-edge for other vaults and passages[21].

At the Main Gate, in 1684, the arches were covered with an additional layer of brick in *terras for the securing of the said arches for this winter.* The smaller sally port arches were covered over with clay and turf, to the same end. In 1685, the final covering of the passages with earth formed part of extensive earthworks carried out that year. Here, this entailed the use of light, or single, rammers. Wharton was instructed: *That the arches over the Gate be covered with good clay well mixed with moss, and that you suffer no ramming over the crown of the arches but what the wheelbarrows and men do, and betwixt the arches over the spandrel to ram the earth with those rammers I had made for the purpose the last year[22].*

The internal fittings of the chambers were included in contracts. The door frames, mantle-pieces, table and benches, and even a communal bed 35ft (c.10.7m) long for the Soldiers Guardhouse, were all of oak. The contract for the construction of the Main Gate had provided for the provision of grates and fire irons, so that the chambers could be immediately put to use on their completion. The Royal Arms were to be set up above the entrance, though this formal adornment was incorrectly executed, and was only to be set up and gilded the next year[23].

The great sea wall

The construction of walls along the south side of the Citadel was a most demanding project. The south curtain was to lie along the Humber shore. The two water bastions were actually to project into the river, and the scarp wall was required to follow their course. Though of massive proportions, recorded as over 3.5m thick at the lowest point where they have been seen, these walls formed only an outer skin, protecting the earthworks behind them from tidal erosion. The difficulties presented both by bad ground and the waterside location of the site at Hull only gradually became clear. This prompted significant development in techniques, both for the construction of foundations, and for the walls above them[24].

The foundations for walls were set in trenches. The difficulties of digging these close to the water's edge were first reported in 1684, at the East Point. This *proved very difficult and dangerous work by reason of the bad ground which (being nothing but sand and ooze) founders upon us.* The excavation of trenches here was *very tedious and dangerous work, the ground at the bottom being very bad and springs of water, which makes the earth to shoot down upon them.* Beckman commented: *I have laid a traverse over the moat to hinder the water to get upon us, which it does apace, and we are perfect quagg-trotters.* These difficulties provided a foretaste of what was to be encountered between 1686 and 1688, as the more extensive works along the Humber shore were attempted. Here, problems presented by groundwater were to be exacerbated by the danger of flooding, by high tides, and by the river itself[25].

The trench for the construction of the water bastion of 1688 was to be *460ft* (140m) *long and 35ft (10.7m) broad in full medium and 8ft (2.4m) deep.* The construction trench for the first water bastion, of 1686, for which detailed documentation has not been encountered, was presumably similar. The trenches were protected by earth dams. In June 1686, a dam failed, allowing water to pour into the trenches. *Mr Holton presuming to make a dam with the earth taken out of the foundation to keep out Humber all along the face, which these high spring tides would not suffer him to do, but on Sunday morning broke quite through, and filled up all the trench digged, for the said foundation, all full of water, and broke down the cross dams at the end of the wall at each flanker, and raised the said frames at the west end of the face which must be taken up again.* A dam was constructed in 1687, for the building of the south curtain scarp, though its form is unknown. The dam for the second water bastion was probably more robust than the equivalent structures built in previous years, not least because of its proximity to the confluence of the rivers

Hull and Humber. A massive box of 1½in. (*c*.37mm) plank was to be framed with beams and secured to long piles. Filled with good stiff rammed clay, it was to stand 12ft (3.7m) high and 12ft thick *in the medium*, for a distance of 607ft (185m)[26].

A breakwater jetty was to protect the water bastions from the full force of the Humber tides. Its construction was urged, in 1686, by Beckman, *because all this side of the Humber is a wasting shore, which is occasioned by the point or nose of Lincoln*(shire), *and the sands on that side, in setting the flowing tides directly in this side, which has considerably wasted the ground on this side the Humber, and being very apprehensive, that when the water bastion is carried out into Humber, that the tide meeting with a sudden opposition will in a very short time waste the ground about the point of the bastion and work under the foundation, which cannot lie deeper than 3½ft* (*c*.1.1m) *at the most, and so the whole bastion will be destroyed, which danger to prevent, the said Sir Martin Beckman has proposed a firm jetty, to be made or carried out from the bank down the Humber to 200ft* (*c*.61m) *in length.* It comprised two rows of driven piles, planked on the inside with 2½in. (64mm) oak boards, and bound at the top by a sill let into the top of the piles, and braced with 40 cross-pieces. The jetty was packed with stone, as a similar, if more permanent, structure to the dams safeguarding the shoreline trenches[27].

The breakwater jetty, the dam of 1688 – and perhaps others, though this is less certain – and the waterside walls of the Citadel all depended on driven piles for their long-term stability. The systematic and extensive use of piling was one of the most striking aspects of the works at Hull. This was a standard requirement of 17th-century waterside fortifications, as at Tilbury, where some have been archaeologically recorded. The designs by de Gomme for Portsmouth include systems of piling and framing. Light piles have also been recorded underpinning later medieval buildings in Hull. It was perhaps the density, scale and extent of piling at the Citadel which occasioned comment. In this respect, the building of the Citadel was locally regarded as an unprecedented enterprise. The 18th-century historian, Thomas Gent, commented how the fortifications were *founded upon large piles, the entire bulks of trees, drove into the earth very deep, joined close together, which took up a great number: the expense of these stupendous works cost above one hundred thousand pounds.* The soft ground encountered along the Humber shore meant that every element of waterside works was to require piled foundations[28].

Piling required heavy specialised gear. At its simplest, this comprised a substan-tial wooden frame, a weight (termed *bell* or *beetle*) to hammer the piles, and ropes and pulleys. The latter would be necessary for teams of men to lift the weight, and then to drop it, for each strike on the pile. The progress of the pile slowed as it reached stable ground; Sir Jonas Moore reckoned: *A 16-hand bell-beetle will not at last drive above half an inch at a stroke or less, if the bottom of the pile comes to touch the firm ground.* In 1683, the equipment left on site at the end of the works included one *beetles and frame for driving piles.* In 1684, *to save charges the carpenter is about borrowing the town's gyn* (engine – a generic term for machinery, in this case for piling). The overseers of piling work in 1685 were to *reassure every particular pile before it be placed or at placing thereof in the gyn or under the bootoll and that they have their due scantling and that no pile be longer than 21ft* (6.4m) *and no shorter than 20ft* (6.1m), *which is a due length for this ground*[29].

An estimate for the breakwater jetty of 1686 is the first source to detail the procedures followed for piling on the Humber shore. It demanded: *192 piles of 26ft* (7.9m) *long, 14in by 12in* (355 by 300mm) *square at the great end shod with iron and driven with a bell of 8cwt to 16ft* (4.9m) *deep.* The contract for the water bastion of 1688 was similarly thorough in its specification of the necessary gear. Having set out the dimensions of piles, the contract required they *shall be drove down with a gyn, whose bell will be no less than nine hundred or one thousand* (408-450kg) *weight, and every pile shall be shod at one end with iron of seven and twelve pound* (3.2-5.4kg) *weights.* A *cuff pile* or collar was to guide the piles on their true course[30].

The first waterside work at Hull was the construction of the Platform adjacent to South Blockhouse, probably in 1682. A detailed design for its foundation occurs in an estimate of July 1682; it is not known whether this was followed in detail. Initially, about 36 piles of 6-18ft (1.8-5.5m) in length were to be driven. They were to be of fir, elm or oak; the longest of 12in by 10in (300 by 250mm) scantling, and the shortest 8in by 6in (200 by 150mm). Once the piles had been driven, a rectangular frame 11ft wide, of fir or oak beams, was to be attached to their protruding heads. The frame was to comprise three *ranging baulks* of 9in by 12in (230 by 300mm) scantling laid along the line of the Platform wall, and cross-pieces set every 6ft. Clay was to be rammed between the timbers, which were then to be covered with 3in. (76mm) oak planks nailed down with 7in. (180mm) spikes. Two or three wooden rails were then to be nailed to the planks, *to hinder the wall from sliding.* The whole foundation was to be two or three inches higher at the front, so that any slippage would be towards the land, rather than out onto the Humber foreshore[31].

Fig 16: East Point: "aerial" view from a crane. East Point (built 1684) is to the left; the right side of the V-shaped re-entrant is the first water bastion (1686), capped by an upper wall (1690). From 1988 excavations by the Humberside Archaeology Unit.

Fig 17: The building of a sea wall: an imaginary view which illustrates the staged construction of a water bastion at Hull, behind a dam (right). A *gyn* (foreground) drives piles; a lattice of timber beams over these is capped with planks, on top of which the wall and its buttresses are built.

Fig 18: The sea wall. Left: Part of the face of the south curtain (built 1687). Right: The upper face and cordon of the second water bastion (1688); lower blocks are held to each other by iron cramps. Scales 2m and 1m long. From 1988 excavations by the Humberside Archaeology Unit.

An estimate for work at East Point was presented at the same time. This envisaged 26 piles, 8 to 12ft (2.4-3.7m) in length. These were to support a frame 10ft (3.1m) in width. The contract for this work, however, of May 1683, increased these specifications in every respect. There were to be 30 piles of 19ft (5.8m) long for every rod (c.2.7m). The frame was to be 19ft wide at its eastern end, narrowing to 12ft wide beyond, with another 26 piles for the rest. The frame was to be lifted at the front by 5in. (127mm). Rubble was to be pounded between the elements of the frame. When the work was actually done, in 1684, an extra 47 piles of 20 to 26ft (6.1-7.9m) long and 9 extra ranging baulks were required for the wider part, and 27 more piles and 8 sleepers for the narrower part. The 8ft piles, which had been envisaged as adequate for the support of buttresses behind the wall, were replaced with piles 20ft long. The increased cost - of £99 2s - arose *from the badness of the ground requiring stronger foundations*[32].

The contract for the first water bastion, of 1686, has not been encountered, but Beckman's instructions to Wharton proposed even denser piling *if the face do prove worse ground than the bastion and northern flanks*. There were to be 40 piles for every rod distance, arranged in five rows, with 10 piles in the front row, 9 in the second, 8 in the third, and so on. This would appear to have intended the exploitation of differential settlement: if structural movement did occur, the wall would settle back against the rampart, rather than toppling outwards into the Humber. The intervals of the frame were to be filled with rammed stone and wood fragments, rather than clay. The frame was also to be protected from infiltrating groundwater: *That no water may run under the foundation, which if it does the whole foundation will be destroyed and consequently the whole work... (a terras mortar) wall must be laid to limit the timber, as is ordered before the foundation so that all the back of the wall be laid in terras half a brick deep only to keep out the backwater till the work is closed; and that as fast as the foundation advances to raise the wall and the clay rammed close to the work that no water may stand near the foundation*[33].

The contract for the second water bastion, of 1688, specified the use of even longer piles: of 26 to 30ft (7.9-9.1m) in length. A width of 13ft (c.4m) was prescribed for the timber frame above them. Wet soil was to be dug out to a depth of 18in. (460mm) round the pile heads and replaced with good clay. There were to be five rows of ranging baulks, which were to be forced down over the piles and into the clay, being morticed to the pile heads if necessary. Cross-baulks were then to be dovetailed with the ranging baulks, being pounded down with wooden mallets. They were to lie 29in. (736mm) apart, more than doubling the density envisaged for the Saluting Platform, only six years earlier. Timber planks 3in. (76mm) thick were then to be nailed over the frame, with three rows of 6in. (152mm) oak *ribbons* spiked to them. A *terras berm* was then to seal the foundation[34].

The brickwork of the scarp walls was built on the level surface provided by the planked capping of timber-framed foundations. This was again to be subject to increasingly rigorous specification. Elements of the scarp have been revealed by excavations at nine points along the south side of the Citadel, and matched the contracts in most discernible aspects. The most striking features of these walls were, firstly, their sheer size, and secondly, the facing of pale, finely-cut limestone ashlar[35].

Beckman initially opined: *that brickwork faced with terras mortar will stand as long and well as the stonework, especially where it cannot be pressed by the violence of the sea, which would lessen this Estimate* (for the Platform of 1682) *to £1,500.* In response to criticism of his designs, in 1683, he stressed this aspect of the site, perhaps in the light of more recent observation. *I have not estimated the brickworks generally through at £6 10s per rod* (2.7m) *but only such walls who requires a great strength to resist the great weight of the earth on the inside and the violent oppression of the sea on the other side, especially at easterly and southerly high winds, which walls requires to be raised with such mortar as is mentioned in my first paragraph of my estimates for Hull... The tide will rise from 4 to 8ft in neap tide and at spring tides from 8 to 12 or 13ft* (2.4-3.7m or 4m) *perpendicular upon these walls which is to be made on the waterside; which is not so much upon any wall now standing near the seaside in England, and when high easterly or southerly winds do arise there must be a sufficient wall to resist the great force the water will produce, which no wall which is yet made at Portsmouth or elsewhere in England will be able to resist especially if the walls should be raised with mortar made of salt water and sand and weak lime*[36].

The Platform was duly built, though no detailed record of its construction has been encountered. It may have occupied a relatively sound parcel of ground close to South Blockhouse. Conditions were worse at East Point. Here, a brick wall was built with separate buttresses or *counterforts* attached behind it – contracts use the colloquial *buttress* rather than the technically correct term of *counterfort*. The terminal of the wall was markedly widened. This was to permit the raising of an elevated look-out at its end. It also supported the earthwork scarp of the eastern defences of the Citadel, which met it on its north-western side. The wall and the buttresses comprised thick skins of coursed brickwork retaining mortared rubble cores. The lower extent of the wall was faced with ashlar. These conventions were followed for subsequent works. The buttresses at East Point, however, were seen to have parted from the wall when revealed by excavation[37].

Later waterside works at Hull saw the contemporary raising of counterforts and walls, to form a single unified structural unit. Larger counterforts were used close to points where the works of one year were to meet those of another, or at salient angles. They were also to be more closely spaced at such vulnerable points. This unity of counterforts and walls is suggested by an enquiry of 1686, which identified a *breach where this fault was found was about 2ft (0.6m) within the buttress and about 3ft (0.9m) into the body of the wall.* It is also implied by the inclusion of *walls* and *buttresses* within a single article of the water bastion contract of 1688[38].

The East Point wall rose as a vertical elevation at the back, and was slightly battered on its outer face; the adjoining element of the water bastion of 1686 appears to have matched it. The design of walls along the curtain built in 1687 is not specified by the documentary sources, but was revealed by excavation. The whole wall was battered front and rear, so as to lie against the rampart behind it. As with the graduated piling enjoined on Wharton the year before, this design ensured that any settlement would enhance the cohesion of the wall and the earthworks behind it. It is also possible that rectangular cavities in the wall were intended to permit localised structural movement to occur without fracturing an extensive run of walling. These may have been a particular precautionary measure favoured by Beckman for his waterside works; a more regular system of triangular cavities was a feature of his work at Clifford's Fort, Tynemouth[39].

Such a canted construction demanded the immediate back-filling of the construction trench. A similar technique was employed for a brick wall built along the flank and face of the west bastion. This was probably that wall recorded as being built to prop up South Blockhouse, also in 1687. The filling of the trench behind the wall required the same level of care as the construction of self-supporting earthworks. Lieutenant Holt was instructed: *That you diligently and carefully see that the earth be very well rammed close to the berm and facing of the scarp (viz.) That for 6ft (1.8m) from the facing of the scarp, the earth be laid loose 4in. (c.100mm) deep well chopped and rammed to 2in, the rest to the extreme of the glacis rammed from 8in. to 4in. (c.200-100mm); the same ramming to be continued on the inside of the wall*

next to the wall between the counterforts for 10ft (3.1m) wide, and the rest of the earth from 12 to 6in. (366-183mm), taking especial care that no wet clay or earth be rammed next to the wall either on the in or outside, for 10 or 12ft (3.1-3.7m) distance from the same[40].

The waterside walls were composite constructions, and the contract for the second water bastion reveals measures taken to waterproof the structure, and to prevent its disintegration. The contract also sought to ensure the use of the best and most appropriate materials. It required: *well wrought mortar made with Knottingley stone lime, fresh water and Paul sand... at every course of bricks in the whole thickness of the wall, for 6ft (1.8m) high from the foundation and from there upward to the top for 6ft deep in the wall from the facing inwards and for the rest every fourth course, as also the whole range of works in hand shall be puttied and levelled with mortar and the nearest front of the wall shall be wrought with the choicest and best burnt bricks six bricks deep.* The basal courses were to be of solidly coursed brick, with the upper parts of hollow, but robust, construction packed with a mortared rubble core. Bricks nearest the front were to be laid in terras mortar[41].

The same level of attention was paid to the stone facing attached to the brickwork. This was to have *a bedding from 8 to 12in. (c.200-300mm) deep in the wall, well bedded in terras and those jointed, cramped with iron 9in. (229mm) long, 1½in (38mm) broad and wide 1⅜in. thick, the hooks in both ends shall go 1¼in deep in the ashlar and these to be well fastened with lead and that every 6ft (1.8m) distance be laid an entire bondstone of 3ft (0.91m) deep in the wall and in even course with the facing continued in every course.* The *bondstones* were closer together than those required at the Platform, which lay 9ft apart (2.7m); and than those at East Point, which were 10ft (3.1m) apart. Excavation revealed that, in so far as the fabric was exposed, these demanding specifications were met in every respect[42].

These ashlar-faced walls usually rose to a height of 15ft (4.6m). At this level they were surmounted by a bull-nosed cordon or *water table* of ashlar, a form which occurred throughout the range of bastioned fortifications. By convention, the cordon often denoted a change in angle from a lower, battered, scarp to a vertical parapet, and was set at the same level as the internal *terreplein*, the surface upon which defenders and their guns would stand. Above the cordon, brick walls were built. These were intended to rise another 12ft (3.7m), but were completed only at East Point, in 1684; elsewhere they achieved a maximum height of about 6ft (1.8m). At East Point, a lower cordon divided stone and brick-faced elevations, while an upper cordon marked the base of the parapet. Elsewhere, a single cordon divided the upper and lower scarp without a change in its angle. The brick walls were faced in Flemish bond, a form favoured for visible elevations throughout the Citadel, though the bonding of corridor walls, or brickwork masked by earth, might be either irregular, or in English bond. English bond had been used for the Henrician defences in the 1540s, and was considered especially appropriate to engineering or military usage because of its reputation for strength[43].

The contract for the completion of the southern scarp with brickwork in 1690 was a very short one. There, 2,617ft (798m) of brickwork was required, to a height of 6ft (1.8m) and a thickness of 9ft (2.7m). There were to be 131 *buttresses* behind it, and their cores could be filled with *cross stones at the back of the wall -* clay packing appeared in some which were exposed by excavation. The facing bricks were to be laid in terras to the depth of a brick and a half. *Angle stones* would mark salient points, with pale limestone providing a contrast with the adjacent brick elevations. All this was to rise *atop of the water table upon the great wall on the Humber side*, and was to be backed with an earth rampart. This was to rise above the level of the wall, with a sloping top, a form technically described as *demi-revetted*, or partially supported. At the end of the year, even Beckman was satisfied; *the finishing of the ramparts towards the Humber or the sea (which wants yet 5½ft [1.7m] of its height) may safely be laid aside till the works be first finished towards the land*[44].

Water all around

The control of water was a vital aspect of the works on the low-lying site at Hull. Drainage, and removal of groundwater, were essential features of every campaign of construction. Once the wide ditches surrounding the Citadel had been begun, these could play a role in carrying water away. Sluices were built between the Citadel moat and the river Hull. At first these were temporary features: control of water levels in the ditch was initially necessary to facilitate the works. A permanent sluice was subsequently built to control and maintain water levels in the ditch, and hence to keep the fortifications in a defensible state.

Immediately west of the Citadel, rickety wooden revetments supported the bank of the river Hull. The poor condition of the riverbank here led to a protracted dispute with the Hull Bench, who sought to evade the cost of its upkeep. To the

east, the banks along the Humber shore required intermittent repair to prevent the site of the Citadel from flooding at the highest tides. Once the ramparts were raised, their stability could also be compromised by surface water standing within the Citadel. A network of *shores* or drains was required to lead it away. This in its turn required extensive levelling and paving, so that water would find its way into the drains, and thence out into the moat.

The first labourers to arrive on the site in 1681 were *set to work to cast up a trench for the conveyance of the water we shall meet with, when the ground is broken*. The year's works entailed the digging of ditches, to a maximum depth of 12ft (3.7m). These inevitably collected groundwater, and flooded. The first operation on site, in early February 1682, was *to repair the sluice to draw off the water*. This was a temporary fixture, whose construction was intended to permit other works to proceed. It took water from the site into the river Hull, to the west. Beckman wrote to the Board in July 1682, *touching a trunk to be made for carrying off the water*. Daniel Green was provided with advances of £10 and £5 for *making a new trunk to carry the water out of the graft into the Haven*, in October, and ironworks were delivered for the new trunk in November. This first stage was completed in December at an overall cost of £41 14s[45].

The temporary *trunk* was removed in 1683; the bank where it had stood was solidly revetted within by angled piles 10in. (254mm) apart, lined with 2in. (51mm) oak planks; earth was then to be rammed to a thickness of 30ft (9.1m) beyond the piles. Its collapse, in 1684, would demand Beckman's immediate intervention: *to strike on the inside 12 piles of 18ft (5.5m) long and line them with double deals and…200 labourers to wheel clay and stone to prevent a perfect breach; this work will cost about £35.* A week later, Joseph Blaides was driving piles to secure a dam here[46].

In April 1683, *we are making a dam to keep out the Haven water in order to lay the trunk. A contract for a trunk for conveyance for the water out of the graft into the haven* was drawn up with Blaides. This was to be a substantial sluice, rising from sill beams, and set into well-consolidated ground. It would not only serve to carry water away during building work, but would afterwards control the level of water in the moat. It was to *be laid 5ft (1.5m) lower than the moat of the new fortification is for the present… see that between the sleepers be well filled and rammed with limestone and rubbish clay and as soon as the trunk is laid to fit dry clay well minced (a) little at a time that is not above 6in. thick and then well rammed… and the same observations when the wings of the same sluice or trunk is placed and that small stakes of 4 or 5ft* (1.2 or 1.5m) *long be driven down 12ft* (3.7m) *broad before the end of the wings and limestone rammed down in the clay, first great and flat stones and between the intervals small ones and that the earth above the trunk be at least so high as any part of the dyke now is at either side.* As, however, *since the trunk is taken 5ft down since Major Beckman left the place and the ground proves worse than when he left it we* (the Board) *do now therefore leave that to you* (the Commissioners) *and the engineer to contrive the best way for a sufficient foundation and the cheapest way you can get it done*[47].

Wings at the inner, moat, end of the sluice had been built by the end of August, though the construction of the outer wings, in the banks of the river Hull, had not been begun. Duxbury was left instructions for *a dam to be made to secure the tide from breaching in.* Blaides declined to begin this work on the outer wings so late in the year, a decision taken in the light of his knowledge of conditions on the river Hull which the local builder Catlyn supported[48].

The next year, *the Commissioners thought it very necessary to have the left wing of the trunk finished this dry season which will cost £79 19s 5 ½d for carpenters work, besides earthwork which is computed to about £60.* Beckman considered the completion of the sluice vital to the drainage of construction trenches, as well as for its future use: *I intend... to finish the sluice on which all our fortune (as well as the Point we are now about) here depends.* This was agreed by the Board. In August 1684, *Mr Blaide the carpenter is now driving the piles for the outer wing.* It was ready in October, when Wharton was instructed: *That the remaining clay before the sluice be removed that the water may have a free passage in and out of the moat.* With the sluice fully operational, the water could be freely drained from the moat. The instructions for Wharton in 1685 set out his first task: *That you open the trench that leads to the sluice or trunks that all the water now in the moat may freely run off, taking care you go not by two feet* (0.6m) *too deep as the trunk lays; and when the water is off, to dam up that narrow passage where the long curtain is cut through*[49].

The wings of the sluice were fixed to the timber revetments along the east bank of the river Hull. The cost *For repairing the banks and jettyworks on the Haven and Humber side* was £13 12s 10d in 1682. Beckman ascribed the collapse of the river bank at Fitch's old sluice to the Bench's neglect, *for the town of Hull takes no more care of its banks, though they ruin it with their cables and anchors.* The Bench was forced to accept responsibility for the repair of revetments along the banks of the river Hull. They did this reluctantly, under threat of losing their Charter, which was only renewed with the relevant clauses added[50].

The union of the town's jettyworks with the new sluice was specified by a contract with Blaides. He was to build *two counter wings for the sluice to join the breastwork which the Corporation will now go in hand with, each wing will extend to 28 or 29ft* (8.5 or 8.8m) *in length, the piles, planks and landties must be of oak, and of the same scantling as those wings that now joins the trunk or sluice.* These were substantial works, entailing 20 piles, planks, tie-beams and ironwork, at an overall cost of £147 6s. The mouth of the sluice in the bank of the river Hull was again to be consolidated. Beckman instructed Wharton: *That you cause immediately stakes of 9 or 10ft* (2.7 or 3.1m) *long to be struck down from the mouth of the sluice down to low water - about 9 or 10in.* (229-305mm) *one from another - about 8ft* (2.4m) *wide, and as fast as the mud is taken away* (?)*from the stakes to ram down... chalk stones and rubbish, and that square and flat stones be laid nearest the mouth very close, and to fill up the small holes or vacancies with small* (?stones)[51].

Duxbury commented: *I believe the wings* (of the sluice) *are so firm, that it cannot be damnified but by their jetty work which, they perceiving now to give way, and bends in and out like a wrinkling nob, makes them more fearful and backward to sign.* The Bench fought an unsuccessful delaying action against accepting responsibility for their embankments. Beckman returned the draft Charter with the necessary articles added, which granted the Bench £18 a year out of the customs of Hull for their upkeep of the banks. The Mayor had dropped dead of a palsy in his shop; and his successor, Alderman Johnston, *being very ill he something delayed their writing.* Five days later, the Mayor was *still so very bad of the gout that he cannot get to the Hall, where there must be a public meeting before any answer can be given.* Two weeks later: *the Corporation will not consent to sign those articles sent down from the Board, but are resolved to cut off their jetty from the wings of the trunk and Mr Mayor without the advice of his brethren (who did that work without his advice or consent) has agreed with Mr Blaides to secure these works cost what it will, for Cataline* (a loaded reference to the builder Catlyn) *will be no more employed, but Mr Mayor is loth to begin upon it without your advice.* The repair of the embankments by the Corporation was under way late in March 1686. Beckman was still engaged in surveys arising from this long-running dispute in 1690[52].

Work on the sluice and in other deep excavations required the use of water pumps. In 1684, Duxbury *agreed for a new pump, which will be done this day and the maker is to finish ironworks and all fixed for 50s, and to serve it, for 4 years, if it fails he is to change it, which with the labourers works to pump out the water will come to £3.* The pump was *well fixed at the mouth of the new trunk, and we have pumped out all* the water which floods there. In August 1684, payment was recorded for two *pumps brought for the use of the works*. These were moveable, and could be turned to various uses; in October labourers were *employed about pumping the water out of the Citadel over the Humber bank from the 13 October to the 18th following*[53].

Flooding from the Humber threatened extensive damage, particularly to the eastern works which gathered pace in 1685. Repairs on the Humber banks in early 1685 entailed a 200ft (c.61m) length of timber jetty works and banks. Further work on the banks was estimated to require timber-work to the value of £10 18s, and £12 9s 4 ½d for earth-moving. The Board ordered the repairs to be done. The Commissioners contracted Theophilus Robinson and John Shields to do the first stage, for £12 4s 6d. The appointment of Duxbury to the Storekeeper's post, in June 1685, meant that there would henceforward be a competent officer of the Board on the spot year-round. Instructions for the year's works stipulated: *That the jetties or breastworks on the Humber be carefully looked after, and by time repaired after any breach therein, having first given (if time permits)... Lord Dartmouth... a particular account thereof.* The equivalent instruction for 1688 would confer greater initiative on the authorities on the spot: *That it be immediately repaired without staying for any order from the Board, but that the Commissioners of the place be acquainted therewith, whose orders you are punctually to observe*[54].

The drainage of surface water within the Citadel entailed the construction of an extensive network of underground drains. Most flowed into the moat. They have been encountered by excavations at the Main Gate; below the floor of the south-eastern sally port passage; leading through the Henrician curtain wall and across the south-western *base flank*; and at the north-western *base flank*. They have been noted above at South Blockhouse and the Castle. Major conduits also figure on the Phillips plan of the Citadel, in 1716, and are probably primary features. In addition, a drain led from the Governor's House. Although rebuilt in the 19th century, this may have served as a domestic sewer, and was probably originally of 17th-century date. The relationship of these channels to each other remains uncertain. With the discovery of so many short lengths, in various locations, it is often difficult to firmly relate their construction to specific documentary sources[55].

Beckmann offered an estimate *for a common shore* of £184 11s 1d in 1683. The contract for its construction the same year specified a brick-built length of 222ft (c.68m), a height of 3½ft (1.1m) to the crown of the arch and a width of 2ft (0.61m). The arch was to be made with Knottingley lime mortar, and the bricks within were to be laid in 3in. (76mm) of terras. The foundation was to be of small rammed rubble capped with Knottingley lime mortar, filling a trench 10ft (3.1m) wide, and paved with 4in. (c.100mm) stone slabs. The outfall was to be stone-paved, with a caulked plank spout, and was secured with an iron grate[56].

The design of drains required in response to localised flooding shows that their specifications might be subject to extensive revision. *As for the drain through South Blockhouse it must be 48 or 50ft (14.6 or 15.3m) in length to be brought through the old guardhouse and so through the west wall of the said house into the moat. The wideness to be from the guardhouse to the west wall of the said house 18in. (c.460mm) within and 2ft (0.61m) high from the upper side of the vault to the under side of the arch and the sides to be a brick in length at each end of the said vault to be a sufficient grate of iron to be let into stone. And through the west wall of the said house to be 10in (254mm) square* which will here be undertaken by one Richard Roebuck for £15 if he finds all materials, but if we find bricks as we have enough of our own he will (do it for) 40s. Beckman revised this initial design, arriving at an estimated cost of £91 18s 6d, including materials. This was to be 140ft (42.7m) long, 2ft high, 1ft (0.31m) wide in the clear, flagged, with an arch and lining in 3in. (76mm) of terras mortar, and the rest with Knottingley lime, on a foundation rammed 9in. (229mm) deep with stone. A cistern or manhole in the middle of the Blockhouse court was to be 15in. (381mm) square[57].

The construction of this drain by Fitch's men was in progress in July 1684. It is clear that this drain was to empty onto the Humber shore, rather than into the moat. In April 1685, Duxbury reported: *That new drain through South Blockhouse is blown up, and the arch broken, so that every high tide coming into the house. There is a spring of water within the old guardrooms near the staircase at South Blockhouse next the wall, which at every tide bubbles up water very fast, I can thrust a stick in 4 or 5ft (1.2 or 1.5m) long, which is all like a bog, and I fear the water soaks under the foundation of the house and it may be the cause of its settling so much, for there are several great cracks all along the staircase from the top to the bottom. It was subsequently repaired*[58].

The direction of water into the drains required extensive levelling. The South Blockhouse drain had been served by over 1,000 square yards (836m²) of paving in the west bastion, at the cost of over £120. In 1686, following emergency repairs over winter involving the support of sagging ramparts and the insertion of drainage spouts, this was accomplished by the wheeling of earth into the Citadel. This cost over £60[59].

A final aspect of water management was its provision for the use of the Garrison. This topic does not figure in the documentation viewed to date. However, the Main Gate was flanked by modest cisterns fed by rainwater from the top of the rampart or from the roof of the gate passage. Later surveys described three cisterns in the angles of the South Blockhouse, with a combined capacity of about 36,000 gallons (163,656 litres). These may have been supplied by *an engine fixed at Hull to make salt water fresh*, which is first recorded in 1690. Its position, near the South Blockhouse, is indicated by the Phillips Plan of 1716[60].

Footnotes

1: Bod. Lib. Rawl. A475, Orders of Commissioners, 14 April 1683; PRO WO46:1, 347, Beckman to Lloyd, 17 April 1683; PRO WO46:2, 54, Instructions for Wharton, 15 October 1684; pers. comm. Andrew Saunders.

2: PRO WO55/1785, Contract, 10 August 1681; PRO WO46:1, 352, Duxbury to Board, 2 April 1683; Bod. Lib. Rawl. A475, Duxbury to Board, 16 September 1685; PRO WO46:1, 347, Beckman to Lloyd, 17 April 1683; Bod. Lib. Rawl. A475, n.d..

3: PRO WO46:1, 347, Beckman to Lloyd, 17 April 1683; PRO WO46:2, Watkinson to Board, 31 July 1683; Bod. Lib. Rawl. A476, item 1, Duxbury to Board, 25 June 1684; *ibid.*, Duxbury to Lloyd, 25 June 1684.

4: PRO WO55/1785, Contract, 24 March 1683; Bod. Lib. Rawl. A475, 15/6/1683; Bod. Lib. Rawl. A476, item 1, Orders of Commissioners, 25 June 1683; PRO WO55/519, Board to Commissioners, 11 April 1688.

5: Foreman and Goodhand 1997, 147-53; Brit. Lib. Egerton Ms. 3359, fo. 1; PRO WO78/1378 (1), profiles of the Citadel ramparts.

6: PRO WO46:2, 227, Commissioners to Board, 25 June 1684; Bod. Lib. Rawl. A476, item 1, Duxbury to Board, 25 June 1684.

7: e.g. PRO WO55/519, Order of Commissioners, 6 October 1686; Bod. Lib. Rawl. A475, Duxbury to Board, 31 May 1686; PRO WO55/1785, Contract, 29 March 1688.

8: PRO WO55/519, Commissioners to Board, 21 November 1687; PRO WO46:1, 310, Duxbury to Board, 5 October 1681; PROWO55/519, Commissioners to Board, postscript, 2 June 1685; e.g. PRO WO46:2, 301, Beckman to Board, 12 December 1684; PRO WO55/1785, Contract, 13 March 1690; PRO WO46:1, 347, Beckman to Lloyd, 17 April 1683; *ibid.*, 335, Duxbury to Board, 2 October 1682.

9: Woodward 1984, 107; PRO WO55/519, Instructions to Wharton, 2 June 1685.

10: PRO WO46:1, 318, Beckman to Board, 26 November 1681; *ibid.*, 319, Beckman to Board, 3 December 1681; Foreman 1998, 66-7; Foreman and Goodhand 1997, 178.

11: PRO WO55/519, Instructions to Wharton, 2 June 1685; PRO WO46:2, 317, Contract, 7 July 1684; Bod. Lib. Rawl. A475, 21, Duxbury to Board, 29 June 1685.

12: Bod. Lib. Rawl. A475, Commissioners to Board, 16 May 1683; *ibid.*, Orders of Commissioners, 23 April 1683; Foreman and Goodhand 1997, 147-153; PRO WO46:1, 347, Beckman to Lloyd,17 April 1683; Bod. Lib. Rawl. A475, Duxbury to Board, 5 August 1685; *ibid.*, Orders of Commissioners, 4 May 1683; PRO WO55/519, Order of Commissioners, 30 October 1686.

13: Foreman and Goodhand 1997, 178; Foreman 1988; Stafford Record Office D (W) 1778/V/64(52), Lambert's Accounts, 28 October 1682; e.g. Gent 1735; PRO MPH554, plan *c*.1807.

14: PRO WO46:2, Watkinson to Board, 31 July 1683; *ibid.* (index), 303, Estimates, 12 May 1685; Bod. Lib. Rawl. A476, item 1, Certificate, 9 April 1685; PRO WO55/519, Commissioners to Board, 21 November 1687.

15: PRO WO46:1, 232, Beckman to de Gomme, 26 April 1683, punctuation slightly amended.

16: Foreman and Goodhand 1997.

17: Foreman and Goodhand 1997, 150-1, 165-6, 179-80, fig. 4.

18: PRO WO46:2, 225, Beckman to Board, 16 June 1684; *ibid.*, 327, Certificate, 29 January 1685; *ibid.*, 334, Certificate, 29 January 1685; Foreman and Goodhand 1997, 179-80; Foreman 1998, 11, 67.

19: PRO WO55/1785, Contract, 24 May 1683; PRO WO46:2, 331 *et seq.*, Certificate, 29 January 1685; Foreman and Goodhand 1997, 167-73; PRO WO46:2, 334, Certificate, 29 January 1685; *ibid.*, 327, Certificate, 29 January 1685.

20: PRO WO46:2, Certificate, 19 January 1685; Foreman and Goodhand 1997; PRO WO55/1785, Contract 24 May 1683.

21: PRO WO46:2, 334, Certificate, 29 January 1685; *ibid.*, 285, Wharton to Board, 18 October 1684; *ibid.*, 327, Certificate, 29 January 1685; PRO WO55/1785, Contract 24 May 1683.

22: PRO WO46:2, 334, Certificate, 29 January 1685; *ibid.*, 301, Beckman to Board, 12 December 1684; PRO WO55/519, Instruction to Wharton, 2 June 1685.

23: PRO WO55/1785, Contract, 24 May 1683; Bod. Lib. Rawl. A475, 21, Duxbury to Plymouth, 29 June 1685.

24: Foreman and Goodhand 1997, 160.

25:     PRO WO46:2, 231, Duxbury to Board, 12 July 1684; *ibid.*, 239, Duxbury to Board, 22 July 1684; *ibid.*, 230, Beckman to Board, 9 July 1684.

26:     PRO WO55/1785, Contract, 29 March 1688; Bod. Lib. Rawl. A475, Duxbury to Board, 30 June 1686; PRO WO55/519, Instruction to Wharton, 3 June 1687.

27:     PRO WO55/519, Commissioners to Board, 17 May 1686; Stafford Record Office, D (W) 1778/I:/1171, Contract, 14 June 1686.

28:     Pers. comm. Andrew Saunders, Patricia Wilkinson; Gent 1735, 178.

29:     PRO WO46:2, Watkinson to Board, 31 July 1683; *ibid.*, 242, Beckman to Board, 23 July 1684; Moore 1673, 76; PRO WO55/519, Instruction to Duxbury, 21 May 1686.

30:     PRO WO55/1785, Contract 29 March 1688.

31:     PRO WO46:1, 220, Estimate, 18 July 1682; Foreman 1997, 60-1.

32:     Foreman and Goodhand 1997, 161-2; PRO WO55/1785, Contract, 24 May 1683; PRO WO46:2, 331, Certificate, 29 January 1685.

33:     Foreman and Goodhand 1997, 165; PRO WO55/519, Instruction to Wharton, 22 May 1686.

34:     PRO WO55/1785, Contract, 19 March 1688.

35:     Foreman and Goodhand 1997, fig. 5; Foreman 1997; Tibbles 1999.

36:     PRO WO46:1, 329, Beckman to Board, 19 July 1682; *ibid.*, 232, Beckman to de Gomme, 26 April 1683.

37:     Foreman 1997, 15, 60-1; Foreman and Goodhand 1997, 160-5.

38:     Foreman and Goodhand 1997, 155-65; PRO WO55/519, Commissioners' Enquiry, 1 October 1686; PRO WO55/1785, Contract, 29 March 1688.

39:     Foreman and Goodhand 1997, 160-5, fig.8, 157-60.

40:     Foreman 1998, 67-8; PRO WO55/519, Instructions to Holt, 3 June 1687.

41:     PRO WO55/1785, Contract, 29 March 1688.

42:     PRO WO46:1, 220, Estimate, 18 July 1682; PRO WO55/1785, Contract, 24 March 1683; Foreman and Goodhand 1997, 155-60.

43:     PRO WO44/100/HK5970 X19, Beckman to Board, 10 December 1690; Foreman and Goodhand 1997; Foreman 1997.

44:     PRO WO55/1785, Contract, 13 March 1690; Foreman and Goodhand 1997, 160; PRO WO44/100/HK5970 X19, Beckman to Board, 10 December 1690.

45:     PRO WO46:1, 307, Beckman to Board, 7 September 1681; *ibid.* (index), 287, 13 July 1682; Stafford Record Office D (W) 1778/V/64(52), Lambert's Accounts, 7 October 1682, 18 November 1682, 4 November 1682, 11 November 1682; Stafford Record Office D (W) 1778/V/64(51), Abstract of Payments, 9 December 1682.

46:     Foreman and Goodhand 1997, 147-9; PRO WO46:1, 322, Duxbury to Board, 7 February 1682; PRO WO46:1, 347, Instructions to Lloyd, 17 April 1683; PRO WO46:2, 256, Beckman to Board, 13 September 1684; *ibid.*, 52, Orders of Commissioners, 17 September 1684.

47:     PRO WO46:1, 352, Duxbury to Board, 1 April 1683; *ibid.* (index), 244, Contracts, 14 April 1683; PRO WO46:2, 347, Instructions to Lloyd, 17 April 1683; Bod. Lib. Rawl. A475, Board to Commissioners, 12 May 1683.

48:     PRO WO46:2, 89, Particular by Lloyd, 30 August 1683; PRO WO46:2 (index), 175-6, Letters from Hull, 24 September 1683.

49:     PRO WO46:1, 231, Duxbury to Board, 12 July 1684; PRO WO46:2, 230, Beckman to Board, 9 July 1684; *ibid.*, 27, Orders of Board, 15 July 1684; *ibid.*, 246, Duxbury to Board, 4 August 1684; *ibid.*, 54, Instructions to Wharton, 15 October 1684; PRO WO55/519, Instructions to Wharton, 2 June 1685.

50:     Stafford Record Office D (W) 1778/V/64(51), Abstract of Payments, 9 December 1682; PRO WO46:2, 256, Beckman to Board, 13 September 1684; PRO WO55/519, Orders of Commissioners, Beckman to Board, various letters 1685-86.

51:     PRO WO55/519, Commissioners to Board, postscript, 2 June 1685; *ibid.*, Commissioners to Mason, 4 July 1685; *ibid.*, Instruction to Wharton, 2 June 1685.

52:     Bod. Rawl. A475, Duxbury to Beckman, 15 February 1686; *ibid.*, Duxbury to Board, 3 February 1686; *ibid.*, Duxbury to Beckman, 20 February 1686; *ibid.*, Duxbury to Board, 22 March 1686; Chancery Judgement 1860, 20, 5 October 1690; KUHRO M393, L1126, L1128.

53:     Bod. Lib. Rawl. A476, item 1, 5, Duxbury to Board, 16 April 1684; *ibid.*, Duxbury to Board, 28 April 1684; PRO WO46:2, 60, Commissioners to Mason, 16 August 1684; *ibid.* 67, 18 October 1684.

54:     Bod. Lib. Rawl. A476, item 1, Estimate, 13 April 1685; PRO WO55/519, Board to Commissioners, 18 April 1685; *ibid.*, Commissioners to Board, 27 April 1685; *ibid.*, Instructions to Wharton, 2 June 1685; *ibid.*, Instructions to Duxbury, 20 March 1688.

55:     Foreman and Goodhand 1997; Foreman 1996; Foreman 1998a; e.g. Foreman and Goodhand 1997, 178.

56:     Stafford Record Office D (W) 1778/V/68, Estimate, 1683; PRO WO55/1785, Contract, 24 May 1683; Foreman and Goodhand 1997, 178, figs 15-16.

57:     PRO WO46:2, 206, Duxbury to Board, 16 April 1684; *ibid.*, 308, Estimate, 19 April 1684.

58:     Bod. Lib. Rawl. A476, item 1, Duxbury to Board, 5 April 1685; *ibid.*, Duxbury to Beckman, 15 April 1685.

59:   Bod. Lib. Rawl. A475, Duxbury to Board, 6 July 1685, 5 August 1685; PRO WO55/519, Orders of Commissioners, 1 May 1686.

60:   Foreman and Goodhand 1997, 173, fig. 14; PRO WO55/714, Report on Fortifications at Hull, 31 March 1811; CTP 1666/7-96, 137.

CHAPTER 8
THE BUILDERS OF THE CITADEL

The building of the Citadel marked a time of transition in both government, and in the arts and sciences, of which the Engineer was expected to have a working grasp. The implementation of this ambitious design depended upon the toil of hundreds of labourers; scores of craftsmen and suppliers; and the supervision of a small but vital tier of foremen and administrators - the latter occupations frequently overlapping - who were responsible for directing their energies.

The overseers

The day-to-day management of the works at the Citadel changed in character between 1681 and 1690. At the outset, the Engineer played an active role, and there is scant evidence for the activities of his subordinates. Overseers are mentioned for the first time in 1683, dealing with earthworks. Some were gunners at Hull, but the intrusion of others was regarded askance, and the appointment of overseers became a contentious issue. In 1686, Beckman acceded to the post of Principal Engineer. This coincided with the opening of a three-year campaign of building, along the edge of the Humber. This ambitious project demanded rigorous control over the quality of work, to be exercised by trusted appointees. These works were costly as well as complex, compounding the need for close supervision. From 1687, formal mechanisms were established to permit this.

The gunners at Hull were prominent as overseers of labourers. This arose from their inclusion on the Garrison establishment as members of the Governor's Independent Foot Company. In 1682, this was stated as comprising 10 soldiers and 10 gunners. This small force had apparently descended, through many changes, from the Governor's personal *retinue*. In 1681, Master Gunner Joseph Osbourne commented that *we have too many lame men in our train*. Gunners' posts provided sinecures for disabled veterans: though equal to the chores associated with the peacetime maintenance of the Garrison, such men were less suited to play an energetic part on a building site[1].

For demolition works in 1681, Beckman had *got Mr Fitch to set day labourers of whom I was overseer and prickmaster* (clerk of works) *myself*, finding that he thereby reduced Fitch's estimate of a cost of between £200 and £300 to little more than £41. There is little indication of how the labour force was managed in 1682. Duxbury's reports described how the Engineer ordered him to employ men on various tasks; he may himself have exercised control over gangs of workers in his capacity as Clerk of Works[2].

In June 1683, the Governor of Hull reported that *our works go on very fast, having most days 100 men at work, who are very carefully looked after by the Engineer, Captain Lloyd*. Lloyd had overseers working under him; Duxbury as an immediate deputy, and others to watch over the labourers. His instructions ordered: *That you will please also to give your orders concerning the works (when you cannot be there) to Mr Duxbury who is to be an immediate officer under you*. The instructions concluded with two points. The first point urged especial care about every stage of brick and masonry work. The second was: *that the overseers of the day-labourers be strictly kept to their duties to see that the wheelbarrows be reasonably filled up and that the men do not stand but in continual action and that the men at the rammers lift up the rammers above the knees and do not stand idle. Upon these two pillars hangs all the works and His Majesty's especial service.* There were six overseers upon the works, each with above fifty labourers under his charge. Two are named: Mr Turberville, newly appointed as Master Gunner at Hull, and Mr Abraham Rogers. Rogers became an overseer to replace Bernard Higgs, who was appointed paymaster at that time. Robert Northern was involved with the paying of labourers, and may also have served as their overseer[3].

A wrangle developed in 1683 over the employment of Mr Edward Raven and Mr Honory Birt by the Commissioners. They were to be paid 15s and 12s per week respectively, as sod-layers, *being both assistants to Mr Wm. Conden*. Lord Dartmouth found *there was no reason for the admitting of such supernumery persons, and is informed that one or both were servants*. There were already sod-layers among the craftsmen who had come to the works from London, to whom Lloyd gave his orders, and who were presumably specialist overseers. The Board stated that it *would have the overseers proportioned to the number of men, about 10 to each overseer*. Such a ratio does not appear at any other time at the Citadel, and may have been that considered appropriate to the execution of craftsmen's work. The Commissioners replied that *we hope as being here upon the place we may be allowed as competent judges of what is fit to be done as those who have informed you*. Between ten and twelve Commissioners were present at meetings held at this difficult time, an unusually high attendance which may underline the vigour of this dispute. They were nevertheless ordered to dismiss the sod-layers, and to observe their orders from the Board and Beckman's directions[4].

Mr Turberville was suspended as gunner and overseer in July. Duxbury was appointed by the Board to examine *touching the abuses given Mr Osbourne by Mr Turberville*, on the occasion of the latter's appointment to Osbourne's post as Master Gunner. Turberville was summoned to the Board. The matter eventually came before the Bench at Hull, and Osbourne's daughter described the *contretemps* between the outgoing gunner and his replacement: *Turberville laid upon her father and had his right hand in her father's hair and the other upon his face; and that the said Turberville (?struck) him upon his eyebrow and... on his back and breast... the said Turberville had ran away*[5].

The Commissioners had been suspected of impropriety in the appointment of the sod-layers for 1683, and Duxbury warned that the selection of overseers for the next year might present similar problems. If earthworks were to be controlled by the Commissioners, *I would desire... that you would be pleased to get new instructions from the Office for the better regulating these works than has been formerly (which is) that you may have sole power of putting in or out Overseers, for I understand every Commissioner expects to put in one of their own, though of mean or no capacity which I hope you will not permit*. The Commissioners appointed Conden as an overseer. Duxbury's point was taken by the Board, which forbade the appointment of overseers until Sir Christopher Musgrave should come down from the Office[6].

First-hand accounts of the works of 1684 suggest that Beckman, Duxbury and the other undertakers were closely engaged with on-site works. Beckman described how *I pray be advised to keep Mr Fitch in London till the works are finished, lest he should come and work us to death; he going too quick for us in all aspects. But now we go on softly and quietly. Excepting only one bricklayer who is very forgetful in laying his bricks without mortar and (I am) therefore obliged sometimes to blow him up and sometimes down his scaffold*. Beckman warned: *I do seriously declare that I will so narrowly look after them that they shall not point 12 apostles in one stroke when the materials come upon the place*. John Fitch himself came up to Hull late in the year, urging his craftsmen to extraordinary efforts. In October, Beckman left Wharton detailed instructions of 14 articles, specifying the remaining tasks to be done.

These included the proviso: *That you allow no overseer over the King's labourers under the number of 15 or 20*[7].

In 1685, Duxbury again drew attention to the limitations of the available staff: *there are but five gunners left, two of which wants three legs, there are now two places vacant, one of which would be very convenient to be supplied by a good sodlayer in the place of Mr Conden (who had died), which Major Beckman knows is so necessary upon all occasions, that the works cannot be done without and I know none more fit than Mr Raven, a soldier in Capt. Lloyd's company who was formerly under Capt. Nicholls, he has been employed upon such service before*. His proposal was to fill the vacant gunners' posts with individuals qualified to assist the ongoing works[8].

Leaving formal instructions for Mr Richard Wharton, one of His Majesty's Engineers, in June 1685, Beckman stipulated: *That our overseers be paid by the week, but by whole and half days, and none to have above 2s per diem nor less than 60 men to look after; that the Major Gunner, Mr Buckely (or Bulkely) and the gunner Sing be continued for that service, being people I know are serviceable..* The payment of day-rates was a similar system to that by which the labourers themselves were paid. Mr Longmire was to be *Overseer of all the carts, for which he is to be allowed 12s a week, and 3s a week as paymaster*. A later contract stipulated that *all such carts as shall be employed therein, shall be full and sufficiently loaded, and that there shall be no want of men to fill the same*. In 1688, Duxbury received 5d a day as an overseer, in addition to his other fees[9].

Raven was indeed employed in 1685, but this was accomplished by piecing together small jobs. The Commissioners found a post for him, *to look after the opening and shutting of the trunks at the sluice, etc., as occasion shall require, for which he is to be allowed 2s 6d a week* - half a labourer's wage was to be allowed for this intermittent service. He also carried out various chores for Duxbury about the stores. Raven contracted for earthworks at the Citadel in 1686, establishing a family connection which continued under his widow thirty years later, when she also contracted for earthwork repairs there[10].

At the close of work in 1685, the Commissioners ordered: *In consideration that the whole works depend upon the managing by good overseers, and having none in view or expectation but Mr Jeremiah Buckely and Mr Andrew Allison (or Allotson) that we can well depend on - who have nothing else to subsist upon - we thought it very convenient for His Majesty's service to allow (them) 6s weekly to the 1st April next... to be paid* unto *Mr John Duxbury in one sum, which he is to pay to the said persons weekly provided they take care to view all the works daily round, and if any deals, or other materials upon* the works *be wanting, that they give an account immediately to the Governor or Commander-in-Chief.* In March 1686, Duxbury was drawing up quarterly pay bills for Mr Allison and Mr Buckely; the latter was *a good overseer, though he is much out of favour with Capt. Copley* (who) *told him his salary might have been saved.* Allison, however, took his duties too far: *We have got a new Controller or Surveyor-General of our works (viz) one Andrew Allison a Scotchman formerly a sergeant at arms, who not only finds fault with our works etc. but talks of it in every alehouse he comes at.* Duxbury agreed with the Governor that *Allison was a foolish fellow, and so he would ever esteem him.* However, *the great grief is to those two overseers, who the Governor and Commissioners think they have too much already for their services and therefore are unwilling to allow them any more,* once spring arrived[11].

The character of the works of 1686-88 dictated closer day-to-day control. Waterside works in 1684 had seen requirements for piling and foundations outstrip the estimates, and had revealed unexpectedly variable ground conditions on the site. Careful record-keeping would be required for further works in such locations: it would be impossible to verify the extent of foundations and the number of piles beneath them when the finished works were measured and certified. Ongoing monitoring was a more flexible and appropriate system than the assessment of progress at its half-way point and at its end, but required more systematic inspection and control of every stage of the work[12].

The construction of a brick wall capable of surviving prolonged immersion was the central element of the works in 1686; this would depend for its strength in part on the use of the correct grades of mortar. Two overseers were accordingly appointed to *look after Mr Fitch's works: one to see the sand fetched and the other to see the lime and sand mixed to the proportion of 36 bushels of lime to 40 bushels of sand.* This concern arose from previous difficulties experienced at Hull. Duxbury was proposed by Beckman: *I am of opinion it is very requisite for His Majesty's service to allow at least one man to be assisting in looking after the bricklayers, carpenters, piledrivers, mortar and terras makers. For want of such a person, I am not only of opinion, but reasonably confident that for the sake of saving His Majesty a few shillings the King will lose many pounds for each such shilling, for 'tis not unknown to any person that have had experience upon great or small works, that the workmen will watch every moment for an opportunity to advantage themselves... you may be pleased to remember you have already allowed me two overseers, but finding not one in the whole county fit for to make*

the least particle of use, I only desire that Mr Duxbury supply both their places. Duxbury duly received formal instructions, setting him alongside Richard Wharton, the junior Engineer, and providing that he should assume Wharton's responsibilities if the latter were indisposed[13].

The post of overseer was a demanding one. Duxbury reported how Wharton and he were *moiling upon the works from 6 to 6 without going off.* A month after his appointment, Duxbury reported his discoveries as an overseer, though writing in his capacity as Clerk to the Commissioners. Having detailed the condition of slabby timber brought in, he also *observed that he* (Fitch) *has employed one Mr Robinson a limer of this town to bring in above 20 (?) of Hull lime and mixed it with the Knottingley lime. Which we cannot conjure to be better than downright cheating His Majesty who pays for Knottingley lime, according to contract and if it had not been detected by the great care and diligence of the Engineer upon the place, and the overseer, who put a stop to it.* His overseer's role was, however, to draw Duxbury into the bruising contest over the competence of the Fitches to undertake the building of the breakwater jetty the same year[14].

An enquiry was held into various defects towards the end of the building season, in October. Richard Elkins, a bricklayer, employed *three or four bricklayers several times about 4 o'clock in the morning to make way for the masons that they might not be obstructed when they came to work.* The difficulty was that work carried out at such an hour could not be monitored. The failure to mortar masonry was identified at one point only; Duxbury and Wharton testified as to the quality of brickwork elsewhere *which work was found to be all very firm and substantial.* Fitch was, however, required to give security of £2,000 for the maintenance of his works. The spirit of individual supervision is glimpsed in one complaint only: *Thomas Elliot declared that he might after an expression Damn you do work well and that he threatened to break their hands if they did not do their work well but positively denies that he said damn you, what care I how the work is done or to that effect*[15].

For 1687, the Board formalised the appointment and responsibilities of overseers, handing down their decision to the Commissioners: *Mr Richard Wharton to be chief overseer of the works and Mr Talbot Edwards to be one other of the overseers from town* (London) *and to employ Mr John Duxbury and Mr Holt who are already upon the place as two more overseers - making in all the number of four overseers for the better managing and carrying on the said works, to whom we have also given order that they shall observe and follow all such orders as you shall from time to time give them in writing under your hand*. The instructions defined a general role concerned with the control of contractors rather than with direct supervision of labourers. Overseers were to ensure the presence of contractors; to prevent sub-contracting or overworks; and were *likewise to take care not to suffer their workmen to work at unreasonable hours or before the due call of the bell*[16].

The overseers had particular areas of responsibility, which were set out by Beckman. Wharton was responsible for timber foundations; Talbot Edwards for the raising of brickwork, and piling; Duxbury for mortar-mixing and the foundation-trenches, both their excavation and their back-filling; and Holt for the ramming of earth against the inner face of the sea wall, and the masonry cladding of its face. Edwards was to *keep an exact account of the number of piles that is or shall be drove of the whole work, comparing every day notes thereof with the master carpenter, that there may not be any dispute about the number when the work is finished*; this was to be cross-checked with Duxbury's own notes[17].

The earthworks of 1687 saw the involvement of soldiers from Colonel Cornwall's Regiment, quartered in the town *for work upon the fortifications*. Beckman reported: *I have had a meeting with the Commissioners who are unwilling to impose upon the soldiers to work at 6d per diem till they have a sufficient order from above for it, because the country people do not nor will not work under 10 or 12d per diem*. As soldiers could not be enrolled as day-labourers, Beckman proposed to set them at piece-work, *or else I fear they will do little good without there be commission officers of their own regiments, as is in all countries but here in England, to make them obey*. The Board recognised *that there is occasion for several principal overseers (viz.) one at every gang to direct the craftsmen where to lay the earth on the rampart, and to look after the rammers, who ought to be commissioned officers to have a command over the soldiers*. Five commissioned officers - Mr Barrett the Town Major, Sergeant Davison, Ensign Moore, Ensign Hastings and Lieutenant Luddrington - were appointed at 3s *per diem*, to command the soldiers. Assistant overseers were also appointed, presumably to supply the necessary expertise: Lieutenant Wharton at 3s, and Mr Pipe the Master Gunner, Mr Fraiston and Mr Conyers at 2s a day apiece. Edmund Pipe was the *late fire master at Tangier*, whose appointment as a gunner at Hull had begun in 1684[18].

For 1688, Duxbury was appointed as fourth overseer, under Mr Jacob Richards, Engineer, first overseer; Talbot Edwards, second overseer; and another unnamed. Instructions reiterated their general responsibilities. Beckman considered, in the light of experience with soldiers on the works, that *many overseers (are) requisite, to look after the men, of whom few are found to do their duty*. The problem was passed on to the Fitches, by a contract signed in May. Beckman was ordered to provide written instructions to the overseers, and the Board approved his *four overseers to be added to the former number for the better dispatch of the works*; they were named as Barrett, Kypton, Wilson and Etherington. The Board ordered the Commissioners to *please some of your number to inspect and see that there be no omission nor neglect of the workmen and overseers in their respective stations during the absence of the said Sir Martin Beckman*. Little is recorded of the progress of the works of 1688. It was to Duxbury, however, that Beckman left a formal Instruction in November: *to see such works finished as is contracted for with Mr Fitch for the present defence of His Majesty's town and Citadel of Hull*[19].

Securing the works

The securing of the works against accidental damage and theft was an ongoing concern. The military character of the site added to these problems. In the light of previous misappropriations at Hull, the Board were sensitive to these issues; when a summerhouse was cleared away in the early stages of the works of 1681, Beckman was warned to take care of the materials. The reuse of broken bricks as infill occurs in the archaeological record of works carried out at this time. In 1682, *the want of a shed to lay up materials* was brought to the Board's attention. The Ordnance stores had been shifted from South Blockhouse to hired rooms to permit the renovation of the Blockhouse, but returned there in September 1682[20].

In October 1682, Beckman noted that two sentry boxes were required, and that a *Corps de Guard* was to be made. The Board ordered the construction of a guardhouse, stipulating that a forge should not be made near it. Payments for this were ordered in December. In February 1684 the door of South Blockhouse was broken down, and some stores were stolen. The Board ordered the Deputy-Governor to place sentries at the door. Duxbury reported: *the Deputy-Governor tells me that there (were) always two sentinels at South Blockhouse, and a guard at South End, and what mischief was done by them, but he not knowing the time, cannot know who to accuse* - the soldiers themselves were the prime suspects, but it was uncertain who was on guard-duty when the break-in occurred. A new door was ready in time for the close of works next winter[21].

In September 1684, an account was received from Beckman *that they are very much pestered in the night time with rogues and thieves which came and break the stages and carried away the tools the workmen should work with withall and if not timely prevented they will do very much more damage.* Two files of soldiers were detailed to provide a pair of sentries to stand guard at the Main Gate of the Citadel, which was under construction at the time. Over winter, the *Commissioners prevailed with the Commander-in-Chief to have a sentry at the Main Gate*[22].

The building of *a small house 7ft (2.1m) square for the security of the apron of the sluice* was ordered by the Commissioners. Beckman urged this lest *some rogue or another (of which we have whole coveys 100 in a covey) throws something down at the passage for the chain which cannot be cleared without digging down 18ft (5.5m) deep and put the King to £100 charge, which such a box will prevent.* The numbering of rogues in coveys of 100 was probably an allusion to the soldiers of the Garrison, and it is clear that cold or hungry soldiers posed a more serious threat to the works over winter than any other enemy[23].

The setting of sentries was one thing, their attendance another. Beckman reported on this, in somewhat relaxed vein, at the end of a busy year: *Here happens very pleasant hunting towards South Blockhouse for hares sometimes. Especially when the sentries turn hares in the sentry boxes at night. For it seems it was not long since Mr Watkinson or sons relating to him had occasion to go early into the stores and had occasion to call to the sentry; but the hare in the box would not answer until an unlucky greyhound comes and starts this new-fashioned sentry out of the box. And away runs the sentry leaving the arms behind and the greyhound and honest Mr Watkinson in full speed after the sentry; but it seems the sentry was well trained and nay to the greyhound lost ground, and then there came another to relieve*[24].

In April 1685, Duxbury reported: *We have lost a considerable quantity of materials this winter, for there are scarce any stages or bridges left within the Citadel, and the shed has been broken twice, and I already miss 23 wheelbarrows which are supposed to have been burnt by the soldiers, and we shall this day tell over all the rest of the stages, and then I shall know perfectly what is left.* For the next winter, the materials were to be lodged *under lock and key in the South House, the Castle and the shed, to preserve them from burning, wherein we had a great loss the last winter.* Despite this, in October 1686, John Fitch complained: *of the great loss and embezzlement of his materials and moved the Commissioners to desire the Governor, Lieutenant-Governor or Commander-in-Chief to command the sentinels to take care of the same and likewise not to suffer any cattle or persons to come upon the works to damnify the same by which much damage has been formerly done.* Sentries were duly posted *at the stone sentinel box on the East Point...at the Main Gate and another on the point of the Castle bastion where the old wall is broken down on Drypool side*[25].

In early 1686, *the soldiers have much damnified the works by running up and down notwithstanding our daily complaints, but now Captain Copley (the Deputy-Governor) is come he will take other measures.* More serious damage could be incurred through animals straying over the site. In December 1684, the Commissioners ordered payment for *fencing to keep the horses out of the works.* The breaking of temporary bridges was to the same end. In March 1688, Beckman instructed Duxbury to keep enough water in the moats to keep animals out, to maintain fences, *and when you find any goats, horses, and oxen at top of the bastion or the wing to cause them to be shot not regarding to whom they may belong, and concerning the damages the law may give to the owner, I will pay the same, provided the owner also gives satisfaction to the King for such trespass and damage*[26].

Craftsmen and trades

The more substantial contractors provided materials, and the majority of craftsmen employed were also their subcontracted workers. The Fitches were the most important contractors at the Citadel. Their workers included plumbers, bricklayers, masons, plasterers and carpenters. These craftsmen were engaged and paid by John Fitch, and so figure only incidentally in the records generated by the Board of Ordnance. The Commissioners directly employed some specialist workers: sod-layers for the cladding of earthworks, or carpenters, particularly for emergency repairs. Local suppliers and craftsmen were most prominent in fulfilling tasks ancillary to those of major contractors, permitting other workers to perform their tasks. They were busiest when the Commissioners were preparing for major campaigns of construction. Coopers, gunsmiths and painters were also engaged for various jobs, usually at the instance of the Storekeeper.

The host of minor tasks carried out by jobbing craftsmen is well illustrated by Captain Collingwood's account of *Moneys disbursed for the flag staff*, in May 1683. Materials cost £2 10s 9d. The itemised labour charges for this modest enterprise included: *1s 8d to William Dawson the carpenter; 6d to the sledman for bringing the staff; 6d to the soldiers for getting the staff upon the top of the house; 1s 10d to soldiers for helping the staff up, 1s to the seamen, 5s 6d to Francis Billet the carpenter for two days work; 1s 6d to the smith for making the clasp; 1s for carpenter's and smith's allowance; and 1s for the carpenters and smith's allowance when they made the mast and that night when they got the mast up on the South House Tho Bedall and myself did attend*[27].

Over thirty local suppliers and craftsmen received contracts and payments for their part in the works between 1681 and 1688. They included four *raff merchants*, or suppliers of plank and spars, and seven carpenters. The most substantial carpenter, Joseph Blaides, was also to supply materials to other contractors. The timber trades were particularly associated with shipbuilding in Hull, an occupation in which the Blaides family were prominent[28].

Raff merchants usually provided materials required for the scaffolding which labourers and craftsmen used in the course of their work, or for other purposes ancillary to the works. John Baumbrough supplied *spar, baulk and deal* in July 1682, and *deals and baulks he sold and delivered* in October. In August, he was paid *for deals etc. for building of a shed*. The overall cost of these services was £25 5s 5d. In May 1683, he provided *100 hanspikes* and *24 slitdeals, for mending of barrows*, costing £3 7s 6d[29].

The later allocation of contracts to raff merchants was slanted towards prominent figures on the local scene. This may hint at a politically motivated attempt to cultivate the support of a particular faction on the Bench of Aldermen, particularly after the accession of James II. In June 1685, Mr Richard Grey was paid £22 *19s for deals, spar etc. bought for the use of His Majesty's new fortifications*, and Mr Robert Nettleton was to receive £18 5s 6d for similar goods. Nettleton had served as Sheriff of Hull in 1684, and Grey occupied this office in 1685. Nettleton was also to serve on the *intruded* Bench of Aldermen appointed under James II between September and November 1688. Alderman Trippitt provided *deals, baulks, spars and other materials for erecting of stages, bridges etc.* in 1687, at an overall cost of £174 1s 6d. Trippett was the least senior of the Aldermen displaced in 1688, but under the new Williamite regime was to become Mayor of Hull in 1689, and again in 1705. Grey was to serve as Mayor in 1691 and 1706[30].

The only other supplier of such standing was William Robinson, who had served as Sheriff of Hull in 1682; two relatives were to hold this office in later years. Robinson is recorded as a lime-burner in the 1670s, when he was engaged in dis-

pute with other tradesmen of the town, and supplied lime to the Citadel works. Another Robinson, John, served on the *intruded* Bench of 1688. The relationship between William Robinson and the Citadel is recorded from 1685. The Board informed Beckman that *you may for His Majesty's service give leave to the Brickmaster Mr Robinson to make use of the ground to make bricks*, and empowered him to negotiate terms with Robinson. The matter had arisen with the removal of 6,000 floors (*c*.55,000m³) of earth from the land taken in for the Citadel, presumably towards its eastern limit. A contract for the manufacture of two million bricks was agreed with Robinson in August 1687, at the rate of 11s for every thousand standard bricks and 20s for every thousand of the choicest and best-burned bricks[31].

Daniel Green was a carpenter and supplier of timber. He was employed in 1682, on the account for the sluice, for which he was paid £10, £5, and finally £12 12s, *for work done in full on the trunk*. He also supplied 81ft (24.7m) of 3in. (76mm) oak plank for lining gun-ports. More extensive work on the sluice fell to Joseph Blaides. He began his involvement at the Citadel in December 1682, when he tendered for the making of gun carriages. The next year, in addition to this task, he was contracted to construct the main sluice between the Citadel moat and the river Hull. An imprest of £40 permitted this substantial task to begin, in May 1683. The building and securing of the sluice were to intermittently occupy him until October 1685. The final closing of his account calculated a cost of £150 12s 10d for the sluice and its riverbank wings[32].

In 1686, with Beckman's support, Blaides competed unsuccessfully against the Fitches for the construction of the breakwater jetty. His last recorded work was the fencing of the road leading into the Citadel, for which he received instalments of £16 and £9 17s 4d in autumn 1686. He may have had some further involvement with works on the riverbank revetments adjoining the sluice, as the order for his last recorded payment for fencing referred to *other work done according to contract made 10 June 1686*. This contract has not been encountered, but on the same day, the Mayor and Mr Catlyn had been ordered *to view the making of the breast works... according to the method of Sir Martin Beckman*. The preference for Blaides as a workman appears to have been on the grounds of his competence, particularly in waterside works, as befitted a shipwright[33].

Mr Lawrence Evans may have taken over Blaides' position as most favoured local contractor. In July 1684, he was to provide *a gyn to drive piles*, suggesting that he was equipped for the execution of large-scale works. Like Blaides, his first recorded employment was a minor one. In September 1684, he was to be paid for a new door at South Blockhouse, and for *the little house of 7ft (2.1m) square to be made of deal boards with a door to secure the apron or shutters of the sluice*. By 1686, however, *Evans the carpenter is ready to lay his frame for the first length* of the timber foundation of the first water bastion. This was, however, disrupted by the failure of a dam keeping the Humber out of the foundations. His responsibility the following year was less crucial: *for making of wheelbarrows and setting up stages and bridges*, and *for making new rams, setting up stages and repairing barrows*. The framing for the second water bastion of 1688 was directed by Beckman and by a Mr Pitts, of whom nothing more is known[34].

Mr John Shields was a carpenter, possibly a wheelwright. He was intermittently employed between 1683 and 1687, as one of the longer-serving craftsmen responsible for the provision and repair of tools. Shields was one of a number of small contractors engaged for this purpose in 1683. His business was intermittently linked to that of the Robinson family, of whom at least three members were employed in various capacities at the Citadel. Luke Robinson was paid £7 for 40 new wheelbarrows in June 1683; Thomas Marshall was also paid £2 13s 4d for wheelbarrows about this time. In July 1683, 50 whole deals and a half deal were left with Duxbury for John Shields. Shields was to repair wheelbarrows at the end of works in 1683; payment for this work was ordered in February 1684, but he was still awaiting his money three months later[35].

Theophilus Robinson and John Shields carried out minor repairs on the Humber banks, being paid £12 4s 6d for this in June 1685. In early 1685, they were to repair 256 wheelbarrows, and haft 34 pickaxes, six double rammers and two single rammers. Their bill itemises this work as follows[36]:

For repairing 40 wheelbarrows that wanted new wheels and bolts, at 18d apiece:	£3
For repairing 66 wheelbarrows that wanted one side of the main frame at 14d apiece:	£3 17s
For repairing 60 barrows that wanted 2 side boards of slit deals and wanted feet at 14d apiece:	£3 10s
For repairing 90 barrows wanting part of the bottoms, ends and pieces of the sides at 8d:	£3
For 34 new helves for pickaxes of ashwood at 4d apiece:	11s 4d
For 6 helves for double rammers at 4d apiece	2s
For 2 helves for single rammers	8d
For mending two hand barrows:	1s

Duxbury, in his capacity as Storekeeper, was still pursuing payment on their behalf a year later, in March 1686. In September 1687, Shields was paid £27 10s for making 150 wheelbarrows at 3s 9d apiece; and in October a further £6 12s for making wheelbarrows and rammers[37].

Carpenters' work would usually require iron fittings to be provided. The contract for the refurbishment of South Blockhouse, for example, which entailed the reconstruction of its timber-framed roof, also required *fourteen hundred pounds weight* (635kg) *of good and serviceable ironwork or thereabouts*. Where, however, such requirements formed part of contracted works, their provision would also fall to the major contractor, and the individual craftsmen responsible for carrying them out are never named. The direct employment of blacksmiths by the Commissioners followed a similar pattern to that of the lesser carpenters. They are not normally referred to as "Mr", in contrast to the merchants, shipwrights and carpenters of the town. The supply of iron fittings was agreed separately, though their cost was listed in the same accounts[38].

Richard Dixon supplied ironwork for the Citadel between July 1682 and September 1683. He first appears in receipt of £3 16s 8d, *for nails, stages, wedges, and other ironworks from the 8th to the 14th July 1682*. His services, defined in similar terms and at similar rates, were recorded by intermittent payments up to October, by which time he had earned £15 5s 3d. In November, this was augmented by a further £11 1s 2d, paid over two weeks, for ironworks for the new trunk[39].

In April 1683, Dixon supplied batches of 1000 *holfitt* nails, and of 500 7in and 4in nails. Four days later, he supplied new bolts at 4d apiece, and charged 1d for mending old ones. *Cottrils* cost 4d a dozen, *forelocks* 3d a dozen, while old iron was 1s per pound. In May, he earned £28 19s, probably all for nails to be used to fasten scaffolding. This was for the provision of 20lbs (c.9kg) of 6in. (152mm) nails and 20lbs of 4in. (c.100mm) nails, both costing £5; ironwork for £3 19s; and 6in. nails, 4in. nails and *kelfitt* nails at £5 for each batch. Further ironwork for the works in June included unspecified goods costing £1 11s; and 500 kelfitt nails, 500 6in. and 500 4in. nails, and 4 dozen bolts and forelocks for the Castle[40].

A bill of £1 16s 6d was to be settled shortly after, and he was also to receive £3 10s 10d *for the Guard Room on the Garrison side*. These were for household iron-work, and provide a good picture of the more usual requirements of smith's work, and of Dixon's day-to-day occupation. The components of the smaller bill are detailed, by *an account of smith's work done in the Castle about repairing a room for the Captain of the Guards by Richard Dixon Smith by the order of the Honble Capt. Copley Lieut. Governor of his Maj's Garrison of Kingston upon Hull*, as follows[41]:

For 400 and a half of 10in. (254mm) nails:	3s 9d
For 2 locks:	2s
For one pair of cross garters for the doors:	7s
All staine head	
For 2...	
For one plate and spikes for the top of the door:	2s 6d
For half a dozen of kellfit nails:	11d
For mending one casement:	6d
For one plate for the door:	2d
For 2 plates and spikes:	8d
For one pair of rings and hooks:	2s 6d
For one dozen of 10in nails	10d
For one dozen of kelfitt nails:	1s 10d
For one plate for the rails at the stairs head and foot 10in long and one other 3ft 8in (c.1.1m) with spikes:	7s
In all:	£1 16s

Lawrence Clerk was apparently a member of a family firm of glaziers. In June 1683, he was paid 6s 5d for his help in the refurbishment of the same room. He charged for 9ft 6in. (0.9m²) of new glass, for mending one top pane with new glass, and for mending and trimming a casement; tasks which would have entailed close cooperation with Dixon. A Samuel Clerk was to be employed mending windows at South Blockhouse, in September 1688, after they had been broken by the concussion from the test-firing of guns[42].

Locksmiths provided a more specialised service, and their charges were correspondingly higher. In 1683, James Atkinson was paid £3 15s 7d, *for a great lock for Myton Gate a hanging lock for Beverley Gate and a lock for sally ports*. John Pinder was paid £3 in early 1684. This was for the repair of the lock on the door of South Blockhouse, which had been broken by thieves. Given its cost, this was presumably a most imposing piece of work requiring a skilled locksmith[43].

Jonathon Snaith (or Smith) was apparently the main supplier of ironworks for 1685. He was paid £1 14s in June, and £13 14s 1d *for ironworks by him delivered... from the 15th of June to the 4th July 1685*, in July. The nature of provision for the following year is unknown. In 1687, however, Thomas Carter, blacksmith, was paid £9 6s 4d *for nails and ironwork done*. This was the beginning of a more profitable engagement with the Citadel. In November, he was favoured by Beckman with a contract *for making of 500 spades according to a pattern sent up to the Office of Ordnance to be paid after the rate of 2s each at the delivery of every 50 spades*. The spades were of Beckman's own design, to be made stronger than usual, for cutting the stiff Hull clays. This contract was apparently the making of Carter. By 1692, he was to secure the post of *Frobusher* at the Garrison, a post involving the cleaning of weapons in store, with an annual salary of £36 *per annum*[44].

Other building trades are not well represented among the minor contractors. Their engagement was usually in response to urgent requirements for unforeseen works, or when major contractors had failed to provide workers or materials. These problems were most significant in 1684. Flooding in and around South Blockhouse encouraged Beckman to press for extensive levelling here. Thomas Goth and John Hewitt were to be paid for paving. The difficulties in supplying stone for other works of the same year encouraged Beckman to contract with *the Mason of this town*, one Mr Roebuck, to arrange alternative supplies. Roebuck was building a new stone sentry box in early 1685, and was later coping parapets at East Point. His initial role as a supplier of materials was in this case to lead to further employment on mason's work[45].

Some specialist services were arranged by the Board of Ordnance in London. In December 1683, the Board contracted with Thomas Moore, a carpenter, *for the providing, furnishing and delivering into His Majesty's stores... the number of 9 new fashioned ship carriages with transoms for iron saker of 9ft long each for the new Saluting Platform at Hull*, minutely detailing every aspect of their dimensions. Another requirement arose in 1683, from *Major Beckman's demand for iron drills to be made to remove the old (Henrician) wall*. Mr Silver *was to make iron drills according to Major Beckman's direction for taking away the old brickwork*. These were probably intended for the drilling of shot-holes to permit the placement of demolition charges. Beckman was to be responsible for extensive demolition works at Tangier over the summer of the same year, and would therefore have had very particular requirements[46].

The maintenance of the arms and stores held at the Citadel was the responsibility of the Storekeeper. When he took over this post in 1685, John Duxbury found these duties had been signally neglected by his predecessor. Such maintenance as proved possible was usually undertaken with local labour. A payment in March 1686 lists some of the headings of his expenditure[47]:

Pay John Langley Cooper 4 days work etc.:	£2 10s 6d
Edward Raven and two labourers to rub over	
holsters, pistols etc. 12d each:	£2 11s
John Harrison lighterman for carrying over	
the old lead round and cross [?burr] shot	
from South End to South Blockhouse:	15s 6d
For labour carrying said lead from South End	
into lighter etc.:	£1 16s 6d
For labourers to get the harness out of the	
stores and drying them in the sun and putting	
them in again:	£1 8s
For posting letters on account of his service:	5s 3d

Coopers were to be recurrently employed to maintain the powder barrels in store. In 1684, payment was made for the storage of newly hooped powder. Thomas Norfolk *wished his money due for cooper's work at Hull may be paid to one Mr Scott.* In 1685, at the time of Monmouth's rising, a cooper was to repair barrels and a gunsmith to clean and repair weapons; *this armourer is a very poor man, and expects his money weekly as he proceeds with his works.* John Langley and George Wilkinson were paid £7 15s *for shifting and hooping* powder in September 1686; as the same bill covered the work of *several labourers cleaning of arms and holsters for 6 months,* at a cost of £8 7s 4d, their work may have extended over a similar period. Langley was paid £3 19s 2d for coopering in September 1688; payment was also listed for labourers hired *to get 100 barrels and 100 beds on shore, putting them into carts and stowing them in the Castle.* Langley and Wilkinson were to be paid £10 2s 6d two weeks later, for repairing 370 powder barrels, while Joseph Goulding was paid for his help in mounting guns, and for *cartage of the powder and beds and old wood.* Such energetic activity was, however, only to occur in extraordinary circumstances, and conditions in the Hull Blockhouses were far from ideal for the long-term storage of any goods[48].

The movement of stores between Hull and other garrisons or the Tower Armouries entailed regular dealings with mariners. In 1683, the Board agreed with David Cosby for the transportation of harness to Hull. The Storekeeper was to pay the freight charge on its arrival. A more regular service was provided by Mr John Huntingdon, the Hull master of the *Speedwell,* and latterly the *Saphire.* He received his first recorded payment, of £2, in June 1683. This was *for bringing the boat* (with coal for the Garrison) *from London.* The next year, now as master of the *Saphire* of Hull, he was to transport nine new gun carriages and a new flag to Hull, at a rate of 5s per carriage. In September he was contracted to transport arms and paper to Hull; they arrived later the same month. In January 1686, Huntingdon petitioned for the overdue payment of £45 12s *due to him for carrying corn powder from Tower Wharf to Hull and £12 for bringing unserviceable powder, drums and small arms from Hull to the Tower.* In 1688, lighterage was *paid to get stores sent from the Tower out of John Huntingdon's ship*[49].

In October 1685, Duxbury was preparing to send unserviceable arms and powder up to London by another ship, under Peter Thompson. However, *we were treating about it, but could not agree for he demanded 18s a barrel, and I told him 12s was enough, upon which he said he would refer himself to the Board for such allowance as was formerly granted to John Huntingdon.* Thompson was a trusted friend and drinking partner of Duxbury's, and he included his own private cargoes in such shipments for the Tower. In thanks for Beckman's help with his appointment as Storekeeper, *I shipped off for you a cask of Hull* (ale) *before Christmas last, but by misfortune the vessel was cast away at Yarmouth pier, but yours among others, being 5 in 7 was saved and sent on board another vessel to London, but I understand that the Master being a knave delivered but 4 of the 5, and not only made them pay extraordinary weight, but kept the cask to himself which when he comes in my way I shall make him pay soundly for. To repair which miscarriage I have presumed to send you another cask of 20 gallons by Peter Thompson which I desire you will be pleased to accept of. I question not his care in the delivery thereof without any charge, and I hope it will prove well.* The beer was apparently sent with a cargo of small arms and old powder being returned to the Tower. In June, a larger consignment, *6 casks containing 24 gallons* (109 litres) *each, being 144 at 10d the gallon for the best beer (which is here called dragons blood)* was incorporated in another cargo shipped by Thompson[50].

The country people

The largest heading of the Commissioners' expenditure was the payment of day-labourers, either to forward agreed contracts or to perform urgent works *on the*

King's Immediate Account. These *country people* were deployed *en masse* for the digging of moats and ditches, for wheeling earth in barrows, and for spreading and compacting it to form ramparts, or to level the site. They also carried out a range of other menial tasks, or provided muscle-power for more specialised craftsmen. These were mostly agricultural workers, for whom the works at Hull provided an alternative to labour on the land, in the East Riding or beyond. They might be supplemented by soldiers of the Garrison, though this help could not be relied upon. On one occasion, a runaway apprentice joined the labourers. He was jailed by the Mayor; the Commissioners, and even the blustering Captain Lloyd, were unable to secure his release[51].

In 1683, Beckman's instructions for earthworks described the tasks that labourers were to perform. Earth was to be dug from the moat, and sods *cut from the ground below the dyke and the river.* Work on scaffolding was possible in fair weather, and the wheeling of earth in any conditions. The minimum necessary number of workers were to provide sods, and to perform ramming for Mr Conden, while the rest brought earth to enlarge a bastion at the Castle, or filled *all the great holes and false ground*[52].

In 1685, Beckman detailed conditions of employment on earthworks in his formal instructions to the overseers: *If workmen be at work at or before 6 of the clock in the morning till 6 at night, there should be times for dinner and breakfast allowed, that the wheelbarrows be well filled, the rammers be lifted up above the knees and no rammer lighter than 70lbs (31.8kg) weight. And that the workmen be kept from idleness, and slow walking with their wheelbarrows, and that the spademen be proportioned to the wheelbarrows according to the several distances. That the workmen be not ill-used, but those that are not serviceable to turn them off from the works being paid for their service according to agreement. That none above 60 and under 15 years of age be entertained, not to have above 9 or 10 pence per diem*[53].

Day-labourers were paid only for the time they were at work. A list of 51 named individuals, hired between 17 and 24 September 1681, shows that a little over half of the gang, 28 men, received five days pay. There were 14 men paid for four-and-a-half days; 4 who worked four days; and 5 who put in three-and-a-half days. If the figures relate to the presence of these labourers, rather than to their performance of a specific task reckoned apart from others - which is possible - they would imply a very fluid pattern of unskilled employment. It follows that there were probably more individuals involved on the works, working as their personal circumstances might dictate, than recorded numbers or costs would suggest. The weather would frequently prevent their useful employment. At the end of May 1686, *the rain, and holidays have much impeded our proceedings* - in that case, the holidays were for the feast of Whitsuntide[54].

The number of labourers employed was reported at some times, and may be inferred from the payments assigned to pay off bills of labourers at others. In 1681, there were from 50 to 300 men at work; more later, as harvest was brought in, releasing labourers for service at Hull. In 1682, there were never more than 170, and more usually less than 100. The works of 1683 saw no less than 210, and a maximum of 475, engaged, until the works foundered in July. The largest team in the later part of the year was 80 men, finishing urgent waterside repairs. These were all years in which earthworks made up the larger part of activity on site. In 1684, a gang of 140 - in September - was exceptional, and payments suggest that the labourers were numbered in tens rather than hundreds. This was a time when craftsmen's work on brick and masonry took priority, and when the numbers of labourers engaged by contractors fulfilling ancillary tasks are often unknown. At the outset of these works, a minimum of 40 or 50 labourers had been required for the digging of foundation trenches[55].

In 1685, when earthworks were the major concern, the earliest recorded payments imply that 220 men were on site in mid-June. The Commissioners noted that *men flock in on us.* There were rarely fewer than 200, and often more, rising to a maximum of 600 in early July. The following year saw effort concentrated on the timber, brick and stone of the first water bastion. Necessary earthworks were contracted out to Mr Raven; the largest team of labourers recorded was something less than 80, and the usual figure was perhaps half that - the calculations for 1686 are particularly uncertain as Raven's profit margin is unknown. In September 1687, the first time in that year for which figures are available, there were reported to be 100 soldiers and 60 country people employed. Through October, the inferred numbers rose from 210 to 720, fell back to 430 in the middle of the month, but rose to something a little under 1,160 by 29 October. The figures inferred from payments in 1688 range from 250 to 300, in April. In June, the Governor reported that *there are many hands and good workmen*; the extent of works in the later part of the year implies a workforce whose size may have approached that of 1687[56] (see appendix).

In September 1681, a late harvest detained the country people. This temporary labour shortage was perhaps compounded by an epidemic ague or influenza, which is thought to have hit Hull and parishes in the north of the East Riding between 1678 and 1681. The Governor refused to allow his soldiers to help with the works; *then the countrymen knowing our want of men mutineered and would not work under 18d a day which hindered us a day or two more.* John Fitch felt that *the people here are dull, lazy sort of people makes me out of love with them.* Beckman complained that *they come and go with the winds and weather*[57].

To recruit fresh workers, *Fitch made proclamations in several market towns.* In 1683, the Commissioners again had difficulty in attracting and retaining labourers, and they were recruited from far afield. Mr Buckley, a gunner and overseer, was paid *for proclaiming the works in the country.* Mr Nibody was paid 30s for his *extraordinary charges in going to several places in the country to raise men for these works*, as was Mr Willoughby. Most unusually, John Hacking was allowed £1 *for bringing his men out of Lancashire*, and 6d for every man he brought. In early June 1685, the Commissioners ordered: *That the works be proclaimed at Hull and Beverley the next market day for men to come to the works*[58].

Enquiry into local wage rates had been undertaken before the works began. The Bench of Magistrates at Hull set the local rates for labourers and workmen. Unskilled porters' and labourers' wages were defined as piece-work rates; in general, unskilled workers could expect between 10d and 14d a day. Master workmen received 1s 8d a day from Easter to Michaelmas Day. Wage assessments in Beverley, in 1679, set 10d as the daily rate for a mower of grass, 5d for ditchers and other common labourers, and 4d for casting a ditch. The summertime rate for labourers at the Citadel appears to have been 12d a day for wheelers and diggers of earth, and 14d for rammers. A gang of day-labourers employed for demolition works, in October 1681, were paid 1s each a day[59].

In October 1682, reduced rates were set from Michaelmass to Ladyday: 10d a day for labourers, and 12d a day for rammers and turf-cutters. This took into account the shorter working day; such seasonal alteration of rates was common practice in the south of England, though less familiar in the North. Similar low-season rates were set by the Commissioners in September 1687: *That the labourers working upon the fortification be allowed 10d per diem for wheelers and 12d for rammers. And for boys 6d per diem to work from 7 o'clock till 5, and no half hours allowed. And that the sergeant commanding the soldiers be allowed 18d per diem... That the labourers shall not be cut off the quarters of days when the wet weather put them off.* Beckman reported: *I have for the present obliged (country people) to take 10d per diem these short days and 12d a man for ramming; but boys who runs with a wheelbarrow as full as the best of them I have ordered with their consent to take from 6 to 8d*[60].

In late June 1683, again with too few labourers, Captain Lloyd allowed them 14d a day from 28 July until Michaelmass. The Commissioners explained that this was because *in this time of harvest they may have more wages in the country.* At this time, women were also serving on the works. This was in keeping with local practice, as women were employed as dock-side porters in Hull. They *were allowed 10d per diem according to their labour we think they deserved as well as the men*[61].

The Board, however, *desired not to allow more than 12d a day to wheelers and 14d a day to rammers as it was formerly ordered... And understanding you have sent out to make proclamation for labourers to come in at 14d and 16d a day, His Lordship and the Board cannot well resent it exceeding their Instructions for they ought not to advance any wages or alter any former orders without the order, consent and approbation by them first received from this Board.* Women's wages were not to exceed 4d a day, and they were ordered to be dismissed, as their employment was *a disparagement to His Majesty's service.* As for workers who refused to work at the set rates: *whosoever offends in that or any other nature are presently to be discharged the works without any further punishment and those that refuse to work this time of harvest shall not be employed at any other time.* It is uncertain how such threats could be enforced when the problem was one of too few hands. As *the moneys for carrying on those works are not come in as we expected and finding by your letter that the harvest coming on does considerably increase the charge, my Lord Dartmouth and this Board do desire you will close the works*[62].

The labourers were paid weekly, at the pay table. Pay day for the labourers was Saturday, at the end of a six day week. This was changed to Friday evening in March 1683, on the Board's order. The Commissioners reported, however, *that we find the men are addicted to be debauched and absent from the works the next day*, and reverted to the previous arrangement. It was initially ordered that: *What moneys happen to be overplus either by men's leaving their pay, or by mistakes, be kept in a purse by itself to be laid out for His Majesty's use, as shall be thought fit by the engineer and the rest of the Commissioners.* It was subsequently ordered: *That what men are unpaid at the end of every pay day, a note be taken of what moneys is left, to remain in the hands of the Clerk of Works, and paid when the men come for it at the sutling house in the presence of the Engineer*[63].

Credit was extended to labourers by the sutler, who provided canteen facilities for the workers, and this arrangement was presumably to ensure that debts owed to him were settled. The sutler's house was run by Mr Felton, who undertook earthworks on the Fitches' behalf. The Commissioners ordered that *if any labourers shall leave the work and run in to (?debt with) the bottle house, that what money is due to them shall be paid to the sutler... so far as the sutler's debt extends.* The bottle house was probably a lightly-built shed. It is uncertain whether this facility remained available after 1684, when Captain Copley was ordered *to satisfy Mr Felton for the sutling house*; and was *to have liberty to dispose of the materials of the sutling house, if no agreement made with Captain Copley.* In 1685, *Whereas several labourers do not appear at the weekly payment and afterwards complaining that they cannot get their monies. It is ordered that whosoever are so unpaid, their monies and the bills are to be left every pay day with the Commissioners who pay that week, to be paid upon the water the next week after*[64].

In September 1681, John Fitch described how he had 145 at the pay table; it is uncertain whether these were paid by Fitch or the Commissioners. It was later ordered that *every Commissioner attend the payment of the labourers according to their turns.* The paymaster was an officer employed by the Commissioners, but one from whom security of £100 was demanded, because of the opportunities for embezzlement. Mr Osbourne, the Master Gunner, initially filled the post. He was succeeded in 1683 by Mr Bernard Higgs. Higgs also helped Duxbury draw up bills for small local contractors, and filled his place when he was called away; for this he was paid 12s a week. Mr Robert Northern received payment for bills of labourers in 1683, and William Longmire in 1685. Instructions issued in 1685 further stipulated the checking of the payroll by an overseer: *That a man of trust, and who gives security, be employed to receive and pay the workmen, and that all bills of payment be countersigned and certified by you* (the overseer) *and the Clerks of the 'Chequer before the bills, warrants or debentures be signed by the Commissioner*[65].

The chronic financial insecurity of the works impacted most directly on the labourers. In December 1681, Duxbury reported *the great clamours of the people for want of their money*; and early the next year *the hardship the countrymen suffer.* The payment of wages depended on the transfer of funds from the Board to the Commissioners. In 1685, Richard Wharton reported that *The men have hitherto been kept at work with fair words and promises, but he* (Mason) *knows not what rhetoric to use them next pay day*[66].

In 1687, soldiers joined the labourers engaged in earthworks. Beckman set out reasons for paying soldiers at a lower rate; these centred on the relative hardships suffered by the day-labourers, and illustrate the conditions under which they lived. *We have taken it upon consideration and the major part (of the Commissioners) finds it not convenient that the soldiers should have less than the countrymen. I must confess I have opposed that opinion by this reason: Viz. The Soldier has at least 4d per diem in ready money if he work or not work, and if he get 6d per diem more when he works he has 14 or 15 pence or more money. The countryman who comes from 10 to 50 or more miles (17 to 80km) to work with his own spade has but 10d more or less per diem, when fair weather, which makes but 5½ days neither, and when it is foul which may continue for 15 or 30 days then he has nothing; but yet must pay 3s per week for his meat and lodging when the soldier on the other side lies in good quarters and receives his subsistence*[67].

Not all labourers could even provide their own hand-tools. Some implements, like rammers, were specialised tools. Wheelbarrows were provided by the Commissioners, or by their undertakers. Some labourers arrived unequipped for work. In 1685, Duxbury was ordered to deliver *20 spades and 20 shovels out of His Majesty's stores under his charge for the present supply of these labourers who have no tools to work with,* and leather buckets *to get the water out of the graft*[68].

Footnotes

1:    CSPD 1682, 535; Bod. Lib. Rawl. A475, Duxbury to Dartmouth, n.d. but filed with January 1686; PRO WO46:1, 319, Osbourne to Board, 22 November 1681.

2:    PRO WO46:1, 311, Beckman to Board, 12 October 1681.

3:    CSPD 1683, 343; PRO WO46:1, 347, Instructions to Lloyd, 17 April 1683; Bod. Lib. Rawl. A475, Commissioners to Board, 17 July 1683; *ibid.,* Orders of Commissioners, 2 June 1683; PRO WO46:1 (index), 41, Orders of Commissioners, 2 June 1683.

4:    Bod. Lib. Rawl. A475, Commissioners to Board, 9 May 1683; Bod. Lib. Rawl. A476, item 1, Commissioners to Board, 25 June 1684; PRO WO46:2, 4, Orders of Board, 14 July 1683; Bod. Lib. Rawl. A475, Commissioners to Board, 28 May 1683; PRO WO46:2 (index), 73, Board to Hull, 2 June 1683.

5:    PRO WO46:2 (index), 44, Orders of Commissioners, 6 July 1683; *ibid.,* 10, Orders of Board, 4 September 1683; *ibid.,* 12, 4 October 1683; KUHRO BRB 8, 64, 8 August 1685.

6:    Bod. Lib. Rawl. A476, item 1, 2-3, Duxbury to Beckman, 12 April 1684; PRO

WO46:2, 25, Order of Board, 1 July 1684.

7:   Foreman and Goodhand 1997, 162; PRO WO46:2, 251, Beckman to Board, 21 August 1684; *ibid*., 242, Beckman to Board, 23 July 1684; *ibid*., 54, Instruction to Wharton, 15 October 1684.

8:   Bod. Lib. Rawl. A476, item 1, fo. 20, Duxbury to ?Dartmouth, 11 April 1685.

9:   PRO/WO55/519, Instruction to Wharton, 2 June 1685; *ibid*., Orders of Commissioners, 11 June 1685; PRO WO55/1785, Contract, 19 May 1688; PRO WO51/37, TBB series 2, 35, 30 September 1688; *ibid*., 166, November 1688.

10:   e.g. PRO WO51/32, TBB series 2, 82b, March 1686; PRO WO55/519, Orders of Commissioners, 1 May 1686; CTB vol. 31, part i, 1716, 180.

11:   PRO WO55/519, Orders of Commissioners, 29 November 1685; Bod. Lib. Rawl. A475, Duxbury to ?Beckman, 22 March 1686; *ibid*., Duxbury to Wharton, 27 March 1686; *ibid*., Duxbury to Beckman, ?8 April 1686.

12:   Foreman and Goodhand 1997, 160-5.

13:   PRO WO55/519, Orders of Commissioners, 1 May 1686; *ibid*., Beckman to Board, 12 May 1686; *ibid*., Instructions to Duxbury, 21 May 1686.

14:   Bod. Lib. Rawl. A475, Duxbury to Hubbald, 12 June 1686; Stafford Record Office D (W) 1778/I/i/1173, Commissioners to Board, 21 June 1686.

15:   PRO WO55/519, Enquiry, 1 October 1686.

16:   PRO WO55/519, Board to Plymouth, 30 April 1687; *ibid*., Instructions to Wharton, 30 April 1687.

17:   PRO WO55/519, Instructions to Wharton, Edwards, Duxbury and Holt, 3 June 1687.

18:   KUHRO BRB 6, 203; Stafford Record Office D (W) 1778/I:/1233, Beckman to Board, 24 September 1687; PRO WO55/519, Orders of Commissioners, 26 October 1687; CTB vol. 7, part 2, 1681-85, 1250.

19:   PRO WO55/519, Instructions to Duxbury, Richards and Edwards, 5 April 1688; PRO WO55/1785, Contract, 19 May 1688; PRO WO55/519, Commissioners to Board, 2 May 1688; *ibid*., Board to Commissioners, 9 June 1688; *ibid*., Instructions to Duxbury, 10 November 1688.

20:   PRO WO46:1 (index), 254, Orders of Board, 18 October 1681; e.g. Foreman 1998, 65-6; PRO WO46:1 (index), 330, Letters to Board, 29 July 1682; *ibid*., 289, Letters from Board, 19 September 1682.

21:   PRO WO46:1 (index), 335, Letters to Board, 7 October 1682; *ibid*., 14 October 1682; *ibid*., 259, Orders of Board, 20 October 1682; Stafford Record Office D (W) 1778/V/64(52), Abstract of Payments, 9 December 1682; PRO WO46:2 (index), 194, Letters from Hull, 16 February 1684; *ibid*., 201, 24 March 1684; *ibid*., 111, Board to Hull, 8 April 1684; Bod. Lib. Rawl. A476 item 1, 5, Duxbury to Board, 16 April 1684; *ibid*., 20 November 1684.

22:   PRO WO46:2, ?264, ?Letters from Hull, 22 September 1684; *ibid*., 301, Beckman to Board, 12 December 1684.

23:   PRO WO46:2, 52, Orders of Commissioners, 17 September 1684; *ibid*., 259, Beckman to Board, 17 September 1684.

24:   PRO WO46:2, 300, Beckman to Board, 6 December 1684, punctuation slightly amended.

25:   Bod. Lib. Rawl. A476, item 1, Duxbury to Board, 13 April 1685; Bod. Lib. Rawl. A475, Duxbury to Board, 7 October 1685; PRO WO55/519, Enquiry, 1 October 1686; *ibid*., Order from Musgrave, 3 October 1686.

26:   PRO WO46:2, 55, Order of Commissioners, 11 December 1684; *ibid*., 301, Beckman to Board, 12 December 1684; PRO WO55/519, Instructions to Duxbury, 20 March 1688.

27:   Bod. Lib. Rawl. A475, Osbourne's Bill, 6 May 1683.

28:   Sykes 1893, 27 September 1693.

29:   Stafford Record Office D (W) 1778/V/64 (52), Lambert's Accounts, 22 July 1682; *ibid*., 14 October 1682; *ibid*., 5 August 1682; Bod. Lib. Rawl. A475, Orders, 7 May 1683; *ibid*., 15, Orders of Commissioners, 23 June 1683.

30:   PRO WO55/519, Commissioners to Mason, 26 June 1685; *ibid*., 13 June 1685; Tickell 1798, 680-1; Short 1998, table 1; PRO WO55/519, Commissioners to Mason, 24 September 1687, 15 October 1687.

31:   Tickell 1798, 680-1; pers. comm. Geoff Percival; Short 1998, table 2; PRO WO55/519, Board to Commissioners, 5 August 1685; *ibid*., Board to Beckman, 24 August 1687, Orders of Commissioners, 26 October 1687.

32:   Stafford Record Office D (W) 1778/V/64 (52), Lambert's Accounts, 7 October 1682-2 December 1682; PRO WO46:1 (index), 260, Orders of Board, 5 December 1682; *ibid*., 291, Letters from Board, 22 December 1682; PRO WO46:2 (index), 314, 3 August 1683; Bod. Lib. Rawl. A475, Board to Commissioners, 4 May 1683; *ibid*., Orders of Commissioners, 20 May 1683; PRO WO55/519, Bill of Works. 7 October 1685.

33:   PRO WO55/319, Commissioners to Mason, 16 September 1686, 16 October 1686; KUHRO BRB 6, 164, 10 June 1686.

34:   PRO WO46:2 (index), 38, Orders of Commissioners, 16 July 1684; *ibid*., 65, Commissioners to Mason, 20 September 1684; Bod. Lib. Rawl. A475, Duxbury to Beckman, 31 May 1686; PRO WO55/519, Commissioners to Mason, 24 September 1687; *ibid*., 15 October 1687; HMC Dartmouth Mss, 136.

35:   Bod. Lib. Rawl. A475, 15, Orders of Commissioners, 23 June 1683; *ibid*., 10 June 1683; *ibid*., 16 July 1683; PRO WO46:2 (index), 313, Contracts, 1 August 1683;

ibid., 105, Board to Hull, 20 February 1684; *ibid.*, 215, Hull to Board, 4 May 1684.

36: PRO WO55/519, Commissioners to Mason, 6 June 1685; Bod. Lib. Rawl. A476, item 1, Bill, 9 April 1685.

37: Bod. Lib. Rawl. A475, Duxbury to Hubbald, 3 March 1686; PRO WO55/519, Commissioners to Mason, 24 September 1687; *ibid.*, 15 October 1687.

38: PRO WO55/1785, Contract, 10 August 1681.

39: Stafford Record Office D (W) 1778/V/64 (52), Lambert's Accounts, 15 July 1682, 27 July 1682, 5 August 1682, 12 August 1682, 15 August 1682, 8 October 1682, 4 November 1682, 11 November 1682.

40: Bod. Lib. Rawl. A475, Order, 23 April 1683, Orders of Commissioners, 27 April 1683; *ibid.*, Orders, 7 May 1683, 19 May 1683, 30 May 1683; *ibid.*, Orders of Commissioners, 10 June 1683; *ibid.*, Order, 25 June 1683.

41: Bod. Lib. Rawl. A475, Orders of Commissioners, 27 June 1683; *ibid.*, Account, 30 June 1683.

42: PRO WO51/37, TBB series 2, 44a, 29 September 1688.

43: Bod. Lib. Rawl. A475, Account, 30 June 1683; PRO WO51/28, TBB series 2, 112, March 1684.

44: PRO WO55/519, Commissioners to Mason, 13 June 1685; *ibid.*, 4 July 1685; *ibid.*, 24 September 1687; *ibid.*, Orders of Commissioners, 21 November 1687; HMC 14, Mss of the House of Lords 1692-93, 189.

45: PRO WO46:2 (index), 70-71, Commissioners to Mason, 20 November 1684; Bod. Lib. Rawl. A476 item 1, Duxbury to Beckman, 15 March 1685; PRO WO55/519, Commissioners to Mason, 7 July 1685.

46: PRO WO46:2, 312, Contract, 6 December 1683; PRO WO46:1 (index), 263, 8 May 1683; *ibid.*, 297, Letters of Board, 8 May 1683; Pepys' Abstracts of Naval Minutes, 46-7, 67-71.

47: PRO WO51/32 TBB series 2, 82b, March 1686.

48: PRO WO51/28 TBB series 2, 151b, June 1684; PRO WO46:2 (index), 240, 22 July 1684; Bod. Lib. Rawl. A475, Duxbury to Board, 20 July 1685; PRO WO51/33, TBB series 2, 27, September 1686; PRO WO51/37 TBB series 2, 44a, 18 September 1688; *ibid.*, 2 September 1688.

49: PRO WO46:2 (index), 14, Orders of Board, 25 October 1683; Bod. Lib. Rawl. A475, Orders of Commissioners, 10 June 1683; PRO WO46:2 (index), 42, Orders of Commissioners, 15 June 1683; *ibid.*, 20, Orders of Board, 315, Contracts, 15 April 1684; *ibid.*, 319, Contracts, 8 September 1684; *ibid.*, 140, Letters from Hull, 29 September 1684; *ibid.*, 33, Orders of Board, 30 September 1684; CSPD 1685-86, 2; PRO WO51/37, TBB series 3, 123, October 1668.

50: Bod. Lib. Rawl. A475, Duxbury to Board, 20 October 1685; *ibid.*, 14 December 1685; *ibid.*, 40 v., Duxbury to ?, 10 February 1686; *ibid.*, Duxbury to Beckman, 15 March 1686; *ibid.*, Duxbury to Board, 19 April 1686, 21 April 1686; *ibid.*, Duxbury to ?, 16 June 1686.

51: Bod. Lib. Rawl. A476, item 1, 2-3, Duxbury to Beckman, 12 April 1684; e.g. PRO WO46:2, 246, Duxbury to Board, 4 August 1684; Bod. Lib. Rawl. A475, Lloyd to Board, 2 May 1683.

52: PRO WO46:1, 347, Instructions to Lloyd, 17 April 1683.

53: PRO WO55/519, Instructions to Wharton, 2 June 1685.

54: PRO WO46:1, 312, Account of Day Labourers, 13 October 1681; Bod. Lib. Rawl. A475, Duxbury to Beckman, 31 May 1686.

55: PRO WO46:2, 119, Board to Commissioners, 17 June 1684.

56: PRO WO55/519, Commissioners to Board, 13 June 1685; HMC Dartmouth Mss, 136.

57: PRO WO46:1, 308, Beckman to Board, 21 September 1681; Kelsall 1938; PRO WO46:1, 310, Duxbury to Board, 5 October 1681; *ibid.*, 318, Beckman to Board, 23 November 1681.

58: PRO WO46:1, 308, 21 September 1681; PRO WO46:2 (index), Letters from Hull, 17 July 1683; Bod. Lib. Rawl. A475, Orders of Commissioners, 2 June 1683; PRO WO46:1 (index), 41, Orders of Commissioners, 2 June 1683; Bod. Lib. Rawl. A475, Orders of Commissioners, 27 June 1683; PRO WO55/519, Commissioners to Board, postscript, 2 June 1685.

59: e.g. PRO WO46:1 (index), 251, 14 May 1681; KUHRO M373; Woodward 1995, 105; KUHRO M373; Kelsall 1939; PRO WO46:2, 4, Board to Plymouth, 14 July 1683; PRO WO46:1, 312, Account of Day Labourers, 13 October 1681.

60: PRO WO46:1, 335, Duxbury to Board, 9 October 1682; Woodward 1995; PRO WO55/519, Orders of Commissioners, 20 September 1687; Stafford Record Office D (W) 1778/I:/1233, Beckman to Board, 24 September 1687.

61: Bod. Lib. Rawl. A475, Orders of Commissioners, 27 June 1683; *ibid.*, Commissioners to Board, 17 July 1683; KUHRO M373.

62: PRO WO46:2, 4, Orders of Board, 14 July 1683; Bod. Lib. Rawl. A475, Board to Commissioners, 20 July 1683.

63: Bod. Lib. Rawl. A475, Orders of Commissioners, 14 April 1683; ibid., 26 May 1683; *ibid.*, 15 June 1683.

64: PRO WO46:2 (index), 75, 30 June 1683; Bod. Lib. Rawl. A475, Orders of Commissioners, 20 May 1683, 26 May 1683; PRO WO46:2 (index), 120, Board to Hull, 24 June 1684; *ibid.*, 39, Orders of Commissioners, 16 July 1684; PRO WO55/519, Orders of Commissioners, 31 July 1685.

65: PRO WO46:1, 308, Fitch to Board, 25 September 1681; PRO WO55/519,

Instructions to Wharton, 2 June 1685; e.g. Stafford Record Office D (W) 1778/V/64 (52); PRO WO46:2 (index), 43, Orders of Commissioners, 24 June 1683; Bod. Lib. Rawl. A475, Orders of Commissioners, 2 June 1683; e.g. *ibid.*, 19 May 1683, 26 May 1683; PRO WO55/519, Orders of Commissioners, 11 June 1685; *ibid.*, Instructions to Wharton, 2 June 1685.

66:     PRO WO46:1 (index), 320, Letters to Board, 12 December 1681; *ibid.*, 326, 29 April 1682; HMC Dartmouth MSS, 128.

67:     Stafford Record Office D (W) 1778/I:/1233, Beckman to Board, 26 September 1687.

68:     PRO WO55/519, Orders of Commissioners, 31 July 1685.

CHAPTER 9

REVOLUTION 1688

The soldiers of the Hull Garrison were divided into a local force of Independent or Unregimented Companies under the Governor and Deputy-Governor, and other detachments, which passed through the town. These included companies posted to maintain the Garrison at an effective level on a long-term basis; and those sent in time of war, or at other times when a strong military presence was required. Some troops were also armed out of the stores at Hull, but would serve elsewhere.

The army increased in size under James II, and its impact on the local scene increased along with the numbers of soldiers in the town. By 1688, there were between 1,000 and 1,500 soldiers billeted on a civilian population of about 7,000. As tension between the Crown and Corporations developed, attention focused on the military presence *per se*, and on its real or anticipated consequences. The loyalties of the Garrison of Hull played a crucial role in the Glorious Revolution of 1688.

The Garrison

Under the later years of Stuart rule, the post of Governor at Hull remained an important one, and the Crown was always to ensure that reliable officers filled the post. Following the removal of the Duke of Monmouth as Governor of Hull, his office passed to John Sheffield, 3rd Earl of Mulgrove. The effective on-the-spot commander of the Garrison, Deputy-Governor Gilby, died in December 1681. Captain Lionel Copley was appointed in Gilby's place. Copley was noted, by Lord Dartmouth, to have been at Hull in December 1678. The Duke of York remarked: *I am glad Copley is at Hull for I look on him as an honest man*. Robert St Clair was commissioned as Captain of the Foot Company in Garrison at Hull, *whereof Colonel Anthony Gilby was Captain*; and was also to be made Deputy-Governor of West Tilbury Blockhouse and Gravesend fort. St Clair is not encountered in records relating to Hull, and was presumably fully occupied with his duties at Tilbury[1].

In November 1682, Lord Mulgrove fell from royal favour. He *was to quit the court all his places and offices being taken from him - Hull is said to be given to Lord Windsor* (the Earl of Plymouth) *and his regiment to the Earl of Chesterfield*. Both men were closely and personally attached to the royal interest. Plymouth was not only a loyal Tory, but also the illegitimate son of Charles II and Catherine Pegge. Chesterfield had in his younger days courted Barbara Castlemaine, an influential mistress of the King[2].

In May 1684, Sir John Reresby, Governor of York, was offered the Deputy-Governor's post at Hull. Reresby declined the offer: *My Lord Dartmouth told me that if I would accept of the Lieutenant Governorship of Hull with the same salary the King gives me at York (£200), he would obtain it for me... but I told him I could not in honour descend from Governor to Lieutenant-Governor. He replied it was as honourable to be the King's Lieutenant in so great a garrison as to be the Governor of a less... I resolved to continue the command I had if it was possible*. Reresby's decision left Lionel Copley in place as Deputy-Governor. This allowed him to settle down; his office was to be confirmed at the accession of James II in early 1685, and, within two years, John Duxbury could report that Copley *now is become a great husband, and lives a very sober solid life*. The consequences of this appointment were to extend far beyond Copley's domestic circle over the next five years[3].

The Royal Warrant of November 1682, appointing Lord Plymouth as the new Governor, also specified his duty *as captain of 20 soldiers there, whereof 10 are to be gunners with an allowance of 10s per day and a fee of 8d per day for each of the said soldiers*. Duxbury was later to claim extra pay as a member of the Governor's Independent Company, as his predecessor, Storekeeper Watkinson, had enjoyed this perk. The Storekeeper and gunners were part of the Governor's command of 10 soldiers and 10 gunners; *in whose Independent Company both this* (Storekeeper's post) *and the gunners, ought to be entered*[4].

Independent Companies supplied two of six companies forming the Garrison. The Independent Companies had formed the fixed element of a mixed force in the 1670s. Their position was defined by the Establishment of 1683-84, an instrument which remained in force until 1700. Each Independent Company had a captain, lieutenant, ensign, two sergeants, a corporal, and a gentleman-at-arms - the company storekeeper. Their uniform was a red coat, lined with blue facings. Some of the men were out-pensioners of the Chelsea Hospital; old soldiers, for whom employment had been found in the *guards and garrisons*. Muster rolls for the Independent Companies at Hull have not been encountered, but the allowance for *fire and candle* at Hull may reflect provision for the guard duties performed by this element of the Garrison. Hull was listed in 1685 as requiring *fire and candle for 8 guards 10s*. This allowance remained the same in 1688, when the Garrison also included two regiments of regular soldiers, and hence must have related only to those soldiers permanently based at Hull. The *guards* were placed at the gates and other locations about Hull, and hence incurred heating and lighting costs for the premises where they were based[5].

Local soldiers were the most effective personnel to perform routine guard duties about the town. Of the eight *guards* listed under the fire and candle allowance, the position of some is known, and others may be surmised. A *Town Guard* was set every night, centred on the Guardhouse in the Market Place, with another at South End. There was also a *Castle Guard*, and a pair of sentries at South Blockhouse. Guardhouses flanked the Beverley Gate, and guns were later brought into the Citadel from Myton Gate and Hessle Gate; all these gates may have had sentries posted. North Gate lay adjacent to the bridge across the river Hull, and was probably also under a fixed Guard. These posts were probably manned by detachments whose members served on a rota. In 1684, two files of soldiers were to provide an extra pair of sentries at the Main Gate of the Citadel. Two lanterns were issued to the relieving guards on Garrison Side, *since in dark nights the ways being bad*. A file was a squad of up to ten men, so a 50-man company might have provided patrols of about half a dozen men apiece[6].

The Army accounts for the Garrison at Hull covered the charge for the Governor, Deputy-Governor, and two companies of Foot - the Independent Companies. For the period 1681-88, their costs were listed as follows[7]:

1680-81: £109 10s
1681-82: £2,742 6s 8d
1682-83: £2,757 11s 8d
1683-84: £2,877 8s 2d
1684-85: £2,339 2s 4d
1685-86: £500 4s ¼d
1686-87: not stated
1687-88: £1,314 16s 11 ½d.

The Storekeeper supplied the companies with ammunition; and the Officer-in-Chief was to deliver accounts showing their usual requirements. On 1 April 1682, every company had been supplied with match. More was required; and was sent in May 1682. From this time, the works on the Citadel were placed under military guard. This provided only imperfect security. Copley investigated theft from the stores held at South Blockhouse, where his Independent Company had provided sentries - and probably the thieves as well. In July, Duxbury was to negotiate a cheap price for a temporary bridge, and *likewise to make a way for soldiers to relieve the guards*. The *removal of the Guard to South Blockhouse* was discussed in September. In October 1682, Martin Beckman proposed *that a Corps du Guard should be provided for the Citadel*. An account of *smith's work done in the Castle about repairing a room for the captain of the guards* was settled in 1683[8].

Additional regular forces brought the garrison up to its full strength of six companies. The Earl of Mulgrove was Colonel of the Holland Regiment (later the 3rd Regiment of Foot, the *Buffs*), as well as Governor. The Holland regiment was distributed in four unequal parts, assigned to garrison duty at Berwick, Portsmouth, Plymouth and Hull. The first mention of the Holland Regiment at Hull was the arrival of a single company in 1679, along with three others from the Duke of Monmouth's regiment. Peter Bristow was assigned to a company of the Holland Regiment at Hull in 1680. Four companies of this regiment were quartered in Hull in 1681-82, and it was to maintain a presence at varying levels over the next few years[9].

Mulgrove's officers included Captain James Stirling, Commander-in-Chief or senior officer of those in Garrison; Sir Ralf Warton; Captain Francis Collingwood and Captain Cornwall. All served as Commissioners for the works on the Citadel in 1681. Mulgrove's soldiers were involved in the early stages of works on the Citadel. In late September 1681, however, *an order which came from the Earl of Mulgrove that no soldiers shall work, who were all struck off for what reason we cannot understand, but that hindered us two or three days*. The Board of Ordnance wrote to Mulgrove about this. Cornwall's company was ordered to Hull from Portsmouth, in the summer of 1682. They then moved to York in November[10].

An inspection of the Garrison was ordered in June 1683. This followed the Rye House Plot, which had intended the assassination of Charles II and James, and a Protestant rising. A general tightening-up of garrisons was ordered by the King, who gave order *to continue our military officers with our companies in the garrison, and in future any officer absent without leave would be faced with absolute cashiering*. Lord

Plymouth was to *inquire strictly into the irregularities and abuses in the matter of companies now in Garrison at Hull, of which His Majesty has been informed.* Four of the six companies *were informed underhand* of the inspection, and attempted to make up their numbers, which were about 25% below their paper strength of 50 men. In the Governor's own Independent Company, under Lieutenant Gower, there were 38 men, 5 allowed to officers, and 3 servants to make up the numbers to 50. Of these, 16 were married, contrary to regulation. Lieutenant Cooke had 37 duty-men; the other four companies were much the same, but were filled up following this enquiry[11].

Plymouth found: *The military officers were not careful in their duty which I hope is well regulated having punished a Lieutenant for it and several common soldiers. The Civil magistrates here* (were) *very negligent of putting the laws into execution against the fanatics the particular I formerly writ to the Privy Seal.* The latter matter was pursued with the Bench, who were cajoled into a show of rigorous law-enforcement against the Dissenters. Plymouth ordered: *That the conventicles, (which he took to be nurseries of faction, etc. and opposite to both divine and human laws) might be suppressed.* Some of the Bench, *hearing the Earl so bitter against the Dissenters, informed against the two Meeting-Houses then in the town, whose Ministers were called Mr Ashley and Mr Charliss. Upon which, the Constables were immediately sent to apprehend them: the former absconded; but the latter was taken, fined, and committed to Prison. Their hearers were sharply rebuked*[12].

Lieutenant Gower, Plymouth's deputy in command of his Independent Company, resigned his post after the shake-up. Gower desired *to assign his employment* to Mr Hutchinson, who took up the post in September 1683. Hutchinson's appointment was requested by Sir Christopher Musgrave, of the Board of Ordnance, his brother-in-law. His tenure was, however, only for a year; Thomas Legard was commissioned as Lieutenant of Plymouth's Independent Foot Company in November 1684. Plymouth also investigated *what methods the former Lieutenants* (of the county) *had taken, in ordering the militia; whereby he might make a more regular improvement*[13].

In 1683, the Governor's Independent Foot Company and four other companies collected arms. The allocation of weapons suggests that the soldiers were divided into three equal groups: a third were equipped with pikes, a third with the old-fashioned matchlock muskets, and the remainder with the more modern flintlocks or firelocks. The arms comprised 36 muskets, which included 17 fire-locks and 17 matchlocks; 16 pikes; 34 collars or bandoliers; one drum and one halberd supplied to Lieutenant Legard, *for the use of my Lord Plymouth's 50,* and the same to the other four companies. The soldiers were under the command of Captain Collingwood; Captain Bristow, who collected arms for the Earl of Mulgrove's recruits; Captain Throgmorton who collected them for his recruits; and Lieutenant Wilkinson, collecting for Sir Hurry's recruits. They were issued with arms out of the stores at Hull[14].

The next year, 1684, the Board ordered: *That a proportion be drawn for sending arms to Hull for part of the Holland Regiment and a letter written to the storekeeper.* The Board wrote in September 1684, *to Mr Watkinson touching the arms sent for 5 companies of the Holland Regiment there.* Captain Collingwood, Major Stirling and Major Morgan of the Holland Regiment continued to serve as Commissioners for the works on the Citadel in 1685. Collingwood, and Captain Titcombe, *Commander-in-Chief* of the Holland regiment, also served as Commissioners in 1687. The Holland Regiment had established a relatively long-standing relationship with Hull, which may have mitigated the irritations associated with a military presence[15].

Stores and Guns

Hull continued to serve as an important depot through the 1680s. As such, it held stores, munitions and guns. These would pass to and fro from the Tower of London, and from Hull to the fortifications at Berwick or Tynemouth, maintaining stores required for routine use. Arms and ammunition would also be issued to Crown forces in time of need. This service became more important from April 1684, when the Ordnance Store at Clifford's Tower in York was destroyed by an accidental fire. The Storekeeper at Hull was an employee of the Board, but cooperated closely with the Governor or Deputy-Governor. Up to 1684, the Storekeeper was John Watkinson. In 1685 he retired, to be replaced by Duxbury, who added this post to his other responsibilities for works on the Citadel[16].

The arms in store included the Train of Artillery for the North. This was distinct from the guns arming the defences, and accompanied troops taking the field in northern Britain, as in 1639-40. It is possible that the Train passed through Hull under the Commonwealth, when the port shipped both siege guns and those captured from royalist strongholds, and when it supplied logistic support for campaigns in Scotland. A muster was taken of the Train at Hull on 1 July 1675. In January 1685, Duxbury complained he was *charged with several stores in the Master Gunner's custody, which belong to the Train delivered to him before my time, by order.* This might suggest that the Train had arrived only after the Restoration, under Watkinson's tenure of the Storekeeper's post and Mr Osbourne's service as Master Gunner. By 1682, Ordnance stores were kept in hired rooms, probably in the town, whence they were to be removed[17].

The guns of the Train were stored disassembled. Beckman wrote in 1682, about *the removing of stores and placing the wheels and carriages of the Train.* With the movement of stores, the carriages *ought to be secured from the weather.* An account of the defects of the Train was sent to the Board of Ordnance, in October 1682. New carriages and horse harness were ordered, and the work given to Joseph Blaides and Mr Blisset. The train carriages were standing a foot deep in water in late 1683; when Watkinson required an order to disburse money for laying up the harness in store[18].

In 1684, four brass guns of the Train were lodged in South Blockhouse. In 1684, the Train comprised 12 brass guns; two culverins of 11 and 10ft; four demi-culverins of 11ft; six demi-culverins, two of 10ft, two of 9½ft and two of 9ft; and also *close wagons ordinary and two tumbrils for the shot*[19].

The conditions at South Blockhouse were far from ideal for the storage of any military *materiel*. In early 1684, Watkinson wrote about the damp condition of powder and powder rooms and the South Blockhouse, where the train carriages were lodged. The *door for the room for the Train guns* was to be rebuilt, and its floor paved. Even with such improvements, there was inadequate internal space. Duxbury enumerated the disadvantages of South Blockhouse as a gun-carriage store: *That room will hold but 8, without the gun, for the room is not high enough to fix a gyn (for lifting gun barrels onto carriages), nor large enough to turn around if they were mounted in the couch. Now those carriages are all cleaned and fixed, I cannot perceive but that they are all good and serviceable. It would be very convenient to have all these lower rooms cleared of the rubbish etc and paved which would contain a great many stores*[20].

In 1685, South Blockhouse flooded again, and guns and carriages were lying in the wet; the guns and carriages all had to be taken out and dried in the sun. The Train is not mentioned again, and, as more stores were brought to South Blockhouse, they may have displaced it. Some ammunition and other heavy goods had been kept at South End, to the west of the mouth of the river Hull, up to November 1684. These were removed to the Citadel in March 1686: *the shed at South House (where the shot, lead and other stores lies) is much decayed and some boards broken down by the weight of the said stores. I have for their better security caused the same to be removed to South Blockhouse and placed with the rest according to their respective natures.* There had been 4,399 round shot at South End, and other stores, and their transfer to South Blockhouse can have left little room for the gun carriages of the Train[21].

In 1683, at the discovery of the Rye House Plot, guns mounted on the defences of the town of Hull were moved to arm the Citadel. Duxbury mounted 7 sakers on ship carriages at the Saluting Platform, where 25 gun-ports stood empty. Two were to come from Beverley Gate, two from Myton Gate, and three from Hessle Gate. Two guns were to be mounted on the Castle. The recently constructed earthworks of the western side of the Citadel were still awaiting guns. At the South Blockhouse half-bastion, 13 guns were wanted. At the Castle half-bastion, *18 are wanted, 49 in all.* At South End and South Blockhouse, there were *24 guns wanting carriages.* In May 1684, *John Hutchinson* was paid *for freight of 9 ship carriages from London to Hull certified by Mr Duxbury*[22].

In August 1685, at Monmouth's rebellion, Duxbury again detailed the state and number of guns on the Citadel's Saluting Platform. Seven sakers still stood there; four culverin carriages were still wanted, either here or perhaps for the Train, together with one six-pounder and saker's ship carriages. *We have made shift to patch up so many carriages that will serve the rest of the guns for the present which all are mounted. We shall want both saker guns and ships carriages for the Saluting Platform where are twenty-five ports but seven mounted... (which) I think ought to be standing carriages*[23].

The guns of the Saluting Platform provided formal evidence that Hull was a defended port. The firing of salutes to visiting ships was a convention signalling the Garrison's readiness to defend Hull. It also, by custom, honoured important visitors, such as visiting circuit judges, or, on occasion, local dignitaries. Salutes marked the sovereign's birthday, accession and death, St George's Day, and November 5, the latter *to commemorate God's great deliverance from gunpowder treason.* An allowance was fixed for such uses, though heavy traffic on the river could result in the gunners exceeding their allowance of powder and match by greeting every ship[24].

In April 1684, the Deputy-Governor was instructed to ensure that such formalities could be more economically observed. Salutes to ships were reduced to *no more than five lesser cannon*, and otherwise were only to be fired for admirals, generals or ambassadors. Captain Collingwood requested the usual monthly allowance - 10 barrels of gunpowder, half a ton of match and 4 qt of paper for the gunners, and, *I do not expect any more guns to be fired until 5 November.* He had *given out orders to the gunners not to salute any merchant ships so that there will be no need of any more powder till the 23rd instant. Being the King's Coronation Day then they will want a supply, which formerly used to be 10 barrels at a time, but now 5 barrels is enough, and as much as they can lay safe in their powder rooms.* These economies could embarrass those with a keen sense of military etiquette. *We had none left to fire upon St George's Day according to the King's Instructions, for which the Governor ordered 21* (gun salute) *and the Dragon frigate coming hither with soldiers, saluted the Garrison with 11 guns, which were answered but with 5 according to the Instructions, but Capt. Hambleton took it as a great affront to have no more*[25].

Soldiers of King James II

Charles II died, and was succeeded by James II, on 2 February 1685. Governor Plymouth sent an express messenger to order the doubling of guards, and to urge a *great care of dangerous persons*, ahead of his own arrival at Hull. However, *By the best enquiries I could make in the counties I came through I met great sadness but as I thought with very peaceable intention. The like I am informed in adjacent parts are of the same temper.* The passing of the old King initially left only the formalities of James' accession to be observed[26].

The Governors of garrisons were responsible for the proclamation of the succession, and the renewal of the commissions of their officers. They were ordered to *call together the officers and soldiers of their garrison and cause the first proclamation to be read to them and commission them the other and that as soon as the same is published they cause volleys of small shot and the cannons of the garrisons to be discharged.* At Hull, the *Governor performed his part. Garrison drawn up in arms at the cross... 3 volleys of small shot... soldiers file by file drawn up and drank the King's health.* An extraordinary *triple discharge of all the great guns in the town and Citadel* was fired to mark the event[27].

While he was in Hull, Plymouth was to attempt to use his influence over the Bench's nomination of Members of Parliament in the first election under James II. He *prevailed with this Corporation and the Trinity House here to make address of congratulation to His Majesty, promising to oppose the election of any person that was for the Bill of Exclusion.* Sir Willoughby Hickman of Gainsborough, a relative of Plymouth, was duly elected, alongside John Ramsden, a merchant of Hull[28].

All the garrison posts were renewed. Plymouth was commissioned Captain of his Independent Company with Thomas Legard as his Lieutenant; and Peter Bristow as ensign *of an Independent Company of Foot in Garrison at Kingston-upon-Hull.* Bristow had been commissioned ensign of a company of the Holland Regiment at Hull in 1680, and his transfer to the locally based component of the Garrison after five years might suggest that he had settled in Hull. Lionel Copley was confirmed as Deputy-Governor; he was also commissioned to be *Captain of an Independent Company of Foot to be raised forthwith.* The new Independent Company under Copley was to incur additional costs for the fire and candle allowance. The daily allowance was 1s for every company. Its annual cost was to rise to £45 14s 0d at Hull, because *there were upon the increase of the forces in 1685 more companies there than allowed upon the establishment, so that the above direction for regulating the allowance for fire and candle could not be punctually observed.* Plymouth was assigned *twenty sufficient soldiers (commanded) there by his deputy etc.* By March, he was back in London, at his house in Picadilly, while Copley commanded at Hull. Alderman Matthew Hardy, a Commissioner for the works on the Citadel, was commissioned as surgeon to the forces in Garrison, in March 1685[29].

In the course of 1685, the accession of James was challenged by rebellions in Scotland and the West Country. The former, under the Duke of Argyll, collapsed almost as soon as it had begun. The latter, under the Duke of Monmouth, bastard son of Charles II and himself formerly Governor at Hull, was more dangerous. Monmouth had been banished on account of his suspected involvement in the Rye House Plot, but was tempted into contesting the throne by the prospect of alliance with Argyll. Monmouth landed at Lyme Regis in early June 1685, soon commanded a force of 7,000 ill-led men, and was proclaimed King of England by the Mayor of Taunton on 18 June. The government raised new forces to put down this revolt[30].

At news of Monmouth's rebellion, Copley armed the six companies in Garrison at Hull. Match and shot could only be supplied to 4 companies. As the new Storekeeper, Duxbury reported: *we have not one bundle of serviceable match to supply the rest... I have according to the Lieutenant-Governor's orders set the armourer about cleaning and fixing his arms being a new company.* The arms were issued by Duxbury: *On Saturday last by order of Captain Copley, I supplied all these 6 companies with 50 and for recourse (viz.) 17 Mus(kets) 17 Snaph(ances) 16 pikes, 34 collars of bandoliers, one drum and one halbert. The officers complained of the badness of the arms, though I gave every sergeant liberty to go in and choose the best in the store, but it being above three years since they were cleaned, they are very rusty, and will always be so without a settled armourer to be continually fulfilling the same*[31].

Monmouth's rising saw eleven regiments raised by the Crown. Not all disbanded after Monmouth was beaten at Sedgemoor, on 6 July, and they were eventually to become the 5th to 15th Regiments of Foot. Hull could play only a modest role in the mobilisation of 1685, and its unfinished defences were hurriedly armed with what guns were available. Sir William Clifton's Regiment of Foot (later the 15th Foot, the East Yorkshire Regiment) was intended to be armed out of stores at Hull, but *we have not sufficient arms to do it, all want fixing and cleaning which the officers are loth to indent for. We have now enclosed all the works on Drypool side, and in a short time will bring it into a good posture of defence, having mounted several guns upon the bastions upon such old carriages as we could pick out to serve for the present, but we have 12 guns more than we have carriages for.* By 20 July, Duxbury had set a gunsmith to clean and repair defective arms at 6d a pair for pistols, and 4d for each musket[32].

The arming of new regiments slowed after the rebels were defeated. The Mayor of Hull received a letter informing him of the government victory, but was *warned to watch and search and apprehend persons, persons travelling up and down not well known... to use diligence therein and for preventing all further rising or disorders.* Mr Richard Thompson junior, *secured in the time of the late rebellion,* was discharged from Hull in late November, giving security to appear at York assizes. On 27 July, Duxbury reported on the plans for arming soldiers and their imperfect implementation: *I was before acquainted with the (?)Rediccorent of the troops of Horse and Regiments of Foot by the Governor who showed me a copy of the King's Warrant for the same which I should have supplied accordingly but now as yours came to me from Sir William Clifton about his arms (for) which I shall want snapphance and muskets.* He received drums from disbanding recruits, and was cleaning pistols for Captain Fairfax's Troop of Horse, in July[33].

By August, the Horse were reduced from 50 to 40 in a troop, and the Foot returned to their peace-time strength of 50 men per company. William Clifton's regiment was disbanded. The Garrison companies were reduced in size, and the arms returned. The officers at Hull required more powder and match than was allowed, *by reason of their extraordinary exercise, many of their soldiers being raw, and undisciplined* - new soldiers used their extra issues in training. Captain Fairfax and Sir Thomas Mauleverer's troops of horse were still to receive their arms. This was because a policing role remained for mounted troops after the defeat of rebels in the field[34].

Hull had taken over the role of depot for units based at York, as well as for the local Garrison. A Lieutenant Williamson failed to return arms issued for his company, *which he says were all broken to pieces, and he wants bandoliers to march with,* suggesting that his company was preparing to leave. In December, *Duxbury at last received the arms hereafter mentioned from Sir John Reresby's reduced Company of grenadiers at York; but there wants the hatchets, grenades, fuses, halberd and drum, when I should have received according to your Honour's order, but I understand Sir John Reresby has retained the same.* The returned arms, equipment for ten men, were listed as follows: *10 carbines slingers; 10 pouches with belts; 10 bayonets with girdles; 10 cartridge boxes with girdles*[35].

Some of the Holland Regiment companies left Hull, to be replaced by other companies of the same regiment. Captain Hatton's company came to Hull in January 1686; Captain Titcombe was the senior officer in Garrison at the beginning of February - both were officers of the Holland Regiment. Three months proportion of powder and match was issued to the companies in January 1686, representing a return to the normal quarterly issue of stores[36].

On 12 November 1685, James had announced his intention to retain his enlarged army. Monmouth's rising supplied the reason for this controversial step. James had declared that the militia was useless - some in the South-West had actually joined Monmouth's rebellion. The standing force was so small that he had now raised it to a greater number, which would be a double charge upon him to maintain. It was true that there were some popish officers in his army, but he hoped that would not cause misunderstanding between him and Parliament. He needed: *A good force of well-disciplined troops in constant pay, that can defend us from such as, either at home or abroad, are disposed to disturb us and even to increase the number to the proportion I have done*[37].

In military terms, James' declaration carried force. Politically, however, it understated the tension attending the establishment of a standing army tainted with his own religious beliefs. The small number of Catholics in the army made for a vicious circle of apprehension. Members of Parliament complained of the unruliness of soldiers, and voiced the traditional complaints that a standing army *debauched the manners of all the people, their wives, daughters and servants. Men do not go to church where they are quartered, for fear mischief should be done in their absence*[38].

Quarters in the town

The *evils of quartering* were an important cause of friction between the Hull Bench and the government. Though barracks might have solved the practical problems of housing soldiers, their provision was thought to increase the risk that the military would become divorced from the civil population. The Bench had entertained the Garrison officers in September 1685; and supplied its customary gifts of barrels of ale for Lord Plymouth, Lord Dartmouth, Secretary Guy, Sir Christopher Musgrave, all of the Board of Ordnance; and for Mr Kynvin, the Corporation's lawyer. These may have been sweeteners to accompany *a letter forwarded to the Earl of Plymouth and as to billeting soldiers*[39].

The post of Town Major, the officer responsible for billeting in the town, was filled by John Johnson, until his death in 1685. He was replaced by Edward Carew, employed by the army *at the sum of 4s a day for finding quarters for the companies of guards*. Carew was succeeded by George Barratt, in December 1686. Barratt's tenure was to see the accommodation of soldiers became an increasingly sensitive issue in the town[40].

The lodging of soldiers had been a familiar aspect of life in Hull since 1643, and had come to supplement the income of poorer inhabitants. In 1687, the Bench rehearsed the recent history of quartering in Hull. *The Corporation has been forced to find quarters for them in private houses at their charge, whereas formerly the constant method (before Theophilus Oglethorpe's regiment [the Holland Regiment] came hither) was for the poor sort of people upon their first arrival of any regiment or company to receive them from the parade into their houses, of whom they had not only lodging, but fire, candle, small beer, washing, salt, pepper and vinegar and all this for 8d a week with which the soldier as well as the poor inhabitants were very well content*[41].

The King ordered that no soldier be allowed free quarter; and that quarters in private houses should only be granted by consent of the householders. In 1686, the government ordered a detailed survey of *all the inns* (and) *alehouses in England with their stable room and bedding*. The survey listed 199 *guest beds* and stabling for 460 horses in Hull. When the Garrison increased, overcrowding was claimed to cause difficulties for the keepers of public houses, which were by law required to accommodate soldiers. They *were forced to lie on the floors, to let the soldiers have their beds, others were forced to place several of these soldiers billeted on them in private houses and to pay 8d, 10d, and some 12d a week for them, to the ruin of many*. This petition perhaps overstated the case. Real difficulties may, however, have arisen with finding room for both soldiers and the unskilled labourers or *country people* when works at the Citadel were under way[42].

In late 1686, Captain Collingwood, in charge of the Garrison companies of the Holland Regiment, sought Captain Birch and Lieutenant Fogg, to find quarters for 500 of their men and officers. It was rumoured that they were to be placed on free quarters: forcibly billeted on the householders of the town. People refused to put them up, unless a Standing Order was issued that they should pay the customary 8d a week for lodging. Early in 1687, four companies of Colonel Cornwall's Regiment (later the 9th Foot) were to pay private quarter in private houses and public houses at 8d a week. Cornwall's Regiment was described as *this unruly regiment*, by Reresby, the Governor of York. The troops left arrears owed to publicans and householders alike, and *a general outcry concerning the great numbers of soldiers in the town*. The townspeople complained that Cornwall's Regiment owed arrears of £127 10s 6d, while the Colonel claimed they owed only £83 4s 4d. The pursuit of the debt presented monumental problems. The Bench's lawyer felt this dispute could only be resolved by trawling through the muster rolls of the regiment to establish the identity and billet of each private soldier[43].

An order from the King and Council duly ordered 8d a week to be paid by men of Cornwall's Regiment in both private and public houses. There were 300 soldiers in public houses, exceeding the available number of beds by 100. Further troops arrived in 1687. James II ordered: *our Royal Regiment of Foot* (later the 1st Foot, or Royal Scots) *to march... to our Garrison at Hull and Beverley where they are to remain until further orders and to do such duty within our said Garrison as our Governor there shall direct, and your officers are to take care that the soldiers behave themselves civilly and pay their landlords and all Magistrates Justices of the Peace constables and our other officers whom it may concern, and hereby assisting them in providing quarters and otherwise as there shall be occasion*[44].

The stated reason for bringing so many soldiers to Hull was their employment as labourers on the Citadel. In September 1687, Beckman had 100 soldiers at work, along with 60 country people. Four companies came from Beverley, *from Lord Dumbarton's Regiment who quartered in Beverley*. Cornwall's Regiment was back in late September. Their return was at James' order, *to work on the fortifications of the Citadel which was making there*. Four officers, suggesting contingents drawn from at least four companies, were to serve as additional overseers on the works: Sergeant Davison, Ensign Moore, Ensign Hastings and Lieutenant Luddrington. The order appointing them was signed by Beckman, three Alderman Commissioners, and Lieutenant-Colonel Purcell, Commander-in-Chief of Cornwall's Regiment[45].

There was a limit to the space to be found for soldiers in the public houses of Hull. One solution proposed by the military was to redefine other commercial premises as public houses. In February 1688, Kynvin, the attorney retained by the Bench, set out the position he was to represent to the Crown in opposing this initiative. He based his case on the government's own survey of accommodation. *To me it seems very plain that supposing there were conveniently to quarter 300 in the public houses, yet that my Lord Dumbarton's 4 companies and Colonel Cornwall's whole regiment ought to pay for private quarters tho' they were in public houses according to his Majesty's orders, since I suppose the 7 companies of my Lord Dumbarton's Regiment there before exceed the 300. And as to what allowances those to be quartered in public houses are for the future to have; I will endeavour that it be settled by His Majesty to prevent further clamours. I find Lord Dumbarton was much dissatisfied with the return that has been made as to the public houses, and nothing will serve his lordship but that brewers, bakers, butchers and brandy shops ought to be esteemed public houses, which he designs very strongly to insist on tomorrow before His Majesty[46].*

In August 1688, the regiment at York was ordered to Hull. There was again an outcry against the large number of troops that were lodged in private houses. The *ad hoc* system for housing soldiers again made the pursuit and collection of arrears owed for their quarters difficult. A petition of the Mayor and Aldermen complained that the Scots Guards had left the town without discharging their quarters in private houses, *£175 being due to several of the poorer inhabitants*. These soldiers were not all kept busy on the Citadel; in 1688 only a fifth of them were available to help, too few to make up more than one labour-gang. Beckman reported, in May 1688, that *the Regiment now here in garrison cannot afford above 10 commanded men out of a company whereof there must be taken 40 men for ramming; the rest being too few for working by task-works[47]*.

As well as providing manpower for the works at the Citadel, soldiers could be set on the more obstreperous Dissenters. Copley, as commander of an Independent Company, was prominent in this activity. He hounded John Baker, a substantial pewterer of the town, who was insultingly termed *the Protestant tinker*. Baker had formerly been at odds with Gilby, Copley's predecessor as Deputy-Governor, not least for his involvement in the investigation of the misappropriation of building materials. Baker's horse and saddle were stolen by soldiers. His cattle were impounded in *Hull Blockhouse*, and the military encroached on his lands. Copley seized the mails, and had them delivered to him at his house, or to a tavern, where he opened them in his search for evidence against Baker. Baker was arrested, but as a substantial merchant of the town was then released on bail by the Mayor. Copley was furious. He wrote to the Mayor: *I desire you will favour me with a copy of the commitment this night, and you will oblige*. Before the court, Copley *complained that Mr John Baker who was confined to his house on Sunday last did not object to his confinement and further that he apprehended a letter sent by the post to the said John Baker on Saturday night before, in which was writ treasonable words thereupon this court thought fit to commit the said John Baker to prison and accordingly a committing was signed by this court for his commitment[48]*.

In 1687, John Baker presented a petition to Parliament, and within the month was granted a writ of *noli proseqi*, a notice that a prosecution *for speaking dangerous words* was to be discontinued. Baker's petition supported James' moves towards religious toleration. This has been variously interpreted. In the traditional view, this was a cheeky ploy by a disputatious Dissenter to claim benefit from policies intended to assist Catholics, who lay at the opposite end of the political and religious spectrum of opinion. According to more recent research, Baker may have been a government spy. According to this view, his petition may have been a serious move to promote alliance between Hull's Dissenters and the government's pro-Catholic interest, against a predominantly Anglican establishment[49].

Whatever Baker's intentions, the matter did not close there. In 1688, an assault was reported against the Postmaster of Hull, George Mawson. Mawson had complained to the Postmaster-General about Copley's interference with the mail, and Copley was told to desist. Mawson was taken by a sergeant and four musketeers to the Guardhouse in Hull, and was tied by the neck and heels for more than two hours. This episode created further protest, as a clear offence by soldiers against a government employee and civilian, and one arising from military intrusion into local affairs. The soldiers' action was roundly condemned in Parliament[50].

Town-Taking day

The disgrace of the Whigs in the last years of the reign of Charles II had permitted the peaceful succession of his brother James. The new government had defended his throne with the help of the army. Concern at James' Catholic faith, whose implications were limited so long as he remained without male issue, was outweighed by a more general fear of civil war. Protestant opinion had been mollified by the agreement that, on James' death, the throne should pass to his son-in-law, the Dutch Protestant Prince William of Orange. This compromise was, however, to be disrupted as James sought to advance his co-religionists to positions of power. The issue was ultimately one of trust. Charles II had successfully maintained a firm division between private inclination and public policy. James II was to fail to strike such a balance, and his autocratic manner and personal piety merely fed suspicion of his political motives.

James admired Louis XIV, whose rule provided a glittering model of the possibilities of absolute monarchy. Under *le Roi Soleil*, France was to become the most powerful state in Europe. In 1683, Louis revoked the Edict of Nantes, a measure which had granted toleration to French Protestants. Louis first purged his army of *Huguenot* officers, and then instigated religious persecutions of his non-Catholic subjects. France had angled for alliance with England through the 1680s, to the dismay of those who saw England's natural allies among the Protestant nations of northern Europe. The association between absolute rule and Catholicism, and the rising power of France, provoked deepening disquiet among English Protestants, and throughout the Anglican establishment.

The influence of Anglicanism was safeguarded by the Test Acts passed under Charles II, which required all holders of public office to take the Anglican communion, thereby signalling their loyalty to the established Church of England under the King. James issued a Declaration of Liberty of Conscience in April 1687, opening a campaign to set aside the Test Acts. Employing powers under the royal prerogative, James issued batches of dispensations to exempt Catholics from the Test Acts. The pro-French Earl of Sunderland was appointed at the head of a Catholic Cabal or cabinet, and his appointment was followed by attempts to place Catholics in positions of influence as admirals, governors, colonels and privy councillors.

Other aspects of royal policy hinted that absolutism and Catholicism converged

in the person of James, and that his admiration for Louis XIV might turn to imitation. In Ireland, the Earl of Tyrconnel, James' Lieutenant-General, purged the army of Protestants; 4,000 discharged soldiers were driven away without even their coats. In America, colonial governments were rolled up into a single body, the Dominion of New England, which was to be ruled under a Governor serving as the King's personal representative. In England, James sought to influence the borough Corporations to nominate Members of Parliament sympathetic to his policies, so that Parliament could be packed with a majority prepared to support them[51].

Plymouth, the Governor of Hull, died in November 1687. He was replaced by Marmaduke, Lord Langdale, of Holme-on-Spalding-Moor, a prominent East Yorkshire Catholic. The Bench arranged a dinner for Langdale and his officers, which he could not attend because of bad weather. The entertainment was postponed until early December, when the Bench chose Christopher Bacon of Ferriby, one of very few Hullshire Catholics - there were only three Catholics recorded in the town of Hull itself between 1676 and 1706 - to serve as intermediary in their first formal meeting with the Governor. Bacon was subsequently to serve as Langdale's agent in his attempts to bend the Bench to support James II. In the light of its past reluctance to enforce laws against Dissenters, the Crown proposed Langdale as Recorder of the Bench, declining the town's nominee. Langdale was duly made a freeman of Hull and, thus qualified to hold municipal office, became Recorder in December 1687[52].

In January 1688, the Queen was reported to be pregnant. James reissued his Declaration of Liberty of Conscience, ordering that it should be read in every church. On 18 May, seven bishops petitioned against this renewed attack on Anglican primacy, and were briefly consigned to the Tower. Langdale informed the government that the ministers of the two churches in Hull had not read the Declaration on the day appointed. On 10 June 1688, a son was born to James. The prospect of a Protestant succession had vanished overnight. A government laced with Catholics, in defiance of laws passed by Parliament, was now engaged in the promotion of absolutist policies under a Catholic dynasty[53].

Parliament was dissolved in July, and James embarked on measures to ensure that a tractable House of Commons would be elected to support him. The temper of the country was to be known by the tone of formal Addresses sent by local authorities to the Crown. Hull's response to James' second Declaration had been both lukewarm and late; and John Baker's own *Address of the Goldsmiths and other Burgesses*, howsoever motivated, outshone it. The Bench then indirectly declined to accept royal control over the nomination of their Members of Parliament, telling the King in a letter *that the election should be free, according to ancient custom*[54].

The trend of events had provoked first deep disquiet, and then, as this went unheeded, conspiracy against a government set on the subversion of English liberties and the Anglican establishment. Six leading peers and the Bishop of London invited William of Orange to invade England and lead a rebellion against James, his father-in-law. Senior army officers, particularly from regiments based near London, and veterans of the Tangiers campaign, were drawn into the plot over the summer of 1688. By September 1688, the Dutch Estates General had agreed that William should lead a force to England to deflect the perceived threat of an alliance between England and France. Thomas Osborne, Earl of Danby and Lord Lieutenant of the West Riding of Yorkshire, was foremost among the conspirators. Danby intended to make himself master of Hull, York and Scarborough, and William's chief advisor. It was probably at his urging that the conspirators advocated a landing in the North, either at Bridlington Bay or south of the Humber. This idea was opposed by advice of seamen, as the North Sea could not be trusted so late in the season[55].

In August 1688, it was rumoured at Court that the French and Dutch were *to set out a great fleet against us*. James, alarmed, ordered all officers to return to their commands, to man the seaports, and particularly that the regiment at York was to go to Hull. On 28 September, James issued *a proclamation setting forth the intention of the Prince of Orange to invade this nation with a strong fleet and a strong army - and His Majesty's officers to be in readiness for the defence of the King and Kingdom*[56].

The reinforcement of the Garrison at Hull was an obvious move. Hull was the principal garrison in the North, a noted hot-bed of anti-Catholic feeling and Dissent, and a convenient landfall for forces setting out from the Low Countries. Lord Sunderland wrote to the Mayor of Hull in mid-September. He ordered that soldiers should be housed in the town. *His Majesty has in regards to the present circumstances, thought fit to send Battalions of Scots Guards and several companies of Lord Montgomery's Regiment of Foot* (later the 11th Foot), *to the town of Kingston-upon-Hull, where there are not sufficient numbers of public houses for the quartering the said battalions and companies, His Majesty does expect from you on this occasion, and all oth-*

ers where the numbers of the Garrison shall require it that notwithstanding the late Declaration (that quarters could only be granted with the householders' consent), *you shall take care that the former practice and usual agreement be continued, whereby all the Garrison exceeding the number of 300 men be lodged in private houses, paying 8d per week, a man, for such necessaries as have heretofore provided for them.* Lord Montgomery, Marquess Powis, was Governor Langdale's son, and a Catholic[57].

Compulsory billeting may have had punitive overtones, but it was not on free quarters, as was later to be alleged, nor was it unprecedented - Parliament's Governor had ordered such measures in 1643. The 18th-century commentators viewed the movement of troops in 1688 as a punishment visited by James on Hull and the Bench. Their affection for free elections was held to have *so enraged him, that, to punish the town, he sent them near 1,200 soldiers, mostly commanded by popish officers.* The account of this descent is a distorted one, empurpled in a Whig tradition: *The tender virgins were threatened to be deflowered; the wives with their children to be murdered. The Magistrates were also in fear of their lives. In the Citadel, the cannons were pointed at the town, ready to fire upon the first dreadful signal; and nothing seemed ready to appear, but horror and destruction. No complaints were regarded by the officers, who said, they must implicitly obey their commanders.* The concrete problems thus described were those of quartering and overcrowding; indiscipline and theft; and the experience of casual intimidation. More lurid expectations closely reflected the traditional objections to a standing army. It is perhaps significant that only one victim of these atrocities could be named: Postmaster Mawson. He, moreover, had fallen foul of Copley, an established figure on the local scene, in the course of the long-standing persecution of Hull's Dissenters[58].

Many soldiers arrived to receive arms and ammunition. Lord Montgomery's companies were in Hull in September and early October 1688. Duxbury received orders, *for delivering out of the stores at Hull arms, and drums for the recruits of the regiment under the command of Viscount Montgomery.* The Regiment of Colonel Henry Gage, the Duke of Newcastle's, was to be armed out of the stores of Hull. This regiment comprised 13 companies, one of grenadiers. Muskets and pikes were provided for 12 companies; 60 fusils or flintlock muskets, *granados*, pouches and bayonets for the grenadiers; and drums, halberts, and ammunition for all. The strength of the army increased dramatically in September and October 1688, reaching a total of 37,218 officers and men. A garrison of two regiments was fixed in Hull: Viscount Montgomery's, with 594 men, and the newly raised regiment of 927 men under Gage[59].

From 5 August to 5 November, guns were moved into position to arm the Citadel. Its Humber front was armed in mid-September: between 12 and 18 September, Joseph Goulding was employed, *drawing the guns and carriages upon the curtains and flanks of the stone wall next to Humber.* More guns were to be removed from Scarborough Castle and Bridlington; though it seems only those from Bridlington arrived. Coopers were repairing 270 powder barrels, and stores from the Tower were brought ashore. The South Blockhouse was issued with beds and more powder (both for guns) in September, and its windows were broken by test-firing in late September[60].

The Governor rode post-haste from London, bearing royal instructions, *For watching the sea coasts; to burn and destroy all places, near to which the enemy should land; to drive away the cattle, and carry every necessary thing away, whereby they might perish for want of subsistence.* These standard provisions in case of invasion had first been invoked in the late 16th century against the threat from Spain. The prevailing mood was reported to be tense. *As to Hull, two parties were in fear: the Protestants, who sided not with the King, thought they should have their throats cut by the soldiers, as they had threatened, in case of the least resistance; whilst they, on the other hand, were as much terrified with the thoughts of the Prince of Orange. The Catholics, of the country, fled from the rage of the incensed rural inhabitants, to the protection of the Lords Langdale and Montgomery (the latter being a colonel) who received them kindly, as being of their persuasion[61].*

The Prince of Orange set sail on 19 October, from the Dutch port of Brill, with a fleet of 655 ships. *'Twas thought, by steering northwards, that they designed for Humber; which occasioned the Lord Langdale to prepare for a siege; but the Prince, though driven back by a violent storm, yet set sail again on the 1 November.* Danby wrote to the Earl of Chesterfield: *that the Prince of Orange if the wind serves well will land in England within the next fortnight and Hull will be delivered up to him and the greatest part of the King's army.* This may have been a genuine misunderstanding, or, alternatively, a ploy to misinform agents of the government: William actually landed on 5 November at Brixham Harbour, near Torbay, Devon, with 11,000 foot and 4,000 horse[62].

The Citadel, and latterly defences on the north side of the town of Hull, saw further measures put in train at Beckman's urging, at a cost of £5,000. Langdale wrote to the Board of Ordnance with these proposals, on 29 October. On 1 November, the Board informed him that they had *received the proposals for an agreement to be made with Mr Fitch for new works to be raised at Hull for the better security of that place amounting in the whole to the sum of £5,000. The Lords of the Treasury (before whom the charge of the said proposal of agreement is laid) have promised all the furtherance that may be expected for carrying on so necessary a work, and have already advanced to that end the sum of £1,000 which shall be forthwith impressed to Mr Fitch for his encouragement.* The Board required that Beckman should draw up a contract to cover this expenditure, and get it signed by Langdale and the Commissioners. On 3 November, the sluices at Hull *were ready for laying the country under water for some miles about that garrison[63].*

On 10 November, Beckman set out his *Instructions for Mr John Duxbury to see such works finished as is contracted for with Mr Fitch for the present defence of His Majesty's town and Citadel of Hull.* The instructions required that the placing of pallisades should be halted, except where they filled gaps left by scaffolding, and that the manufacture of *stockadoes* should halt at 2,000, though 4,000 had been contracted for. The country people were to complete the clearance of moats for *lodgements*, and works on a *large half bastion before the North Gate and Town Bridge* were to be continued by the townsmen and country people; various other provisions were also made for this new fortification. Fitch was to have *no hand* in these works. Care was to be taken that the sluices were working and secure. This is the only occasion in the 1680s when townsfolk were recorded working alongside country people as labourers, and confirms that this was an anxious time[64].

James belatedly raised further forces, which concentrated as a field army of 30,000 at Salisbury. This left the North guarded only by troops in garrison, and the field lay open to the conspirators to act there. Danby wrote to William that on 21 November he would secure York. On 22 November, Danby took York for William. A meeting was held under pretence of drawing up a loyal address to the King. The meeting was interrupted by a Mr Tankard, who ran into the hall, crying that the Catholics had risen and had fired on the militia. The Governor was seized, and the conspirators declared for a *free Parliament[65].*

A week later, Danby wrote to Sir John Hamner, Lieutenant-Colonel of Montgomery's Regiment in Hull. *If you are willing and can help us in our design, so far as to make us masters of Hull I engage that £5,000 shall be placed to you in a month after it is done besides the just merits you will deserve from your Prince, which shall not want my recommendations of it as it deserves, and you shall not want 1,000 men to your assistance, if other things be all prepared for it.* The handsome offer underlines the importance attached to Hull. How Danby intended to find this extraordinary bribe so quickly is uncertain. The figure of £5,000 had been cited only three weeks before by Beckman, as the cost to be incurred by emergency works at Hull. Beckman himself was a veteran of Tangiers, and it is entirely possible that he had become aware of his colleagues' involvement in conspiracy against James. Danby may also have been aware of the decision of the Lords of the Treasury to allocate such a sum, which was half the cost of a full year's building work at the Citadel. Whatever his allegiance, and like many involved in these events, Beckman left no written evidence of his loyalties at the time. Danby wrote to William from York on 1 December: *I am in some hope of securing Hull but dare not assure myself of it*[66].

Hull was indeed seized, on 3 December. Hamner replied to Danby the next day. *My Lord, in answer to your Lordship's letter, I can only say that we have thought fit to secure the Lord Langdale, the Lord Montgomery, the Major of the Duke of Newcastle's, with all such officers as are known papists, and take the town into the Lieutenant-Governor's hands who heartily joined with me. We have done it without effusion of blood and to the satisfaction of the town. My Lord I intend suddenly to kiss your hands at York, or else send an officer on purpose if I cannot be spared and leave this place with security. This is returned by your own messenger with the submission of my Lord, of your most humble devoted servant John Hamner.* At the foot of the letter was added, *Our Governor Captain Copley presents his most humble service*[67].

Other reports confirm that the coup at Hull was at the instance of the deputy-commanders of the Garrison. *Upon the revolting of the forces in Hull, the Lord Langdale the Governor and Marquess Powis his son whose regiment was there were seized by Copley, Deputy-Governor and Sir John Hamner, Lieutenant-Colonel, but they have since been given their liberties, which I hope to be a good precedent.* To achieve this, Copley and Hamner must have had confederates. One was Captain Humphry Herbert (or Fitzherbert). Herbert sought reward for his part: *being a captain of a foot company in the garrison at Hull (he) was very instrumental in securing that garrison*[68].

The mechanics of the coup are described only by Thomas Gent's *History*, whose Whiggish bias has been noted above. The sequence of events is held to have begun with the disarming of Catholic adherents of the Duke of Newcastle at York, on 22 November. The Duke of Newcastle's Regiment is implied by Gent to have then marched to Hull. These newly-raised troops had actually been armed

out of stores at Hull in October, and were reckoned part of the Garrison there. On 3 December, Gent claims, the Catholic officers *laid a plot to secure the Protestant officers, with their adherents, by changing the rounds. Lord Langdale, that night, gave out, that Lord Montgomery would take the rounds of Captain Copley, who was a Protestant. This coming to his ears, by the adjutant's telling it to Fort-Major Barrett, he was so much affronted, that he vowed if the Lord Montgomery offered such an indignity, he would lay him by the heels.* The most credible element of the tale would seem to be Copley's bristling objection to interference with his responsibility for Guards about the town.

Gent's account continues: *But, to prevent any such design, and be rather beforehand, he discoursed with Hamner, Carvill, and other Protestant officers, and they consulting with the Magistrates, it was unanimously agreed, to call the soldiers of their party to arms, etc. and seize upon the chief heads of the papists.* Gent noted that Copley consulted some officers of Montgomery's Regiment, and that there was collusion between the Bench and Copley. The involvement of Town-Major Barrett was pivotal, as his office frequently brought him into contact with the Bench. The conference perhaps took place in the house of an Alderman, later the *Olde White Hart Inn*, on Silver Street. The *plotting chamber*, upstairs in the Olde White Hart, is traditionally associated with Sir John Hotham's defiance of Charles I in 1642. Hotham, however, had acted on the orders of Parliament, and his defiance had been public. The building associated with this legend, moreover, post-dates the Restoration. The treasonable events of 1688 provide a more credible context for the tale[69].

There were but few words about it. In two hours time the Market-Hill was covered with armed men; who were spirited up, by hearing they were called to defend the King and Protestant religion. The Lord Langdale knew nothing of it, till he was suddenly seized by a Guard, under Captain Carvill; who plainly told him, he was come to secure his Lordship, as being a Roman Catholic; and had no right to govern, according to the laws of the land. The Governor, in amazement, replied: What, Captain! Is not the King's dispensing power to be admitted of? - No, said the other bluntly. Why then, said his Lordship, I have no more to say at present; and so was made prisoner.

The *Market-Hill* was the Market Cross, which had been rebuilt in the centre of the Market Place, in 1683. This lay only yards from the Guardhouse, on the south side of Marketplace, where Postmaster Mawson had been tortured. It is uncertain whether support of the King would have rallied Hull, though the defence of Protestantism chimed with local predisposition. It may be speculated that Copley's *party* was built around his own Independent Company of the Garrison, which he had commanded for seven years, and that it was his command of this distinct local force which permitted him to act where and when he did.

Gent's account concludes with the rounding up of other Catholic officers; his description of this concluding act in the drama again undermines his allegation that they had planned a preemptive *coup. The Lord Montgomery was secured by Captain Fitzherbert; and Major Mahoney, by Fort-Major Barrett. The inferior Catholic officers, hearing the soldiers were under arms; they ran, for fear of blame, to their respective posts, where they were secured. Next morning, one of the Protestant Captains marched forth, with 100 men to relieve the Guards; and seized the popish officers, with others of their persuasion, who little dreamt of what had been transacted in the night. Thus the Town, Fort and Citadel, being secured by Captain Copley, he then set the prisoners at liberty.*

The Bench Books of the town are silent on the matter. The Bench of Aldermen had been formally turned out of office by the Crown on 22 September, in favour of a short-lived *intruded* Bench which left no record of its proceedings. Officially, the Corporation were informed of the coup after the event. *The Town's husband is ordered to pay £1 13s 7d for what was drunk in the Town's Hall on this 3rd of this instant... when the Lieutenant-Governor of this and the rest of the Mayor and Aldermen to acquaint them they had* (taken) *the Lord Langdale, the Governor, officers and Roman Catholic officers belonging this said garrison.* There is also a hint that soldiers had to be reined in; Copley was *to give notice by beat of drum that they do not go to several houses in town and violently take away and spoil their goods and break and spoil their houses and loot the like*[70].

The anniversary of the *coup* was to be celebrated for many years to come, *as Town Taking Day.* The rewards granted to those involved confirm the importance of their achievement. Hamner declared he had not received Danby's offer of a bribe until after the taking of Hull. He became Colonel of his regiment on 31 December, and was to serve as a brigadier in Ireland in 1689. Sir John Hotham, an active Parliamentarian and grandson of the former Governor, was initially named as Governor in Langdale's place, though he died soon after. He had left England in 1684 and had returned with William, which brought him political rehabilitation and his new post. Danby became the next Governor of Hull, and

also Duke of Leeds, Earl of Carmarthen, High Steward of Hull, and Lord Lieutenant of the East, West and North Ridings of Yorkshire. His brother, Charles Osborne, became Deputy-Governor and MP for Hull[71].

Deputy-Governor Copley, most spectacularly, was rewarded with the Governorship of Maryland and Virginia. As a sop to the sentiments of the Whigs, six Commissioners set off in the summer of 1689 to visit Hull, *for reforming abuses in the army,* with orders to *disband any officer, soldier, troop or company or regiment* which looked to be technically or politically deficient[72].

Footnotes

1: Stephens and Lee vol. 18, 13-15; CSPD 1679-88, 229; HMC Dartmouth Mss, 41; Dalton 1960, 188; CSPD 1681-82, 33.
2: CSPD 1682, 528; Williams 1994, 14; Stephens and Lee, vol. 54, 23-4; vol. 62, 175-7.
3: Browning 1936, 337; Bod. Lib. Rawl. A475, Duxbury to Board, 27 March 1686.
4: CSPD 1682, 535; Bod. Lib. Rawl. A475, probably January 1686.
5: Childs 1976, 41; Lawson 1969, 14; PRO WO24/8, part 8, fo. 22, January 1685; PRO WO24/8, part 5, Establishments.
6: CSPD 1676-77, 331; PRO WO55/519, Order by Musgrave, 3 October 1686; Bod. Lib. Rawl. A476, item 1, 5, Duxbury to Board, 16 April 1684; Hull City Council 1987, fig. 5; Evans and Sitch 1990; Bod. Lib. Rawl. A475, ?January 1686.
7: CTP Extra vol. 7, pt 1, 1679-88, for 1688.
8: PRO WO46:1 (index), 256, Orders of Board, 14 February 1682; *ibid.,* 257, Board to Watkinson, 1 April 1682; *ibid.,* 325, Letters to Office, 12 April 1682; *ibid.,* 326, 20 May 1682; *ibid.,* 257, Orders of Board, 30 May 1682; *ibid.,* 330, Duxbury to Board, 24 July 1682; *ibid.* (index), 334, Letters to Office, 25 September 1682; *ibid.,* 336, 14 October 1682; Bod. Lib. Rawl. A475, Account, 30 June 1683.
9: Blaxland 1972, 112; CSPD 1679-80, 165; CSPD 1679-80, 461; KUHRO M363.
10: PRO WO46:1 (index), [?]309, Letters to Office; CSPD 1682, 285; PRO WO46:1 (index), 254, Orders of Board, 1 October 1681; Browning 1936, 280.
11: Williams 1994, 165-8; Childs 1976, 42; CSPD 1683, 319, 343.
12: KUHRO BRB 8, 41, 52, L1029; CSPD 1683, 343.
13: CSPD 1683, 429; CSPD 1683, 339; CSPD 1684, 218; Gent 1735, 178.
14: Bod. Lib. Rawl. A475, Order, 1683.
15: PRO WO46:2 (index), 137, Board to Hull, 6 September 1684; *ibid.,* 263, Letters from Hull, 21 September 1684; *ibid.,* 28, Orders of Board, 22 July 1684.

16: RCHM 1972, 176-79.

17: CSPD 1675-76, 194; Bod. Lib. Rawl. A475, Duxbury to Board, 15 January 1685; PRO WO46:1 (index), 259, Orders of Board,19 September 1682; ibid., 20 October 1682.

18: PRO WO46:1 (index), 289, Letters from Office, 3 October 1682; ibid., 335, Letters from Hull, 19 September 1682; Stafford Record Office D (W) 1778/V/64 (52); PRO WO46:2 (index), 311, Board to Hull, 12 June 1683; ibid., 184, Letters from Hull, 4 November 1683.

19: PRO WO46:2 (index), 39, Orders of Commissioners, 16 July 1684; Bod. Lib. Rawl. A475, Duxbury to de Gomme, 15 August 1685; Stafford Record Office D (W) 1778/V/71 (184), Account of Ordnance, 1684-85.

20: Bod. Lib. Rawl. A476, item 1, fo. 25, Duxbury to Board, 19 April 1685, punctuation slightly amended; PRO WO46:2 (index), 52, Orders of Commssioners, 6 September 1684; ibid., 190, Letters from Hull, 12 January 1684.

21: PRO WO55/519, Board to Duxbury, 19 March 1685; PRO WO46:2 (index), 339-55, Estimates, 12 May 1685; Bod. Lib. Rawl. A475, Duxbury to Board, 22 March 1686; ibid., Duxbury to ?, 30 April 1686.

22: PRO WO46:2 (index), 96, Board to Hull, 11 October 1683; PRO WO51/28 TBB series 2, 114, 16 May 1684; PRO WO46:2, 452, Account of Ports for Guns, ?1684 (alternatively, August 1685).

23: Bod. Lib. Rawl. A475, Duxbury to Board, 15 August 1685.

24: BRB 5, 69, 189, 176; PRO WO46:1, 319, Osbourne to Board, 22 November 1681.

25: PRO WO46:2 (index), 111, Board to Hull, 8 April 1684; Bod. Lib. Rawl. A476, item 1, Duxbury to Board, 30 May 1684; ibid., 5, 16 April 1684; ibid., 28 April 1684.

26: CSPD 1684-85, 278.

27: CSPD 1684-85, 3; KUHRO BRB 8, 119; de la Pryme, pt. 2 [1986], 111.

28: CSPD 1684-85, 14, 23; Gillett and MacMahon 1980, 183-4.

29: CSPD 1684-85, 23; CTB pt. 3, vol. 8, 1619; CSPD February-December 1685, 67; HMC 11th report, Dartmouth Mss, 123; CSPD February-December 1685, 61.

30: Williams 1994, 182-3.

31: Bod. Lib. Rawl. A475, Duxbury to Board, 6 July 1685; ibid., 21, Duxbury to Plymouth, 29 June 1685.

32: Williams 1994, 178-195; Bod. Lib. Rawl. A475, Duxbury to Board, 11 July 1685; ibid., 5 August 1685.

33: CSPD February-December 1685, 252, 395; Bod. Lib. Rawl. A475, Duxbury to Board, 27 July 1685.

34: Bod. Lib. Rawl. A475, Duxbury to Board, 5 August 1685; ibid., 17 August 1685; ibid., Bod. Lib. Rawl. A475, 1 December 1685.

35: Bod. Lib. Rawl. A475, Duxbury to Board, 7 September 1685.

36: PRO WO55/519, Orders of Commissioners, 29 November 1685; Bod. Lib. Rawl. A475, Duxbury to Board, early 1686; PRO WO55/519, Commissioners to Board, 1 February 1686; Bod. Lib. Rawl. A475, Duxbury to Board, 13 January 1686.

37: Williams 1994, 178-95; Browning 1936, 394; Williams 1994, 196.

38: Fraser 1979, 319; Williams 1994, 197.

39: KUHRO BRB 6, 146, 149, L1106.

40: Sykes 1893, 3 January 1685; CSPD 1684-85, 272; PRO WO55/519, Enquiry, 1 October 1686; CSPD January 1686-May 1687, 329.

41: KUHRO M382a.

42: CSPD February-December 1685, 217; KUHRO M386; PRO WO30/48/1686, fos. 49-50; KUHRO M382a.

43: KUHRO BRB 6, fo. 172, 2/12/1686; KUHRO M380, 1687; Browning 1936, 470; KUHRO M380, 381, 382a, L1113.

44: KUHRO BRB 6, 203, M381, M382a.

45: Stafford Record Office D (W) 1778/I:1233, Beckman to Board, 24 September 1687; HMC Dartmouth Mss, 134; BRB 6, 203, M382; PRO WO55/519, Orders of Commissioners, 26 October 1687.

46: KUHRO L1112.

47: KUHRO M386; PRO WO55/519, Commissioners to Board, 2 May 1688.

48: Childs 1987, 35; KUHRO L1115, BRB 6, 133.

49: CSPD 1687-89, 550; Short 1998; Gent 1735, 185-6.

50: Browning 1944-51, vol. 1, 447-8.

51: Williams 1994, 198-202.

52: CSPD 1687-89, James II, 45; Aveling 1960, 65; Short 1998; KUHRO L1109, BRB 6, 196.

53: Gent 1735, 184; Williams 1994, 198-202; CSPD 1687-89, James II, 216.

54: Gent 1735, 185-6.

55: Williams 1994, 204-6; Browning 1944-51, vol. 2, 401.

56: Browning 1936, 506, 511.

57: KUHRO M386.

58: Gent 1735, 186-7.

59: Fortescue 1903, vol. 3, 1880, 566; Browning 1944-51, vol. 2, 401; CSPD 1687-89, James II, 314, 310.

60: PRO WO51/37, TBB series 3, 123, 29 October 1688; ibid., 124, 5 November 1688; PRO WO51/37 TBB series 2, 44a; CSPD 1687-89, James II, 319; PRO WO55/37, TBB series 3, 123, 7 November 1688; PRO WO55/37, TBB series 2, 44a, 29 September 1688; TBB series 3, 123.

61:     Gent 1735, 188-9.
62:     Gent 1735, 188; Browning 1944-51, vol. 2, 135.
63:     PRO WO55/519, Board to Langdale, 1 November 1688; HMC 10, Powis Mss,
        397.
64:     PRO WO55/519, Instructions to Duxbury, 10 November 1688.
65:     Speck 1988, 188-204.
66:     Browning 1944-51, vol. 2, 132-3, 144.
67:     Browning 1944-51, vol. 2, 147.
68:     HMC 70, Hastings Mss 11, 206; CTB 1556/7-1696, William III, 37.
69:     information D. Neave.
70:     Short 1998; KUHRO BRB 8, 231-2.
71:     Tickell 1796, 583-9; Dalton 1960, vol. 5, 7; KUHRO BRB 8, 233; Roebuck 1980,
        63; CSPD 1689, 48; CSPD 1691, 254; Browning 1944-51, vol. 1, 485-6; CSPD
        1690, 68.
72:     CSPD 1690, 12; Childs 1987, 28.

CHAPTER 10

HULL AND A NEW REGIME

The Glorious Revolution and the constitutional settlement which followed resolved domestic political issues first raised by the Civil War. The coronation of William and Mary, however, drew England into closer engagement with the continental politics of the Age of Kings. These focussed on the rise of France as a European superpower. The conflict between William and James was crucial from an English perspective, but in a European context was a side-show, fought out in its most peripheral land. Opinion in England was not generally to follow the finer points of this struggle. Throughout the 18th century, anti-Catholicism and xenophobia were to provide a rabble-rousing formula for unscrupulous politicians. The cause of the House of Stuart, Jacobitism, was invariably tarred with a Popish brush. The succession of foreigners to the English throne brought further involvement in wars on the Continent, and a risk of riot and the recurrent need for troops to put down disorder at home.

Two strategic doctrines were available to England in her dealings with Europe, and were developed in the reign of Queen Anne. The first position, favoured by the Whigs, was a continental doctrine, whereby England would involve herself on the European mainland. A strong army was necessary to pursue this policy. The alternative would become known as the *blue water* theory, and was favoured by Tories. This saw the Navy as England's first line of defence. In this view, the army and any land-based military establishment was ancillary to the fleet, and, moreover, posed a peacetime threat to English liberties. Hull, as a strategic fortified port and Garrison, with an increasingly prosperous maritime community, straddled this divide[1].

The flight of James II to France in the closing days of 1688 ended war on English soil. It was with French encouragement that he resumed the struggle for his throne in Ireland. James landed at Kinsale, County Cork, in March 1689, and 100,000 Irishmen rallied to his cause. The Dutch had declared war on France a month before. William was to draw England into their struggle against Louis XIV. On 13 February 1689, William assumed the appointment of Commander-

in-Chief. With Parliament's support, he raised 6 regiments of horse, two of dragoons, and 25 of foot. Some of these units were raised only for service in Ireland. A Williamite foothold in Ireland, centred initially on Londonderry, was to be expanded in the course of 1689. Scottish Jacobites were defeated at Killiecrankie and Dunkeld, and the war between William and James was fought out in Ireland[2].

The Irish war was to be decided by William's victory at the battle of Aughrim, in 1691. This encounter saw Dutch, Danes, Germans, Scots, English, *Huguenot* Frenchmen and Protestant Irish in the Williamite ranks. Ranged against them were not only Catholic Irish, but French soldiers under a French general, and Englishmen loyal to James. In 1695, English and Dutch soldiers fought together against the French at Namur.

King William's Wars

A Bill of Rights set out the liberties won in the Glorious Revolution of 1688, and forbade the maintenance of a standing army in peacetime, while the Mutiny Act regulated the behaviour of soldiers in time of war. The ironic consequence of William's accession for Hull, however, was a renewed influx of soldiers. These were foreign troops hired by William for service in Ireland, and English soldiers passing to the Continent or elsewhere. More troops were stationed in the ports of England between 1691 and 1693, against the threat of invasion posed by a French fleet at Brest, and an army in Normandy. Fifteen new regiments were raised over the winter of 1693-94, specifically for an abortive expedition against Brest[3].

The army was a deeply unpopular institution. Recruitment was at its lowest ebb in the 1690s; there was scant enthusiasm for service in William's wars, fought as they were on behalf of the Dutch. Recruits were drawn from amongst criminals and the lowest orders of society, and it was in William's army that flogging was introduced as a disciplinary measure. His wars were to last nearly nine years, at an annual cost of a little under £5,000,000, leading to the establishment of the National Debt[4].

The first contingent to arrive in Hull, in November 1689, was a force of Danish troops. A sum of £12-13,000 was to be sent to Hull, *so that the soldiers will be able* to discharge their quarters and pay duly on their march. *Exact discipline* was to be observed. The first payment, of £2,000, was drawn from customs collected at Hull. Three transports packed with horses and men anchored in the Hull Roads, awaiting disembarkation. The troops arrived in poor condition following their voyage, and were unable to march immediately to Chester on their way to Ireland, as had been planned. The Prince of Wurtemburg arrived at Hull in December 1689, as one of the commanders of the polyglot force William was assembling for his Irish campaign[5].

Some of the troops who landed were unable to clear their quarters for lack of money. Those quartered in Hull included dragoons, who were placed in taverns and inns because of the stabling these provided for their horses. In 1691, three English regiments were to sail from Hull to Moordijck, to fight in Holland. They were part of a force of 5,580 foot and 240 horses. It was proposed to transport them at a rate of 15s per head. It is uncertain how long they waited for passage, for *without ready money the services cannot be undertaken.* In April 1692, it was proposed to send 1,000 arms to Hull, to supply the militia of Yorkshire[6].

Payment at the rate set for the fire and candle expenses of the Independent Companies continued at Hull. These charges, together with Copley's pay as Deputy-Governor, were borrowed from John Fitch in 1690. These costs were met, as usual, nearly a year in arrears. Towards the end of the year, the Treasury ordered the issue *of any disposable unappropriated moneys in the Exchequer to the Earl of Ranelagh for clearing the garrisons of Hull, Cinque Ports, Plymouth and Berwick to January last £2,119 13s 11 ½d*[7].

Regular Garrison troops were initially provided by the Duke of Newcastle's Regiment, continuing a service begun in 1688. In 1691, the Mayor; Charles Osborne, Hull's Member of Parliament and new Deputy-Governor; and Lord Carmarthen, the Governor, engaged the lawyer Nicholas Baker. He was to petition the Privy Council over the payment of costs for quartering for the year. A force of 100 soldiers was *thought sufficient to be a guard in the town for the safety thereof.* This strength reflected that of the Independent Companies, while the Bench's appeal blurred the distinction between the demands for army accommodation, and the requirements of the town for its own policing and guards. The Town Major, George Barrett, received a royal bounty of £40 in August 1691, as the officer responsible for tackling the problems of housing soldiers in the town[8].

The Governor reported to the Mayor: *I have tried all manner of ways that are possible for the adjusting relating to the quarter in private houses.* This was reduced to 4d a week by the Mutiny Act of 1689, halving the rate charged for James' soldiers. Colonel St George ordered more beds to be made available in the new barracks at the Citadel. It was hoped that *the Barracks be convenient to lodge them except a number sufficient to be a guard in the town for the safety thereof, which may not be above 199 men.* This figure reflected the findings of the 1686 survey of inns, which had listed that number of *guest beds* in Hull. The Bench may have hoped that the number of soldiers to be housed in the town could be matched with the accommodation known to be available[9].

Companies from the Duke of Bolton's Regiment, raised for the war in Ireland, were quartered in Hull. The Exchequer issued £1,000 for *the present supply of eight companies quartered at Hull,* in February 1693. In January 1694, there were still *eight companies now in this Garrison... the alehouse keepers have not beds to lodge them all nor are they without ruin of more than one half of them able to keep them at 4d a day or pay them 3s 6d a week for every private continual and 7s per week for a sergeant and 4s 6d a week for each corporal.* Mr St Quinten, the other Member of Parliament for Hull, had lent money, *for paying the soldiers' sustenance.* The Bench was forced to pick up this charge, at a cost of £118 14s per week. Later in the year, the Bench borrowed £238 from Mr George Dickinson, the Collector of Customs, to pay a fortnight's subsistence, so as to relieve the burden on the innkeepers. Bolton's Regiment maintained a presence in Hull up to 1696, though its second battalion was at war on the Continent. At this time, facing the prospect of invasion by the French, there was intense activity: *The embargo on ships here is put into execution. The Citadel, Garrison and all defences are prepared and the military officers and soldiers very active on searches etc.* Companies of Sir John Jacob's Regiment, which was divided between Hull, Berwick and Carlisle, filled out the Garrison. Its core remained the Independent Garrison Companies, while contingents of regulars moved from garrison to garrison on a fixed rotation[10].

The Bench petitioned the King, setting out its traditional account of the evils of quartering. Jacob's companies *have been subsisted...by the keepers of public houses within this town, whose number exceed not above 80; the greatest part whereof are poor widows of seamen whose husbands have been lost at sea in Your Majesty's and their country's service, the payment of the subsistence the poor ale house keepers have so long continued, that many of them have been ruined broke up and left houses and employment... so that these eighty public houses' keepers scarce 40 of them can quarter any sol-*

diers, and these the least of them not above two in a house and the most not above one soldier. While the innkeepers of Hull were thus inconvenienced, *the barracks within the Citadel will very well contain betwixt 2 or 300 soldiers.* This appeal was made in the knowledge that companies of Sir Henry Belasyse's Regiment were due to replace Jacob's men. Belasyse's Regiment had formerly been in Dutch service, and may have been especially unwelcome for this reason. The repayment of the innkeepers was ordered from the Treasury in July 1696; £2,000 was allocated to Jacob for quarters at Hull, Berwick and Carlisle, in February 1697[11].

A currency crisis in 1696-97 further hampered the government's ability to meet its obligations, and the civilian population of strategic towns was virtually expected to pay, support and feed the army. This arrangement led to great resentment against the soldiers. In May 1696, the Bench found *that it would make a great disturbance and be the impoverishment of many poor alehouse keepers*, and so borrowed £80 for this purpose from a Mr Sugar, at 6% interest for 6 months. From December 1696 to April 1697, they provided subsistence for the companies of Colonel Board and Captain Austin, of Lord Lucas' Regiment. Payments were made to the Regimental Agent, *the said bills delivered into the hands of the Mayor*. In April 1697, Hull was still providing subsistence for Jacob's Regiment. In 1697, the Bench was repaid £705 for one month's subsistence for Jacob's Regiment, and the £238 owed since 1694 for Bolton's. These sums had been raised from the Town Chest, on the issue of six-month bonds, or borrowed from wealthy citizens. Along with urgent payments, the occasional older debt surfaced. In 1699, £64 was received for the quarters of Sir John Hamner's Regiment, which had been owed since 1692[12].

Some officers found congenial private lodgings; an inventory of the goods of John Field, an Alderman and former Mayor who died in 1691, was written *in the Colonel's chamber*, in Field's house. Practical difficulties could, however, attend quartering in private or business premises. Postmaster Mawson already had good reason to feel uncomfortable in the company of soldiers. He was *so overburdened with soldiers that he cannot possibly attend the new service of his office, we therefore desire that you will ease him so far as you can by taking off the soldiers' quarters from him or at least so many of them that they may not be an encumbrance upon him in the discharge and execution of this office*[13].

In early 1697, four companies of Sir Henry Belasyse's Regiment were ordered from Hull, and companies of Colonel Churchill's Regiment were to bring the Garrison back to its normal strength of six companies. Late in the year, a battalion of Scots Guards landed at Hull, and marched from there to Scotland. Three weeks subsistence money was ordered for them, and a week's money for two battalions of the Royal Regiment of Foot - the combined strength of the two regiments totalled 26 companies. In this case, the soldiers had landed at Hull, but were only to stay for a short while before continuing on foot to their destination[14].

Correspondence on the subject of payment for quartering continued into 1698 between the Mayor and Osborne. In 1697, the Treaty of Ruyswick suspended hostilities in Europe, and dictated a staged reduction of the English army to 7,000 men. Though its implementation took several years, the treaty immediately lifted the burden of soldiers in transit, and permitted the remainder to be more evenly spread between the English garrison towns. By 1700, sensitivities aroused by quartering at Hull were specifically recognised by the government. The Deputy-Governor was informed that: *The King is willing that dragoons at Leeds and Wakefield should quarter about Hull, if there should be a conveniency for it... It would not be well if they should remove thither and a complaint be made from Hull*[15].

Casual violence was recorded within the Garrison, but it was usually between soldiers, rather than being directed at the civilian population. In 1690, Lieutenant Franklin was tried for killing Captain Cony; and in 1695 Ensign Allgood was killed by Ensign Bulmer; in both cases deaths may have arisen from duelling. In 1693, a Lieutenant of Captain Heemskirk's company was shot, and another two soldiers were shot in July, though records of courts martial have not been encountered. Complaints against the insolence of officers and soldiers were made to the Governor in 1690, 1696 and 1697. The impressing of soldiers, who were formally all to be volunteers, was a more provocative expedient. The Duke of Bolton's Regiment was alleged to have forced away 60 to 70 householders before it sailed for Flanders. In 1697, a woman was to give witness against three soldiers committed to gaol. Their trial was under consideration early the next year by the Mayor and Osborne, suggesting the matter was a sensitive one[16].

The material grievances arising from a military presence were as acute as under James II; indeed, the income to be derived from it by poorer households had been reduced. Now, though, these grievances lacked the *frisson* of suspicion with which James' policies had been viewed. From 1698, the baptism of soldiers' children figures in the Parish Registers of Drypool. Among the first soldiers' children to be born there was *Hugh son of Hugh Scot Gentleman, officer at the Berwick, bapt. November 2.* His father commanded a company of the Holland Regiment rotating between Hull and Berwick[17].

A shrunken Garrison

The 18th century opened with the Grand Alliance of England, Holland and Austria, led by the Emperor Leopold, ranged against France. Allied armies waged war in Europe, led by John Churchill, Duke of Marlborough. A further 12 regiments of Foot were raised for this conflict, which continued until 1713, when it was ended by the Treaty of Utrecht. King William died in 1703, to be succeeded by Queen Anne, who herself died without issue in 1714. The succession of George I was greeted with sporadic rioting by Jacobite mobs. This disorder saw the movement of troops into key towns like Hull. In late 1715, James Stuart, son of James II and known as the Old Pretender, landed in Scotland. English Jacobites were unwilling to move from riot to rebellion: though a Highland army marched as far south as Preston, Lancashire, they failed to rally English support. Jacobite defeats, at Preston and at Sherrifmuir in November 1715, effectively ended the threat to Hanoverian rule. In February 1716, James Stuart returned to France[18].

In 1700, under pressure from Parliament, expenditure on the army was slashed, and the old Garrison Establishments were disbanded. Henceforward, the policy of *no standing army* was to be upheld, and the army voted by Parliament was to be sufficient to garrison only the most important fortresses. This was the end of the Independent Companies at Hull. The Garrison Establishment henceforward comprised the Governor, Deputy-Governor, Surgeon, Master Gunner and six Gunners, at an annual charge of £674 2s 6d. The Mutiny Act of 1703 regulated billeting, and henceforward, *quartering in no private house whatsoever* was to be allowed[19].

Military activity in Hull centred on the implementation of security measures. In July 1703, Captain Middleton, a Jacobite exile returned from France, was arrested at Hull. An Act of 1696 *for the better security of His Majesty's person* had declared it to *be High Treason for any English subject to come to England without leave.* He was, however, to be well-treated until his *bona fides* could be established. Middleton complained: *I am 73 years old, in a strange place, with little money or credit.*

Following confirmation that he had returned on hearing of an amnesty published in Scotland, he was released. In 1704, an Austin Belson was detained for three weeks, as he was travelling without a pass. He wrote to a Member of Parliament to challenge his arrest, and was subsequently discharged to sail to London aboard a warship. In November 1704, a return of sick and wounded prisoners included some held at Hull[20].

Under the fire and candle regulations, £63 was allowed for the Hull Barracks in 1705. The Deputy-Governor wrote to the Secretary at War, *setting forth the hardship of the garrison there, for want of a better allowance of fire and candle which has been reduced from £473 to £63 per annum.* The lack of Guards led him to press *the necessity of a porter to keep the gates of the town and the Citadel at an allowance of 12d a day, which duty is now under the care of a sentinel to the dangerous consequence of the garrison and defrauding the Queen of her customs.* Fire and candle allowances were increased, initially by £174 in 1706; then by £195 5s; the allowance for 1707 came to £237 for Hull Barracks. The payment of fire and candle was, however, to lose its strict relationship to the numbers of soldiers actually on duty. In 1713, General Sutton was to appeal against alteration of the rate, on the grounds that his pay as Governor was less than that received by Governors at Plymouth and Portsmouth, *where also the perquisites far exceed the small one he only enjoyed* in the form of fire and candle[21].

The parish registers of Drypool Church include few references to soldiers or their dependants between 1700 and 1708. This suggests that relatively few occupied the barracks at the Citadel over this period. In 1708, with French support, James, the *Old Pretender*, attempted an invasion of Scotland. Orders were left at Hull for 10 battalions of troops expected to land there, part of a force of 8,000 men sent to uphold the Protestant succession in England. Entries in the Drypool registers referring to soldiers increased from early 1709. They mentioned soldiers from five companies under Captains Julius Stirk, Callis, Bonifeur, Barkham and Wilper. Stirk served as a Lieutenant in Colonel Charles Churchill's Regiment of Marines; while Callis was an officer of Sir Richard Tempest's Regiment of Foot. From 1709, Joseph Wightman's Regiment provided Garrisons at Hull and Berwick[22].

The Garrison continued to hold prisoners captured in naval engagements, left by Navy ships putting in at Hull. In 1709, payments for the Garrison expenses of the previous year included £186 10s 8d for prisoners of war. In March 1708, Admiral

Byng had scattered a French fleet sent to assist the Old Pretender. One ship, the *Salisbury,* was taken as a prize, and several prisoners were to be carried to Hull, where the Deputy-Governor should *receive them into your custody and keep 'em safe until further order.* In March, Rear-Admiral Baker was to *proceed into the river Humber... to deliver into the charge of the commanding officer at Hull all the French soldiers and non-commission officers*[23].

Appointments of ancillary staff marked the renewed growth of the military presence at Hull. In 1711, provision of a chaplain to the Hull Garrison was considered, and John Taylor was appointed to this post. In 1712, Blanchard Waide was appointed surgeon to the Garrison, succeeding his father Benjamin. Wightman was involved in disbanding the regiments of Sir Charles Hotham and Colonel Clayton in 1712, travelling to Hull, Newcastle and Berwick. In 1714, he was described as *Major-General Joseph Wightman, Brigadier Commander-in-Chief the Forces in North Britain,* under the heading of expenses for the usual staff of the Hull Garrison. Elements of Colonel Charles Willis' Regiment (later the 30th Foot) were in Hull in 1714-15, and at least one of their officers was still in the town two years later[24].

In October 1715, news of a more dangerous Jacobite rising in Scotland reached Hull. Lord Rich Irwin, of Temple Newsome, Leeds, had become Governor of Hull the same year, with General John Jones as his Lieutenant. As Deputy-Governor - bearing the title of Colonel - Jones asked the Mayor *to assist me with some men towards strengthening the town's guards.* The rump of the Established Garrison was itself under strength; *we have only six gunners allowed here, of whom but four are now fit for duty.* The Governor was invited to dine with the Bench on November 15, probably to discuss measures for the defence of Hull[25].

The Governor implemented orders for the arrest of suspected Jacobites. Lord Dunbar and Sir Marmaduke Constable, prominent East Yorkshire Catholics, were detained. *I have clapped sentinels on their doors, which they think severe.* As a Catholic, Constable refused to swear oaths denying his beliefs, and was imprisoned in Hull, and then York, until the end of 1716[26].

The Bench was equal to the apprehension of other suspicious persons, as the government ordered. James Ellerker, a Catholic from Hullshire, was committed to prison, as *dangerous to the government,* in 1715. He was not discharged until the following year. Sarah Darkin uttered treasonable words, that: *the Pretender was the right heir to the throne.* She was brought before the Bench, found against, but acquitted. James Dobby, a mariner of Newcastle-upon-Tyne, was dealt with more harshly. Having drunk a health to *King James III,* he was found guilty and sentenced: *to stand in the pillory for an hour at noon in the Market Place of this town. He should pay £20 to the King and find security for his good behaviour for twelve months*[27].

The Bench also assured the political rectitude of officers of the Garrison. Two officers took the oath appointed by law at the Michaelmass Quarter Sessions of 1715. After this, all the officers produced certificates showing they had taken the Anglican Communion, and that they subscribed to a Declaration Against Transubstantiation, proving their rejection of Catholic doctrine. By the Epiphany Sessions of 1717, 24 officers of Lord Irwin's Regiment had subscribed. So, too, did Master Gunner George Marshall, and Lieutenant Barnes of Willis' Regiment[28].

Town Major Barrett reported the situation at Hull, in late November 1715. Twelve companies of Colonel Lucas' Regiment were in Garrison. There were also a number of half-pay officers in Hull. Three transport ships had arrived, *with 700 Dutch which will give some trouble but it is the occasion of a great deal of money to be spent in the town, the transports will sail with the first fair wind for Edinburgh.* The barracks were equipped to hold 180 men, and were actually occupied by 100. Lucas' men, *which did duty in the town are in private quarters, and pay every week, a hundred relieve the barracks every month so with humble submission I think it is rather an advantage than a burden to the town of Hull.* A 100-man force in the town would be equivalent to the strength of the old Independent Companies, and their duties were fulfilled in rotation[29].

Barrett's review of quartering at this time suggests that Hull had reached a sensible accommodation with its military community. The Mutiny Act prohibition of quartering in private houses had perhaps been only nominally respected. *It has always been the custom in this Garrison when any company march in, the public houses in the Town give them quarters for the first night only and afterwards they go into private or poor people's houses and pay each soldier sixpence per week for his lodging which is a great help to the poor inhabitants of this town.* The rate of 6d a week represented a compromise between the 8d due under James II, and the 4d set by the Mutiny Act of 1689. More Dutch soldiers were in Hull from April 1716. Their pay is reflected in the large figure of £1,016 6s 11d for Hull Garrison. And, it was not only poorer householders who profited from their stay. At the end of the crisis,

Hull ships conveyed 3,189 men and sick men and 58 horses back to Holland in July 1716, at a cost to the government of £1,195 17s 6d[30].

Lucas' Regiment was supplemented by Wightman's Regiment of Foot in 1716. This regiment had 450 soldiers in nine companies, with a company of 50 grenadiers. In October, Lucas' Regiment marched out of Hull, to be replaced by Lord Irwin's Regiment, which had come from *North Britain* to relieve them. The departure of Lucas' men was preceded by no less than five weddings of soldiers in August. It may be surmised that Barrett's arrangements for quartering had promoted very amicable relations between some soldiers and their hosts[31].

The finest fortification

The role of the Citadel under William and Mary was set out by Sir Martin Beckman in December 1690. *Now how necessary 'tis that this fortress be finished to keep therein a sufficient magazine for the northern parts of this kingdom, all men of experience cannot but be sensible thereof; and I am well assured that no monarch, prince or state has been nor can be safe in their government without tenable fortifications for their magazines, and security for the respective seaports. The old saying in England, for its objection has been and yet is, that England is an island and the royal fleet is the ramparts; this argument was in reasonable force when the French was inconsiderable at sea and the Dutch alliance beaten out of it; and suppose we may continue in that happiness, yet troubles at home would be uneasy to the governments notwithstanding a naval force; but if the seaports were well fortified, all attempts from abroad and at home, would be of no value.* The next 30 years would not see his advice followed, and the defences of Hull enjoyed little more than the most necessary level of maintenance, and sometimes not even that[32].

The status of Hull as a magazine actually diminished after 1688. The Glorious Revolution had seen gunpowder stockpiled at Hull, and arms and stores brought in from the lesser fortifications of the region. By 1695, however, Hull held only 228 barrels of powder. This compared with 416 barrels at Berwick, and 2,520 at Tilbury and Gravesend. It was the external aspect of the fortifications that commanded the attention of all who viewed them[33].

The earliest illustrations of the Citadel are eye-level views from the south, east, north and west. These were drawn by Beckman, in 1688, before its southern

defences had been raised to their full height. The striking visual impact of the new fortifications is confirmed by 18th-century prospects which show its completed form, particularly those favouring a mariner's view of the town and the Citadel from the Humber. The defences also made a deep impression on visitors to Hull[34].

In 1695, Edmund Gibson considered the present state and recent history of the defences: *on the east side of the river, is built a strong Citadel begun in the year 1681, and including the Castle and South Blockhouse. It has convenient apartments for lodging a good many soldiers, with distinct houses for the officers; has also an engine for making salt water fresh, and is well furnished with ordnance. But yet the strength of the town does not consist so much in its walls or fortifications, as in its situation: for all the country being a perfect level, by cutting the sea banks they can let in the flood and lay it for five miles (c.8km) round under water, which the Governor of the place, at the late Revolution had designed to do, if the then Prince of Orange had landed there, as was once thought, for he had caused several flood-gates to be made, and pitched upon certain places about the town and on the bank of the Humber, for cutting[35].*

The diarist Celia Fiennes, visiting two years later, first considered the town defences. *We enter the town of Hull from the southward over two drawbridges and gates, there is the same entrance (in) another part of the town by two gates and two drawbridges, there is also a third entrance by two gates and two drawbridges from Holderness.* The entrances she described included Beverley Gate, North Gate and, her own route, Hessle Gate. She also noted the *ditches around the town to the landward and they can by them float the grounds for three miles (c.5km) round which is a good fortification.* Fiennes then turned her attention to the Citadel. *The garrison and platform which is the fortification to the sea is in a very uniform figure and were it finished is thought it would be the finest fortification that could be seen, it's walled and pallisaded; I walked round it and viewed it and when I was on the water it seems to run a great length and would require many soldiers to defend the half moons and works[36].*

In September 1689, the Commissioners of Excise and Custom were *asked not to press Mr Fitch for such money as he is to pay them... all by reason that (the) King is indebted to the said Fitch in a considerable sum for the works of Hull.* Large sums listed up to 1692 on Hull's account represented the clearance of debts owed to John Fitch. These instalments were of £14,221 17s 3d in 1690; £16,072 7s 3 ¼d in 1691, and £7,823 12s 2 ¼d in 1692. The Board of Ordnance reported to the Treasury, in October 1693, that they were in arrears of £157,000, without any

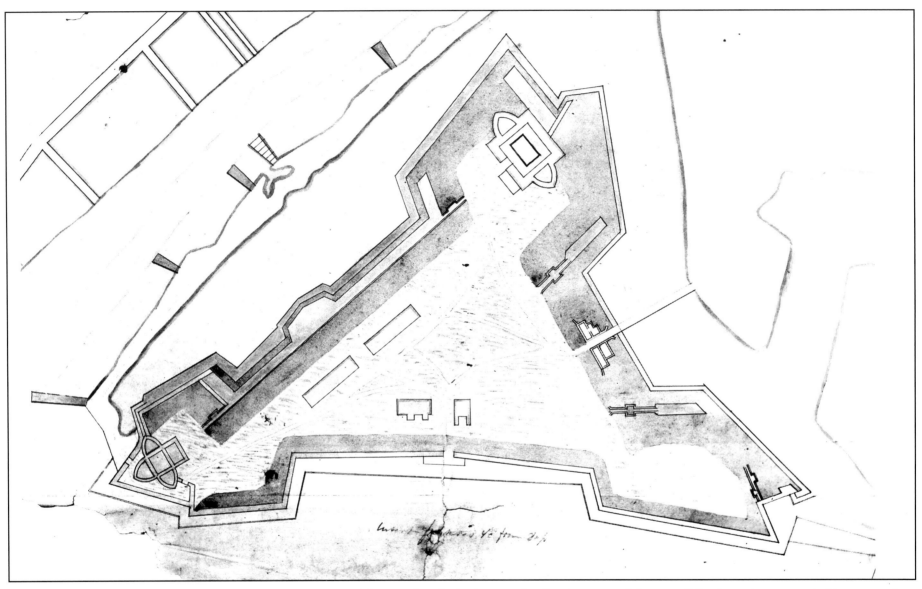

Fig 19: A plan of the Citadel, before 1735; and perhaps copied from earlier draft plans, as details of casemated features differ from those recorded by excavation. From the collections of Wilberforce House Museum, Hull.

ordinary budget to cover the maintenance of fortifications, which had consequently fallen into decay. At Hull, in September 1693, the lease of *waste ground betwixt the Northgates... the drawbridge and sally port* was to be renewed. This was part of the northern defences raised in 1688, and was rented by the shipbuilder Benjamin Blaides[37].

Jonathan Jennings was paid an annual salary of £45 12s 6d, as *overseer of the works at Hull*, recorded from December 1692. He is also listed as a member of the *descent train* of engineers. Between 1692 and 1715, charges listed for Hull represent only the limited works which the Board of Ordnance could manage. The financial limitations afflicting central government lent particular vigour to their attempts to pass costs onto the Bench, as with those arising from the repair of revetments along the river Hull. The banks continued to suffer from damage caused by the launching or mooring of ships in the increasingly congested port. For 1692-93, the charge for Hull was £104 7s 7 ½d; for 1694-95, £107 1s 3d; and for 1695-96, £949 8s 8 ½d. The latter figure suggests an unusual level of expenditure, on what is not known. Repairs at Hull for 1696-97 amounted to £25 8s 6d, with £58 16s 2d listed as a separate item, for *repairing the gunners lodgings*. The latter entry may refer to the casemated chambers at the Main Gate of the Citadel[38].

From March 1695, the Board of Ordnance had been pressing the Bench to carry out repairs at South End; *finding it to belong to the town we are positively resolved not to meddle with the repair of it*. The Bench was similarly resolved. In April 1697, they drafted a letter concerning the repair of *the breastwork at the Artillery Yard, South End*. In July, the Governor reported the dire condition of the town walls behind this battery, and the urgent need for repairs. Work here was not undertaken, as the Bench were still seeking ways to pass responsibility for repairs at South End to the Crown two years later. The issue remained unsettled for another ten years or so, and the Hibbert View of 1737 and the Buck View of 1745 both show extensive breaches in the southern town walls, with a timber fence separating the battery from the town[39].

In 1697-98 expenses of £78 22s were recorded, for *Hull barracks and guardhouse and upholding the works and repairing the main sluice broken down by high tides*. The first two of the three items relate to expenses incidental to housing soldiers. Expenses for 1699-1700 were £292 2s 2d, for the *King's Royal Citadel, Beverley Gate, and North Gate etc.* These may have included work on riverside revetments, perhaps mending them in the vicinity of the sluice. In 1699, Mr John Charlton,

Surveyor-General of the Ordnance, was sent to inspect *a breach of a wharf caused by the tide in the fortifications of Henry VIII*, which was afterwards repaired. Two estimates for repair of fir breastworks, dated to September 1699 and submitted as tenders for the work, specified the requirements: six iron-shod 30ft (9.1m) piles and six 16ft (c.4.9m) piles; three *landties*; a 16½ft (c.5m) *camshot*; twelve 17ft (c.5.2m) planks; ironwork; and labour including the driving of the piles. The costs were variously estimated, at between £18 5s 6d and £28 18s[40].

A further tender details extensive repairs required at the Citadel, at an estimated cost of £75 16s 10d, and gives a most valuable impression of its condition in 1699. Minor items related to the barracks. Furniture within required repair or replacement: mendable pieces included 35 cupboards, 19 tables, 28 *forms*, and 58 bedsteads; 13 new bedsteads, 7 cupboards, 11 tables and 17 new *forms* were also wanted. The roofs of the barracks, officers' lodgings, Governor's house, and Guards required torching with lime and hair[41].

The fortifications were in worse condition. Along the waterfront wall of the south scarp, terras and lime were needed, *to prevent the stones from falling out, the joints being so extraordinary wide, and for putting in the stones which are already out*, at a cost of £6 10s. A man was required, *to cut and trim the quickset hedge top and bottom which is above 300ft (c.91m) in length at the east bastion the same being almost ruined for want of right dressing*, at a charge of £1 10s. This was the first reference to a hedge, forming an obstacle before the main ramparts; it remained a feature of the eastern defences in 1735. Earth was to be cleared out of 80 gun-ports, *which are so sloped up by the falling of the earth into them from the sides of the embrasures that they are become unserviceable till cleared*. Six sentry boxes were to be repaired. Timely action was required *for repairing the bridge that goes into the Citadel which is so ruinous that it is dangerous going over in the wintertime (yet a small repair at present will prevent accidents)*. It was also recommended that 10 rod (c.27m, or possibly double that length) of hurdle work, comprising 10ft (3.1m) planks of fir or oak, should be set about the berm, backed with stiff clay, *to secure the upper berm, or bank on which the bastion stands from being washed away by the water in the moat, the lower berm being already gone and if not timely prevented from going further may become very chargeable*. The powder rooms were damp through neglect.

The armament of the Citadel

On June 27, 1692, a directive ordered that guns at the Citadel in a fit condition were to be used to supply ships of war. The guns were to be dismounted, and lighter guns - *drakes* and *taper-bored* guns - were to be mounted in place of those taken. This exchange was to equip ships fitting out to escort a large convoy bound for the Mediterranean. No record of the armament of Hull over the next seven years has been encountered, though it is likely that some smaller guns were replaced; *taper-bored* guns do not appear in the next survey of guns, though *sakers* - equivalent to *drakes* - were listed[42].

The armament of the defences of Hull was surveyed in July and August 1699. *An Account of Ordnance* detailed the number, type, length, weight and mounting of guns in and around Hull and the Citadel. The serviceable, repairable or unserviceable condition of their carriages was listed; as was the provision of beds and coins - the wooden platforms on which each gun stood and the tackle used for moving it. Some guns were named according to long-established convention, others according to the weight of their shot. The Account indicates the strength of the batteries at Hull, and confirms that the Citadel was now the main defence for the town, albeit one weakened by inadequate maintenance. The distribution was as follows: numbers in brackets refer to guns whose carriages were defective, or guns listed without carriages[43].

In the Town South End:	*3 culverins, 1 demi-culverin, 1 saker, on standing carriages.*
Main Guard in the Town:	*2 sakers, on ship carriages.*
Beverley Gates:	*1 (1) brass saker.*
North Gate:	*1 saker, 2 (1) 12-pounders, on standing carriages.*
North flanker:	*3 (2) demi-culverins, on standing carriage.*
Under the Castle:	*1 6-pounder, 2 sakers, on standing carriages.*
North bastion to the Castle:	*1 12-pounder, 2 demi-culverins, on standing carriages.*
South bastion:	*5 (2) 12-pounders, 2 demi-culverins, on standing carriages.*
South flanker to the Castle:	*3 (2) 6-pounders, 3 sakers, on standing carriages.*
South House bastion:	*2 culverins, 1 12-pounder, 2 demi-culverin, on standing carriages.*
South House flanker:	*3 (2) sakers, on standing carriages.*
Saluting Platform:	*14 sakers, 11 on ship carriages and 3 on standing carriages.*

Half-bastion of the Sea:	*5 sakers, 4 (2) 12-pounders, 3 (2) demi-culverins, on standing carriages.*
Flanker to the Sea:	*4 (3) culverins, on standing carriages.*
Curtain to the Sea:	*4 (2) culverins, 1 (1) 12-pounder, on standing carriages.*
East Point:	*2 demi-culverins and 1 demi-culverin cut, on standing carriages.*
Ditto:	*3 (1) culverins, on standing carriages.*
Facing Drypool:	*2 culverins, on standing carriages.*
Over the Main Guard west of ditto:	*1 culverin, on standing carriage.*
Main Guard Door:	*1 (1) 12-pounder, on standing carriage.*
East Flank:	*3 (1) demi-culverins, on ship carriages.*
Ditto:	*2 sakers, on ship carriages.*
West flank:	*1 (1) culverin cut, 2 (2) demi-culverin cuts, 4 (1) sakers, 1 (1) demi-cannon cut, 1 (1) culverin, on ship carriages.*
Upon the South House:	*3 (3) demi-culverin of which two were on standing carriages and one on a ship carriage, 4 (1) sakers on ship carriages.*
Brass saker upon the bridge for exercise:	*1 saker on standing carriage.*
Brass ordnance:	*2 (2) culverins, 4 (4) demi-culverins.*
Unmounted in Citadel:	*6 (6) sakers.*

Iron Ordnance mounted in the town and new fortifications: 2 demi-cannon cuts, 25 culverins, 14 12-pounders, 25 demi-culverins, 4 6-pounders, 43 sakers.

The characteristics of the guns may be summarised as follows. Most guns had a similar *point blank* range. This would apply for close-in defence, when canister or grape shot were to be used as anti-personnel weapons, or to tear the sails and rigging of ships. Maximum ranges were defined for the use of solid iron shot[44].

Name	Wt of shot (in lbs)	Calibre (inches)	Close range (yards)	Max.Rg (yards)
Demi-cannon	27	6	340	1,600
Culverin	15	5	400	2,000
12 pounder	12	Figures not listed		
Demi-culverin	9	4.5	380	1,800
6-pounder	6	Figures not listed		
Saker	5	3.5	300	1,500

The South End battery mounted mainly heavy guns, which could project a notional 59lbs (*c*.27kg) of shot against enemy ships. This was the only significant armament in Hull itself. The Main Guard in Marketplace mounted two guns. The muzzle of one of these is illustrated as protruding from the north wall of the Guardhouse by a view of *c*.1700, and in such a location would have fired canister or grapeshot, to suppress civil disorder. The field of fire from the Guardhouse had been obstructed by the reconstruction of the Market Cross in 1683, and ship carriages for the guns there would have made their deployment difficult. Beverley *Gates* - alluding to the inner and outer drawbridges - had only a single brass saker; North Gate was more powerfully armed, but the exact location of guns is not specified in either case[45].

The listing of guns at the Citadel was ordered in a counter-clockwise direction, beginning with the northernmost batteries. The *north flanker* was a *base flank* battery. Together with guns *under the Castle*, it was positioned so as to control the landward approach to North Bridge and Hull from the east. The lack of carriages for the larger guns effectively halved the power of these batteries. The *North bastion to the Castle* may refer to more guns here, or alternatively to guns on the face of the bastion, facing the river Hull and the town. This position, however, lacked embrasures in 1716[46].

The *south bastion* might refer to guns along the north bastion face, looking eastwards. Alternatively, together with the *south flanker to the Castle*, they may have formed a two-tier arrangement, with lighter guns occupying the *base flank*. If so, together they could project a notional 90lbs (*c*.41kg) of shot at vessels attempting to enter the mouth of the river Hull. This manoeuvre entailed the use of cables attached to the *Dolphin* outside the river mouth, so as to warp vessels against the contrary flows of the Hull and Humber, and a ship attempting this would present a near-stationary target.

The *South House bastion* guns may have occupied some of ten embrasures along the west face of the bastion and in its upper flanks, supplemented by *sakers* in the *south house flanker*. The Saluting Platform mounted 14 *sakers*. The ship carriages here would be more resistant to salt-spray. In peacetime, it was these guns which saluted visiting ships.

The *half bastion of the sea* probably refers to the face of the west bastion, adjacent to the Saluting Platform. Dispositions here are again uncertain. These guns could deliver 58lbs (*c*.26kg) of shot; yet had the carriages been in better order, the power of this battery would have been nearly doubled. The *flanker to the sea* also had only one serviceable carriage; its fire covered the shoreline before the Citadel. Guns were only sparsely distributed along the south curtain. The poor state of gun carriages along the south side of the Citadel might suggest that they had formed part of the complement rushed into position in November 1688, and that they had subsequently been allowed to deteriorate.

At East Point, guns were listed in two groups of three. The Gent view, of 1735, was to depict two guns on ship carriages and two or three embrasures at the re-entrant end of the west water bastion. Three guns on each side of the re-entrant may be inferred. They were intended to cover the shoreline to the east, and to engage approaching ships. Together, they could project a notional 57lbs (*c*.25kg) of shot, forming a strong battery[47].

The guns *facing Drypool* were probably on the north face of the east bastion. The *Main Guard* was the entrance to the Citadel in the centre of its east curtain. The strongest eastern batteries were in the flanks. The *east flank* guns covered North Bridge. The *west flank* mounted nine guns, though the Phillips plan illustrated seven embrasures here in 1716, so there may have been a second tier of guns on the main rampart. Potentially a powerful battery, none of the big guns here had serviceable carriages.

Guns were mounted *upon the South House*, occupying the platform on the roof of South Blockhouse as they had since 1684. All were unusable: probably the result of their exposed position and the failure to maintain them. South Blockhouse now served as a store rather than as a working element of the defences. The twelve dismounted brass guns may represent elements of the Artillery Train. If so, *sakers* had replaced the six *demi-culverins* which had made up part of the Train in 1684[48].

The Account of Ordnance is important for its portrayal of the Citadel as an armed gun platform at its most formidable. Overall, its armament was similar to that which had defended Hull in 1643. The Blockhouses had lost their role as gun platforms, though their suitability for this role was to be occasionally reconsidered in the course of the 18th and 19th centuries. The failure to maintain gun carriages, a problem throughout the era, significantly detracted from the power of these modern defences. An estimate prepared in 1699 detailed necessary repairs, to the wheels, axles, and chocks of gun carriages mounted on the defences, and to equipment of the Train, gun by gun, at an estimated cost of £60 9s[49].

The concept underlying the design of the Citadel had been overtaken by the Glorious Revolution. Under the settlement of 1689, England avoided absolutism and the corollary violence of revolt and repression. The west curtain facing the town of Hull, the single most powerful battery at the Citadel, had been entirely disarmed by 1699. The Citadel's function of assuring domestic tranquillity had been lost even before its completion.

A fortress decayed

While a skeleton Garrison was maintained at the Citadel, routine repairs could at least be envisaged, and there is evidence of piecemeal works. A short series of detailed estimates dated to the early 18th century survives, from which the deteriorating condition of the defences may be inferred. These were encountered among municipal papers at Hull, which tends to underline the reviving role of the local community in the upkeep of the royal fortifications.

In March 1700, the Deputy-Governor was urged *to take some care about your drawbridges*. Hull saw £248 15s 6 ½d spent on *Gates, drawbridges, barracks and storehouse* for the year, so this recommendation may have been followed. In November 1701, the state of defences around the town was addressed. An estimate listed *work necessary to be done, at several parts of the moats joining and the outbridges of the town of Hull, both for the security of the same, and the prevention of ill people getting in and out at unseasonable hours as they used to do*. This specified 206ft of *blinds* to be made, with posts, rails and boards; the scouring of the town moat in several places to its proper width of 20ft (6.1m) broad and 3ft (0.9m) deep; and brickwork *to keep up the banks next the bridges which by their constant falling down choke up the highway*. Dams were to be made to enable work in the moat. A *new door with a sloping wing to the water at one side of the same* was to be positioned *before the narrow bridge of the sally-port at the North Gate of the town*, with its lock and ironwork. The estimated cost was £46 5s 6d[50].

Repairs in 1700-1701 cost £44 8s 8d for Hull Garrison. This figure comes close to that of £46 17s offered by an estimate of 10 February 1701, for repairing damages done at Hull, *by violent storms and extraordinary tides*. These repairs were to entail two carpenters' work over a week on the replacement of 42ft (c.13m) of sills and 100 deal planks which had been washed away, and the carriage and ramming of earth on the Humber banks. Repair of breastworks along the river Hull, near North Blockhouse, was also required[51].

In May 1701, an estimate specified minor repairs to *the main sluice next the Haven to prevent further damages that may happen by the water*. The necessary work entailed the provision, repair and pitching of planks; and six days work by William Walker and John Hart, carpenters, who were to receive 2s 6d and 2s a day respectively. The overall cost was estimated at £4 19s 10d. Another £10 5s, however, was required for the mending of a breach in riverbank revetments nearby. The breach was 65ft (c.20m) long, 15ft (4.6m) deep and 10ft (c.3.1m) wide, and was to be dug out and cleared. Deals were to be spiked to piles, which had apparently survived in place. Earth was then to be rammed by a five-man team of labourers over a period of nine days[52].

An estimate of June 1702 was for repairs required: *for the security of the ramparts belonging to Her Majesty's Garrison... and for the prevention of ill people leading rubbish, and dirt, as frequently they do, upon the said ramparts*. This entailed a fence, with locks and ironwork *for a barrier at each wing to open upon any occasion*, at a cost of £9 12s. William Walker was again to serve as carpenter, at a fee of £1 for 8 days work[53].

In May 1703, Edward Raven, a participant in works at the Citadel since 1685, and an overseer, offered his estimate of the cost for repairing a stone sentry box. This enumerated materials as a *chalder and a half of lime*, 1,500 new bricks, 12ft (3.7m) of stone, 30 iron cramps and 8 stone (c.51kg) of lead; labour costs included 23 days for a bricklayer and his labourer - costing £2 6s for the bricklayer and half as much for his labourer - and 16 days of mason's work at 2s 6d a day. Raven's total costing was £11 13s 7d; another tender arrived at a cost of £14 7s 3d. The number of bricks required suggests that the sentry box was in danger of parting from its position on a brick-faced rampart. The second estimate also stated that *all the passage both stone and brick was forced to be taken up as also the wings*, though the exact relation of these features to the sentry box is uncertain. This was one of two or three watchtowers, set at the south-east, south-west, and possibly the north, salient angles of the Citadel[54].

No actual expenditure at Hull is listed by the Treasury Bill Books between 1701 and 1708-9. This period saw the defences of Hull neglected. A further estimate, dated to May 1703, dealt with further requirements for planked repairs and rammed earthworks, *from the main jetty to the second jetty* along the east bank of the river Hull. It also allowed for repair of the *two dams and Humber bank breast-work* at the East Point of the Citadel[55].

In 1705, being requested to report on the fortification of the North, the Board of Ordnance found *this office under great difficulties, not having any person here proper to undertake that service*. They wished *Your Grace could spare any engineer from abroad who might perform that service... In the meantime we are in hopes either Mr Ayres or Mr Povy - who have small employments in this office will be fit to survey and draw plans of the northern garrisons - though we are afraid they are not able to make proper observations for new fortifying them.* The officers capable of directing work were away at the wars. Nor was a major contractor available; John Fitch had recently died, and the Board was unwilling to re-grant his monopolistic niche. At Hull, Town Major Barrett acquired the overseer's post on the death of Edward Raven in 1707, and also for a time held the *frobushers* position. His salary for the latter, however, was stopped by the Board, because he had failed to maintain the arms in store[56].

In 1708, the year of James Stuart's landing in Scotland, the Governor was asked what quantity of powder could be lodged safely at Hull; it was found that 1,000 barrels could be stored. Following this enquiry, five store-ships were sent for Hull and Berwick to improve the military supply of North Britain, in April. Hull, along with Portsmouth and Plymouth, was to hold the largest stocks of powder for the Navy, rendering Hull an important supply base for North Sea squadrons. In 1709, ammunition, arms, and tools were sent to Hull and Berwick by sea, along with plank and timber for the mending of gun carriages. William Idle had taken up the Storekeeper's post in 1689. With the restocking of Ordnance stores at Hull, complaints reached the Board that Idle was absent from his duty. He had *found he was a great deal out of purse, because his bills had not been passed by the Board*[57].

When Treasury payments on Hull resumed in 1708-9, £322 7s 5 ½d was required for repairs. £140 10s 1 ½d was spent in 1711; repairs in 1712 cost £75 0s 10 ½d, with a distinct sum listed for *Discharge Kingston upon Hull* of £52 11s 11d – perhaps as repayment for costs incurred locally. The latter sum may have related to the long-delayed repairs at the South End battery. Town and Crown had gone to law on this point in 1697; and by 1709 the town had begun repairs there. The only other item known in more detail is an estimate by Jonathan Gill of £6 4s 5d for the repair of windows in the officers rooms, Barracks and Castle[58].

In 1713, *repairs to fortifications at Hull* cost £657 13s 6 ½d; in 1714, £259 2s 5 ¼d; the *Reparation of Castle etc.* cost £108 0s 3 ¼d in 1715. In July 1713, Engineer Richards reported to the Ordnance on the danger posed by the tides and rolling shingle to Blockhouse Point, referring to the Saluting Platform. This report may have resulted in some part of the heavy expenditure for 1713 and 1714. The most substantial works related to this report comprised *the repair of the south-west corner of the Saluting Platform by the South Blockhouse in the Citadel of Hull against Humber*. Richard Roebuck prepared an estimate for this, in February 1714. He also addressed other problems about the defences. Roebuck was another craftsman who had formerly been employed on the works, as a mason in 1684-85. He proposed that 36ft (*c*.11m) of ashlar facing should be reset with terras and iron cramps. Another 50ft (*c*.15m) of ashlar was to be reset in terras; the entire stone-clad south front of the Citadel was to be repointed, and subsequently pointed annually at a charge of £10 *per annum*. The cost of initial works was set at £37 3s 1 ½d[59].

More expensive repairs were required at the Garrison sluice. Forty Stockholm deals were wanted, *to repair the sides and bottom of the main sluice next the Haven where the deals are torn up and rotten the whole being 100ft (c.31m) in length*. Planks were required, *for outsides of the sluice and repairs within where the plank is broken to pieces*. *Ground joists* or sills were required, comprising 120ft (*c*.37m) of oak. The sluice doors required waterproofing by *lathering, caulking and pitching*, and earth was needed, *to fill and ram in the bottom and sides of the sluice to prevent the water getting under as also to make dams*. Iron spikes would fasten the timber. Four carpenters and four labourers would be required. These charges, amounting to £44 6s, would be further augmented if the *crosswork* of the adjoining revetments were to be mended. Both the originator and the recipient of the estimate appear from the layout of the document, however, to have been aware that this charge properly fell to the Bench.

Other estimates were for works amounting to wholesale renovation of the Guardhouses of the town. One carpenter's estimate details internal works on Guardhouses *of the town and Citadel*. It is uncertain whether the *Main Guard* was that in the Market Place, or the entrance to the Citadel itself. It required a door-frame; 16yds (c.15m) of cornice - from its low cost of only 16s, probably internal woodwork; *window shuts* and a new door and table for the guardroom, at a cost of £7 5s. Beverley Gate Guard needed a new door and door frame with lock and ironwork, for £3 9s. At Myton Gate Guard, a door-frame and door were needed; also a new roof, with a 24ft (7.3m) wall-plate timber, 16 20ft (c.6.1m) spars, 3 baulks, pantiles, with laths and nails provided; altogether costing £8 10s. At North End Gate Guard, a new door and roof required similar works and materials. Richard Davis proposed tiling at the coal house at South End; plastering at the Main Guard; tiling and brickwork at Myton Gate and North End Guard; and raising a chimney at the latter. The overall charge was £18 6s. Davis additionally estimated for £5 3s 6d worth of brickwork and tiling at the Barracks. An estimate of £20 15s 9d was offered for posts and rail fencing at the Citadel. Jonathan Gill offered to mend assorted window-panes and casements at the officers rooms, Barracks, Guardhouses and South Blockhouse, at a charge of £2 9s 6d.

The Jacobite rising of 1715 was met only by improvised remedies for widespread deficiencies. Lieutenant-Governor Jones found it necessary to use *one of the drawbridges which was taken down from the town* for the Citadel. He wrote to the Board of Ordnance: *as to putting the Citadel in a posture of defence and hope to be honoured with your directions,* on 12 October. Town Major Barrett was paid £42 as an overseer, suggesting that a gang of labourers was employed; and a further £45 12s 6d *for working the engine for making salt water fresh.* The Storekeeper, now Ralph Jackson, was also serving as *Frobusher,* at a salary of £40 and a bonus of £10. He had previously served as an overseer at Portsmouth, and was to remain at Hull until his death in 1732[60].

Payments recorded in 1716 may also relate to works carried out at this time: all were minor. Richard David, a bricklayer, repaired grates at the Citadel, perhaps at the outfalls of its drains. Jonathan Gill carried out glazing. Mary Raven, the widow of Edward, raised floors - in this case a measure of earth - and made a blind earthwork at the end of East Point, probably to protect the flank of the battery there. John Shipman was paid for repairing beds and bedding. The charge of these works amounted to £20 13s 5d[61].

In January 1716, the Board sent Captain Thomas Phillips to carry out their long-deferred survey of northern fortifications. In July, Phillips found *the defence works at Hull at a standstill for want of orders from the Board of Ordnance,* and beseeched

Lord Irwin, the Governor, to take the matter up with the King. The cost of *reparations* listed at Hull, in 1717, was £150 8s 2d. A further item, £750 8s 2d for both the payment of labourers and the fitting up of the Field Train at Hull, suggests that more extensive earthworks had been undertaken. These may, however, have comprised consolidation rather than new works; later plans do not record any major features to be ascribed to this period[62].

Phillips' visit was ultimately more important to the historians than to the defenders of Hull. He made a detailed plan of the town and its environs, which was the first to approach a modern level of accuracy. In keeping with his purpose, he paid particular attention to features of military significance. Among these were an *old demolished redoubt* east of the Citadel, which preserved the lines of an earthwork guarding one of the sluices of *c.*1688; outworks *now resumed by the proprietors* outside Hessle Gate; and at the *great half-bastion* in front of North Gate. Copies of his survey were eventually to be lodged in both local collections and the Public Record Office[63].

In 1720, Daniel Defoe rehearsed much the same points of strategy that Beckman had considered 30 years before. Like all others, he noted the strength of Hull's location. However, he considered the origin of the Citadel in a novel light. *King Charles II, on occasion of the frequent Dutch Wars in that reign had once resolved to appoint a station for a squadron of men of war here, with a yard and dock, for building men of war in the Humber; and in this occasion, resolved to make it strong, in proportion to the necessity of those affairs; upon which a large Citadel was marked out on the other side of the river; but it was never finished. The greatest imperfection as to the strength of Hull in case of war is, that lying open to the sea it is liable to bombardment, which can only be prevented by being masters at sea, and while we are so there's no need of fortification at all; and so there's an end of the argument on that subject.* Defoe had misconstrued both the design and setting of the Citadel in the light of contemporary opinion. He had, however, cogently summarised the underlying reasons for its neglected state[64].

Footnotes

1:     Corelli-Barnett 1970, 148.

2:     Williams 1994, 212-20.

3:     Childs 1979, 192; Ogg 1955, 366, 392.

4: Childs 1987, 124; Ogg 1955, 170.

5: CSPD 1689-90, William and Mary, 322; CTB vol. 9, 66; CSPD 1689-90, William and Mary, 326; CTP 1656-7/1696, 82.

6: CTP 1556-1696, 76, 82; KUHRO BRB 6, 549; CTP cont. 1557-1698, 20; CSPD 1692, 254.

7: PRO WO51/40, TBB series 2, 89, 28 March 1690; CTB vol. 9, part 1, 839; CTB vol. 9, part 1, 866.

8: Dalton 1960, vol. 2, 222; KUHRO L1147-9, L1151, L1156; CTB vol. 9, part 1, 1259.

9: KUHRO L1147.

10: Fortescue 1903, vol. 3, 566; CTB vol. 10, part 1, 484; KUHRO BRB 6, 334, 350, 365; HMC Buccleuch Mss. 2, pt. 1, June 1694; KUHRO M405; Childs 1987, 107; Ogg 1955, 396; Hist. Mss. Comm. 55, vol. 8, 80; CTB vol. 11, 391; Childs 1979, 173.

11: KUHRO M405; Williams 1994, 213; CSPD 1696, 271.

12: Childs 1987, 97-8; Wilson 1965, 220; KUHRO BRB 6, 392, 442, 408, 411, 350, 419, 393, 445; Tickell 1798, 681.

13: KUHRO DM, 17 February 1691, L1162.

14: KUHRO L1175; CSPD 1697, 487; CTB vol. 13, 43.

15: KUHRO L1175, L1176; Rogers 1977, 69; CSPD 1700-1702, 261.

16: Gent 1735, 191; KUHRO L1163A, L1170, L1177; Childs 1987, 109; KUHRO L1170, L1177.

17: YPRS 125, Drypool vols 1-5, 21 December 1698, 6 May 1699, 2 November 1699; Dalton 1960, vol. 5, 325.

18: Lenman 1980, 115-19.

19: Scouller 1966, 83; CTB vol. 15, 1700, 329-30; Corelli-Barnet 1970, 143.

20: CSPD 1703-4, 58, 95-6; CSPD 1704-5, 565-6, 188.

21: PRO WO24/38, fo. 15, 1705; CTB 20, pt 1, 1705-6, 505; CTB 20, pt. 1, 767; CTB 20, pt. 2, 1706-7, 92; CTB 20, part 1, 1706-7, 148; HMC Portland Ms X, 91, 1713.

22: YPRS 125 Drypool, vols 1-5, 15 December 1700; 17 January 1701, 9 November 1701; 4 December 1703, 10 November 1706, 26 January 1708, 3 January 1709; HMC House of Lords Mss 1708-10, 8, 1708, 40, 46; Lenman 1980, 153; YPRS 125 Drypool vols 1-5, 24 March 1709; Dalton 1960, vol. 5, 130; HMC House of Lords Mss 1708-10, new series 8, 269.

23: CTB vol. 23, part 2, 280; HMC House of Lords Mss 1708-10, 74, 299.

24: CTB 1711, vol. 25, part 2, 71; Dalton 1960 vol. 5, 183; CTB vol. 26, pt. 2, 542; CTB vol. 28, part 1, 134; Farmer 1901, 136; KUHRO Quarter Sessions Book CQ2 1693-1787, Epiphany 1716, fo. 56.

25: KUHRO BRB 6, 761-2; HMC 55, vol. 8, 93-4; KUHRO BRB 6, 655.

26: HMC 55, vol. 8, 93; Clay 1915, 180.

27: KUHRO Quarter Sessions Book CQ2 1693-1787, fo. 55; ibid. fo. 52 facing.

28: KUHRO Quarter Session Book CQ 1693-1787, fo. 51 facing, fo. 56; Farmer 1901, 136.

29: KUHRO L1242.

30: CTB vol. 30, part 1, 1716, 129; ibid., part 2, 1716, 375-6.

31: CTB vol. 30, part 1, 1716, 129; HMC 55, vol. 8., 93-4; YPRS 125 Drypool vols 1-5, 5 August 1716 to 25 August 1716.

32: PRO WO44/100/HK5970 X19, Beckman to Board, 10 December 1690.

33: e.g. PRO WO51/37, TBB series 2, 44a, 19 September 1688, 29 September 1688; PRO WO51/37 TBB series 3, 123, 7 November 1688; PRO WO46:3, 131, 5 September 1695.

34: Brit. Lib. Add. 33233, 1-5; e.g. Gent 1735; Hibbert 1737; Buck 1745.

35: Woodward 1985, 42.

36: Woodward 1985, 49; Morris 1984, 99.

37: CTB vol. 9, part 1, 363; CTB Pt 2, 12 March 1690; Declared Accounts Ordnance, Charles Bertie Treasurer, 289, pipe 2675, 30 June 1690; Declared Accounts Ordnance, Charles Bertie Treasurer, 291, pipe 2676, 30 June 1691; Declared Accounts Ordnance, Charles Bertie Treasurer, 292, pipe 2677, 30 June 1692; CTP continua 1557-1695, 324; KUHRO BRB 6, 325.

38: HMC 14, House of Lords 1692-93, 189; KUHRO L1159, L1244; Declared Accounts Ordnance, Charles Bertie Treasurer, 292, audit bundle 1857, roll 103; CTB vol. 18, Charles Bertie Treasurer, 294, pipe 2680, 30 June 1695; CTB vol. 18, Charles Bertie Treasurer, 295, pipe 2681, June 1696; CTB vol. 18, 1695-1702, 524.

39: KUHRO L1167, BRB 6, 372; PRO WO46:4, Danby to Romney, 5 July 1697; KUHRO L1186.

40: CTB vol. 18, 1695-1702, 535, 578; Chancery Judgement 1860, 26-7; KUHRO DDE 6 15/13, Ext. fos 64, 68, Book B.

41: KUHRO DDE 6 15/13, fo. 62, Ext. fo. 62, Book B, 16 September 1699.

42: CSPD 1692, 339; Ogg 1955, 388.

43: PRO WO55/319, 31 August 1699.

44: Hogg 1963, 20-34.

45: Tindall Wildridge 1884, 27, plate 7.

46: Phillips Plan 1716.

47: Humberside Libraries 1974; Foreman 1989, 41.

48: Stafford Record Office D (W) 1778/V/71 (184), Account of Ordnance of the Train, 1684.

49:    KUHRO DDE6 15/13, Entered Fo. 65 Book B, 16 September 1699.

50:    CSPD 1700-2, 261; CTB vol. 18, 1695-1702, 180; KUHRO DDE6 15/13 fo. 226, Book B, 29 November 1701.

51:    CTB vol. 18, 529; KUHRO DDE 6 15/13, fo. 260, Book B, 10 February 1701.

52:    KUHRO DDE6 15/13, fo. 173, Book B, 10 May 1701.

53:    KUHRO DDE 15/13, Book B, 3 June 1702.

54:    KUHRO DDE6 15/13, Book B, fo. 67, 15 May 1703; Thew 1784, plan.

55:    KUHRO DDE6 15/13, Book B, fo. 27.

56:    PRO WO46/6, 29065, 22 May 1705; Tomlinson 1973, 64, 232.

57:    HMC House of Lords Mss 1708-10, 47, 259, 162; Tomlinson 1973, 129; HMC House of Lords Mss, new series viii, 269; Hogg 1963, 232, 62, 98.

58:    CTB vol. 23, part 2, 197; CTB vol. 25, part 1, 256; CTB vol. 26, part 1, 1712, 206; PRO WO46/4, Danby to Romney, 7 July 1697; KUHRO L1167, L1186; KUHRO BRB 8, 527, 626, February 1712; KUHRO DDE 6 15/13, 4 October 1712.

59:    CTB vol. 27, part 1, 1713, 237; CTB vol. 28, part 1, 1714, 192; CTB vol. 29, pt 1, 1714-15, 120; Tomlinson 1973, footnote 10, citing BM Stowe Ms. 477, 10; KUHRO DDE 6 15/13.

60:    HMC 55, vol. 8, 93-4; Hogg 1962, 180, 183; YPRS 125 Drypool 1-5, Parish Registers, 16 January 1732.

61:    CTB vol. 31, part 1, 1717, 180.

62:    Porter 1889, vol. 2, 145-6; HMC 55, vol. 8, 98; CTB vol. 31, part 1, 1717, 171; CTB vol. 31, part 1, 1717, 188.

63:    Foreman and Goodhand 1997, fig. 2; e.g. versions of Phillips plan PRO MR 1228, MPHH 85 [1-2].

64:    Woodward 1985, 56.

CHAPTER 11
COMPLACENCY AND CRISIS

After the alarms of 1715, the maintenance of the defences was effectively abandoned for a generation. The Treaty of Utrecht, in 1713, dictated a halving of the number of guns in all fortresses. This would have reduced the armament of the Citadel to about 50 guns. In 1750, a Return of Ordnance listed 28 eighteen-pounders, 14 nine-pounders and 20 three-pounders at Hull. Visitors to Hull in the 1690s had been impressed by the strength of the Citadel. Those who recorded their opinions in the 1730s remarked, rather, upon the decayed state of the fortifications and their Garrison[1].

An Invalid Garrison

In November 1715, the forces available for the defence of Hull had included a number of half-pay officers. From 1719, Captain John Massey and Lieutenant Mathew Draper were listed as half-pay officers at Hull, and as officers of *Invalids*. They were still at Hull in 1721. In 1724, Ensign Peter Pidget and Henry Harmen Vandeck were officers of an Independent Company of Invalids. In 1739, an old quarter-master of dragoons was also listed in the town. In 1724, an anonymous visitor described the Garrison as follows: *Brigadier Stanwix is Governor, and Colonel Jones Deputy-Governor of a Garrison which consists of four companies of Invalids of 45 men each. The fortifications are old and decayed and little store of arms.* When George II succeeded to the throne in 1727, the Garrison officers were invited to join the Bench in polite and formal celebration. They were to attend Holy Trinity and have a sermon preached with the Town's Musick attending in their proper place; followed by entertainment with wine and eatables at the Corporation's charge[2].

In 1681, Charles II had founded the Royal Hospital, Chelsea. The Hospital was completed only after Charles' death, and provided a retirement home for soldiers who had served twenty years or more in his small army. By 1690, 472 Hospital places were filled, and a further 107 out-pensioners drew allowances. This level of provision was to be overwhelmed by the veterans of later wars. Old soldiers who were fit filled the ranks of Invalid Companies. These first provided guards for the Royal Palaces, so as to release regulars for service in the field. At the emergency of 1715, 25 more companies of Chelsea pensioners were formed to take over garrison duties. They were initially to provide garrisons for Edinburgh, Stirling and Dumbarton. They wore a plain red coat with blue facings and linings, yellow buttons, a red waistcoat, and blue breeches. A tricorne hat with a yellow binding completed their outfit[3].

Burials recorded at Drypool between 1717 and 1732 included about 30 soldiers, but neither wives nor children of soldiers are identified over the same period. This could be the result of delicacy on the part of the parish clerk: association with common soldiers was not a matter to take pride in. It might alternatively hint that the soldiers were a body of older men. In 1733, the defences of Hull were described by another visitor, who was clearly unimpressed: *The Citadel is its best defence, having a double tier of guns, a wide ditch before it, and what is more terrible, a company of Invalids within. This was once accounted the strongest fortress in England but now the walls are tumbling down, and the ditches a common lay-stall; why these or others especially northwards are suffered to run to ruin, is the alteration of our proper and natural strength since the Union, which doubtless is the fleet*[4].

In 1715, two out of six gunners at Hull were unfit for duty; the allotment of their posts to disabled seamen was a custom of long standing. They occupied quarters within the Citadel Barracks; gunners appear in the Drypool registers, their burials being recorded in 1719, 1720, 1723 and 1724. The death of so many tends to suggest that these, too, were elderly men. Two were Master Gunners: Joseph (?)Butterfly in 1720, and Thomas Thompson in 1723. The Storekeeper, Ralf Jackson, died in 1732, still in office. Deputy-Governor Jones, commanding officer, and perhaps among the younger members of his staff, was himself aged 59 by 1720. In 1730, he bought a large house in Porters Entry, facing Hull's High Street, and died at the age of 87, in 1748, having achieved the title of Governor shortly before his death[5].

The condition of the Citadel matched that of the Garrison. The only action to keep up the fortifications was taken by the Bench. In 1726-27, *the East Jetty on the Garrison Side opposite to the Horse Staithe* was to be examined, with a view to shortening it. In 1728, *the part of the South End which is between the jetty and the wooden steps* was to *be extended with a wall of brick of convenient thickness – to be done by 1*

July next. In 1731, two Aldermen *viewed the long jetty without Myton Gates and the breastworks adjoining*, which *were much out of repair and ordered to be repaired*; the *South Jetty on Garrison Side* was also to be repaired. Further repairs to wooden breastworks at South End were ordered in 1733 and 1736, and to the Garrison-Side jetty in 1735. A view dated to 1735 shows that the bridge to the Main Gate of the Citadel had been removed. Embrasures were reduced to hummocks, while horses grazed or rolled on the ramparts. Hibbert's *South East Prospect of Kingston Upon Hull*, of 1737, shows twelve guns mounted at the Saluting Platform of the Citadel, and two before the South End Battery. While this view is questionable in matters of detail, it suggests that the lower south front of the Citadel had been clad with planks. A plan outlining limited improvements, drawn by Thomas Fearnside in 1743, suggests that the Board of Ordnance at least had Hull in mind at that time[6].

From 1733 to 1740 the families of soldiers again appeared in the Drypool Registers: the burial of twelve soldiers, five children, and one army wife are recorded over this eight-year period. George Barratt Gent(leman) died in December 1734, and, as a resident of the town rather than the Garrison, was buried at St Mary's, Lowgate[7].

Hull and the "Forty-five"

In 1743, George II led his soldiers to victory at Dettingen. In 1744, the assembly of a French invasion fleet at Brest promoted anxiety throughout England. The fleet, however, was destroyed by gales, resulting in the collapse of French plans. The English army was again engaged in Flanders in 1745, leaving the country denuded of trained troops. It was now, with French help, that Charles Edward Stuart landed in the western Highlands of Scotland on 25 July 1745. Charles Edward was the grandson of James II: known to enemies as the Young Pretender, and to the Highlanders who flocked to his standard as Bonnie Prince Charlie. His revolt was to pose a far more significant threat to Hanoverian rule than that of his father in 1715[8].

Jacobite forces took Edinburgh. As they marched south, panic gripped the English boroughs and shires. On receiving news of the Scots' advance, the Bench, under Mayor Froggatt, sent a loyal address to the King, on 13 September. This was graciously received. Deputy-Governor Jones and the Bench agreed that

Hull should hold out. On 20 September, the Duke of Newcastle, Secretary of State for the Southern Department and effectively Prime Minister of the day, contacted the Earl of Malton, Lord Lieutenant of the West Riding. Newcastle proposed to arm the Yorkshire Regiment of volunteers with arms and ammunition out of the stores at Hull. As this supply alone was insufficient, more munitions would be sent to Hull. The Highland clans swept away the half-trained government troops of General John Cope at Prestonpans, on 21 September 1745[9].

On 24 September, the Mayor and Deputy-Governor informed Newcastle of their decision, asking for commissions for officers. The Mayor added that the moats around the town could not be filled with water until they had been cleansed, and hoped for orders to that end. About 25 September, the opening of the sluices to flood the land around Hull was considered or rumoured, though this was not done. A commission appointed Froggatt as Captain of a company of gentleman volunteers. As, however, his mayoral term ended on 30 September, a new document was required for his successor, William Cookson. It was nearly two months until it arrived, placing him under the Deputy-Governor's orders[10].

The Lord Lieutenant of the East Riding was Lord Irwin, brother to the former Governor of Hull. Irwin left his house at Temple Newsome, near Leeds, and established himself at Beverley in October. He was armed with a Crown directive, *for searching forthwith to cause all arms belonging to papists, non-jurors or other persons that shall be judged dangerous to the peace of this kingdom within your lieutenancy to be seized and secured*. There were no Catholics in Hull, and only 437 in the whole of the East Riding; the Clerk of the Peace made little effort to secure presentments against this harmless minority[11].

As Lord Lieutenant of the East Riding, Irwin commanded the County Militia. However, he regarded the raising of the militia as an expense to the county without good effect. In their place, volunteers were to be raised, and supported by public subscription. He had no jurisdiction over Hull, which in peace was self-governing as a Town and County Borough, and in time of emergency was commanded by the Governor or his Deputy. Perhaps because he misunderstood this position, Irwin took particular exception to the grant of a commission to the Mayor, and to the enrolment of Hull gentry with the town's forces rather than his own[12].

Newcastle ordered land carriage of arms to Hull, and on 7 October notified the Earl of Malton that 1,500 arms were on their way. Delays in their supply were held to be the result of the failure of the Lords Lieutenant to appoint an agent at the Tower, whence the arms were sent. Newcastle reminded the Lords Lieutenant *that it is at least 150 long miles to Hull and I believe not the best of roads* - though the supply of Hull was customarily by sea, for just this reason. The Deputy-Governor and Mayor of Hull were to achieve more by informal collaboration than formal mechanisms controlled by royal officials unaware of local conditions[13].

By early October, preparations had begun at Hull for the repair of *dykes and ditches*, on which 3,000 people were said to be involved. The gentry and merchants of the town lent a hand to keep up civic morale. Workers were summoned by beat of drum every morning; some were paid as labourers at 1s a day, while volunteers distinguished themselves with cockades in their hats. The Bench requested technical help; on 8 October, the engineer Peter Henry Bruce arrived. His inspection the following day found that: *the moats had been deepened, the ramparts repaired, the embrasures restored and the magazines placed in order. In fact it seemed as though the work had been guided by a skilled engineer. He had nothing to do but to follow in the lines so ably begun, and with the help of all concerned Hull was soon declared to be in a fit state to resist all attack*[14].

The frigate *Success*, under Captain William Thompson, was ready to sail with a cargo of arms and stores for Georgia when news of the Scots was received. The Lords Lieutenant of Yorkshire proposed that it put into Hull, and that these resources be devoted to the defence of the town. Newcastle approved this measure, in the light of the disaster at Prestonpans. Thompson made over to Captain Buttery, commander of one of the companies raised by the town, *20 nine-pounder cannon with all things appertaining to them, at the request of the Mayor and Burgesses*. His ship is held to have been equipped with smaller guns, forming a floating battery to provide flanking fire. Where this was is uncertain: the Humber tides would not permit a vessel to maintain station in that river; a mooring between the Citadel and North Bridge would have been the only practicable position on the river Hull[15].

The Mayor was commissioned to name the captain, lieutenant and ensign of a body of gentleman volunteers. A force of regimental strength was mustered. Robert Pease, a substantial merchant of the town, was to serve as Captain. Twelve companies of 60 men apiece were assembled. They were to be armed once the muddle over provision of muskets by the Board of Ordnance had been resolved,

by 2 December. The gentry and nobility of the County raised funds to pay for volunteer levies. Regular sergeants, corporals and drummers were placed in charge of the companies to instruct them in drill, musket drill, and to impart a modicum of discipline. It is possible that this training was provided by the Invalids - they were at any rate to render this service to the militia in later years. The Master Gunner at Hull, John Shipman, had his small complement of full-time gunners. Four artillery companies, composed of the Wardens and Brethren of Trinity House, would provide further crews for guns[16].

The Bench also dealt with other measures relating to security. Unlike previous occasions, when this had merely entailed the prosecution of those who muttered disloyal sentiments, some genuinely suspicious cases came to light. Gerard Labort (or Jaques Labarrt) was arrested by a constable at the turnpike. Suspected of being a French spy and emissary of the Pretender, he was brought before the Bench and imprisoned. He had visited every East Coast port between Berwick and Hull before being detained. A farmer's son from Northumberland was brought as a prisoner to Hull, on 23 November. He had been caught with a sealed purse of 120 guineas, contributions from Catholic gentry to the rebels ensconced in Carlisle[17].

General Henry Pulteney, one of Hull's two Members of Parliament, now served as Governor of Hull. In late November, Pulteney was informed that the Duke of Ancaster's Regiment had been ordered to Hull, and that he was to find billets for them. He could only place one company in the Citadel, which was already occupied by four companies of Invalids. Ancaster's Regiment would remain in Hull for about a year. Pulteney commented on the poor relations between the Mayor, the Deputy-Governor and Lord Lieutenant Irwin: the *unfortunate misunderstandings amongst them... might have been of bad consequence had the enemy made their approaches to us at the instant*. The Earl of Scarborough's Regiment was also to reinforce Hull[18].

Carlisle fell to the rebels in November, and the victorious march of the Highlanders continued. As in 1715, they marched down the western side of England, to Preston, and finally to Derby. Though English Jacobites failed to rally to their cause, the invaders were able to withdraw unmolested to Scotland in December. Once the issue of quartering had been raised, the goodwill of the Hull Bench was lost. Further expense on the defences now appeared futile - the Bench maintained that if they wanted them, the Lord Lieutenant or Governor should see that new works were paid for. On 8 December, the Governor found the Bench refusing to bear the expense of caulking Thompson's ship, in return for his help in arming Hull. Towards the end of the month, the *grumbling of one or two Aldermen who had unwarily drawn in a small number of the town to find fault about the fortifications being insufficient*, was reported to Newcastle[19].

The Board of Ordnance considered the further improvement of the defences. A plan, dated 30 December 1745, outlined *works to be done at the Citadel at Hull*, marked on Fearnside's survey of 1743. These were comparable to the *ad hoc* measures of 1688. Oak palisades were to be set along the Humber shore before the Citadel, where the stakes were to be tipped with iron to prevent the approach of boats. Towards the land, they were to be set in the ditch; as storm-poles below the parapets to prevent escalade; and across the entrance to the Citadel, which now lay next to the Saluting Platform. The planking of the edges of the moat was also advised, to prevent the moat further washing away the berm before the ramparts. A sluice and drawbridge were to be made near the Saluting Platform. A gap in the south curtain, where the quay lay, was to be closed, and a sally port provided in its place[20].

Deputy-Governor Jones reported that the Citadel had been fortified by February 1746. Later plans show a line of stakes along the centre of the landward moats; the sluice at the Saluting Platform; and the blocking of the gap at the centre of the south curtain. Other works may, from their character, be attributed to this period, though documentary evidence for them has not been encountered. It was perhaps at this time that the wings holding ramparts back on either side of the former Main Gate were rebuilt – their new form appears on the plan of 1743 - and repairs are suspected elsewhere around the perimeter of earthwork defences. The ground-floor gun-ports of South Blockhouse were rebuilt. Rectangular Henrician gun positions were redefined by thin brick walls, to form splayed embrasures typical of mid-18th-century work[21].

In the event, the only enemies Hull saw were prisoners. Their accommodation merely compounded the problems presented by the quartering of soldiers. In January 1746, some Scots of the Highland Army were confined at Hull. They joined 150 Irish soldiers and officers in French service, who had been captured at sea, in December 1745. In February, the prisoners were transferred to the Citadel. Complaints about their living conditions were relayed to Hull by the Duke of Cumberland, the newly-appointed commander of the army in England.

In early March, another 36 Spanish soldiers joined them, and Newcastle warned that more prisoners should be expected. The Mayor pointed out that if prisoners were given the liberty that Cumberland proposed, there would be insufficient forces in Hull to prevent them mutinying. They were to be permitted to walk about the Citadel in the daytime, and their officers were to be lodged in quarters appropriate for gentlemen. The officers were then paroled and sent home, while the soldiers remained in Hull until late in the year. The casemated guard-chambers at the Main Gate of the Citadel were later described as the French prison, and it was probably in this damp and overcrowded setting that the common soldiers were held[22].

In January 1746, General Hawley was defeated at Falkirk. The King, enraged by this reverse, ordered that the best ten regiments serving in Flanders should return to England. Dutch and Hessian troops were despatched under the provisions of the same treaty which had been invoked in 1715: seven out of ten battalions were foreign troops. On 7 March, a fleet of transports carrying reinforcements for Cumberland's army put in at Hull. This unscheduled halt followed reports that French warships had been spotted by Scarborough colliers. A significant force of soldiers probably occupied the Citadel barracks: the burials of eight soldiers, a lieutenant, and two gunners - all with English names - were recorded between 26 January and 24 May 1746[23].

Under Cumberland, the veterans of Dettingen and Fontenoy pursued the Highlanders to Culloden, and the Jacobite army was annihilated there on 28 April 1746. The emergency ended with this victory, and the volunteer companies at Hull disbanded shortly afterwards. The crisis had exposed the inefficiency of central government; the inadequacy of the county militia; and bickering and rivalry between royal appointees and the Bench. The defence of Hull had been organised at the initiative of the Mayor and Deputy-Governor, with the help of citizens bearing spade and musket, and the maritime community of the town. These forces would never have been capable of engaging the rebels in the field. It is an open question whether, had the sluices indeed been opened, Hull would have been able to hold besiegers at bay as it had in 1642 and 1643[24].

The East Riding militia

The population of Hull was now growing with the revival of the town's trade. Increasing numbers of the poor were housed in the cottages and slums of a warren of dingy courts. The courts sprang up within plots defined by medieval property boundaries, running back from Hull's long-established streets. Thirteen constables elected by the Bench controlled the civil population[25].

In 1750, the *New and Present State of England* reported that 25 Independent Companies of Invalids, each of 52 men with officers, served in England's garrisons. At the outbreak of the Seven Years War, in 1756: *the four foot companies of Invalids with their bayonets fixed were drawn up in the Market Place, and the officers at the head of each company who all made a very handsome appearance.* In 1759, the monthly return of the Garrison at Hull enumerated three Invalid Companies, under Major Hind, Captain Shadwell and Captain Edwards. Each company included a captain, lieutenant, ensign, two sergeants and a drummer; a total of 114 men were in Garrison, so the companies must then have been considerably under strength[26].

The Invalid Companies continued to be supplemented by a contingent of regulars. This was probably a single Regiment of Foot, with the allowance of fire and candle continued for them. Between 1747 and 1759, the Drypool registers record the burials of 30 soldiers, a sergeant, a lieutenant and five soldiers' wives from the Citadel barracks, along with a single Gunner and a Gunner's wife. The burials of ten children, though the baptism of only one, are also recorded[27].

The renewed outbreak of war galvanised Parliament into passing the new Militia Act of 1757, which finally superseded the Restoration Acts. The East Riding Militia had been under the command of Danby in 1689, when it had comprised eight companies of foot, and totalled 679 men. In 1704, Hull had provided £1 18s to John Bielby of Beverley for a coat for their principal in the East Yorkshire Militia, and the repayment of £1 10s from Mr Wilbert of Beverley was recorded the following year. The Bench Books are elsewhere silent on the matter of militia. They had not been raised in 1715, and 1745 had seen volunteers raised while the militia was not. Despite its efforts in 1745, under the 1757 Act, Hull was still not to have its own militia; rather, it was to contribute towards forces under the command of the Lieutenant of the East Riding[28].

In July 1757, representatives of the Bench met the Deputy-Lieutenants of the East Riding to discuss the raising of militia. Each parish was to draw up lists of able-bodied men, from which those liable for service were to be selected by drawing lots. These provisions were widely misunderstood, the labouring classes fearing that they were intended to provide conscripts for service overseas. Rioting swept the East Riding between 10 and 15 September 1757. A mob in Beverley insisted that the constables return the lists and pay them money, or they would burn the town. Politicians distrusted the militia because it enhanced the influence of the aristocracy who commanded it, and owed its loyalties to county institutions rather than to the King. If, on the other hand, it achieved an efficient standard, the militia would pose the same constitutional problems presented by a standing army[29].

Hull and the East Riding contributed a regiment of 460 infantry, which was eventually embodied on 1 January 1760, for an initial term of five years from the passage of the Militia Act. Muster lists do not survive. The officers included Captains William St Quentin and Henry Maister; and Lieutenants Francis Bielby, James Barry and Charles Pool. A Mr Taylor was to be treasurer of funds raised in the town and county, for support of the wives and families of militiamen. The East Riding militia was to wear scarlet kersey coats with buff facings, red breeches, white leggings, waistcoats and shoes. Soldiers raised in Hull were to serve for two years, until 1762, in Newcastle-upon-Tyne, under their Colonel, Sir Digby Legard. After this, they disbanded[30].

The militia never served in their home area. In 1761, two battalions of the North Riding Militia spent the summer watching the coasts and travelling about the county. They were at Hull, Richmond, Masham, Gilling, Scarborough and Beverley. In September 1761, at Hull, their Colonel, Sir Ralf Milbanks, was given five guineas by the Bench for the celebration of the marriage of His Majesty. The end of the Seven Years War saw attempts to abolish the militia, but it survived as an institution after 1763, training by companies or half-companies. In 1769, a further Militia Act made the militia a permanent feature of English life. England was again at war with France and Spain. To combat this threat, 30,000 militia took up stations. In May 1778, the East Yorkshire Militia were inspected at York, under their Colonel, Henry Maister, before marching south[31].

From ditches to docks

In July 1746, the Bench commissioned *a report of John Grundy on the condition of the ditch circumscribing the walls and ramparts of the town.* Grundy *viewed the land walls and ramparts of the town and found so much warped and silted up by dirt and soil*

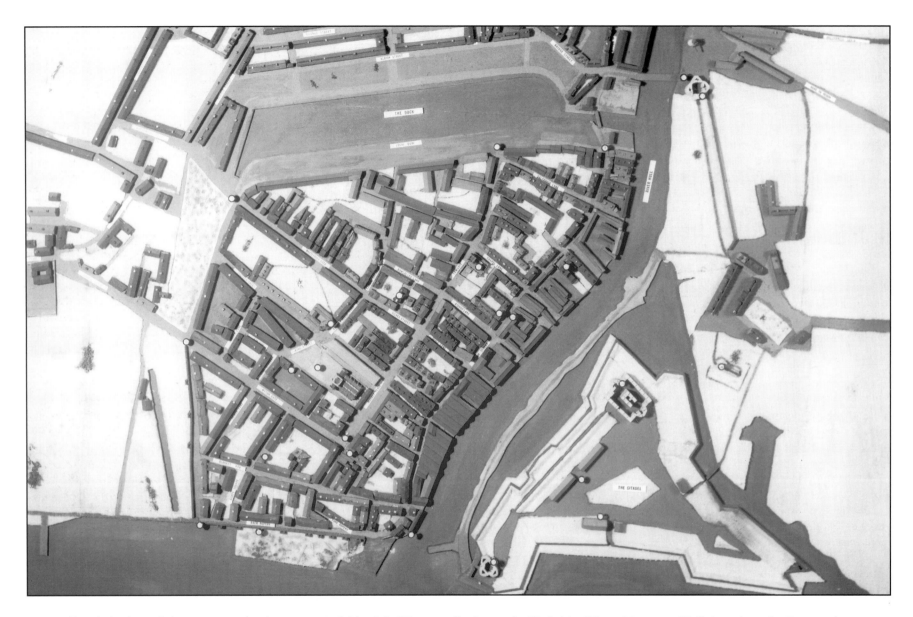

Fig 20: Hull and the first of the Town Docks, in 1791. Model by J.G. Watt, on display at the Yorkshire Water Museum, Hull, based on the Bower plan.

from the common shore from the town which empty themselves therein, and from sediment also left in it by occasionally taking in the tides at a clow or shuttle (shutter) *under Hessle Gate, that its bottom is now higher than the outfall or mouth of many of the said common shores whereby drainage of the town is not only obstructed, but also the foul water is retained along the said ditch for want of a proper outfall into the Humber in a stagnated state, and has become extremely noisome, putrid and unwholesome to the adjoining inhabitants in particular, and also to the town in general.* His report dealt mainly with the inner moat about the town, a relict of its medieval defences[32].

The survey proceeded in a clockwise direction, enumerating sewer arches of between 3ft and 9ft width under Hessle Gate; Myton Gate; Postern Gate - *a very large shore*; Beverley Gate, and leading to this, *Whitefriar Gate* – formerly fed by a sewer from the Land of Green Ginger; and North Gate. Sluices at Hessle Gate and North Gate had connected, respectively, with the rivers Humber and Hull; the latter *has long since been stopped up and disused.* Also, *Near the North Gate is a stock or tunnel with a shuttle of about 12 or so inches* (c.300mm) *wide which serves in case of need to communicate with the outer ditch.* High tides would rise between 6ft (1.8m) and 10ft (c.3.1m) above the level of water in the ditch. The outer ditch, part of the defences constructed in 1640, carried fresh water, but could not be used to flush the inner ditch as the base of the latter was now silted to a higher level.

Grundy proposed new sluices, *at the mouth of the tunnel under Hessle Bridge,* and a *draw door at the mouth of that at the North Gate.* Water would enter the moat at high tide at North Gate, and would wash away the town's sewage through the Hessle Gate sluice. Alternatively, the levels between the outer and inner ditches should be adjusted, so that the clean water in the outer ditch could be brought by a tunnel to flush the inner ditch. The lowest level of provision would be for all sewers to be directed into the Humber. The defensive works of the previous autumn had been devoted to the outer ramparts and ditches. Even so, in 1752, John Wesley came to Hull, and was *quite surprised at the miserable condition of the fortifications, far more ruinous and decayed than those at Newcastle, even before the rebellion. It is well there is no enemy near*[33].

In 1756, the town laid claim to ownership of the town ditch. In June 1756, an entry in the Bench Books recorded: *that from thence to the crook at Hessle Gate is proper ground for an additional harbour... That from Hessle Gate to the Long Jetty is also a proper place for a further addition to the harbour.* The outbreak of war, and pro-

tracted wrangling over the position favoured for a new dock and Legal Quay, or customs wharf, meant that nothing came of this plan. The land between the inner and outer ditches about the town was acquiring a range of uses incompatible with any continuing defensive use. In July 1763, *Land known by the name of Tilery Close* was bounded by a tan yard and associated premises of John Martin to the north; by lands and tenements belonging to James Holmes and others to the south; *by a certain ditch called the Outward Moat on the west,* and *by another ditch called the Trundle on the east... in occupation of the proprietors of the waterworks.* Tilery Close lay on the west side of the town. Its proprietor, Henry Denton, was to be held responsible for the scouring of all *sewers ditches and watercourses belonging to the said demesne.* To the east, by 1766, the northern extent of the Henrician wall, *an old wall or line of defence,* and the North Blockhouse, were *now both in ruins*[34].

A new dock was necessary because of the increasingly congested state of the Haven in the river Hull itself. Only the western bank of the river was available for the loading and unloading of ships, the other side being occupied by the Citadel, and lying in the jurisdiction of Drypool rather than Hull. It was a considerable advantage - for merchants - not to have a Legal Quay, where customs officers might operate effectively. Hull had enjoyed an exemption from operating a Legal Quay since 1559, forcing any inspection of cargoes to be carried out by officers scrambling across vessels tied up at the private quays and staithes of the town[35].

The Bench unsuccessfully sought to control this development. In 1771, the Recorder was *desired to draw a proper memorial for obtaining the walls, ditches, ramparts and bastions about the town for the Corporation.* In 1772, the Bench assured the Governor, General Honeywood, *that this Corporation will be very glad to make him any satisfaction for any privileges he* (i.e. the Crown) *may loose by such a grant.* In 1773, however, the Treasury determined *that they would be trifled with no longer, and would make a port at Gainsborough* (in Lincolnshire), *if the Legal Quay was not soon built at Hull.* This threat to Hull's trade brought a long-running debate to a head, and in 1774 the Dock Act was passed by Parliament, creating the Hull Dock Company[36].

The Dock Act vested all the walls, ditches and defences west of the river Hull in the Hull Dock Company. In 1774, the town walls from Beverley Gate to North Gate were levelled, leading to the discovery of an ancient cemetery below *the half moon redoubt opposite Lowgate.* The first dock was dug on the line of the northern defences, between North Bridge and Beverley Gate. The Dock Company was to finance the venture. In 1775 the foundation stone was laid, and three years later the first of Hull's Town Docks was completed. Initially known simply as the Dock, or the New Dock, it was to be renamed Queen's Dock in 1854. This set an important precedent for the conversion of the encircling defences of the town to an entirely different use[37].

Further docks were proposed in 1784, as the success of the first venture became clear. Defences on the western side of the town stood in ruinous condition: *Myton Gate within the earthen ramparts, from whence on either side extends a wall built of same, the greater part in ruins.* It took another 23 years of wrangling between vested interests before the passage of a second Dock Act, in 1802. This was for a dock linked to the Humber, taking in the defences between Hessle Gate and Myton Gate. It was preceded by an Act of 1801, which permitted the removal of the southern defences; the Act also specified that the earth excavated from the Humber Dock should be placed on the Humber foreshore. New streets - Humber Street, Wellington Street and Pier Street - would be laid out on this reclaimed ground. To make way for the docks, the defences between Beverley Gate and Myton Gate were removed between 1784 and 1791, and the relict of the western defences was demolished soon after 1800. Humber Dock opened in 1809. A third dock, Junction Dock, would be opened in 1829. It linked the first and second Town Docks, and completed the new perimeter of the Old Town[38].

Through negotiation with the Crown, the Corporation built a new Guardhouse, again in the north part of the town. In 1786, they declared themselves willing to erect *a guard house of equal dimensions with the present one, on a piece of ground belonging to them on the south side of the High road the distance of fifty feet (c.15m) from the ground pointed out to them by the Engineer.* In 1789, they took up the land, and the new Guardhouse appeared on plans of 1791 and 1817[39].

The development of the Town Docks had further grave consequences for the Citadel. Changes in the currents of water close to the confluence of the rivers Hull and Humber were brought about by these massive campaigns of construction. This altered the pattern and rate of silt deposition in the Humber. The accumulation of *growths* before the southern side of the Citadel accelerated rapidly. The process may be followed in a series of plans of Hull, of 18th and 19th-century date. The result was that the massive coastal fortification of the 1680s was progressively stranded, as the shoreline moved out into the Humber. The stone-faced scarp, which was to have been defended with obstacles against landing parties in small boats in 1745, could be approached dry-shod 50 years later[40].

Wooden walls

In 1779, a combined French and Spanish fleet sailed down the Channel, bringing the prospect of invasion to the attention of all. The Bench considered that Hull was defenceless against this threat; and asked the Board of Ordnance to place the town in a posture of defence. They suggested that outlying batteries should be placed at Paull Cliff and Skitter Point which faced it on the opposite shore to the east, controlling the navigable channel in the Humber; and at the Artillery Ground, or South End. This represented a first step towards a return to a strategic approach to the defence of the town, as had been envisaged by Henry VIII. The High Steward of Hull offered to provide the town with twenty 18-pounder guns, to be placed at South End and at Marfleet. Marfleet was to mount six guns, and a small battery was also to be established at Paull. Hull initially declined the offer, on the grounds that it could not be accepted without explicit royal approval[41].

The correspondence on these matters was between the Mayor, on behalf of Hull, and the High Steward of Hull, for the Crown. The Governor and his deputy were not drawn into the discussions, and it is apparent that as the physical fabric of the defences had been whittled away, their responsibilities had diminished with them. Charles Watson-Wentworth, Lord Rockingham, became High Steward in 1766, and was a forceful advocate for the town during the 16 years he held office. The King expressed satisfaction at Rockingham's proposal to arm the town with a gift of artillery – the six guns proposed at Marfleet - and was assured *that attention will be paid to the security of that part of the coast.* Rockingham wrote to the Mayor in October 1777, indicating his willingness to help the town in any way: *as the town and port of Hull is so an object to all the trading and manufacturing parts of Yorkshire, that I shall always feel anxious to assist and pay every attention to its welfare and security.* Twenty eighteen-pounders were dispatched by the Board of Ordnance, and were placed as a battery on the south curtain wall of the Citadel, where remained in 1798. Rockingham also stressed the danger of a maritime assault, and was one of the first to remark on the vulnerability of Hull, despite its Citadel. *If ever an attack is made by ships upon Hull, almost every shell fired by the enemy will come directly into the town of Hull even though batteries at the Fort (Citadel) or at the Artillery Ground (South End) may well repel an enemy*[42].

The real grounds for concern were highlighted in the autumn of 1779, by the exploits of John Paul Jones. Jones was an American captain, serving the colonies in revolt. He commanded crews of different nationalities, with the support of France. His mission was to harry English merchant shipping around the coast of Britain. Jones' flotilla comprised the *Bonhomme Richard*, the *Alliance*, the *Pallas* and the *Vengeance*, and had taken shipping and prisoners without hindrance by the Navy. The English response was a traditional one. HMS *Serapis*, a 40-gun frigate commanded by Captain Richard Pearson, and the *Countess of Scarborough*, a sloop armed with 20 guns under Captain Pierce, were detailed to escort merchant ships travelling in convoy[43].

On 19 September, Jones was taking prize ships off the Northumbrian coast. Newcastle was alarmed, though Jones did not follow his initial plan to attack that town. The Bench was already concerned for the safety of shipping and, on 21 September, wrote to the Admiralty as to their *apprehension of the trade which it daily expects from the Baltic*. On the morning of 22 September, Jones captured two Hull pilot boats off Spurn Point. From his prisoners, he learned that a large Baltic convoy was close at hand. This had enjoyed an uneventful passage of the North Sea, and had divided at Whitby. Forty merchant ships were bound for London, while the rest sailed northwards. Jones determined to attack the south-bound element of the convoy[44].

Hull flew red flags to alert ships of the danger of enemy action. Warning had been brought by William Foster, of Bridlington. Bridlington Piers, it was reported, were full of ships sheltering from Jones; some had had their rigging shot away, and one ship had sunk in the harbour entrance. The Northumberland militia were called out, and dispatched to the cliffs and shore to guard against a landing[45].

Captain Pearson sighted the enemy ships at about 1 pm on the 23 September. He tried to turn his convoy back towards Scarborough, sailing close to the shore. He placed the *Serapis* between the convoy and Jones' flotilla, which was hampered in its attempt to overtake the convoy by a light wind, which favoured larger ships with a greater area of sail. By about 6 pm, with the sun setting, the *Serapis* and the *Bonhomme Richard* were ready for action. The battle between them lasted about three and a half hours, and was watched by crowds that flocked to the cliffs and beaches of East Yorkshire. Soldiers, too, stood to arms. The Vicar of Hornsea was among the onlookers, and recorded the dying stages of the battle between 11

pm and midnight. The *Countess of Scarborough* fought a two-hour battle against the *Pallas*, and struck its colours at about 7.30 pm. Jones boarded the badly damaged *Serapis* from the *Bonhomme Richard*, which had been wrecked in the engagement and was to sink on 25 September. Jones limped back across the North Sea to the Texel, off the Dutch coast, with his prizes and prisoners. Through a combination of good luck and worsening weather he evaded further British ships which were searching for him along the English coast[46].

Jones was an outlaw and a pirate in law. He was hailed by his American compatriots, however, and even in England was regarded as a hero in some quarters, receiving the accolade of celebration in ballad and song. He entered the national mythology of the United States of America as a founding father of its navy. The captured British captains were released in 1780, and faced a court martial on their return. They were, however, acquitted. The achievement of Jones in defeating the British overshadowed the fact that Captains Pearson and Pierce had fulfilled their mission of protecting the Baltic convoy. Captain Pearson was given the Freedom of Hull, and was presented with a silver cup and two boxes of oak. Some English sailors of the *Bonhomme Richard* were less fortunate: having swum ashore at Filey, in the heat of the battle, they were eventually to appear before the Mayor and Magistrates of Hull[47].

The Admiralty acknowledged the capture of the two British warships on 27 September. The merchants of Hull remained strongly in favour of the convoy system for the protection of their ships, as the larger part of their trade was with Northern Europe, particularly the Baltic. They considered the protection of their trade imperative. Privateers continued to operate off the north-east coast throughout 1781, and the town's trade suffered some diminution as a result[48].

The Admiralty ordered a sloop and several cutters to cruise the area. A constant watch was to be maintained by frigates and a cutter operating along the northern coast. The convoy system would be kept up. The Secretary of State informed the King of the concerns felt at Hull. A Colonel Bramham was ordered to view the Humber and the adjacent coast, and to report the best measures to be taken for their security. He advocated the use of armed hulks as floating batteries. The first two ships appointed were *proved to be faulty and ordered into dock*. Two more were sent. One was to moor *before the town to act as a floating battery, the other was ordered to keep nearer the Humber mouth, to serve as a floating battery and in a sailing state in order to answer the use of the one as need required; as well as to be able to sail out to sea or return again and form herself into a battery as occasion serves.* The floating batteries were ordered to be discharged and sold in January 1783, and in February their commanders were ordered to proceed to the Thames[49].

In March 1782, Lord Carmarthen warned of the immediate probability of the Dutch attempting a landing on the eastern coast of the kingdom. It was understood that their fleet was out, but he thought Newcastle and Sunderland were more at risk than Yorkshire. In July, Lord Shelbourne's first action on taking up Lord Rockingham's position on the latter's death was to send a circular to all the principal towns. He suggested the immediate enrolment of volunteers for national defence. An advertisement asked for gentlemen to officer these companies, and for other persons to offer their services[50].

A meeting convened in Hull on 12 May, to determine emergency plans for the defence of the town. The meeting found the government plan impractical. As alternatives, they proposed the allocation of a private to every company of the present militia, or a local militia raised by ballot but embodied for the summer season only. The Bench offered to subscribe £500 towards raising men for defence of town and county. A month later, the offer had been rescinded. This was perhaps because the threat of invasion was thought to have passed. Peace talks were in progress in November, and a treaty was signed in September 1783. There followed a decade of peace, during which Hull celebrated a growing prosperity, and in 1788 the centenary of Town Taking Day, its historic liberation from the threat of military rule[51].

Footnotes

1: Dorman 1990, 14.
2: KUHRO L1242; HCSP WO 1740-49, Army vol. 16, 117; Crowther 1992, 12; KUHRO BRB 6, 744.
3: Neuberg 1989, 139-40; Fortescue 1903, vol. 2, 6; Lawson 1969 vol. 3, 133.
4: YPRS 125 Drypool vols 1-5, Parish Registers; Crowther 1992, 13.
5: YPRS 125 Drypool vols 1-5, Parish Registers; BRB 6, 766; BRB 7, 182; Hull Courant, August 1748.
6: KUHRO BRB 6, 766; BRB 8, 744, 747, 766, 785, 805, 820, 833; PRO WO78/1378 [3].
7: YPRS 125 Drypool vols 1-5 Parish Registers; Sykes 1893, 464-79.

8: Corelli-Barnett 1970, 190; Lenman 1980, 236; Rogers 1977, 22.
9: Smurthwaite 1993, 201-2; ERYCRO DDGR 38/103: A Relation of the Battle of Prestopans 1745 by an officer concerned and taken prisoner by the Rebels; KUHRO BRB 7, 77; McLynn 1980, 137.
10: HMC 55, vol. 8, 107; McLynn 1980, 136; KUHRO BRB 7, 78, DM/5/5/4/2, 25 November 1745.
11: Leeds City Council 1951, 31; KUHRO DMT/5/8/4/1; Aveling 1960, 46, 50, 65.
12: Norfolk 1965, 7; Gillett and McMahon 1980, 210; McLynn 1980, 139.
13: McLynn 1980, 137-8.
14: York Courant 15 October 1745; Northampton Mercury 28 October 1745; McLynn 1980, 136; Porter 1889, vol. 2, 158.
15: McLynn 1980, 136; KUHRO BRB 7, 82.
16: KUHRO DFP 466/473; McLynn 1980, 137-8; PRO WO17/789/9/1; YPRS 125, vol. 2, Parish Register of Drypool, 31 July 1746; Norfolk 1965, 8.
17: KUHRO BRB 9, 83; KUHRO Quarter Sessions Book 1737-58, CQ3 fo. 71, 1745; McLynn 1980, 135-6, 140.
18: McLynn 1980, 139; KUHRO BRB 9, 82, 74.
19: McLynn 1980, 139-40.
20: PRO WO78/1378(3).
21: McLynn 1980, 140-1; e.g. PRO MPHH 97 [3-4]; Foreman 1997, 15, fig. 8; Foreman and Goodhand 1997, 172-3; e.g. Woodward 1987, 63-4.
22: McLynn 1980, 140-1; Thew Plan 1784.
23: Rogers 1977, 22; Corelli-Barnett 1970, 192; YPRS 125 vols 1-5 Drypool.
24: Norfolk 1965, 8.
25: KUHRO BRB 9, 106.
26: Hull Courant, 25 May 1756; PRO WO17/789:1.
27: PRO WO17/789:1, Monthly Return, 1 July 1759; YPRS 125 Drypool vols 1-5, Parish Registers;
28: Norfolk 1965, 6; KUHRO BRB 8, 528, 546.
29: KUHRO BRB 9, 288; Neave 1996c, 124-5; HCCRO LT/4 31757; Rogers 1977, 28; Corelli-Barnett 1970, 168.
30: Norfolk 1965, 10-11; ERYCRO LT/8/1; KUHRO BRB 9, 304, 5 June 1760.
31: Bell-Turton 1906, 46; KUHRO BRB 9, 331; Rogers 1977, 30; Norfolk 1965, 11.
32: KUHRO BRL/2732, M449.
33: Crowther 1992, 16.
34: KUHRO BRB 8, 258; L1284; BRB 9, 250, 362-3, 365; M822; Chancery Judgement 1860, 37.
35: Jackson 1972, 235.

36:    KUHRO BRB 9, 407; BRB 8, 407-8; Jackson 1972, 242.

37:    Sheahan 1864, 444; Gillett and MacMahon 1980, 222; Jackson 1972, 243.

38:    Crowther 1992, 25-6; KUHRO BRL 1387/2016, Gillett and Macmahon 1980, 224; Allison 1969, 417.

39:    KUHRO BRB 10, 21, 86; Hargreaves plan, 1791.

40:    Humberside Libraries 1974; Foreman and Steedman 1997.

41:    KUHRO BRB 9, 487; BRL 1368/10-11; BRB 9, 496.

42:    Stephens and Lee vol. 60, 49; KUHRO BRL 1386/10, 11; Tickell 1798, 892.

43:    Jackson 1972, 137; Howes 1989.

44:    KUHRO BRB 9, 94; BRL 1386/1 and 3.

45:    Gillet and MacMahon 1980, 247; Whytehead Letters, uncatalogued collection in ERYCRO, Beverley Local Studies Library.

46:    Whytehead Letters; KUHRO BRL 1386/7.

47:    Morrison 1959, 154; Walsh 1978, 167.

48:    KUHRO L 1779; Jackson 1972, 39; KUHRO L1298, L1300, L1302-3, L1307-10; Jackson 1972 appendix, 342, 400, 402.

49:    KUHRO L1312, BRL 1386/87, BRL 1386/114, 13 July 1781; PRO WO47 (index), 1783.

50:    KUHRO BRL 1386/154.

51:    KUHRO BRB 9, 571-4.

CHAPTER 12

FACING THE THREAT OF FRANCE

The French Revolution, in 1789, opened the last wars in which the defences of Hull would play a part. In November 1792, a Revolutionary Decree *offered help to all those nations who desire to overthrow their King*. In February 1793, the French Republic declared war on Britain, and, more menacing to Hull, launched a successful invasion of the Low Countries. In December 1796, a landing in Ireland was prevented by storms. The next year, a force of 1,400 men landed at Fishguard, Wales. The invaders surrendered when it became clear that, unlike the Irish, the Welsh would not rise against English rule. The United Irishmen led another rebellion in 1798, encouraged by France.

With the new century, the threat of revolutionary war gave way to the more formidable danger of attack by Napoleon. After Trafalgar (1805), British sea-power could prevent a full-scale invasion. As a major depot, Hull supplied the North Sea squadron of the Royal Navy, playing a part in national defence. The risk of raids, however, continued to threaten Hull and other coastal towns. The long coastline of East Yorkshire forced development of a strategy whereby a trip-wire guard on the coast would alert defending forces, which could then engage the enemy on ground of their own choosing.

After Waterloo, the contest between commercial and military interests for the use of defences at Hull was to resume. The defences were to be further weakened by the encroachment of commercial facilities. The extension of docks to the east of the Citadel sealed its fate, as its batteries could no longer protect the port against attackers entering the Humber. The Citadel was razed in 1864, and with it disappeared the last visible traces of the 17th-century defences of Hull.

A strategy for regional defence

In March 1793, a French privateer was sighted off the East Yorkshire coast. Invalids from the Citadel, and soldiers under Captain Caleys – perhaps including men from the 42nd Foot, in quarters at Hull – were marched to Patrington. From this central point, they could intercept a party landing anywhere on the South Holderness coast. In July 1793, Samuel Thornton, one of Hull's Members of Parliament, proposed to the Mayor that a frigate or some other armed vessels should protect the town and the Humber. In February 1795, the Bench asked *for a sufficient naval force independent of convoys, to be sent down with all speed to protect the town and neighbouring coast and to rendezvous in the Humber*. The Duke of Leeds wrote to the Mayor about the defence of Hull, the Humber and the coast of the East Riding. By February 1797, the 64-gun *HMS Standard*, and *HMS Lion* and *Director*, were stationed in the Estuary. In 1798, the guard ships *HMS Nonsuch* and *HMS Redoubt* were on station; they fired warning shots in an attempt to detain the home-bound whaler *Blenheim*, an episode in the long-running fight between Hull sailors and the press-gang[1].

A popular rising could hardly be expected in Holderness. Hull, however, remained a prime target for a raid conducted as an economic act of war: the value of property in the town was conservatively estimated at £5 million. *Since the French possessed themselves of Holland, this coast has been considered in danger, and the town of Hull on account of its wealth and vicinity to Holderness an enemy's probable point of attack*. In March 1797, General Scott advanced ambitious proposals for the enclosure of Hull and its docks with a new line of defence. A plan was drawn up by Captain D'Arcy of the Royal Engineers. The *Hull Lines* were intended to secure the town against an attack by an enemy force which might approach from the east, or from the north[2].

The Lines were to form a jagged earthwork *enceinte* of ditch and bank running north from the Humber, beyond the west side of the town, to a northern spur with tenaille front, on the west side of the river Hull. They would continue on the eastern side of the river Hull, returning southwards to the Humber. Their outer ditch would join the Barmston and Holderness Drains; the former was a new feature, the latter an older dyke to the east. The drains would assist defence, by inundation if the need arose, of the countryside beyond the Lines. The completion of the ravelin before the east front of the Citadel was to bring it into the Lines as their south-eastern anchor. Scott's scheme was unanimously endorsed by the Bench, on 28 March 1797. The town, however, considered *that the defence of the town was of national concern, and the expense of such works as may be deemed necessary should be defrayed by the government*[3].

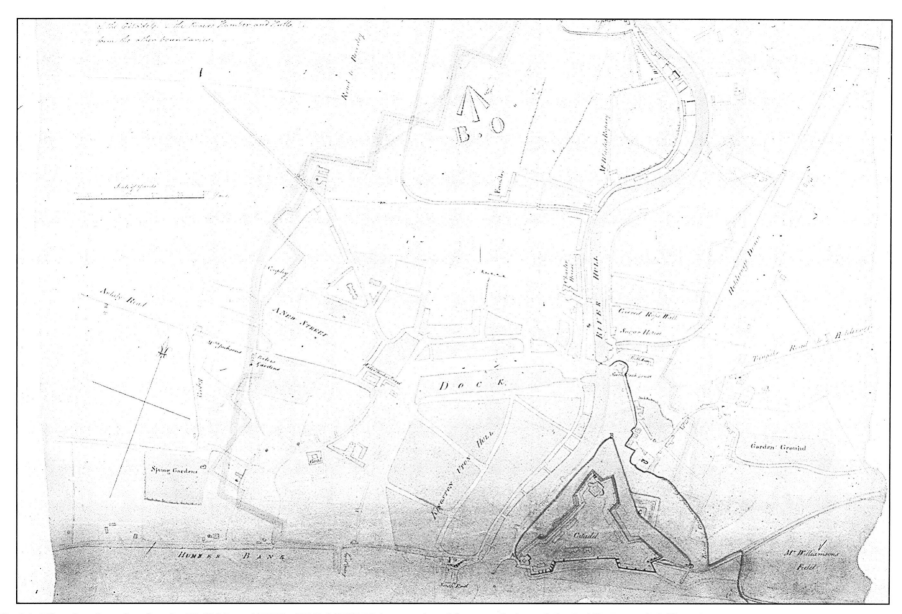

Fig 21: The abortive plan for the Hull Lines (1797); PRO MPH 504, reproduced by permission of the Public Record Office, Kew.

By August, D'Arcy had compiled a detailed schedule of repairs and new proposals for the eastern part of the Lines, at an estimated cost of £1,516 12s 2d. However: *To ascertain the value of the land they will occupy in addition to the Government Ground is only in the power of an Act of Parliament. As every landowner in this neighbourhood expects to see his fields laid on... when the Citadel is demolished to make room for the extension of the Dock. A Plan they are very fond of contemplating and will not allow it to be superseded by a scheme for more fortifications unless they are under the influence of an alarm of the enemy being landed within fourteen miles of Hull. In all I proposed I depended on Martial Law and the necessity of the times for assistance, but if that necessity no longer exists, perhaps it would be better to look out for some other situation on the Humber for the Depots of Yorkshire, than to attempt to free the Citadel of Hull from the investiture of private property that at present surrounds it*[4].

General Scott declined to recommend works to strengthen the Citadel, *unless the inhabitants of Hull continued at their own expense the works proposed from the river Hull to the Humber, nor would he march any men in to Hull for its defence while it remained an open town*. By the end of April, the Bench had informed General Scott that they were unable to raise a sufficient sum to fortify the town. D'Arcy commented: *This is the history of the rise and fall of Plan A*. A range of factors had calmed popular fears: *moving from Hull for fear of the enemy is now no longer practiced*; the militia had been bolstered by supplementary forces; naval defence had been improved, and peace talks were under way[5].

New proposals for the region were set out in about 1803, by Major-General Mulgrave, commanding the Yorkshire Military District. Mulgrave indicated a decisive shift away from a strategy based on fixed defences. *The plan... of erecting batteries and throwing up entrenchments, on various points of the coast, I by no means approve, as such fixed points of defence might be easily avoided by the enemy...I should approve instead of any settled batteries, an establishment of horse artillery, consisting of four medium twelve pounders, and two howitzers of proportionate calibre to travel with them; which should be so disposed near the two great leading roads* (from Hornsea to Beverley, and from Spurn Point to Hull), *as to be rapidly transported to any quarter where the enemy might appear to point their descent*. A camp of 1,000 infantry at Dimlington, with three guns, would deploy to Kilnsea against troops landing at Spurn. An enemy march towards Patrington would be met by inundation, and steered towards an obstructed line of march. This was to be strengthened *by circles or districts, with some village pointed out in the centre of each, where the country people, who are disposed to act offensively, may assemble with their arms, and receive carbine cartridges, which will fit the ordinary bore of fowling pieces. In each of these alarm posts I shall place an officer who has seen service, from one of the regiments of line, as far as they can be spared, who will be charged with the care of directing the country people in harassing the enemy on their flanks and rear*. Mulgrave considered *the officers of militia cannot be employed with effect in a service of this nature*. A further *corps* at Hedon and Paull would support the Dimlington camp. In the event of landings at Hornsea or Bridlington, the enemy *would be exposed to very strong posts, at Skipsea and other places, protected by meres and drainages, extending parallel to the road*. If all else failed, the river Hull would provide a line of defence[6].

The Humber tides, of 6 knots, impeded both attack and defence of the river, making the proper siting of land batteries important. The navigable channel could be controlled from Paull. Posts at Paghill (cited by Mulgrave as a distinct location, though normally identified with Paull) and Boreas Hill could support Paull, and dominated the sluices on which defence by inundation depended. Mulgrave derided proposals to improve the Citadel: *The money expended on an estimate to widen the ditch at Hull Citadel; and to prevent an escalade at a point where no escalade would be attempted by any military man of experience and discretion, would be much better applied to secure the advantages which nature has prepared at Paghill.*

At Hull, *the Citadel presents its feeble bastions, and useless batteries, which point across, but do not enfilade the channel. The Citadel, under its present circumstances is totally useless as a means of defence... should an enemy in flat boats pass fire and land above Hull, the Citadel would become worse than useless; as neither defence nor retreat would remain to the Garrison. The western tenaille, from the north to the South Blockhouse, has no guns, nor the means of mounting any; and the whole interior of the Citadel is commanded within musket shot from the houses on the opposite side of Hull river. The north bastion, and eastern façade, which point towards the great road from Bilton to Hull town, are so completely masked, by the town and church of Drypool, that they could not in any situation see an enemy advancing by that road*. Defences beyond Drypool would most conveniently comprise guns deployed from the Citadel when an alarm was raised.

Mulgrave's final recommendation was *for flag staves and proper officers on the coast, to carry into effect, the Admiralty signals*. Beacon fires along the coast were reinstated: at Hornsea, Cowden, Withernsea, Dimlington, Kilnsea, Welwick, Patrington, Keyingham, Atwick and Tunstall. Many of these posts figured in Mulgrave's contingency plans to counter invasion, as the bases from which a mobile land campaign was to be waged. Beacons were initially manned by local men, though this duty later devolved upon soldiers, probably members of the militia. From 1796, the system was updated with the erection of signal stations at Spurn Point, Hornsea and Flamborough Head. These were under the command of a naval officer, and were regularly inspected[7].

In August 1803, Captain Chapman of the Royal Engineers assessed positions for new Humber batteries. At Paghill/Paull, five or six heavy guns could be mounted on traversing carriages; a couple of guns near White Booth Roads, on the opposite bank, extended the time enemy ships would have to endure an enfilading fire. A site at Paull Cliff was acquired, and a redoubt built. A jury was called under the Defence Act to decide whether its proprietor, Major Hugh Blaydes of the 3rd Regiment of West York Militia, had demanded an exorbitant price. By April 1805, there were batteries at Whitby, Scarborough Castle, Bridlington Quay, Paull Cliff and Spurn Point, north of the Humber; and at Stallingborough and White Booth Road on the south bank. *A Report of Iron Ordnance in Hull Garrison and its dependencies*, in May 1805, considered eleven 18-pounders, fourteen 9-pounders – one totally unserviceable - and sixteen 3-pounders, one of which was *an old gun on her carriage in the Blockhouse yard unserviceable these many years past*. A near-contemporary return for Hull Garrison and South End listed a total of 50 mounted and dismounted guns. They included five 24-pounders; seven serviceable and eight unserviceable 18-pounders; three serviceable and fourteen unserviceable 9-pounders; and six working 3-pounders with twelve unserviceable: of 22 usable guns, nine were *very old but serviceable*[8].

The new role for the Citadel was as base for *the brigade of medium 12-pounders*. This force was installed, along with four light 6-pounders and two 5½in howitzers, by May 1805. The draught horses and drivers for the guns were in hired stables, awaiting the completion of new stables at the Citadel. In 1809, the mobile artillery at the Citadel numbered between 180 and 240 officers and men; 236 horses; ten 6-pounders – half light and half heavy – and a pair of howitzers; and a dozen ammunition carriages. The Paull battery was crewed by 38 officers and men. In March 1811, Paull was being prepared to mount six 24-pounders on traversing platforms. Batteries on the south side of the Humber, at Skitter and Stallingborough, were also to be up-gunned at this time, with five and four 24-pounders respectively[9].

The Militia

The scheme for defence on land depended on the deployment of militia along with regular forces. Though of unproven military value, their presence was important in relieving the fears of the propertied classes. They played a direct role in the maintenance of law and order, and in the suppression of riot. Indirectly, their presence reduced the pressure to embark on more expensive schemes. The Militia fell under the command of the Duke of Leeds, as Lord Lieutenant of the East Riding[10].

The Militia was embodied by an Act of 1792. At the outbreak of war, 50,000 militiamen were balloted and formed up in their own counties, along with 40,000 Fencible Cavalry. A man balloted for militia service, which though under military discipline was restricted to home service, could pay £20 to secure a substitute to serve in his place. A Militia Act of 1794 empowered the Lord Lieutenant to raise Supplementary Companies to augment the County Militia. For the Supplementary Companies, a fixed quota was demanded of each county, and no exemptions were permitted. The East Riding Supplementary Militia was called into being in 1796. Local fishermen and mariners enrolled in the Sea Fencibles, under Captain Edwards of the Royal Navy[11].

A further Act of 1794 permitted Independent Volunteer Companies to be raised. Unlike the Militia, they were not to be posted for duty outside their home county. Recruitment to the Volunteers was swollen by those seeking to evade the militia ballot, effectively draining men and resources from more regular forces. They were privately funded by patriotic organisations, and were paid 1s a day for at least 20 days of exercise every year. A meeting was held in Beverley, where it was decided that a voluntary subscription should be the proper means of providing local defence. The fort at Bridlington Quay was to be repaired out of the subscription, and was to be manned by a company of 100 infantry who would also defend the coast and neighbourhood. The Board of Ordnance was to be asked to provide guns and ammunition for the fort[12].

In keeping with its independence from the East Riding, Hull took its own notable part in the Volunteer movement. In 1794, the Royal Hull Volunteer Infantry assembled five companies under Lieutenant-Colonel Christopher Machell. The Hull Trinity House Volunteer Artillery Company numbered about 60 seamen, under Captain Benjamin Metcalfe. Prince William of Gloucester, nephew of the King and General Commanding His Majesty's Forces in the Northern District, reviewed the military at Hull, in November 1795. As the first royal visit to Hull since 1665, this provided a fillip to civilian morale. The forces reviewed included the Surrey Militia, in Garrison at the Citadel; the Volunteers; and a troop of Hanoverian Cavalry. The *Hull Gentlemen and Yeomanry Cavalry* mustered a troop under Captain William Hall, mainly Hull men. The Bench subscribed 100 guineas for Hall's troop in 1796, and urged the inhabitants of the town and County to do likewise. In 1798, a further *Armed Association* of three companies was formed in Hull[13].

The Volunteers took up joint responsibility for the policing of Hull itself, sharing this duty with the Garrison. In April 1796, riots against the price of flour broke out in Market Place, and the Magistrates read the Riot Act on two successive days. The Nottingham Militia joined the Volunteer Artillery, Volunteer Infantry and Hall's Troop of Volunteer Horse in putting down the riot. The zeal and firmness of the Volunteers was commended – most came from classes less troubled by the price of bread than the rioters. In summer, when most regular soldiers were encamped in the countryside, Volunteers took over guard duties: *Much praise is due to them as to the readiness they evinced on taking this duty in the absence of the militia*[14].

In 1798, a Lieutenant Loten, commanding a press gang, was attacked by a sailor. The mob joined in. The 4th and 5th West Yorkshire Militia, the Hull and Cottingham Volunteers, the Armed Association and the Yeomanry Cavalry were called out to quell the riot, and patrolled the streets for a further three hours until order was restored. The Volunteers also patrolled in small bands at night, supplementing the efforts of the town's constables, and taking suspicious characters into custody. By 1803, the Mayor was to request the Colonel of the 69th Foot, in Garrison, for a detachment of 30 men for the day-to-day purpose of keeping the peace. It was coming to be expected that routine policing, as well as any breakdown in public order, was to be dealt with by the military[15].

The traditional disdain for professional soldiers was a dangerous attitude to maintain towards militiamen chosen at random from amongst craftsmen and labourers, especially when revolutionary ideas were in the air. In 1798, two privates at Hull, from the Nottinghamshire Militia and the Northampton Militia, received 500 lashes apiece, *for uttering some seditious expressions*. The Nottinghamshire Militia was regarded as *undisciplined*; some men possessed writings from Radical Clubs which they had joined before being balloted. A private soldier's pay was 8d a day, of which 4d went towards his subsistence. This was a time of rising prices, and unwelcome guests could not be fed at this price. Some soldiers cried in their beds for lack of food, or deserted through hunger. In May 1798, pay rose to 1s a day, enabling soldiers to buy meals to supplement the bread or biscuit provided by the Army. In 1800, soldiers received a further 1d a day, in lieu of small beer formerly provided as part of their subsistence[16].

The increase of militia from 1793 forced the government to take an interest in the accommodation of troops. Political objections to the building of barracks remained: they were *unconstitutional*; they would become *Universities for Praetorian Bands*; soldiers housed together would be vulnerable to agitators and subversion. Barracks, however, were urgently required at Hull. In 1795, the Surrey Militia complained of the lack of proper quarters and the expense of providing lodgings. In 1797, the North Yorkshire Militia, with 757 men, lodged seven companies in the North Blockhouse, which was fitted out to provide makeshift lodgings. Eight men from each company were billeted in Sculcoates, four companies were in the Citadel barracks, and one company was sent on detachment to Hedon. The same year, the Hull Advertiser reported that 2,000 soldiers were temporarily quartered on the innkeepers of Hull. In 1799, the innkeepers petitioned that cavalry and artillery horses be billeted in livery stables, as accommodating them prevented them from putting up other travellers[17].

A centrally directed programme of barrack building began, under Colonel de Lancy. This was under the auspices of the War Office; Royal Warrants took this function from the Board of Ordnance, vesting it in the Barrack Department. Temporary barracks were established at Hull by 1807. The largest lay to the north of the Old Town, in the vicinity of the North Blockhouse, at the Ropery of Frost & Co, and nearby at Lime Street. The premises of a Dr Alderton, near Sculcoates Church and at the end of the north ropery, were fitted out as barracks. The government also rented the Humber Bank Barracks, a building near the moat of the Citadel, with its own wharf, for £200 *per annum*. A general return for barracks at Hull in 1800 listed the builders' account at £5,401; there is no indication of exactly how these costs were incurred. In 1805, the rents for temporary barracks at Hull amounted to £1,929 13s. It was reported at this time that some barracks in Hull were overcrowded, though the premises were not specified. Todd Campbell served as a civilian Barrack Master for Hull, with a brief to carry out thorough monthly inspections[18].

In 1803, only 141 men were listed as sick from a Garrison numbering 3,768; this low proportion suggests that, overall, conditions were tolerably good. By 1811, an isolation hospital had been set up in a house on Beverley Road, and other hospitals in Hodgson Street, on the Humber Bank, and at *the Groves*, in Sutton. In later years, a significant proportion of soldiers buried at Drypool, the parish church serving the Citadel, were recorded as having died at one or other of the military hospitals outside the town[19].

Up to 15,000 soldiers guarded the coasts of the East Riding, of whom between 3,000 and 4,000 were in Hull. The full panoply of defensive measures was in place by 1800. The underlying weakness of all the new forces was their amateur status and the inexperience of their officers. In 1801, the Admiralty met renewed anxiety by stationing three ships in the area: *HMS Nonsuch* anchored in White Booth Roads, supported by *HMS Redoubt* and *HMS Nautilus* in the Humber. On October 1 1801, the Peace of Amiens brought an uneasy truce between England and France. Infantry regiments were rapidly reduced, the militia marched home and disbanded, and all voluntary forces were suspended.

Many of these men would be recalled to the colours within a couple of years. The Hull and County Volunteer Infantry reformed in 1803, and expanded to a force of 900 men in 12 companies and a rifle company. In 1808 it disbanded, making way for the East Riding Local Militia. This had an establishment of 1,000 men, and served until 1816; Hull contributed the 4th battalion, under Lieutenant John Wray. In 1809, the Hull and Sculcoates Corps of Volunteer Infantry could draw on 832 local militia volunteers; 553 were liable to serve from the town parishes of Holy Trinity and St Mary's, and 110 from the County of Hull beyond. The Sea Fencibles also reformed in 1803, and 385 men crewed a flotilla of 20 sloops under Royal Navy officers, each boat being armed with a pair of 18-pounder Carronades and a long 6-pounder[20].

The Invalids remained an element of the fixed Garrison at Hull. A Captain Leonard Brown, from Jersey, was appointed in the place of Captain Adams, who had died, in 1798. Brown's company gave three days pay as a contribution to the local war effort, amounting to £161 18s. They were now part of a national force of 70 companies, styled the Regiment of Invalids. The Regiment was disbanded in 1802. In July, Brown's company *disembodied*, and the company of Captain Grant was to disband as soon as it could be replaced by a regular regiment. Among those discharged were three sergeants: aged 80, 68 and 64 years, who had

served respectively 64, 46 and 44 years. Invalid gunners were retained, as their skills remained important to the manning of forts; a year later, the Return of the Royal Artillery in the Yorkshire District listed one Major Gunner, one Bombardier and nine gunners of Invalid Artillery. The burial of *Alexander McPherson, Sergeant and pensioner* was recorded at Drypool, in April 1806. The main force under Mulgrave in 1803 was of regular militia: the 1st, 2nd and 3rd West Yorkshire Militia, with a combined strength of 2,069 men[21].

The Drypool Parish Registers show that, from 1803 to 1807, 29 soldiers based at the Citadel married local women. Over the same period, there were 25 baptisms of children *belonging to the Garrison*. The burials of 41 soldiers and gunners; 35 soldiers' children and 12 gunners' children, and 7 soldiers' wives, were recorded at Drypool. The soldiers were mostly from Militia serving at Hull on a rota – the 2nd West Yorkshire, North Lincoln and (if distinct) 3rd Lincolnshire, East Suffolk, Cumberland, Westmoreland, 2nd Surrey, and 3rd West Yorkshire Regiments; two soldiers of the 69th Foot of the Line, the Warwickshire Regiment, were also listed. The numbers of gunners and soldiers buried were almost equal; the disproportion in the mortality of wives and children hints that living conditions were far worse for those families who chose to accompany militiamen. Gunners were described as of South Fort in one case, but were usually of the Artillery Regiment, or simply the Artillery. A soldier of the 68th Foot left a brief account of his time in Hull, in 1807. *At Hull our duty was very hard, having to mount guard three times in the week. The whole of the troops used to parade every morning in George Street at eleven o'clock; those who mounted the Main, Garrison and South End guards had to undergo the severe inspection of the brigade major, who was a constant plague and torment to the soldiers*[22].

In September 1807, 833 men of the Sussex, Cumberland and 1st West Yorkshire Regiments in Garrison provided about 200 volunteers for service in Line Regiments, towards a quota of 250. Contingents from the Kings German Legion, the Royal Engineers and Artillery, and the Warwickshire and 2nd Royal Regiments of Foot were in Hull at the time. In 1808, the Garrison comprised the Hereford, Royal Cumberland and 84th Regiments of Foot; in 1809 the Royal Lancashire and Cumberland Regiments were at the Citadel[23].

The Garrison Return for July 1809 listed 173 officers and men of the Artillery, 350 men of the Royal Hertford Militia and 629 men of the Royal Cumberland Militia. On Christmas Day 1809, there were 620 men of the Royal Cumberland

Militia and 573 of the Royal Westminster Militia in Garrison, along with the Artillery. From 1810, the Depot Battalion of the 65th Regiment of Foot was stationed at Hull, whence it dispatched contingents for service overseas. The half-yearly Return of the Regiment's Women and Children, for June-December 1810, listed 16 women legally married; 4 boys and 9 girls under 10 years of age; and 3 boys and five girls over 10. In 1812, the rank and file of the battalion included 22 lads from 15 to 18 years, and one drummer and 4 rank and file boys under 15. At this time, the Royal Denbigh, the 33rd Foot and the Carlow Regiments were also at Hull. In 1813, the 4th Irish Dragoons and the Royal Lincolnshire Militia joined them in Garrison. In 1814, the Acting Sergeant Major of the 65th witnessed the wedding of a soldier to a widow; one, perhaps both, were probably of his own regiment[24].

The less comprehensive Parish Registers for the period 1808-15 (no records have been encountered for 1811, no marriages are listed, nor are men's units, and other lists may be partial) record the deaths of 31 soldiers, two gunners, three or four soldiers' wives, and 26 of their children. Register entries from March 1814 recorded age at death. Most Garrison children who died in 1814-15 were infants or toddlers: 4 were new-born, and of 13 children, the oldest were 4 and 9 years old[25].

The Citadel and the Napoleonic Wars

The priority afforded to strategic defence left the Citadel ancillary to a wider regional scheme. It was to fulfill three distinct roles, for which extensive provision was made: as a defensible work; as depot and arsenal, and as a barracks. Improvements to stores further reduced the military effectiveness of the defences surrounding them.

D'Arcy's survey of 1797 had identified about 21 embrasures at the Citadel. A plan of 1807 illustrated 77 embrasures, though most were rendered as poorly defined or degraded openings, and included some which had stood empty since at least 1699. Wider ramparts, the repair of 16 platforms, and nine new platforms, were required if guns were to be mounted. In 1805, five platforms were constructed from *small and useless stone platforms in the Citadel*. Expenditure on *common stone platforms* was recorded between 1805 and 1807, at an overall cost of £137 18s 6d. *Traversing platforms and kerbs* cost £128 2s 9d in 1804, with further minor

expenditure, 1807-10. At the Citadel, these were relatively insubstantial features, with kerbs built in brick. Three traversing guns were positioned at salient angles of the Citadel. Other embrasures, probably on the south front, were repaired with stone between 1811 and 1813. The South End battery, on the opposite side of the river Hull, remained important: *The guns of this battery will not only form a respectable crossfire with those from the Citadel, but are of great consequence; as they enfilade the channel for shipping.* These separate sites *afford each other reciprocal support*[26].

Reversing the deterioration caused by a century of neglect made the repair of the Citadel itself an expensive business. Over the period 1804-15, almost £16,300 was laid out by the Board of Ordnance, and this excluded works on the accommodation within. Between 1807 and 1809, the greater part of £1,963 was spent on *repairing parapets and ramparts*; another £392 15s 4 ¾d was then spent on the *repair of parapets*. The building of a counterscarp, 1806-10, lining the outer face of the moat, cost £7,111 17s 11 ¾d. This brick-built wall rose from a piled and framed timber foundation of similar form to that below the sea-walls of the 1680s. Repair of the escarpment revetment – where is unknown – cost £442 6s 4d. The Saluting Platform saw two bouts of repairs, in 1806 and 1812-13, costing £144 18s 7 ½d. Major works entailed the draining of the moat, which was provided with a deeper central slot, or *cunette*. The cunette cost only £31 1s 10d; its extension along the south front, 1808-11, cost £666 16s 1 ½d. Palisades were provided, at one time or another, at the south front forming a breakwater, at the former Main Gate, at the west bastion and at the west entrance. The fortifications were *generally in good condition with the exception of 8 embrasures on the South Front*, by March 1811[27].

Having conceded that Hull would continue as the depot for the Yorkshire Military District, the Board of Ordnance set about the improvement of the storage facilities within. In 1805, they maintained floating Magazines at Hull, and temporary Magazines at York, Selby and Armyn. By July 1807, a new Great Powder Magazine stood immediately adjacent to the Castle, while Garrison Magazines were lodged in the casemates at the former Main Gate. The new magazines comprised five brick-built and slate-roofed rooms, capable of holding 440 whole barrels, 7,480 half barrels and 1,530 quarter barrels of powder; the casemated magazine could take 500 whole barrels and 920 half barrels. The same year, a naval expedition to Copenhagen was fitted out from stores at Hull. Smaller casemated chambers were used by the Garrison; the north-east sally port magazine, the largest such chamber, was *occupied by the regular militia at Hull, for*

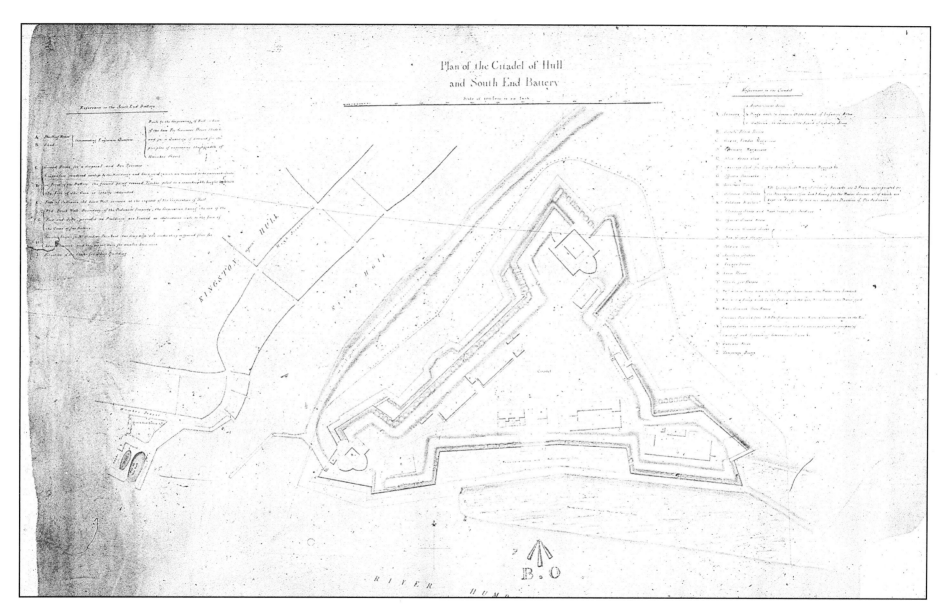

Fig 22: The Citadel (1807), as chief depot of the Yorkshire District; PRO MPH 554, reproduced by permission of the Public Record Office, Kew.

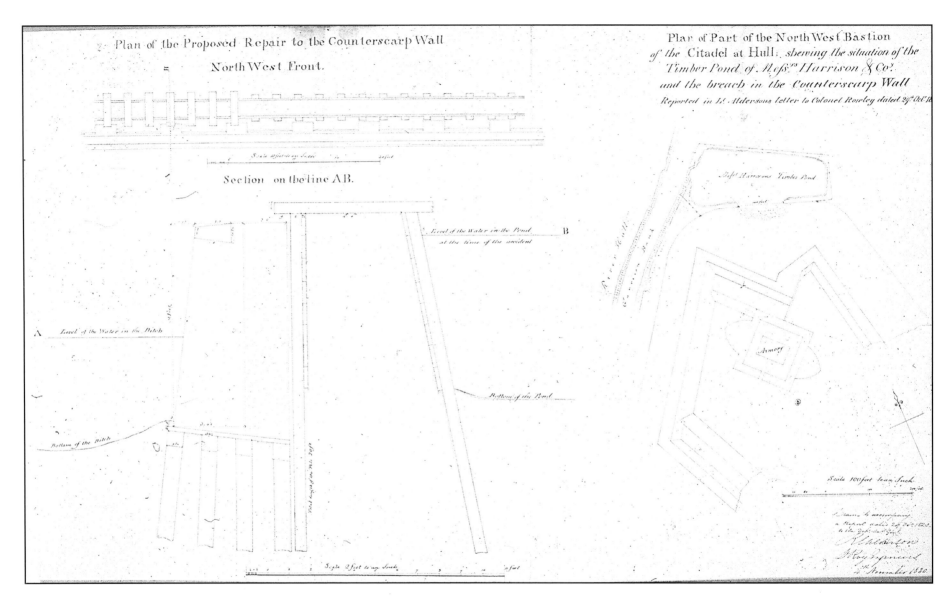

Fig 23: The counterscarp wall of 1806-10, with proposals for repair following its partial collapse (1820); PRO MPH 986 [5], reproduced by permission of the Public Record Office, Kew.

service ammunition. The smaller sally ports, however, were *formerly fitted up for the reception of powder but are so damp as to render them improper for any kind of perishable stores*. A brick-built shed, built in about 1811 in the *base flank* west of the Castle, was subsequently and variously described as a laboratory shed, cooper's shop and shifting house. This was ancillary to the new magazines, from which it was prudently separated by the main rampart[28].

An Act of Parliament of 1802 provided for a road leading to the north part of the Citadel, to be built and maintained by the Corporation. Substantial sums were laid out by the Ordnance in 1804-5 and 1808-10, for making roads, at an overall cost of £1,203 11s 6d. In 1807, a temporary bridge was recorded as giving access to new magazines. In 1809-10, expenditure of over £463 was recorded towards a *new communication through the north curtain*, a more permanent bridge. This passed across the *base flank* to the east of the Castle, bringing about the final redundancy of that battery[29].

In 1806, at South Blockhouse, *a total alteration is taking place with respect to the dimensions of the rooms etc*. These works were described a year later: *the roof of the old Blockhouse… was taken off, and an interior wall pulled down. It is reported as about to be fitted up as a naval storehouse, in which it was proposed to keep a constant supply of stores; capable of furnishing six sail of the line and twelve frigates, in case of emergency*. The refurbishment entailed the removal of galleries within the thickness of the walls, so that the space could be used for stores. The reduction of the walls to the thickness of their outer skin dictated the insertion of four substantial pillars or posts to support the roof. By 1811, South Blockhouse contained eight ground floor rooms and one large upper room, which were *now fitting up to receive Ordnance stores of various descriptions*[30].

The Castle had been converted to serve as an Armoury by 1805. The upper rooms in the bastion towers could hold 20,000 stands of infantry arms apiece, and the upper galleries 3,000 stands of cavalry arms. The ground floor rooms included a forge, two workshops and further vacant storerooms. Other stores were held in *the blue store shed*, a timber-framed and weatherboarded pan-tiled building close to South Blockhouse. By 1811, there were also a tiled brick Engine House for the Ordnance Fire Engine. A post-built Wagon Shed to shelter 30 wagons was erected in the later part of 1810. A Forage House was constructed of timber and roofed with tile[31].

The soldiers' barracks at the Citadel had been built to house 200 men in 1688, yet, in 1797, the Citadel was reported as having *enclosed barracks for four hundred men*. Ancillary facilities, in 1807, included cleaning sheds and wash houses for soldiers at either end of their barracks; a soldiers' kitchen between the barracks; a soldiers' privy; two wells with pumps - not used to supply drinking water - and three cisterns. In 1811, the Citadel was held to offer accommodation for one field officer, three captains, eight subalterns and 465 men, 292 men in double bedsteads. This was without significant augmentation of its permanent building stock. The Ordnance retained an office in the southern end of the barracks, along with the Master Gunner, further reducing the space available for soldiers. A gravel parade ground was laid out on the central area of the interior, by May 1811, taking up most of the open space remaining. After serving as an emergency barrack, the ruinous North Blockhouse had been demolished in 1803, its materials realising over £800 at auction[32].

The Citadel was provided with a new privy for the soldiers, on the south front, in 1806. The only recorded provision before this had been a wooden *house of office*, which had been perched on the tip of the Saluting Platform, whence the tide scoured away ordure. Growths of mud before the Citadel had choked a sluice at the south-west corner of the Citadel since its installation *c*.1745, and particularly since the building of the Town Dock. The blocked sluice prevented the privy draining. By 1811, this led to a *project for remedying the nuisance caused by the Privy… It having become so bad as to be extremely distressing to the troops in barracks during the prevalence of a southerly wind*. An embankment was to be formed *with old oak piles to be drawn from the Citadel, filling in between the piles with earth well rammed, and deepening and widening the cunette 170ft in length*. In June 1816, the low level of water in the moat, *which exhales the most putrid miasma*, was held to be responsible for an outbreak of cholera. Earth-closets were also provided; the brick tank serving one has been excavated in the lee of the ramparts of the west bastion; its final filling was dated to *c*.1790-1820. A drain apparently serving the Governor's House, whose repair post-dated the laying of the parade ground in 1811, may also have served as a domestic sewer[33].

Shelters and stables for the mobile artillery at the Citadel were to take up much of the remaining internal space. In May 1805, Lieutenant-Colonel Burton, of the Royal Artillery, *found the Car Brigade of light 6-pounders, parked in a small close, near to the stables hired for the accommodation of its horses*. They were awaiting the construction of sheds near the Castle. *The Heavy Brigade of medium 12-pounders, and its ammunition, has been under proper sheds in Hull Citadel during the winter. The Car Brigade is now drawn up near to the Heavy one, but not covered, and the horses of the Car Brigade have taken possession of the one of the new stables that are at present finished.* Chapman, commanding the Royal Engineers for the Yorkshire District, was urged to complete the sheds at the end of May. This also provided material for other repairs; he had *from time to time laid all the spare earth dug out from the foundations of the stables, magazines etc. in a central situation so as to be convenient for the repairs of the south front and for the reformation of the parapets of the west and north fronts.* Stables were constructed for 302 horses. By 1811, store rooms, a harness room, a dark room (for the treatment of frightened horses); and rooms for a wheeler collar-maker, a carriage smith and the farrier reduced the stabling to 264 horse standings. A small harness store, and a granary, both brick-built and tiled, had also been built by 1811, as separate structures nearby. The stables were extensive: four ranges occupied most of the interior of the east bastion, and most of the ground between it and the officers' barracks to the west[34].

The stables and associated structures were of ephemeral construction. Excavation has shown some parts of buildings marked by shallow slots, post positions and light brickwork. Their position was merely evidenced by the limits of cobbled surfaces elsewhere. This light construction facilitated their removal after 1815. A schematic plan of 1817 suggests that half of these ranges had already been removed. By 1831, only one wing of one stable block remained. These were workshops associated with the eastern pair of ranges; they were to be recorded in 1850 as the Barrack Store[35].

The peacetime Garrison

In the decades following Waterloo, the Citadel was occupied by the depot battalions of a series of Regiments of Foot. Over the period 1816-25, soldiers of the West Norfolk Militia (so described in 1818) or 54th Foot, and of the 80th, 88th, 52nd, 22nd, 66th, 15th, 73rd, 65th, 17th and 56th Foot were recorded by the Drypool Parish Registers. Some regiments made a greater impression than others on the local community – the 52nd were especially notable in this respect, marrying 21 local girls between September 1820 and June 1821. When they left Hull, in June, led by *the gallant Colonel Sir J. Colbourne,* they were *accompanied by the regrets and esteem of the inhabitants.* In the first 10 years of peace, there were 50 Garrison weddings; and the burials of 31 soldiers, 5 women, and 48 of their children, the latter mostly infants under one year old. High infant mortality highlights the insanitary nature of life in barracks, yet also suggests that women and children could be nearly as prominent in an army community as they were in the courts and slums of the overcrowded town[36].

The forces replacing the 52nd included two troops of the Queen's Dragoon Guards; *the novelty of horse soldiers in Hull excited considerable interest, and the parade ground opposite the Neptune Inn, the headquarters, was daily crowded with admiring spectators.* The Garrison more normally comprised infantry. The coming and going of recruits and detachments meant its strength varied widely from one month to the next. In September 1825, the 56th Foot had 132 rank and file, 4 drummers and 5 sergeants at Hull, under the Governor and Deputy-Governor. Over the following year, of over 300 officers and men; *there are 203 non comm. officers and men billeted on the Innkeepers in the vicinity of the Garrison.* The *Garrison total* was 652 men, indicating that another battalion was also at Hull. In February 1826, Hull Citadel was held to offer space for 456 men. Companies were detached to serve at Bradford, Halifax and Brigg. In 1827, contingents of the 5th, 40th and 71st Foot were described as depot battalions with officers recruiting. In March, the Garrison stood at over 500, but, from April, at only 194 officers and men, with 46 detached to Brigg, Lincolnshire, 4 recruiting, and *2 privates in the hands of the Civil Power.* From 1828 to 1830, there were between 184 and 387 men in Garrison, of the 83rd, 7th, and 80th Foot[37].

As well as the soldiers, the Town Major, Surgeon, a Lieutenant of Royal Engineers, and one master gunner and two gunners of the Invalid Artillery were listed as part of the establishment at Hull. Although he had an office at the Citadel, from before 1826 the Engineer occupied a residence at South End, where he had charge of seven 10-pounders on its South Front, mounted on wooden garrison carriages. In 1831, Lieutenant B.W. Marion of the Royal Engineers was at South End. The other Garrison functionaries were Lord Cathcart, the Governor; Robert Simpson, Fort Major; Alex G. Carte, Barrack Master and Storekeeper; Thomas Higins, Ordnance Armourer and George Woolfe, Master Gunner. The Governor's post was an honorific one, and the other Garrison posts were to become similarly undemanding positions. No Royal Engineer was listed on the Garrison staff by 1843. The Town Major died in 1844, and, as the demand for quartering soldiers had diminished, his post was not filled. Alexander Carte, a married man and father, was a keen sportsman, and a founder member of the Kingston Garrison Archers in 1825. The club flourished and, by 1835, absorbed its civilian counterpart, the Hullshire Bowmen. Carte was to devote his later years to the invention of life-saving rockets, buoys and belts; from 1847, his *different inventions for saving life from shipwreck… may be seen every day, from 11 to 12 o'clock, at the Citadel, Hull*. Master Gunner Wolfe commanded a small band of Invalid gunners, for whom duty at the Citadel provided the customary working retirement[38].

From 1830 to 1850, the 33rd, 53rd, 22nd, 37th, 60th, 73rd, 87th, 38th, 48th, 40th, 90th, 57th and 81st Regiments of Foot supplied elements of the Garrison, most units staying a year or two before moving on. Between 1830 and 1834 there were no burials of children recorded, and only a single marriage. The Garrison remained, however, vulnerable to epidemic disease. The decade 1836-45 saw the burial of 42 soldiers, 43 of their children, and 3 army wives. Of these deaths, about half occurred in 1839-40. Barrack Master Carte lost 5 young children in December 1840, and, unusually, one death in the Garrison at this time was specifically ascribed to cholera – outbreaks of cholera in the town were identified in 1832 and 1849. The following eleven years, to 1856, saw a further 48 soldiers, including several aged retainers, and 35 children buried. In 1845, the 48th Foot made way for the 90th; the rotation was of particular interest as the outgoing and incoming contingents traveled by special train. The 48th, *including officers and their ladies, and the wives and children of the troops*, numbered 435. Of the 90th, 250 men *were accompanied by 150 women and children*. In March 1846, the 90th departed, with *308 soldiers, 55 women, 3 children above twelve, 44 above three, and 47 under three years of age. In addition there were six horses and three dog carts*. The years 1846-47 saw the deaths of 18 children and 17 adults, and 1849-50 the burials of 12 soldiers, 2 women and 10 children[39].

In time of war, a uniform turned many pretty heads; a correspondent to the Hull Advertiser had satirically declared an outbreak of *Scarlet Fever* in 1804, in tribute to this perennial attraction. Veterans of the Peninsula, and latterly of Waterloo, were lionised; and their exploits celebrated in the theatres of the town. In peacetime, marriage between the daughters of gentry and officers was common, and approved. Common soldiers' dependants were less well-regarded. In 1843, Lieutenant-Colonel A.H. Trevor, who was to serve at Hull two years later, complained in a letter to the Naval and Military Gazette, that *these wretched creatures are allowed to crowd into barracks with their starving children – some with families of 5, 6, 7 and 8… taking up the room, bedding, tables, fires of the men – destroying their comfort and all attempts at cleanliness – making the soldiers discontented and driving them*

frequently to the canteen and the beershop and frequently to desertion. Soldiers' wives are generally the greatest nuisances, and I have had more trouble to control their conduct and behaviour than I can describe. But, more casual contact with civilian women could be dangerous: between 1837 and 1847, 273 soldiers of every 1,000 were hospitalised with a sexually transmitted disease. In 1849 alone, 627 women in Hull were charged with prostitution. In 1854, the discovery of an infant corpse on the bank of the river Hull led one of the town's doctors to remark that *the practice of procuring abortion is very prevalent in Hull*. Contact between town and Garrison was normally unimpeded. The gates of the peacetime Citadel stood open; it was only in exceptional circumstances, as when a suspicious death prompted fear of cholera in August 1831, that they would be temporarily closed[40].

The Garrison was intermittently called on to repress disorder in the troubled years which followed victory over Napoleon. In 1815, soldiers were called to put down a riot by seamen, who were demanding an advance in wages, and other *illegal purposes*. In 1816, a local currency crisis saw violence, the reading of the Riot Act, and the military called out again. The Bench suggested that a *military zone may be permanently stationed at Hull to be at all times ready to assist the civil power in suppressing riots*, additionally expressing fears for the safety of the Citadel magazine. At the election of 1820, the troops were confined to barracks, *in consequence of the extensive depot of arms and ammunition in their charge*. In September 1832, the agitator James Acland stirred up a near-riot with his demands that the Corporation elections be held on a Sunday. A prearranged signal agreed between the Magistrates and the military – the hoisting of a black flag on St Mary's Church tower – summoned a squadron of cavalry and 100 infantry from the Citadel, successfully discouraging further disorder. Three years later, it was suspected that the Duke of Wellington had held troops ready to suppress the riots expected during contested elections in Hull. These troops, however, had been marshalled no closer than Wetherby. The officers and soldiers of the Garrison made their own intermittent appearances before the Magistrates, the men typically on charges of drunkenness or brawling; their superiors for *the silly irregularities of some youthful officers*. In the 1830s, the theft of door-knockers was a favourite autumnal sport – in one week in 1836, 19 such incidents were reported in Drypool[41].

From 1835, the establishment of a civilian Police Force lifted the duty of maintaining public order from the army. The first Chief Constable of Hull, appointed in 1836, was Andrew McManus. He was a former officer of the 88th Foot, the

Connaught Rangers, a unit which had quartered at the Citadel in 1819. The Police were involved in a number of bruising encounters with soldiers. Both officers and men regarded a policeman as ranking below a private soldier, and were consequently unwilling to be restrained by one. In 1842, an soldier was heard to threaten a policeman that he would *serve the blue b—- out in the same way they did in Newcastle*, suggesting that such clashes were part of a more widespread antagonism between serving soldiers and policemen – who were typically retired soldiers themselves. In 1843, two officers of the Garrison were tried by court-martial and cashiered for their part in *disturbances in the town*. In 1846, further incidents led the military to promise to send out *piquets* every evening, so as to control the behaviour of soldiers. As the Hull Police Force grew – from 77 in 1836 to 130 by 1850 – the assaults by drunken soldiers on police officers also increased. As late as 1856, an attempt by policemen to arrest two unruly grenadiers in Queen Street led to the assembly of 5,000 people; the soldiers escaped, with the crowd apparently enjoying the policemen's predicament[42].

The military presence provided a range of diversions to compensate for the localised rowdiness of soldiers. Victory at Waterloo was celebrated by fireworks at Hull, with a military band to play *appropriate pieces* for each item of the display. In 1824, more than 4,000 tickets were sold to spectators of a balloon ascent from the Citadel; another ascent was advertised in 1841. In 1835, a review of the 22nd Foot at the Citadel attracted *many inhabitants to witness the spectacle*. In July 1826, the band of the 56th Foot opened evening concerts for the season at the Botanic Garden. There was concern that, in 1836, the Tory officers of the Garrison attended *a great political dinner and ball at Beverley*, and allowed the regimental band to play there. Public band concerts, however, became regular and popular fixtures: in 1837, the band of the 37th played every Tuesday at the Botanic Garden. In 1841, the band of the 73rd were to play three times a week throughout their stay; twice a week at the Hull Zoological Gardens, and once a week at the Botanic Garden. Rivalry between locals and soldiers was most successfully addressed on the cricket pitch. In 1833, matches were held between the 53rd Foot – the first Regiment to be noted for the rape of door-knockers - and the Hull Union Cricket Club. A match in 1852, between the Garrison and Hull, *was graced by the presence of a large number of the fair sex*. In 1855-56 the army was represented by the West York Militia, and Hull by the Hull Town Cricket Club[43].

A final tussle

The building stock at the Citadel contracted after 1815. Scant change was recorded through the 1830s. By 1842, ancillary structures had begun to surround the barracks, while formal gardens were laid out between the southern rampart of the Citadel and its outer ditch. By 1845, the barracks had been connected to a supply of piped water; and by 1850 were provided with long washhouses. Living conditions at Hull were probably better than in many stations; between 1825 and 1843, there were usually fewer soldiers than places for them to stay, though women and children would swell the paper strength of a depot battalion[44].

The encroachment of civil and commercial property had long been recognised as compromising the defensibility of the Citadel. In 1793, plans had been drawn up for a new dock which was intended to take up the northern part of the Citadel. Massive ponds for the treatment of timber were dug nearby. In 1820, the overfilling of a timber pond immediately north of the Citadel resulted in the collapse of a stretch of the counterscarp wall lining the outer side of the moat. Further damages were reported to the counterscarp in 1833 and 1838. By 1840, the military were fending off requests to use the moat itself as a timber pond: *the Ordnance has already given up to commercial uses the ground outside the fort... and having arrived at the brink of the ditch it is I think time to pause – and reflect that, whatever may be the value of these defences in a military view, and however well disposed the Board may be to facilitate the execution of a matured plan for improving the accommodation of the port, these considerations do not apply to the request of an individual to be granted the use of the ditch for a purpose which, while injurious to the Ordnance interests, can have no other object than his own particular benefit*. Less than two years later, it was reported that the Government had set a price of £250,000 on the Citadel, should the Dock Company seek to buy its site for a new dock[45].

The first plan to show the new dock in approximately the position it was to occupy is dated to 1829. Its development was set in train before the sale of the Citadel. By 1843, the proposed dock and tide basins to the east of the Citadel were plotted as *cuttings*, and the Humber foreshore was lined by *wood piling*. Excavations for docks and timber ponds would be accompanied by extensive reclamation of mud growths, whose limits were defined by timber jetties and piles projecting into the Humber, a process which would leave the site of the Citadel entirely divorced from its coastal setting. The excavation of the dock began in 1845, and the first stone was laid a year later. The Victoria Dock was to open in 1850, setting in train further developments along the Humber bank. By 1856, a pair of jetties defined a triangular area of reclaimed ground at the mouth of the river Hull. In 1857, an iron shipbuilding works was established immediately south of the Citadel, and industrial facilities would subsequently encroach onto its site[46].

The withdrawal of the military was preceded by a last review of the defensive value of the Citadel. In August 1846, it was noted that an armament of seven 18-pounders was mounted. There were a total of 13 flagged platforms for guns available, in poor condition; the traversing platforms of Napoleonic vintage were also unserviceable. Piecemeal repairs were recognised as inadequate, and in December a comprehensive report on the armament of Hull was prepared by Colonel Whingates, of the Royal Artillery[47].

The Citadel was to be *considered as a sea battery*. The Humber channel permitted *vessels of war of a large class* to approach to within 700 yards. The tides, formerly a significant factor aiding defense, could now be overcome. Steam vessels *lashed to Men of War…would accomplish the distance from the Spurn to the town of Hull in less than three hours*, and could then maintain station to bombard, or to cover a landing. South End Battery, the historic complement to the Citadel in controlling the mouth of the river Hull, was *now almost useless, the embrasures being nearly masked by the walls of a dry dock recently constructed*. The *River Humber Front* of the Citadel would need to be lined with 32-pounders and 8 inch shell guns, against the *heavy ordnance and large calibre which the ships of an attacking force would bring against it… these pieces should be 18 or 20ft distant from each other*. Mortars might be placed on the Saluting Platform, an open location, or could alternatively be moved from one place to another. The other sides of the Citadel were to provide flanking fire in support of the Humber front, and to deter sneak attacks.

The disadvantages of the scheme were striking. Tall buildings along High Street to the west would present good cover for attackers, just as the spoil from dock excavations to the east closed the defenders' view in that direction. A complement of 109 guns would be required, almost all heavier than those in place, and most requiring the construction of *dwarf traversing platforms* for their deployment. This was recognised as special pleading: *A calculation of the armament for the Citadel cannot be based on the usual rules for army fortresses… the chief feature of this Citadel is its character as a sea battery, and as such it should be in a state to provide a successful result from a contest with the heavy ordnance, and concentrated mass of fire which ships of war of large classes can bring against it*. Whinyates' survey closed with

passing reference to the site on Paull Cliff, highlighting its long-known advantages. His findings were passed to the Board in January 1847, with minor reduction of the suggested numbers of guns, and reiteration of demands for the reconstruction of forts at South End and Paull. The only work at the Citadel which may be linked to these proposals was the provision of a small Regimental Magazine, sheltered behind the southern ramparts[48].

It has been asserted that the military occupation of the Citadel ended in 1848; this overstates what appears to have been a more gradual winding-down of the military presence. In August 1850, tenders were invited *for the paving at the rear and ends of the soldiers barracks, and for taking up, renewing and relaying the flag pavement and channel stones within the boundary wall of the new magazine*. The musters of the Royal Invalid Artillery in 1851 listed three gunners; Major Gunner George Wolfe died, aged 77 and resident at the Citadel, in 1852. The last recorded muster of Invalid gunners was in 1857. The *customary half-yearly inspections* of troops quartered in the Citadel were reported as continuing up to October 1853. The 28th Foot were replaced by a detachment of the 34th in February 1854. The *company of artillery, for some time stationed in Hull*, left for Woolwich, and thence for the Crimean War, in January 1855[49].

The replacement of regulars by the militia, freeing troops for the Crimean War, may more accurately mark the beginning of the end of the military occupation. The West York Militia were in Garrison from 1855 to 1856, leading ladies and gentry through the customary whirl of military balls, reviews and cricket matches. The Drypool Parish Registers attest continued military residence at the Citadel until May 1856. In 1859, a new generation of patriots formed the East Yorkshire Rifle Volunteers and the 4th East Riding Artillery Volunteers. The latter were granted the use of the South Blockhouse as their headquarters, and used the open areas of the Citadel for their drill. On 12 March 1859, a 12-gun salute marked the wedding of the Prince of Wales, the last time guns were fired at the Citadel[50].

The site of South End Battery was sold in 1855. The Board of Ordnance made over the Citadel to the Commissioners of Woods and Forests in 1858. While the future of the site was considered, it served as a store for timber, the principal commodity imported through the Victoria Dock. In 1859, a Bill of Sale of Crown Lands described the Citadel and its foreshore as an area of nearly 60 acres, with a Humber frontage of 1,600ft. The site included *an extensive range of buildings and erections*, which were to be pulled down as a condition of purchase, *and the ditch and counterscarp walls (being in length about 4,000 yards) and containing a very large quantity of good bricks with landings, gun platforms, and 11 capital pumps and cisterns.* In February 1859, the Corporation offered £105,000 for the site, with the stated intention of retaining it as a recreational area for the people of Hull. The offer was rejected and the Corporation took the issue of the ownership of the site to the Court of Chancery in 1860. The case revisited the protracted disputes between the later Stuarts and the Bench over responsibility for maintenance of the river banks. The Attorney General found against the town, in 1861, on the basis of Crown possession of the Citadel since 1700, and the Corporation was ordered to pay the costs of the suit[51].

The site was sold as a single lot. The buildings of the Citadel were razed in 1863-64, and a network of streets was planned. Few of these appear to have been laid out. The archaeological dating of material sealing Citadel-period structures suggests that the area became a convenient dump for refuse over the next few decades. The Citadel foreshore was extensively reclaimed by 1863. The buildings associated with the iron shipbuilding works of Martin Samuelson, and its successors, were to occupy the southern part of the Citadel for the rest of the 19th century. Timber stacks covered much of the remainder of its area, together with extensive railway tracks for the movement of wood. The dockside facilities were modernised through the later 19th century, and, by 1920, Victoria Dock was to occupy 25 acres, timber ponds 24 acres, and open timber storage 130 acres[52].

Between August 1940 and May 1942, wartime bombing devastated the area; the raids between 7-9 May 1941 were especially damaging. Victoria Dock never fully recovered, and in 1964 the entrance to the dock from the river Hull was closed and remodelled. Victoria Dock was closed on 1 February 1970, and its basin and half-tide basin were filled. The construction of a dual carriageway across the site in the 1970s was not accompanied by formal archaeological works, though the naming of the road as Garrison Way commemorated its former use. On its north side, between the new road and the river Hull, a light industrial zone has become established. The remainder of the area to the south remained derelict until ground investigations began in the 1980s, in advance of extensive urban regeneration[53].

Only from 1987 did the unsuspected survival of the Citadel come to light. It was then immediately clear that its major structures had defied all efforts to remove them in the 1860s. Rather than being thoroughly demolished, masonry and ramparts had merely been razed to ground level. This left over half the original extent of the 17th-century structures, and their entire foundation system, intact. The tops of the most massive walls often lie only inches below the modern land surface. Later excavations have also encountered significant elements of clay rampart, often surviving to at least *c.*1m in depth. These deposits are less visually striking than the masonry elements of the fortifications. Their value lies rather in the detailed documentation of their construction: the material incorporated into them can be confidently dated to within a decade, and sometimes to a particular year.

The age of the bastioned fortress was an age of kings. Such monuments are rare in England. In part, this was because of the more slender resources available to the English Crown, compared to the great continental monarchies of the 17th and 18th centuries. In part, it is a tribute to the wooden walls of an island people. Yet, finally, we have few Citadels because 17th-century England saw the first modern revolution against absolute rule, and saw that revolution defended. Hull, with its traditionally independent outlook, played a crucial part in these events. The defences commemorate the men - and women - who built them and lived in them. They also remain as a monument to the prisoners detained behind their grim walls in times of repression, and to a community which was never to be bridled by bastions and guns.

Footnotes

1:     KUHRO BRB 10, 173; BRL 1387/112; L1367; BRB 10, 272; Credland 1995, 20.

2:     PRO WO55/714, 4 August 1797.

3:     PRO MPH 505 Plan, 13 March 1797.

4:     PRO WO55/714, 1 August, 3 August 1797.

5:     PRO WO55/714, 4 August 1797.

6:     PRO WO30/59, 57-72, Proposals for the defence of the Humber, *c.*1803.

7:     Poulson 1821; Hebditch 1947, 109-151; ERYCRO LT9/54.

8:     PRO WO55/714, Chapman to Mulgrave, 17 August 1803; ERYCRO LT 4/7, 21 January 1807; PRO WO55/714, Report by Master Gunner Wright, May 1805; *ibid.*, Return of Iron Ordnance, 23 May 1805.

9:     PRO WO55/714, 27 May 1805; *ibid.*, Burton's report, 20 April 1805; PRO WO17/827, Monthly returns, Hull Garrison, 25 July 1809, 25 August 1809; PRO WO55/714, Royal Engineers Report, 31 March 1811.

10:     Norfolk 1965.

11:     Norfolk 1965; ERYCRO LT 7/22 Hull Schedule F, 1807.

12:     Norfolk 1965.

13:     KUHRO BRB 10, 242; *Hull Packet* 1795; KUHRO BRB 10, 272; Norfolk 1965.

14:     KUHRO BRB 10, 251; *Hull Advertiser* 30 April 1796, April 1798.

15:     KUHRO BRB 10, 301; *Hull Advertiser*, January 1799; KUHRO BRL 1385-6.

16:     Emsley 1975; *Hull Advertiser*, August and September 1798; Bell-Turton 1906, 427; Corelli-Barnett 1960, 241.

17:     Breihan 1990, 165-7; KUHRO L1372, L1136; *Hull Advertiser*, 11 February 1797, 20 May 1797; KUHRO BRB 10, 319.

18:     Suddaby 1907, 31; *Hull Advertiser*, November 1804, June 1805; HCPP 1806, vol. 6, 224; *ibid.* vol. 2, 1806-7, 213, 236; *Hull Advertiser*, January 1811; PRO WO46/111, 1804-5.

19:     PRO WO17/872:2, Yorkshire District and Depot Monthly Returns, Hull Garrison, July 1803; *Hull Advertiser*, 13 January 1810.

20:     *Hull Advertiser*, 25 January 1798, 10 July 1802, 24 July 1802; YPRS Drypool 125 Parish Registers; ERYCRO LT/722 Muster Rolls, 1804, 1807; ERYCRO Muster Rolls Hull, 6 January 1809; ERYCRO LT2 4/18, 9 October 1803.

21:     *Hull Advertiser*, 10 July 1802, 24 July 1802; YPRS 125 Drypool Parish Registers; PRO WO17/872, Return of detachment of Royal Artillery in Yorkshire District; PRO WO17/872:2, 1803-9, Yorkshire District and Depot, both 1 July 1803.

22:     YPRS 1-5, Drypool Parish Registers; Suddaby 1907, 30.

23:     *Hull Advertiser*, 5 September 1807; Suddaby 1907, 31.

24:     ERYCRO Parish Registers PE/107/34-PE109/29, cited by Payne 1996, appendix 6; YPRS 125 Drypool Parish Registers; *Hull Advertiser*, 5 September 1807.

25:     PRO WO17/872 Yorkshire District and Depot Returns, Hull Garrison, 1809; YPRS 125 Drypool Parish Registers; PRO WO17/185 no. 4, Monthly returns of 65th Regiment of Foot Depot Hull; Suddaby 1907, 32; ERYCRO Parish Registers PE 109/29, 22 August 1814.

26:     PRO MPH 504, Plan, MPH 554, Plan, 22 July 1807; PRO WO55/714, Estimate, 1 August 1797; PRO WO55/714, Chapman, 12 September 1805; PRO WO55/715, Account of Expenses 1804-15; Foreman and Goodhand 1997, 155-6, fig. 6; PRO WO44/195, Royal Engineers, York, 28 August 1846; PRO WO55/715, Captain Arnold, 15 December 1811.

27:     PRO WO55/715, Account of Expenses 1804-1815; PRO MPH 986[5], 1820, Proposed Repairs; PRO WO55/714, Arnold to Handfield, 31 March 1811.

28:     PRO WO55/714, Burton's Report, 20 April 1805; PRO MPH 554, Plan, 22 July 1807; PRO WO55/2319, Lands and Rents at Hull, *c*.1806; PRO WO55/714, Royal Engineers' Report, 31 March 1811; Gillett 1988, 46-50; Foreman 1988, 3; PRO WO55/1833, Book 302, Ordnance Lands, 1811; PRO WO55/2319, Lands and Rents Hull *c*.1806; Foreman 1995, 32-3.

29:     42nd George III Cap. 91, Sec. 51; PRO MPH 554 Plan, 22 July 1807; PRO WO55/715, Account of Expenses 1804-15.

30:     PRO WO55/2319, Lands and Rents Hull, *c*.1806; *Hull Advertiser*, 5 September 1807; Foreman 1997, 12; PRO WO55/714, Engineer's Report, 31 March 1811.

31:     PRO WO55/714, Burton's Return, 23 May 1805; PRO WO55/2319, Lands and Rents Hull *c*.1806; PRO MPH 554, Plan, 22 July 1807; PRO WO55/714, Engineer's Report, 31 March 1811; PRO WO55/1883, Book 302, 1811.

32:     PRO WO55/714, D'Arcy, 4 August 1797; PRO WO55/1883, part 1, Accommodation at Hull, 1811; PRO WO55/714, Arnold, 14 May 1811; PRO MPH 554, plan 22 July 1807; PRO WO55/714, Engineer's Report, 31 March 1811; *Hull Advertiser*, 19 February 1803.

33:     PRO WO55/715, Account of Expenses 1804-15; PRO WO55/714, Arnold, 27 June 1811, 1 July 1811, 7 August 1811; *Hull Advertiser*, 1 June 1816; Foreman 1997, 13-14; Foreman 1998.

34:     PRO WO55/714, Burton's Return of Ordnance, 23 May 1805; PRO WO55/714, Drummond, 27 May 1805; PRO WO55/714, Chapman, 12 September 1805; PRO WO55/1883, book 302, 1811; PRO WO55/714, 31 March 1811; PRO MPH 554, Plan, 22 July 1807.

35:     Foreman 1987, 24-5; Atkinson 1998; Cragg plan, 1817; PRO MPH 976, Plan, 1831; Ordnance Survey Plan, 1854.

36:     YPRS 1-5, Drypool Parish Registers; ERYCRO PE 109/31, Parish Registers; *Hull Advertiser*, 8 June 1821.

37:     *Hull Advertiser*, 13 June 1821; PRO WO55/1883, Yorkshire District Returns; PRO WO17/789, Monthly Returns Hull Citadel; *ibid.*:1, Monthly Returns Hull Citadel.

38:     PRO WO55/1883, Yorkshire District Returns; White 1831, xxxviii; Suddaby 1907a, 21; Credland 1992; PRO WO17/789, Hull Garrison Returns 1759-1844, August 1843.

39:     Suddaby 1907, 33; YPRS 1-5, Drypool Parish Registers; ERYCRO PE 109/33, Parish Registers; *Hull Advertiser*, 30 June 1845, 20 March 1846.

40:     *Hull Advertiser*,12-18 August 1831, 15 May 1804; Suddaby 1907, 28; Payne 1996, 33-4; Neuburg 1989, 89.

41:     KUHRO BRB 9, 104, BRL/2198, 21 September 1816; KUHRO BRL 2314, 31 March 1820; Suddaby 1907, 24; *Hull Advertiser*, 12-18 August 1831, 4 October 1833, 11 October 1833, 6 January 1835, 28 October 1836.

42:     *Hull Daily Mail*, 1936; Payne 1996, 29-30; Suddaby 1907, 33.

43:     Payne 1996, 32-3.

44:     PRO MPH 976, 1831; MPH 1016, ?1843; Goodwill and Lawson, plan, 1842; PRO WO44/563; Ordnance Survey plan, 10ft to the mile, 1853; Payne 1996, appendix 1.

45:     Hull Local Studies Library, Hull Dock Co. plan, 1793; Craggs plan, 1817; PRO MPH 986 [5]; PRO WO44 (index), Northern District, 1838; PRO WO44/534, Victor to Board, 17 December 1840; *Hull Advertiser*, 15 July 1842.

46:     Hull Local Studies Library, Hull Dock Co. plan, 1829; Hartley plan, 1843; Foreman and Steedman 1997; Thompson 1990, 32-5; Evans and Sitch 1990, 24.

47:     PRO WO44/195, Commander Royal Engineers Yorkshire District to Inspector General of Fortifications, 28 August 1846, 3 September 1846, 12 September 1846, December 1846.

48:     PRO WO44/195, Director-General of Artillery to Board, 11 January 1847; Ordnance Survey plan 1853; Foreman 1988, 30-1.

49:     Allison 1969, 417; *Hull Advertiser*, 9 August 1850, 14 October 1853, 17 February 1854, 27 January 1855.

50:     *Hull Advertiser*, 18 August 1855, 19 January 1856, 5 April 1856, 10 May 1856; HCCRO PE 109/69; Norfolk 1965, 35; Saunders 1907.

51:     *Hull Advertiser*, 3 November 1855; Allison 1969, 417; KUHRO 1866K, no. 6, filed 14 May 1860.

52:     Atkinson 1998; Thompson 1990; Credland 1982; Hull Local Studies Library, Hull Dock Co. plan, 1863.

53:     Thompson 1990, 127-8, 32.

WORKMEN AT THE CITADEL, 1681-88.

Where numbers of labourers are cited as *c.* a figure, this has been estimated from payments of Bills of Labourers, *pro rata*, usually rounded off to the nearest five men. Direct citations are similarly approximate in most cases. Most payments were for a weekly wage-bill.

Date	Workers	Where employed	Money paid	Reference and comments
5..9.1681	Carpenters	?	-	PRO WO 46:1, 306
7..9.1681	4 Carpenters / 2 Bricklayers / Labourers	Repairing drawbridge / Repairing parapet / Trench for drainage	-	PRO WO46:1, 307, Beckman
21..9.1681	100 Labourers	Half bastion at S. Blockhouse	-	PRO WO46:1, 308, Beckman
25.9.1681	120-145 Labourers	Turfing; Half bastion at N. Blockhouse	-	PRO WO46:1, 308, Duxbury, Fitch
5.10.1681	150 Labourers	Turfing Half bastion at S. Blockhouse	-	PRO WO46:1, 310, Duxbury – Soldiers taken off works; labourers then strike for pay-rise
12.10.1681	Labourers	Demolition	-	PRO WO46:1, 311, Beckman
13.10.1681	51 Day-workers	Demolition	-	PRO WO46:1, 312, Beckman
22.10.1681	300 Labourers	Turfing Half bastion at S. Blockhouse	-	PRO WO46:1, 314, Beckman
16.11.1681	Plumber / 150 Labourers	Roofing S. Blockhouse / Ramparts and ditches	-	PRO WO46:1, 316, Duxbury
23.11.1681	260 Labourers / Carpenters, Plumber	Bastion at S. Blockhouse / Roofing S. Blockhouse	-	PRO WO46, 318, Beckman – workers "come and go with the winds and weather"
26.11.1681	300 Labourers	Turfing Half bastion at N. Blockhouse; two others begun	-	PRO WO46:1, 318, Duxbury
28.11.1681	100 Labourers / Plumbers / Carpenters	Moat on Drypool side / Roofing S. Blockhouse, pipes / Gun platforms	-	PRO WO46:1, 319, Duxbury
3.12.1681	50-60 Labourers	2 Half bastions on Humber	-	PRO WO46:1, 319, Beckman
13.3.1682	100 Labourers / Bricklayers, Masons	Moats, Castle bastion / S. Blockhouse parapet, indoor lath, plaster & floors	-	PRO WO46:1, 324, Duxbury
29.4.1682	Labourers	S. Blockhouse, Moats	-	PRO WO46:1, 326, Duxbury – "slow going"
15.7.1682	c.80 Labourers	-	£21 0s 9d	SRO D(W) 1778/V/64 (52), Lambert
22.7.1682	c.115 Labourers	-	£29 12s 9d	SRO D(W) 1778/V/64 (52), Lambert
24.7.1682	150 Labourers	Half bastion at S. Blockhouse	-	PRO WO46:1, 330, Duxbury
29.7.1682	c.120 Labourers	-	£30 0s 2d	SRO D(W) 1778/V/64 (52), Lambert
5.8..1682	c.105 Labourers	-	£26 16s 8d	SRO D(W) 1778/V/64 (52), Lambert
12.8.1682	c.135 Labourers	-	£34 19s 2d	SRO D(W) 1778/V/64 (52), Lambert
19.8.1682	c.54 Labourers	-	£13 10s 0d	SRO D(W) 1778/V/64 (52), Lambert
31.8 - 2.9.1682	c.28 Labourers	Embrasures, S. half bastion, Oprill to bring up guns	£6 9s 7½d	PRO WO46:1, 288, Duxbury / SRO D(W) 1778/V/64 (52), Lambert
9.9.1682	c.65 Labourers	-	£16 17s 4d	SRO D(W) 1778/V/64 (52), Lambert
16.9.1682	c.80 Labourers	-	£20 6s 3d	SRO D(W) 1778/V/64 (52), Lambert
23.9.1682	c.95 Labourers	-	£23 15s 0d	SRO D(W) 1778/V/64 (52), Lambert
30.9.1682	c.85 Labourers	-	£21 8s 8d	SRO D(W) 1778/V/64 (52), Lambert
2.10.1682	90 Labourers	Filling old moat, and gaps	-	PRO WO46:1, 335, Duxbury
7.10.1682	c.70 Labourers	-	£17 11s 0d	SRO D(W) 1778/V/64 (52), Lambert
9.10.1682	c.135 Labourers / Rammer and Turfcutters	Half bastion at Castle	£29 16s 8d	PRO WO46:1, 335, Duxbury – Labourers rates reduced to 10d a day, 12d for Rammer and Turfcutters, between Michaelmas & Ladyday
14.10.1682	c.125 Labourers	-	£26 8s ½d	SRO D(W) 1778/V/64 (52), Lambert
21.10.1682	c.95 Labourers	-	c.£19 2s	SRO D(W) 1778/V/64 (52), Lambert
28.10.1682	c.105 Labourers	-	£21 5s 8d	SRO D(W) 1778/V/64 (52), Lambert
4.11.1682	c.125 Labourers	-	£26 9s ½d	SRO D(W) 1778/V/64 (52), Lambert
11.11.1682	c.155 Labourers	-	£32 0s ½d	SRO D(W) 1778/V/64 (52), Lambert
18.11.1682	c.170 Labourers	-	£35 7s 8d	SRO D(W) 1778/V/64 (52), Lambert
20.11.1682	Labourers / Bricklayers / Carpenters & Smiths	New Guardhouse / As above / New Trunk	£40 7s 8d	PRO WO46:1, 340, Duxbury – cost includes deals for Stages
25.11.1682	Labourers / Bricklayers	/ New Guardhouse	£46 19s 10d	SRO D(W) 1778/V/64 (52), Lambert
2.12.1682	Labourers / Bricklayers	-	£33 4s 4d	SRO D(W) 1778/V/64 (52), Lambert
	Carpenter	New Trunk	£12 12s 0d	
9.12.1682	c.55 Labourers	Fetching materials to New Guardhouse	£11 18s 1d	SRO D(W) 1778/V/64 (52), Lambert
1.4.1683	180 Labourers	Castle Half bastion & Saluting Platform	-	PRO WO46:1, 345, Duxbury
7.5.1683	New Sodlayers	-	-	PRO WO46:1, 349, ?Duxbury
11-12.5.1683	c.440 Labourers	Saluting Platform finished; Bastion at S. Blockhouse almost finished; Curtain (W) 36ft thick	£92 3s 4d	PRO WO46:1, 351, Lloyd / Bod. Lib. Rawl. A475, Commissioners
14.5.1683	400 Labourers	Turfing S. bastion; Parapet Castle Bastion	-	PRO WO46:1, 352, Duxbury – "we are much distracted of this wet weather"
16.5.1683	400 Labourers / 3 Sodlayers	Turfing	-	Bod. Lib. Rawl. A475, Commissioners
19.5.1683	c.210 Labourers	-	£43 0s 6d	Bod. Lib. Rawl. A475, Commissioners
20.5.1683	c.455 Labourers / 3 Sodlayers	-	£94 13s 8d	Bod. Lib. Rawl. A475, Commissioners – Sodlayer's assistants to be dismissed
26.5.1683	c.455 Labourers	-	£94 13s 8d	Bod. Lib. Rawl. A475, Commissioners
2.6.1683	c.300-320 Labourers	-	£62-5 8s 6d	PRO WO46:2, 41, Commissioners
9.6.1683	c.370 Labourers	-	£76 0s 0d	PRO WO46:2, 42, Commissioners
10.6.1683	c.475 Labourers	-	£98 15s 6d	PRO WO46:2, 42, Commissioners
18.6.1683	-	W. Curtain, Castle Bastion parapet; Half bastion against Drypool Church, Berm	-	PRO WO46:2, 151, Duxbury
23.6.1683	c.335 Labourers	-	£68 8s 4d	Bod. Lib. Rawl. A475, Commissioners
25.6.1683	100 Labourers	-	-	CSPD 1683, Plymouth – "Our works go on very fast"
27.6.1683	-	-	-	PRO WO46:2, 44, Commissioners – Labourers to have 14d a day until Michaelmas
17.7.1683	300+ Labourers	-	-	Bod. Lib. Rawl. A475, Commissioners
20.7.1683	-	-	-	Bod. Lib. Rawl. A475, Board – Works to close
27.9.1683	c.40 Labourers	Trunk; Jettywork at Saluting Platform; Mending Bastion	£8 14s 11d	PRO WO46:2, 95, Board
5.10.1683	c.35 Labourers	Earthwork at Trunk	£6 13s 8d	PRO WO46:2, Commissioners
16.10.1683	c.80 Labourers / Carpenters	Finishing earthworks / Repairing Jetties	£16 13s 8d / £4 17s 3d	PRO WO46:2, 48, Commissioners
16.4.1684	Labourers	Pumping out water	£3 0s 0d	Bod. Lib. Rawl. A476 item 1, Duxbury – includes 50s for the pump
28.4.1684	Labourers	Pumping; Small repairs	£4 15s 9d	Bod. Lib. Rawl. A476 item 1, Duxbury
16.5.1684	Labourers / Gunners	Removing guns from Town Gates to S. Blockhouse	£10 4s 4d	PRO WO51/28 TBB series 2, 114
11.6.1684	Labourers, Masons	Drain at S. Blockhouse	-	Bod. Lib. Rawl. A476 item 1, Duxbury
17.6.1684	Labourers	-	£17 17s 2d	PRO WO46:2, 23, Board
25.6.1684	30 Labourers	Main Gate & Guardhouses' Foundations	£9 5s 6d	PRO WO46:2, 227, Duxbury – Beckman paid labourers on his "undertaking" foundations
30.6.1684	35 Labourers	Foundations at East Point	£9 10s 0d	Bod. Lib. Rawl. A476 item 1, Duxbury
9.7.1684	5 Bricklayers	Main Gate	-	PRO WO46:2, 230, Beckman
12.7.1684	Labourers	Foundations; Cutting Ramparts for Sally Ports; Pumping water from Moat	£247 19s	PRO WO46:2, 231, Duxbury – Beckman's contract for foundations (sum cited) was used to cover cost of these other works
22.7.1684	Bricklayers, Masons / Labourers / Carpenters	Arches at Main Gate / Foundations / Piling at East Point	-	PRO WO46:2, Duxbury – Comments on the "very tedious and dangerous work" on foundations
24.7.1684	c.95 Labourers	Cutting Ramparts for Sally Ports; Pumping at East Point	£23 12s 6d	PRO WO46:2, 131, Board – Fitch ordered to pay these costs from money sent him
4.8.1684	c.30 Labourers	Raising Moat at East Point; Pumping and digging for Wing of New trunk	£7 15s 8d	PRO WO46:2, 246, Duxbury – these smaller teams employed on the King's Immediate Account
9.8.1684	c.25 Labourers	Raising Moat at East Point; Sloping down South Bastion	£6 12s 6d	PRO WO46:2, 59, Commissioners
11.8.1684	Bricklayers	Main Gate; East Point wall	-	PRO WO46:2, 248, Duxbury
16.8.1684	?c.40 Labourers	Sloping Rampart at S. Blockhouse; New Trunk	£10 5s 1d	PRO WO46:2, 60, Commissioners – may include cost of 2 pumps and cobbles
25.8.1684	Bricklayers, Masons / Carpenters	Main Gate / Piling at East Point	-	PRO WO46:2, 252, Duxbury
30.8.1684	Labourers	-	-	PRO WO46:2, 61, Commissioners

Date	Workers	Work	Cost	Source
6.9.1684	c.40 Labourers	-	£9 15s 8½d	PRO WO46:2, 62, Commissioners
13.9.1684	200 Labourers	Mending breach at Old Trunk	About £35	PRO WO46:2, 256, Beckman
15.9.1684	c.35 Labourers / Bricklayers / Carpenters	Guardhouses, Sally Ports / Piling and Frame, East Point	£8 15s 0d	PRO WO46:2, 258, Duxbury – Payment for Day Labourers and "other things"
20.9.1684	Labourers	-	-	PRO WO46:2, 64, Commissioners
22.9.1684	Masons	Arch of Main Gate	-	PRO WO46:2, 264, Duxbury
27.9.1684	Labourers	-	-	PRO WO46:2, 65, Duxbury
29.9.1684	Masons / Carpenters	East Point wall / Sally Port doors	-	PRO WO46:2, 276, Duxbury
4.10.1684	Labourers	-	-	PRO WO46:2, 66, Commissioners
8.10.1684	Plasterers / Carpenters	Inside Sally Ports / Doors; Lining Guardhouses	-	PRO WO46:2, 277, Duxbury – Notes "the want of Masons which is a great obstruction"
11.10.1684	Labourers	-	-	PRO WO46:2, 67, Commissioners
18.10.1684	Labourers / Masons	Pumping water from Citadel over the Humber Bank / East Point , Wall face (E.)	-	PRO WO46:2, 67, Commissioners / PRO WO46:2, 285, Wharton
25.10.1684	Labourers	-	-	PRO WO46:2, 68, Commissioners
29.10.1684	Bricklayers, Masons / Carpenters / Fitch's Labourers	East Point, Wall face (E) / Lining Rooms; Doors / Great Drain Foundation	-	PRO WO46:2, 288, Duxbury – "This frost and snowy weather has hindered the bricklayers from working these 3 days"
1.11.1684	c.30 Labourers	Levelling Sally Ports	£6 12s 6d	PRO WO46:2, 68, Duxbury – includes cobbles
5.11.1684	Bricklayers, Masons	East point; Sally Ports' & Main Gate's Wings	-	PRO WO46:2, 289, Duxbury – reports further delays and damage, due to "This great storm"
12.11.1684	Masons	East Point Water Table; Chimney for Guardroom, Main Gate; Sally Port	-	PRO WO46:2, 291, Duxbury – Weather "so various and wet that we could not work 2 whole days"; Stone not yet come
15.11.1684	c.8 Labourers	Levelling S. Bastion & Gate Passage; wheeling cobbles	£3 0s 3d	PRO WO46:2, 69, Duxbury
18.11.1684	Masons / Carpenters	Hewing in a shed / In Guardhouse Rooms	-	PRO WO46:2, 54, Commissioners – All except indoor work to halt because of weather
20.11.1684	1 Labourer / 3 Pavers etc.	Gather and store materials / New S. Blockhouse Door; / Paving of Bastion & Entrance	- / £27 3s 0d	Bod. Lib. Rawl. A476 item 1, Duxbury / PRO WO46:2, 70-1, Commissioners
22.11.1684	Labourers	-	-	PRO WO46:2, 71, Commissioners
26.11.1684	?Masons	East Point Parapet	-	PRO WO46:2, 299, Commissioners
3.12.1684	Masons / Bricklayers / Carpenters / Fitch's Labourers	Cornice at Main Gate / Outer Wings, Main Gate / Drain foundations etc.	-	PRO WO46:2, 298, Duxbury – Notes concern at setting stone in frosty weather
5.12.1684	Labourers	-	-	PRO WO46:2, 72, Commissioners
6.12.1684	Masons	Hewing stones in Vaults	-	PRO WO46:2, 300, Beckman
10.12.1684	Masons / Labourers	Main Gate Sedims; Coping Wings / Covering Works; Fencing	-	PRO WO46:2, 300, Beckman
11.12.1684	c.15 Labourers	Covering works; Fencing	£3 2s 0d	PRO WO46:2, 55, Commissioners
16.12.1684	Labourers	-	-	PRO WO46:2, 72, Commissioners
5-9.4.1685	Bricklayers / Carpenters	Pointing recent works / Repairing wheelbarrows etc.	- / £14 2s 0d	Bod. Lib. Rawl. A476 item 1, Duxbury
13.4.1685	Gunners / Bricklayers / Masons	Moving & Cleaning Carriages / Pointing / Finishing Stone Sentry Box	-	Bod. Lib. Rawl. A476 item 1, Duxbury
19.4.1685	Painter / Labourers & Gunners	Priming Doors / Moving Carriages, mounting Guns; Draining Moat	- / £19 11s 10d	Bod. Lib. Rawl. A476 item 1, Duxbury / PRO WO55/519, Commissioners – paid 6 June
27.4.1685	2 Carpenters	Repairing Humber Banks	£12 4s 6d	PRO WO55/519, Commissioners
11.6.1685	1 part-time Labourer	Opening & closing Trunks	2s 6d pw	PRO WO55/519, Commissioners
13.6.1685	1 Painter / c.220 Labourers	Painting Carriages etc. / Levelling, Clearing Moat & Room in S. Blockhouse	£7 7s 4d / £55 10s 8d	PRO WO55/519, Commissioners
20.6.1685	c.285 Labourers	-	£71 9s 2d	PRO WO55/519, Commissioners
27.6.1685	c.360 Labourers	-	£90 11s 4d	PRO WO55/519, Commissioners
4-6.7.1685	c.280-300 Labourers	Scarp of Berm; Curtain Rampart; Levelling in Citadel	£70 2s 4d	PRO WO55/519, Commissioners / Bod. Lib. Rawl. A475, Duxbury
7.7.1685	Mason	Coping East Point Parapet	£22 8s 0d	PRO WO55/519, Commissioners
11.7.1685	400 Labourers	Enclosed Drypoolside works	-	Bod. Lib. Rawl. A475, Duxbury
13.7.1685	400 Labourers	-	£113 17s 4d	Bod. Lib. Rawl. A475, Duxbury
27.7.1685	400 Labourers	Drypoolside Curtain Rampart of Bastion	£155 19s 9d	Bod. Lib. Rawl. A475, Duxbury
31.7.1685	Mason / 40 Labourers	Cramping Parapet, East Point Getting Water out of Moat	-	PRO WO55/519, Commissioners – Tools provided for labourers who had none
17.8.1685	350 Labourers / Carters	East Bastion Scarp, Berm and Base Flank; Scarp of Curtain and Base Flank; Levelling	£99 3s 2d	Bod. Lib. Rawl. A475, Duxbury – Weekly cost for Labourers, Carters etc.
26.8.1685	c.360 Labourers	-	c.£90	Bod. Lib. Rawl. A475, Duxbury
29.8.1685	c.75 Labourers	-	£18 1s 7d	PRO WO55/519, Commissioners – Wet weather reduced work and costs
7.9.1685	c.380 Labourers / Carters	Scarp of second Base Flank	£96 17s 6d	Bod. Lib. Rawl. A475, Duxbury
16.9.1685	c.270 Labourers	Base Flanks & their gun-ports	£69 1s 4d	Bod. Lib. Rawl. A475, Duxbury
7.10.1685	50 Labourers	Securing the works	-	Bod. Lib. Rawl. A475, Duxbury – Works closed, though resuming shortly after
14.10.1685	Labourers	Parapet begun, Drypoolside	-	Bod. Lib. Rawl. A475, Duxbury
20.10.1685	c.180 Labourers	-	£47 0s 0d	Bod. Lib. Rawl. A475, Duxbury
12.1685	Labourers	Taking Match from vessels into S. Blockhouse Stores	8s 0d	PRO WO51/33, TBB Ser. 2, 186b
8.1.1686	Labourers	Carrying from vessel to Stores	4s 6d	PRO WO51/33 TBB Ser. 2, 186b
10.2.1686	Labourers	Berm, E. Curtain, near Drain	-	Bod. Lib. Rawl. A475, Duxbury – Emergency repairs over winter
20.2.1686	Labourers	Berm etc.	-	Bod. Lib. Rawl. A475, Duxbury
3.1686	2 Labourers & others / Cooper / Lighterman	Work cleaning in stores etc. Re-packing powder Moving Stores from S. End to S. Blockhouse	£9 1s 6d	PRO WO51/33 TBB Ser. 2, 82b
8.5.1686	Labourers, Carpenters & Smiths	Works and goods Dec. 1685-May 1686	£33 0s 11¼d	PRO WO55/519, Commissioners
22.5.1685	c.15 Labourers	Drainage; Boring ground; Digging out/ filling at Bastion	£19 13s 8d	PRO WO55/519, Beckman
31.5.1686	Carpenters / Bricklayers / Raven's Labourers	Water Bastion, Frame & Water Bastion, W. Flank Levelling	- / £30	Bod. Lib. Rawl. A475, Duxbury / PRO WO55/519, Commissioners (5.6.1686)
12.6.1686	Raven's Labourers	Repairing Blind, E. Bastion; Levelling	£24 17s 6d	PRO WO55/519, Commissioners – Continuing contracts with Raven
14.6.1686	Carpenters, / Bricklayers	Water Bastion	-	Bod. Lib. Rawl. A475, Duxbury
26.6.1686	Raven's Labourers	Levelling	£30	PRO WO55/519, Commissioners
30.6.1686	Carpenters / Bricklayers / Labourers	Water Bastion	-	Bod. Lib. Rawl. A475, Duxbury – Reporting breach of dam and blowing up of wooden foundations
3.7.1686	Raven's Labourers	Levelling	£30	PRO WO55/519, Commissioners
9. 1686	Coopers & Labourers	Shifting etc. over 6 months	£16 2s 4d	PRO WO51/33 TBB Ser. 2, 27
11.9.1686	Raven's Labourers	Filling Old Moat at Castle with earth from New Moat	£17 18s 0d	PRO WO55/519, Commissioners
18.9.1686	Raven's Labourers	-	£19 16s 1d	PRO WO55/519, Commissioners
25.9.1686	Raven's Labourers	-	£11 16s 2d	PRO WO55/519, Commissioners
6.10.1686	Raven's Labourers	Levelling; w/earth from Moat	£11 10s 4d	PRO WO55/519, Commissioners
30.10.1686	Raven's Labourers	Digging round Berm for pavers; Enlarging Moat to raise Rampart	£18 2s 6d	PRO WO55/519, Commissioners
2.9.1687	c.75 Labourers	-	£18 16s 2d	PRO WO55/519, Commissioners
20.9.1687	Labourers, Soldiers / Carpenters	Earthworks, Sodwork Stages; repairing Tools	-	PRO WO55/519, Commissioners
24.9.1681	100 Soldiers / 60 Labourers	Earthworks	-	SRO D(W) 1778/I:/1233, Beckman
1.10.1687	c.210 Labourers	-	£43 4s 0d	PRO WO55/519, Commissioners – ?Includes Soldiers; estimated at rate of 10d per day
8.10.1687	c.720 Labourers	-	£150 19s1d	PRO WO55/519, Commissioners
15.10.1687	c.430 Labourers	-	£89 10s 0d	PRO WO55/519, Commissioners

15.10.1687	Carpenter	Making rams; Stages; Repairs	£20 2s 0d	
22.10.1687	c.770 Labourers	-	£160 4s 1d	PRO WO55/519, Commissioners
26.10.1687	Soldiers, Craftsmen	Ramparts	-	PRO WO55/519, Commissioners
29.10.1687	c.1160 Labourers	-	£238 15s 2d	PRO WO55/519, Commissioners – As above, Soldiers with Labourers at 10d per day
7.4.1688	Carpenters Labourers	Repairing Materials etc.	£54 8s 11d	PRO WO55/519, Commissioners
14.4.1688	Carpenters Labourers	-	£61 19s 6d	PRO WO55/519, Commissioners
21.4.1688	c.280 Labourers	-	£60 0s 10d	PRO WO55/519, Commissioners
2.5.1688	40 Soldiers+ (?Total c.100?)	Ramming	-	PRO WO55/519, Commissioners – 10 Soldiers per company of the Garrison regiment to work
6.6.1688	Carpenters	West Water Bastion, Frame	-	Hist. Mss. Comm. Dartmouth Mss, 136
18.9.1688	Cooper	Powder barrels	£3 19s 2d	PRO WO51/37 TBB Ser. 2, 44a
19.9.1688	c.4 Labourers	Landing & stowing Stores	10s 0d	PRO WO51/37 TBB Ser. 2, 44a
10.11.1688	Labourers & Townsmen Bricklayers	Half bastion at North Gate Palisades at Citadel Second (W) Water bastion	-	PRO WO55/519, Beckman

179

BIBLIOGRAPHY AND REFERENCES

Abbreviations

BL	British Library
BM	British Museum
Bod. Lib.	Bodleian Library, Oxford
BRB	Bench Record Books, Kingston upon Hull Record Office
BRL	Bench Record Letters, Kingston upon Hull Record Office
CCAM	Calendar of Committee for the Advancement of Money 1642-56
CSPD	Calendars of State Papers Domestic
CTP	Calendars of Treasury Papers
CTB	Calendars of Treasury Books
D	Deeds relating to property, Kingston upon Hull Record Office
DMT5	Coroners Report 1850, Kingston upon Hull Record Office
DNB	Dictionary of National Biography
ERYCRO	East Riding of Yorkshire County Record Office, Beverley; formerly HCCRO
HCCRO	Humberside County Council Record Office
HCSP	House of Commons Session Papers, Barracks, 1806-7
HMC	Historic Manuscripts Commission (Calendars): House of Lords Manuscripts, Dartmouth Manuscripts, Powis Manuscripts
KUHRO	Kingston upon Hull Record Office
L&P	Calendars of Letters and Papers
LPFD	Calendars of Letters and Papers Foreign and Domestic
L	Letters, as listed in Stanewell's Index to collections of Kingston upon Hull Record Office
M	Deeds, Letters and Miscellaneous Documents, as listed in Stanewell's Index
PRO	Public Record Office, Kew, London
Rawl.	Rawlinson Manuscripts, Bodleian Library, Oxford
TBB	Treasury Bill Books
WO	War Office papers, Public Record Office, Kew
YAS	Yorkshire Archaeological Society, Proceedings (19th-century transcripts)

Works cited

Allison, K.J. (ed.) 1969
Victoria History of the Counties of England (VCH), *A History of the County of York, East Riding Vol. 1: The City of Kingston upon Hull*, Oxford University Press, London.

Allison, K.J. (ed.) 1989
Victoria History of the Counties of England (VCH), *A History of the County of York, East Riding. Vol. 6: The Borough and Liberties of Beverley*, London.

Atkinson, D. 1998
Trial excavations in South Bridge Road, Kingston upon Hull 1997, Humber Archaeol. Rep. *21*, photocopied report, Hull, Humber Archaeology Partnership.

Aveling, H. 1960
Post-Reformation Catholicism in East Yorkshire 1558-1790, East Yorkshire Local Hist. Soc. Ser. *11*.

Ayers, B. 1979
Excavations at Chapel Lane Staith 1978, East Riding Archaeologist vol.5, Hull Old Town Rep. Ser. *3*.

Barclay, S. 1992
Espionage: This business of Hull, *Military History*, Vol. 8, no. 6, February 1992, Leesburg, Virginia USA, Empire Press.

Bartlett, J. 1971
The medieval Walls of Hull, *Hull Museums Bulletin 3-4*, 1-28.

Bell, R. 1849
   Memorials of the Civil War, correspondance of the Fairfax family, 2 vols, London, Richard Bentley.

Bell-Turton, R. 1906
   The History of the North Yorks Militia, (reprinted 1973, Stockton).

Bellamy, J.M. 1971
   The Trade and Shipping of Nineteenth Century Hull, East Yorkshire Local Hist. Soc. Ser. *27*, (reprinted 1979).

Bennett, A. 1988
   The Goldsmiths of Church Lane, Hull, 1527-1784, *Yorkshire Archaeol. J. 60*, 113-26.

Binns, J. 1986
   Scarborough and the Civil War 1642-1651, *Northern Hist. 22*, 95-122.

Binns, J. 1991
   Captain Browne Bushell, North Sea Adventurer and Pirate, *Northern Hist. 27*, 90-105.

Blashill, T. 1903
   Evidences Relating to the Eastern Part of the City of Kingston upon Hull, Hull, Brown and Sons.

Blaxland, G. 1972
   The Buffs, the Holland Regiment, London, Leo Cooper Ltd.

de Boer, G. 1973
   The two earliest maps of Hull, *Post-Medieval Archaeology 7*, 79-87, Pls 10-12.

Boyle, J.R. (ed.) 1882
   Memoirs of Master John Shaw written by himself in the year 1663-4, Hull, Peck.

Boyle, J.R. 1905
   Charters and Letters Patent granted to Kingston Upon Hull, Hull, Hull City Council.

Boynton, L. 1967
   The Elizabethan Militia, London, Routledge.

Breihan, J.R. 1990
   Army Barracks in the North East in the Era of the French Revolution, *Archaeol. Aeliana* (5th Ser.) *18*, 165-76.

Brooks, F.W. 1939
   A Medieval Brickyard at Hull, *J. Brit. Archaeol. Assoc.* (3rd Ser.) *4*, 151-74.

Brooks, F.W. (ed.) 1951
   East Riding Muster Rolls, 1584, *Yorkshire Archaeol. Soc.* (Record Ser.) vol. *116*, Miscellanea 5.

Browning, A. (ed.) 1936
   Memoirs of Sir John Reresby, Glasgow, Jackson.

Browning, A. 1944-51
   Thomas Osbourne Earl of Danby and Duke of Leeds, 3 vols, Glasgow, Jackson.

Bruce, J. (ed.) 1839
   Historie of the Arival of Edward IV in England, Camden Soc. 1, London, 1-30.

Bruce, L. 1980
   The Jacobite Risings in Britain 1689-1746, London.

Butler, L. 1991
   Sandal Castle Wakefield, Wakefield, Wakefield Hist. Publ.

Carlton, C. 1992
   Going to the Wars. The experience of the British Civil Wars, 1638-1651, London, Routledge.

Chancery Judgement 1860

In Chancery, 1860 K. No. 6, filed 14 May 1860, Between the Mayor Aldermen and Burgesses of the Borough of Kingston-upon-Hull Plaintiffs and Her Majesty's Attorney General Defendant; *The Answer.* (Consulted at Hull University Brynmor Jones Library; together with Kingston upon Hull City Council 1858).

Childs, J. 1976

The Army of Charles II, London, Routledge and Keegan.

Childs, J. 1979

The Army of James II and the Glorious Revolution, Manchester University Press.

Childs, J. 1987

The British Army of William III, 1698-1702, Manchester University Press.

Civil War Tracts

Kingston upon Hull City Council Local Studies Library, *c.*40 bound vols.

Clarendon, Edward, Earl of, [1712]

The History of the Rebellion and Civil Wars in England, 6 vols (1643 siege of Hull in vol. *3*), Oxford, Theatre.

Clay, J.W. 1893

Yorkshire Royalist Composition Papers, *Yorkshire Archaeol. Soc. Record Ser. vols 15-17.*

Clay, J.W. 1915

The Gentry of Yorkshire at the Time of the Civil War, *Yorkshire Archaeol. J. 23,* 349-94.

Colvin, H.M. 1982

History of the Kings Works vol. 4, 1485-1660, part 2, London, HMSO.

Corelli Barnett, T. 1970

Britain and her Army, 1509-1970, a military political and social survey, London, Penguin.

Credland, A.G. 1992

Archery in Hull and Beverley in the 19th century with notes on the origin and progress of the sport, *East Yorkshire Local Hist. Soc. Bull. 46* (Summer 1992), 8-11.

Credland, A.G. 1995

The Hull Whaling Trade: an Arctic enterprise, Beverley, Hutton Press.

Crowther, J. (ed.) 1992

Descriptions of East Yorkshire: de la Pryme to Head, East Yorkshire Local Hist. Soc. no. *45.*

Daiches, D. 1973

Charles Edward Stuart. The life and times of Bonnie Prince Charlie, London.

Dalton, C. (ed.) 1960

English Army lists and Commission Registers 1661-1714, 3 vols, London, Francis Edwards.

Dickens, A.G. 1964

The English Reformation, London, Batsford Ltd.

Dickens, A.G. 1938

New Records of the Pilgrimage of Grace, *Yorkshire Archaeol. J. 33,* 298-308.

Dockray, K. 1992

The Battle of Wakefield and the Wars of the Roses, *The Ricardian,* vol. 9, no. *117,* June 1992.

Dorman, J.E. 1990

Guardians of the Humber 1856-1956, Humberside Heritage Publ. *16,* Hull, Humberside County Council.

Duffy, C. 1975
Fire and Stone. The Science of Fortress Warfare 1660-1860, London, David and Charles.

Duffy, C. 1979
Siege Warfare, London, Routledge and Kegan Paul.

Eddy, M.R. 1976
Hull Castle - Preliminary Report, unpublished typescript (summarised by Cherry, J. in Post-Medieval Britain in 1976, *Post-Medieval Archaeology 11*, 97).

Ellis, S. and Crowther, D.R. (eds) 1990
Humber Perspectives: a region through the ages, Hull, Hull University Press.

Emsley, C. 1975
Political Disaffection and the British Army in 1792, *Bull. Inst. Historical Res. 48*, 130-45.

English, B. 1979
The Lords of Holderness 1086-1260: a study in feudal society, for Hull University by Oxford University Press.

English, B. 1990
The Great Landowners of East Yorkshire, 1530-1910, Hemel Hempstead, Harvester Wheatsheaf.

Evans, D.H. 1995
The Archaeological Potential of the Myton Gate in Hull, photocopied report, Hull, Humberside County Council.

Evans, D.H. 1999
Excavations at the Beverley Gate, and other parts of the town defences of Kingston upon Hull, article for *Post-Medieval Archaeology*.

Evans, D.H. and Sitch, B. 1990
Beverley Gate - The Birthplace of the English Civil War, Beverley, Hull City Council and Hutton Press.

Fairfax, Lord Thomas, [1884]
Short Memorials of the Civil War, *Yorkshire Archaeol. Soc. 8*, 207-22.

Fairfax, Sir Thomas, [1910]
Short Memoirs of Sir Thomas Fairfax written by himself during the great Civil War, Knaresborough, Hargreave.

Farley, A. (ed.) 1783
Domesday Book, Record Commission, 3 vols [indices by Ellis, H. 1816-33, 3 vols].

Farmer, J.S. (ed.) 1901
Regimental Records of the British Army 1600-1901, Bristol, Crecy Books.

Firth, C.H. 1902
Cromwell's Army, A History of the English Soldier during the Civil wars, the Commonwealth and the Protectorate, (1st edn.) London, Methuen.

Firth, C.H. (ed.) 1906
Margaret Duchess of Newcastle: *Life of William Cavendish Duke of Newcastle*, London, Library.

Firth, C. and Davies, G. 1940
The Regimental History of Cromwell's Army, Oxford, Clarendon Press.

Fletcher, A. 1981
The Outbreak of the English Civil War, London, Arnold.

Foreman, M. 1987
An investigation of the archaeological potential of the Hull Citadel, photocopied report, Beverley, Humberside County Council.

Foreman, M. 1988
Hull Citadel 1988, photocopied report, Beverley, Humberside County Council.

Foreman 1989
The Defences of Hull, *Fortress 2*, 36-45.

Foreman 1994

A Desk-Based Assessment and Project Design for Archaeological Evaluation of the Sammy's Point Redevelopment, Hull, photocopied report, Beverley, Humberside County Council.

Foreman 1995

Trial Excavations in Tower Street, Hull, photocopied report, Hull, Humberside County Council.

Foreman, M. 1996

Further Trial Excavations in Tower Street, Hull June 1996, photocopied report, Hull, Humber Archaeology Partnership.

Foreman, M. 1997

Trial Excavations at Sammy's Point, Kingston upon Hull March 1997, photocopied report, Hull, Humber Archaeology Partnership.

Foreman, M. 1997a

Hull UWWTD Scheme Archaeological Evaluation Shafts 10 and 11: Hull Citadel, NAA 97/31, photocopied report, Barnard Castle, Northern Archaeological Associates.

Foreman, M. 1998

Further Excavations at Sammy's Point, Kingston upon Hull, April-May 1998, Humber Archaeol. Rep. 29, photocopied report, Hull, Humber Archaeology Partnership.

Foreman, M. 1998a

Hull UWWTD Scheme: Archaeological Monitoring at shaft T3A, typescript report submitted to Northern Archaeological Associates, 1998.

Foreman, M. in prep.

Excavations and Survey at Hall Garth, Beverley.

Foreman, M. and Goodhand, S. 1997

The construction of Hull Citadel, Post-Medieval Archaeology 30 (for 1996), 143-185.

Foreman, M. and Steedman, K. 1997

An Archaeological desk-Based Assessment for the Humber Tidal Defences (Victoria Dock), Humber Archaeology Report 17, photocopied report, Hull, Humber Archaeology Partnership.

Fortescue, J.W. 1903

A History of the British Army, 16 vols, London, Macmillan.

Fraser, A. 1979

King Charles II, London, Weidenfeld and Nicholson.

Frost, C. 1827

Notices relevant to the early history of the town and port of Hull, Hull, J.B. Nichols.

Gardiner, S.R. 1893

History of the Great Civil War 1642-1649, 4 vols, London.

Gent, T. 1735

History of the Royal and Beautiful Town of Kingston upon Hull, (facsimile edition 1869, Hull, M. Peck and Sons) London.

Gillett, E. 1988

The Humber region at War 1793-1815, Humberside Heritage Publ. 12, Hull, Humberside Leisure Services.

Gillett, E. and MacMahon, K.A. 1980

History of Hull, (2nd edition 1989), Hull, Hull University Press.

Hadley, G. 1788

A New and Complete History of the Town and County of Kingston upon Hull, Hull, T. Briggs.

Haigh, P.A. 1997

The Military Campaigns of the Wars of the Roses, (paperback edition; first publ. 1995) Stroud, Sutton Publishing.

Hale, J.R. 1965
>The Early Development of the Bastion: an Italian chronology 1450-c.1534, in Hale, J.R., Highfield, J.R.L. and Smalley, B. (eds) 1965, *Europe in the Late Middle Ages*, London, Faber and Faber.

Hebditch, Mrs. 1947
>Late 18th and early 19th century papers relating to the organisation of the country against a possible invasion, *Yorkshire Archaeol. J. 36*, (for 1944-47) 109-15.

Hill, C. 1980
>*The Century of Revolution 1603-1714* (2nd edn.), Walton-on-Thames, Nelson.

Hime, W.L. 1903
>*History of the Royal Regiment of Artillery, 1815-1853*, London, Longmans.

Hirst, J.H. 1913
>*The Blockhouses of Hull, and who went there*, Hull, A. Brown and Sons.

Hogg, O.G.F. 1963
>*English Artillery, 1326-1726*, London, for Royal Artillery Institution.

Horrox, R. 1978
>*The Changing Plan of Hull, 1290-1650*, Hull, Kingston upon Hull City Council.

Horrox, R. 1983
>*Selected rentals and accounts of medieval Hull 1293-1528*, Yorkshire Archaeol. Soc. Rec. Ser. *141* (for 1981), Leeds, University of Leeds Printing Service.

Hoskins, W.G. 1976
>*The Age of Plunder, the England of Henry VIII 1500-1547*, London, Longman.

Hughes, Q. 1974
>*Military Architecture*, London, Evelyn.

Hughes, Q. 1989
>Review of Humberside County Council, Hull Citadel 1988 (Foreman 1988, above), *Fort 17* (1989), 10-11.

Hull Advertiser 1794-1854
>Microfilm rolls, Beverley Local Studies Library.

Hull Directory, 1791
>Hull, facsimile reprint 1885, Peck and Son.

Hull Courant
>Newspaper, 1746-48.

Hull City Council 1987
>*The Archaeology of the Beverley Gate, Hull: interim report*, Hull, City Planning Dept. with Archaeology Unit, Humberside County Architect's Dept.

Hutton, R. 1985
>*The Restoration, A Political and Religious History of England and Wales 1658-1667*, Oxford, Oxford University Press.

Jackson, G. 1972
>*Hull in the Eighteenth Century. A Study in Economic and Social History*, University of Hull.

Kear, D. 1986
>Clifford's Fort and the defence of the Tyne, *Archaeologia Aeliana 5* ser. *14*, 99-134.

Kelsall, R.K. 1938
>The General Trend of Real Wages in the North of England During the Eighteenth Century, *Yorkshire Archaeol. J. 33*, 49-55.

Kelsall, R.K. 1938a
>*Wage Regulations under the Statute of Artificers*, London.

Kelsall, R.K. 1939
    Statute wages during a Yorkshire epidemic, 1679-81, *Yorkshire Archaeol. J. 34*, 310-16.

Kenyon, J.P. 1978
    Stuart England, London, Allen and Lane.

Kenyon, J.P. 1988
    The Civil Wars of England, London, Weidenfield and Nicholson.

Kingston upon Hull City Council 1858
    Statement Relative to the Title of the Citadel and Fortifications of Kingston upon Hull, printed for the Public Park and Recreation Grounds Committee, June 1858, Hull.

Lambert, J. 1891
    Two Thousand Years of Guild Life: full accounts of Guilds and trading companies of Kingston upon Hull from the fourteenth to the eighteenth century, London, Simpkin, Marshall, Hamilton, Kent and Co.

Lankester, E. (ed.) 1846
    Memorials of John Ray, London.

Latham, R. (ed.) 1983
    The Diary of Samuel Pepys, Vol. X, Companion, London, Bell and Hyman.

Laver, J. 1948
    British Military Uniforms, London, Penguin.

Lawson, C.P. 1969
    A History of the Uniforms of the British Army, 5 vols, London, Davis.

Leeds City Council 1951
    Temple Newsome House, Leeds, Libraries and Arts Committee of Leeds Corporation.

Lenman, B. 1980
    The Jacobite Risings in Britain in 1689-1746, London, Eyre and Methuen.

Malachowicz, E. 1977
    Fortifications in Poland, *Fort 3*, 53-62.

Markham, C.B. 1870
    Life of the Great Lord Fairfax, London, Macmillan and Co.

McLynn, F.J. 1980
    Hull and the 45, *Yorkshire Archaeol. J. 52*, 135-42.

McNicol, P. 1987
    The Sieges of Kingston upon Hull in 1642 and 1643, Hull, Kingston upon Hull City Council.

Miller, K., Robinson, J., English, B. and Hall, I. 1982
    Beverley: An Archaeological and Architectural Study, RCHM(E) Supplementary Series 4, London, HMSO.

Moore, Sir Jonas, 1673
    Modern Fortification, (1st edn. consulted; 2nd edn. 1689), London.

Morley, B.M. 1963
    Henry VIII and the Development of Coastal Defence, London, HMSO, Dept. Environment Ancient Monuments and Historic Buildings.

Morris, C. 1984
    The Illustrated Journeys of Celia Fiennes, 1682-1712, London, MacDonald and Co.

Muller, John 1744
    A Treatise Containing the Elementary Part of Fortification, Regular and Irregular, London.

Myres, J.N.L. 1935
    The Teutonic settlement of England, *History 20*, 250-62.

Neave, D. 1983
    William Catlyn 1628-1709, *Bull. East Yorkshire Local Hist. Soc. 28*, autumn 1983, 8-10.

Neave, D. 1996a
  The Pilgrimage of Grace, in Neave, S. and Ellis, S. (eds) 1996, 120-21.

Neave, D. 1996b
  The Civil War in the East Riding, in Neave, S. and Ellis, S. (eds), 122-23.

Neave, D. 1996c
  Anti-Militia Riots, in Neave, S. and Ellis, S. (eds), 124-25.

Neave, S. and Ellis, S. (eds)
  An Historical Atlas of East Yorkshire, Hull, University of Hull Press.

Neave, D. and Waterson, 1988
  Lost Houses of East Yorkshire, Beverley, Hutton Press.

Neuberg, V. 1989
  Gone for a Soldier. A History of Life in the British Ranks from 1642, London, Cassell.

Newman, P. 1985
  Atlas of the English Civil War, London, Routledge.

Nicholson, J. 1887
  Beacons of Holderness, Driffield, Printed for the author by T. Holderness.

Norfolk, R.W.S. 1965
  Militia, Yeomanry and Volunteer Forces of the East Riding 1689-1908, East Yorkshire Local Hist. Soc. no. *19*.

Ogg, D. 1955
  England in the Reign of James II and William III, Oxford, Oxford University Press.

O'Neil, J. 1945
  Stephen von Haschenperg, engineer to King Henry VIII, and his work, *Archaeologia 91*, 137-55.

Oppenheim, M. 1896
  The Administration of the Royal Navy, London, Lane.

Palliser, D.M. 1983
  The Age of Elizabeth 1547-1603, London, Longman.

Parsons, D. (ed.) 1836
  The Diary of Sir Henry Slingsby of Scriven Bart., London, Longman.

Payne, K. 1996
  "Scarlet Fever": The Town of Hull and the Citadel Garrison 1795-1856, Unpublished undergraduate dissertation, Humberside University, April 1996.

Peacock, E. 1874
  The Army Lists of the Roundheads and Cavaliers (1642), London, Chatto and Windus.

Pepper, S. 1976
  Planning versus fortification: Sangallo's project for the defence of Rome, *Fort 2*, 33-49.

Porter, W. 1889
  History of the Corps of Royal Engineers, 2 vols, London, Longmans, Green and Co.

Poulson, G. 1841
  The History of Holderness, 2 vols, Hull and London, vol. *1* R. Brown and W. Pickering, vol. *2* Thomas Topping.

de la Pryme, Abraham [1986]
  A History of Kingston upon Hull, 2 vols, Hull, Kingston upon Hull City Council and Malet Lambert High School.

Raistrick, A. and Jennings, B. 1965
  A History of Lead-Mining in the Pennines, London, Longman.

RCHM(E) 1972
   An Inventory of the Historical Monuments in the City of York, vol. 2, the Defences, London, HMSO.

Reckitt, B. 1952
   Charles the First and Hull 1639-1645, Howden, Mr Pye Press.

Reid, S. no date
   Officers and regiments of the Royalist army, 4 vols, Lea on Sea, Partizan Press.

Rodriguez-Salgado (ed.) 1988
   Armada: An International Exhibition to commemorate the Spanish Armada , Nat. Maritime Mus., London, Penguin.

Roebuck, P. 1980
   Yorkshire Baronets 1640-1760: Families, Estates and Fortunes, Hull, Hull University Press.

Rogers, H.C.B. 1977
   The British Army of the 18th Century, London, Allen and Unwin.

Rogers, P.G. 1966
   The Fifth Monarchy Men, London, Oxford University Press.

Ross, W.G. 1984
   Military Engineering During the Great Civil War 1642-49, London, Trotman (reprinted from Professional Papers of the Corps of Royal Engineers, vol. *13*, 1887).

Routledge, F.C. (ed.) 1970
   Calendar of the Clarendon State Papers preserved in the Bodleian Library, Oxford, 5 vols (vol. *4*, 1657-1660), Oxford.

Roy, I. (ed.) 1964
   Royalist Ordnance Papers, *Oxford Record Soc. no. 15*.

Rushworth, J. 1721
   Historical Collections of Private Passages of State 1625-1648, 6 vols, University of Hull Archives (Rushworth Coll.).

Ryder, I.E. 1989
   The Seizure of Hull and its magazine, January 1642, *Yorkshire Archaeol. J. 61*, 139-48.

Saunders, A.D. 1960
   Tilbury Fort and the Development of Artillery Fortification in the Thames Estuary, *Antiq. J. 40*, 112-74.

Saunders, A.D. 1976
   Deal and Walmer Castles, London, HMSO.

Saunders, A.D. 1980
   Tilbury Fort, London, English Heritage.

Saunders, A. 1989
   Fortress Britain: Artillery Fortification in the British Isles and Ireland, Liphook, Beaufort.

Saunders, R. 1907
   A History of the Royal Garrison Artillery (Volunteers), Hull, Walker and Brown.

Schoerer, L. 1974
   No Standing Armies, U.S.A., John Hopkins University Press.

Scott, D. 1883
   The British Army from the Restoration to the Revolution, 3 vols, London.

Scouller, R.E. 1966
   The Armies of Queen Anne, Oxford, Clarendon Press.

Sheahan, J.J. 1864
   History and Description of the Town and Port of Kingston upon Hull, General and Concise, London, (2nd edition 1866, Beverley, John Green).

Shelby, L.R. 1967
   John Rogers Tudor Engineer, Oxford, Oxford University Press.

Sheppard, T. 1902
> Relics of the Civil War, *Hull Museum Publ.* no. 7, April 1902, 11-12.

Sheppard, T. 1904
> An old Hull gunsmith, *Hull Museum Publ.* no. *20*, June 1904, 38.

Sheppard, J.A. 1958
> *The Draining of the Hull Valley*, East Yorkshire Local Hist. Soc. no. *8*.

Short, M.J. 1998
> The Corporation of Hull and the government of James II 1687-9, *Bull. Hist. Res. 71*, 172-95.

Singleton, F.B. and Rawnsley, S.R. 1986
> *A History of Yorkshire*, Chichester, Phillimore.

Smith, R.D. 1988
> Towards a new typology for wrought-iron ordnance, *Internat. J. Nautical Archaeol. Underwater Exploration 17.1*, 5-16.

Smith, R.D. 1993
> Port Pieces: The use of wrought-Iron Guns in the Sixteenth Century, *J. Ordnance Soc. 5*, 1-10.

Smith, R.D. 1995
> Wrought iron swivel guns, in Bound, M. (ed.), *The Archaeology of Ships of War*, Internat. Maritime Archaeol. Ser. vol. *1*, 104-13.

Smith, V.T.C. 1997
> The defences of London during the English Civil War, *Fort 25*, 61-81.

Smurthwaite, D. 1993
> *The Complete Guide to the Battlefields of Britain with Ordnance Survey Maps*, Michael Joseph Ltd.

Speck, W.A. 1988
> *Reluctant Revolutionaries. Englishmen and the Revolution of 1688*, Oxford, Oxford University Press.

Spiteri, S.C. 1993
> Illustrated glossary of military architectural terms, *Fort 21*, 105-14.

Spiteri, S.C. 1994
> *Fortresses of the Cross: Hospitaller Military Architecture (1136-1789)*, Malta, Heritage Interpretation Services Publication.

Stamp, A.H. 1991
> *Cottingham and the Civil War*, Cottingham Local History Society *13* (transcript of BM Egerton MS 2647).

Stanewell, L.M. 1951
> *Hull Corporation, City and County of Kingston upon Hull, Calendar of Deeds, Letters and Miscellaneous Old Documents*, Hull, Hull Corporation.

Stephens, L. and Lee, S. (eds.) 1885 onwards
> *Dictionary of National Biography*, 63 vols, London, Humphrey Milford, Oxford University Press.

Stone, L. 1972
> *The Causes of the English Revolution 1529-1642*, London, Routledge and Keegan.

Suddaby, J. 1907
> The Old Hull Citadel: the last century of its existence, *Hull Museum Publ. 20* (March 1907), 23-33.

Suddaby, J. 1907a
> A Hull Inventor of Life-Saving Appliances, *Hull Museum Publ. 20* (March 1907), 15-22.

Sykes, J. (ed.) 1893
> The Registers of Saint Mary's Church Hull, *Yorkshire Archaeol. J. 12*, 464-80.

Thompson, M. 1990
> *Hull Docklands: an illustrated history of the Port of Hull*, Cherry Burton, Hutton Press.

Tibbles, J. 1999
Humber Field Archaeology Watching Brief no. 291, Victoria Dock Primary School, February 1999, Unpublished developer-funded report, Hull, Humber Archaeology Partnership.

Tickell, J. 1798
The History of the Town and County of Kingston upon Hull, Hull, Thomas Lee and Co.

Tindall Wildridge, T. 1884
Old and New Hull: A series of Drawings of the Town of Kingston upon Hull, Hull, Peck and Son.

Tindall Wildridge, T. (ed.) 1886
The Hull Letters; printed from a collection of documents found among the Borough Archives in the Town Hall, Hull, 1884, during the progress of the work of indexing... 1625-1646, Hull, Wildridge and company.

Tomlinson, H. 1973
The Ordnance Office and the King's forts, 1660-1714, Architectural History 16.

Tomlinson, H.C. 1979
Guns and Government. The Ordnance office under the later Stuarts, London, Royal Hist. Soc.

Travis-Cook, J. 1890
Notes relative to the Manor of Myton, Hull, A. Brown and Sons.

Tucker, J. 1972
The role of the Navy, in Tucker, J. and Winstock, L.S. 1972, 74-8.

Tucker, J. and Winstock, L.S. (eds) 1972
The English Civil War: a military handbook, London, Arms and Armour Press.

Walker, J. 1934
Yorkshire Plot 1663, Yorkshire Archaeol. J.. 31 (1932-34), 349-359.

Walsh, J.E. 1978
Night of Fire, New York, McGraw-Hill Book Co.

Walton, C. 1894
History of the British Standing Army 1660-1700, London, Harrison.

Watson, J.C. (ed.) 1960
The Oxford History of England: the reign of George III, 1760-1815, Oxford, Clarendon Press.

White, W. 1831
Directory of Hull, Sheffield, White.

Williams, N.T. St John,
Redcoats and Courtesans: the Birth of the British Army 1660-1690, London, Brasseys.

Wilson, C. 1965
England's Apprenticeship 1603-1763, London, Longman.

Woodward, D. (ed.) 1984
The Farming and Memorandum Books of Henry Best of Elmswell 1642, London, Oxford University Press.

Woodward, D. (ed.) 1985
Descriptions of East Yorkshire: Leland to Defoe, East Yorkshire Local Hist. Soc. Ser. 39.

Woodward, D. 1995
Men at Work: Labourers and building craftsmen in the towns of northern England, 1450-1750, Cambridge Studies in Population, Economy and Society in Past Time 26, Cambridge, Cambridge University Press.

Woodward, F.W. 1987
History of the Royal Citadel, Plymouth, Plymouth, Devon Books.

INDEX

Dawson, William: 108
Defoe, Daniel: 146
Denton, Henry: 155
Dickinson, Mr George: 135
Dighton, Gervase: 52
Dixon, Richard: 110-11
Dobby, James: 138
Dobson, Alderman William: 49
Dodson, Edward: 40
Dorman, A.: 49
Drake, Joseph: 42-3
Draper, Lieutenant Mathew: 149
Duckenfield, Robert: 47
Dumbarton, Lord: 126
Dunbar, Lord: 138
Duncan, Lieutenant-Colonel Thomas: 49-50
Durer, Albrecht: 11-12
Duxbury, Andrew: 67
Duxbury, James: 66-7
Duxbury (or Duxbery), John: 65-9, 73-4, 76-7, 79, 85, 99-100, 104-8, 110, 112, 115, 119-22, 124, 128-9
Dymoke, Captain Thomas: 26

Edward I, of England: 2
Edward II, of England: 2
Edward III, of England: 2
Edward IV, of England: 5
Edward VI, of England: 16-17
Edwards, Captain: 153
Edwards, Captain (RN): 163
Edwards, Talbot: 63, 75, 106-7
Elizabeth I, of England: 17, 23
Elkins, Richard: 106
Ellerker, James: 138
Elliot, Thomas: 106
Elton, Major (or Lieutenant-Colonel) Richard: 41-2
Elvidge, Ensign: 51
Etherington: 107
Evans, Lawrence: 78, 109-10

Fairfax, Captain: 124
Fairfax, Colonel Charles: 42

Fairfax, Frances: 28
Fairfax, Lord Ferdinando: 29-30, 34, 36, 39-40
Fairfax, Sir Thomas: 29-30, 33, 39-40
Fareside (or Fairside), Mr: 58, 64
Fauconberg, Lord: 53
Fearnside, Thomas: 150, 152
Felton, Mr: 72-4, 88, 115
Ferries, Thomas: 23
Field, Alderman John: 136
Fielding, Colonel Edward: 25
Fiennes, Celia: 139
Fitch, Mr John: 57-9, 64-5, 67-8, 72-9, 81, 85, 87-8, 99-100, 104-9, 114-5, 135, 139, 145
Fitch, Sir Thomas: 59, 64, 72-5, 77-8, 85, 107, 109, 115, 129
Fitzgerald, Colonel: 51
Flaherty, Captain Morrough: 50
Fogg, Lieutenant: 125
Foster, William: 157
Foxley, Thomas: 16
Fraiston, Mr: 107
Francis I, of France: 6
Franklin, Lieutenant: 136
Frogatt, Alderman (and Mayor): 150
Frost and Co.: 164

Gage, Colonel Henry: 128
Garlike, Theophilus: 52
Gate, Sir Henry: 13
Gee, William: 49
Genew, Henry: 57
Gent, Thomas: 92, 130-1, 143
George I, of England: 137
George II, of England: 149-50
Gibson, Edmund: 139
Gilby, Captain Anthony: 47, 48, 50-3, 57-8, 119, 126
Gill, Jonathan: 145
Glemham, Sir Thomas: 26, 28
Gloucester, Richard, Duke of: 5
Gloucester, Prince William of: 163
Goffes, Colonel: 40
de Gomme, Sir Bernard: 56, 58-9, 61-3, 67, 72-3, 75, 77, 84, 87, 92
Goodgroom, Richard: 47
Gorrel, Edmund: 18

Index of Places

Index of Officials and Bodies, Civil and Military

Index of Ships' Names

Also from  **Kingston Press**

FORGOTTEN HULL

Graham Wilkinson and Gareth Watkins

Hull's social history is brought to life in this fascinating pictorial record of the city, showing what it was like to live in Hull between the 1890s and 1930s.
Forgotten Hull is a magnificent collection of over 100 meticulously researched historical photographs of the city and surrounding area, faithfully restored and reproduced from the original glass plate negatives and mounted prints of the Hull Corporation Health Department.

Forgotten Hull price £12.75

ISBN 1 902039 00 9

DAN BILLANY

Valerie A. Reeves and Valerie Showan

Born in 1913 into a poor Hull family, Dan Billany fought tenaciously to achieve his ambitions - a university degree, a job as a teacher and eventually fame as a best-selling author in Britain and the USA. *Dan Billany - Hull's lost hero,* is a carefully researched biography contrasting his adventures as a soldier, a prisoner of war and as a fugitive on the run in Italy with the inner turmoil of a man coming to terms with his homosexuality - a life cruelly cut short and enormous potential unrealised.

Dan Billany price £6.25

ISBN 1 902039 01 7

LOST PUBS OF HULL

Graham Wilkinson and Paul Gibson

A unique insight into Hull's social life is revealed in this pictorial reminder of the variety of types and styles of pub which featured as part of the city's landscape.
Lost Pubs of Hull, containing more than 100 photographs, many published for the first time and each thoroughly researched, is a tribute to many of the city's fondly remembered institutions, as well as a nostalgic step back in time.

Lost Pubs of Hull price £12.75

ISBN 1 902039 03 3

Orders and Enquiries

Kingston Press,
Hull Central Library,
Albion Street
Kingston upon Hull
United Kingdom
HU1 3TF

Telephone: (01482) 616814
Fax: (01482) 616827
E-Mail: kpress@hullcc.demon.co.uk